STUDIES IN JUDAICA

STUDIES IN JUDAICA

in
Honor of
Dr. Samuel Belkin
as
Scholar and Educator

Edited by Leon D. Stitskin

KTAV PUBLISHING HOUSE, INC.
NEW YORK

YESHIVA UNIVERSITY PRESS
NEW YORK

Library of Congress Cataloging in Publication Data

Stitskin, Leon D   comp.
    Studies in Judaica.

    Includes bilbiographical references.
    1. Judaism--Addresses, essays, lectures. 2. Belkin,
Samuel. 3. Musar movement. 4. Repentance (Judaism)
5. Revel, Bernard, 1885-1940. I. Belkin, Samuel.
II. Title.
BM42.S716   296   74-7242
ISBN 0-87068-257-1

TABLE OF CONTENTS

FOREWORD

This Anthology of *Studies in Judaica* dedicated to the commemoration of Dr. Samuel Belkin's thirtieth anniversary as President of Yeshiva University contains in the main the learned essays that we published at our Department of Special Publications. Fifteen years ago, Dr. Belkin asked me to assume the responsibility of publishing a series of *Studies in Torah Judaism* which would constitute a philosophic basis for the formulation of a rationale of Judaism grounded in our biblical, halakhic and philosophic sources. We initiated the series with Dr. Belkin's essay on "The Philosophy of Purpose." As the acknowledged exponent and spokesman for traditional Judaism, Dr. Belkin's study initiated the classical character and unique insights which have marked the nature of the series since its inception.

Five years later we began a parallel series of *Studies in Judaica* as well as the publication of scholarly books designed for students in Judaica, research and scholarship. The primary thrust in this series was to recreate for contemporary scholars some of the classical works of our sages and philosophers, augmented by a critical appraisal of their writings and rendering them relevant to contemporary scholarship.

This Anthology, dedicated to our revered President whose scholarly counsel and constant encouragement has made the Yeshiva University Press an international forum for the elucidation of traditional Judaism, consists in the main of translations and evaluations of some of the works of our classical scholars published in our series of *Studies in Judaica*. Some of the essays have been condensed for inclusion in this volume.

LEON D. STITSKIN, *Editor*
Yeshiva University Press

1

DR. SAMUEL BELKIN AS SCHOLAR
AND EDUCATOR

ON THE OCCASION OF HIS 30th ANNIVERSARY
AS PRESIDENT OF YESHIVA UNIVERSITY

by LEON D. STITSKIN

A.

Two verses in the Bible dealing with two senses of the word Reason denote two currents of thought according to some scholars which had their beginnings in ancient Israel and developed into a more formal expression in what came to be known as the Palestinian and Alexandrian Hebrew Traditions. In the Book of Psalms (CXI, 10) we read: "The beginning (or the principal part) of Reason is the fear of God." On the other hand, in Proverbs (IV:7), a comparable statement reads: "The beginning (the principal part) of Reason is to acquire Reason."

It is obvious that we have here a conscious consideration of Reason and its place in Biblical times. The existence of Reason as a crucial element in life was recognized but its relative place and weight were subject to debate. One school held that Reason was simply a faculty, an aid, a guide in carrying out the commandments of God. The absolute and ultimate is the command of God. Reason is but a quality in one's mind subordinated to the fear or Will of God. In this sense it serves as a discipline in the practical conduct of life by helping to explicate the Torah's commandments through drawing inferences or pointing to necessary connections and through supplying an additional motive for moral behavior by demonstrating its pragmatic consequences. This school of thought, which limited the scope of human reason and denied its ability to pierce beyond the veil, affected chiefly the Jews in Palestine and Syria who wrote in Hebrew and Aramaic and developed its formal expression in the Book of Kohelet (Ecclesiasties)[1] and in the Ecclesiasticus of the Apocrypha, where we find again the affirmation: "The beginning of wisdom is the Fear of God" (I, 14). Ben Sira thus carried on the old Hebrew tradition of the absoluteness of God's Word and of His direct control of all that happens in the world. Only the Torah manifests God's Presence. For unlike the connotation of Torah as teaching, as implied in the Book of Proverbs, to Ben Sira it meant divine legislation. This tradition was followed by the Palestinian Midrashic and Rabbinic literature for whom Reason was a useful and illuminating instrument, but there was nothing ultimate about it. Only the Torah, says the Midrash Rabbah in its opening commentary on the first verse in the Bible, was the blueprint for Creation (Gen. R. 1).[2]

On the other hand, in the Book of Proverbs, the exhortation is: "The beginning of Reason is to get Reason." Reason in this sense is a possession, as we find in a subsequent chapter of Proverbs (VIII:22-24), "It was God Himself Who got me as a possession at the begining of His course, before His works of old. From eternity was I enthroned, from the beginning, from the antecedents of the earth. When there were no abysses was I begotten, when there were no fountains heavy with water."

The personal and separate identity of Reason could hardly be made more clear. It appears to be the same as God's Reason and as such capable of reading His Thoughts. This conception in the philosophical discourse of personified Reason has several implications. It raises Reason to a cosmic function projecting the structure of the world itself as rational. Rationality ties up together all existing things. It is not simply by the mere Will of God that the world is good and promotes goodness but because the world is the creation of Reason. Hence the appeal to man must be to be rational in order to succeed.

This notion implies further that Reason is elevated to a revelation which Reason itself makes to individual men—a mystical revelation inasmuch as it comes to each man for himself. Moreover, this remarkable hypostasis of Reason as an almost co-eternal being beside God brings it into a relation to the Divine Authority which addresses man through the phenomena of life and even of the inanimate world. As an independent existence in virtue of its own nature, Reason calls upon men as the creation of Reason to be rational as it is rational.

This doctrine of personified Reason was pursued in the Wisdom of Solomon[3] and in the Apocalypse by the Book of Enoch[4] and in philosophy by Philo's *Logos*. That *logos* in Philo means Reason is plain throughout his writings, especially in his *Allegorical Interpretation* (I, 19). That it is also hypostatized and assumes an ontological content is evident from his "Confusion of Tongues" (41), where he refers to it as the Logos of the Eternal which must of necessity be imperishable, incorporeal, differing in nothing from the Divine Image (*ib.*, 62, 63).

Scholars differ, however, as to the origin of Philo's doctrine of the Logos. His close contact with the Stoic system led many scholars to conclude that he accepted the Stoic *loga spermatika* or Reason as the active principle in the universe working on the passive principle, unqualified susbtance (Diogenes Laertius, VII, on Zeno, 134). Other scholars, however, could not accept this view inasmuch as in the Stoic system Logos is the same as God, is identified with God, the *pneuma*, a notion which Philo did not accept. They held therefore that Philo's Logos was derived from the Palestinian Aramaic "Memra" which the Targum translated as the Word of God and which they also personified and used to avoid crass anthropomorphism. But "Memra," it must be noted, never meant Reason, but as we pointed out, Philo's Logos was as much Reason as word. Still others maintained that Philo's *Logos* combined the Platonic doctrine of ideas, the Stoic *pneuma* which permeate the cosmos and Jewish angelology. But this combination resulted in an intricate mixture perforated with contradictions concerned with the relationship of these divine powers to God.

To us, however, the question of the source of Philo's *Logos* is more than of theological or historical importance. It goes to the very heart of the problem of the philosophic enterprise in Judaism. Inasmuch as to Philo philosophy was not merely a means for an exposition of his ideas or an exercise of the inquiring human mind but a complete scheme of thought in which Judaism as a whole was conceived as a philosophic doctrine, it is crucial to investigate the source of his ideological construct. If the method and content of his writings have their roots in the Palestinian tradition—although clarified and elucidated by Hellenistic influences—then Judaism pursued a current of philosophic thought concomitantly with the halakhic process projecting an organic character of its own. If, on the other hand, we assume his sources on the metaphysical status of Reason or philosophy are exclusively of the Alexandrian tradition, then we shall have to attribute *Mahsevet Yisrael* to alien cultures grafted upon the body of Jewish thought modes.

I

Dr. Belkin's comprehensive scholarship on Philo which for its originality and thoroughness is uniquely impressive and revolutionary, throws light on this crucial philosophical problem. Although the major thrust of Dr. Belkin's scholarship on Philo has been on the latter's midrashic material, his major thesis has ramifications in every area of Philo's intellectual pursuits. Dr. Belkin as a consummate Talmudic and Greek scholar has been probing into the specific sources and primary texts of Philo's midrashic work such as his *Midrash Sh'elot u'Teshubot al Bereshet u-Shemot,* "Questions and Answers on Genesis and Exodus" and others. He amassed vast materials from rabbinic traditions—the Talmud, Midrash Rabbah, Midrash Tehilim, Midrash Tadsche, The Mekilta—demonstrating Philo's dependence upon the primary texts of those ancient rabbinic passages. He shows the similarity of those texts with Philo's work not only in exposition but also in method and phraseology.[5] Some of those traditions go back to the third century before the common era, and Philo made use of those ancient primary texts that may have been solely in the possession of Alexandrian scholars but emanated from Palestine. He often elaborates on the midrashic comments but in most cases helped to elucidate them, make the texts more comprehensible. "Standing alone, passages in Philo and rabbinic literature," writes Dr. Belkin, "are not sufficiently lucid or intelligible but when placed side by side do shed light on one another."[6]

In sum, Dr. Belkin has demolished the notion prevalent for centuries that there were two divergent currents of thought of very different origins—the Palestinian and the Alexandrian—and the two were diametrically opposed to each other. Dr. Belkin's assumption constitutes not only a unique contribution to technical scholarship but goes to the very heart of the Hebraic philosophic enterprise. One may conclude from his investigations that by the same token Philo's *Logos,* which denoted the metaphysical status of Reason, goes back as well to ancient Hebraic sources with which he was thoroughly acquainted and were not the product of pure Hellenistic formulations. As a matter of fact the same Book of Proverbs, which is cited by some scholars as the primary source for the Alexandrian philosophic tradition of projecting Reason as the source for knowledge, also speaks of "The Fear of the Lord is the beginning of Understanding" (Prov. I, 7). Apparently the Book of Proverbs as well as the Jewish Wisdom literature generally pursued a notion of Reason which was essentially and distinctively Jewish. It regarded Reason in several senses: (1) as a speculative philosophical instrument, (2) as a motivational force demonstrating utilitarian consequences, (3) as a faculty for moral cognition, but most important of all (4) metaphysically as a constituitive ultimate being. This was Saadia's notion of Reason as well as Bar Hiyya who asserted "that any potential object which reason affirms its realization must have already changed to actuality" (Heg. ha-Nefesh, p. 5).

Accordingly, Dr. Belkin's scholarly works on Philo which will soon be compiled into several volumes constitutes a major contribution to Jewish thought in keeping with Maimonidean doctrine that Judaism was a many-faceted scheme of thought consisting of Biblical, rabbinic, and philosophical tradition—all blended into a perfect synthesis of the Judaic enterprise.

II

This leads me to another aspect of Dr. Belkin's scholarly works. In 1958 Dr. Belkin launched the first of Yeshiva University's new series of *Studies in Torah Judaism* with a monograph entitled *The Philosophy of Purpose* which marked a significant event in Jewish rethinking. At a time when religious philosophy was faced with an onslaught of growing skepticism as a result of technological advances on the one hand and a moral decadence on the other, Dr. Belkin's exposition offered a radical restatement of the position of traditional Judaism which attempted to fill the void. Putting the mark of emphasis on human existence Judaism espouses, he argued, a philosophy of purpose. In such a mode of discourse the primary interest is not in origins or causes but in spiritual effects and man's destiny. "Rather than attempting to prove the creation of the world by God," he asserts, "the Torah concentrates on improving the quality of man's response to God. Both Philo and Maimonides stress the fact that even the actions of God in this world depend on the moral actions of man."

By the same token the Divine Commandments must be viewed as the embodiment of a high moral purpose. "The purposeful philosopher," he says, "attempts to define their meaning of man and to divine the purpose which is fulfilled by their utilization. There is a moral and spiritual purpose to the law at a deeper level of meaning not immediately apparent to the teachings of the Torah. A purposeful outlook is involved in the assignment of the ultimate value of the observance for man's fulfillment. While it cannot always explain the beginnings, it posits its meaningfulness and motivation in terms of ends and purpose for man."

In this personalistic sense, Dr. Belkin understands the *Beratia* in *Erubin,* recording the dispute between the School of Shammai and the School of Hillel. The problem revolved around the question whether it would have been better had man not been created. Both schools finally agreed that "since he has been created, it behooves him to search his deeds." Thus the primary concern of Judaism is not with being and non-being but with the existential meaning of the human condition. The crucial requirement of our day is the redirection of world ideology towards a spiritual interpretation of man. As the writer puts it: "We need a philosophy which emphasizes not the likeness of man and beast, but the likenesses of man and God . . . which looks upon man not as mere biological and chemical mechanism, but as a divinely endowed human being who has a higher moral and spiritual purpose in life."

The excellent exposition which initiated the Yeshiva University Press is a profound and far reaching study providing answers to contemporary problems and pointing to new and mature directions for traditional Judaism. Drawing extensively on Jewish sources, the essay has been translated into Hebrew and Yiddish and laid the ground-work for his future works reflecting insights that are so relevant to contemporary thought.

III

Clearly, Dr. Belkin has not only distinguished himself as a famed expert on Philo and as a philosopher of Purpose but there is a third aspect to his scholarship in the Talmudic discipline. As a brilliant and profound *rosh yeshiva,* Dr. Belkin has pursued a unique approach in terms of method and content in the study of the Talmud and Halakhah. The method is one of textual analysis which brings to bear a stream of learned insights upon the halakhic process and helps to resolve many involved textual inconsistencies in a scholarly manner.

Intertwined with this method of textual analysis which he has introduced in his "shiurim," is Dr. Belkin's basic concept of halakhah which governs his methodology. He argues that while the term ha-lakhah projects a notion of an elaborate legal system, it is funda-mentally different from general jurisprudence. Jewish law "which has its origin and is deeply rooted in religious convictions," Dr. Belkin writes, "looks upon law as a moral guide and as a means of learning how to obey the Divine Word of God" (*In His Image,* p. 214). It is the embodiment of Judaism's spiritual concepts and the corpus of practices, which the halakhah prescribes is related to some "higher law" or ethical ends based upon God's attribute of mercy.

This notion of halakhah has many implications. For one thing, it repudiates an exclusive sociological or economic motivation for rab-binic legislation. The author emphatically states, "The disagreements between the Sadducees and the Pharisees, as recorded in the Mishnah and reported by Josephus, had almost no direct bearing on political, sociological or economic problems of the day. Through ingenious and fanciful interpretations it is possible to read sociological and economic motives into these controversies. But basically, the Pharisaic-Sadducean differences are concerned purely with ritual laws and beliefs, belief in angels, resurrection, immortality, free will, the authority of the Oral Law, and literalism. True, if one desires, one can credit such ritual matters as handwashing, defilement of sacred writings, and the religious calendar of differing political views. However, such speculative theories can never approach the true essence of historic Judaism nor can they explain the Pharisaic understanding of the emphasis in the rabbinic code upon the *demos,* the individual and the sacredness of human personality created in the Image of God. Unlike any other legal system which is designed chiefly for the protection of society even if in the process injustice is done to individuals, Judaism's rules of conduct are primarily concerned with the concept of individuality— the protection and advancement of the individual. The Halakhah is not theology but rather anthropology—the knowledge of man and his development in order that he may be transformed into "In His Image" (*ibid.*).

Moreover, other judicial systems operate in the framework of two contending parties, the plaintiff and the defendant. In the rabbinic code of law, the defendant is his own plaintiff. Jewish Law represents a voluntary discipline. Its high standards are constantly prodding us on to live more nobly in order that we may fulfill ourselves. In our judicial system we always appear, as it were, in court without an official summons to judge our own actions and embark upon a course of improvement. Dr. Belkin makes the point that even the high priest on the holiest day of the year publicly confessed his errors and proclaimed before all that as a human being he was subject to frailties that need to be rectified. It is interesting to note in this regard that while the confession of the ordinary worshipper may have been in private, it was incumbent upon the high priest to proclaim it publicly, thus indicating that before God all men are equal. No one stands above the law.

Finally, the ultimate purpose of Halakhic Judaism is to develop conscience Jews. This can be accomplished only when we learn to view every act no matter how commonplace and insignificant in cosmic, Halakhic, God-centered terms. Halakhah conceived of the moral imperative not in the abstract but in the practical application of ethical values in the daily routine of living. The ethical verities have relevance when translated into human activity or endowed with legal as well as moral sanctions.

B.

DR. SAMUEL BELKIN AS EDUCATOR

Manifestly, the three areas of Dr. Belkin's scholarship have augmented his role as the acknowledged scholar and spokesman for traditional Judaism and spurred his herculean efforts to create the greatest citadel of higher Jewish learning in the world. This brings us to a consideration of another area of his achievement, as the foremost educator and dynamic architect of Yeshiva University. The past three decades under his inspiring leadership have witnessed the school's phenomenal growth, unprecedented expansion, widespread program of research, and high quality of excellence and intellectual integrity unmatched in the annals of our history. The fact is inescapable that never in the history of our people since the days of Yavneh and the Golden Age of Spain to the Lithuanian Yeshivot have so many students been exposed to the teachings of two cultures under one roof as we find today at Yeshiva University. Of a total of over eight thousand students enrolled in courses leading to nineteen degrees and diplomas, fifty-two hundred of them are engaged in a unique dual academic and Jewish studies program. Such a program of synthesis combining modern sciences and arts with our Judaic heritage serves to moralize scientific invention and intellectualize the basic tenets of our faith by which Judaism and mankind can survive. It is fortifying to note that more than eight thousand alumni, graduates of our colleges and graduate and professional schools, are contributing knowledge and skills in communal and religious leadership, industry, medicine, government, law, the sciences, social service and education. Indeed every segment of the nation and the Jewish community is being served by the graduates of this vibrant reservoir of learning established and guided by the foremost educator of our time.

In his burning zeal to establish Yeshiva University as a living monu-
ment of Torah, culture and service, Dr. Belkin was guided by three
basic educational motivations which direct the current of this fountainhead of learning: (1) Centrality of Torah learning and practice;
(2) The advancement of the arts and sciences and their infusion with
our spiritual heritage; and (3) Serving the nation and the Jewish
community by a professional alumni, and trained leaders imbued with
skills, ethics and spiritual vision.

I

In charting the course which the American Jewish community must
follow in order to retain its identity and vitality, Dr. Belkin draws
upon his scholarly historical background. In a very apt analogy, he
compares our community to two similar communities of the past—the
Jewish community of Alexandria and the Jewish community of Spain,
during the Golden Age. He points out that while both were living in
vibrant communities, only the Jewish community of Spain made a
lasting contribution to the Rabbinic and Scholarly literature, which is
part of our present heritage. The reason for this lies in the fact that
the Jewish community in Spain made use of the original sources of
Jewish learning and knowledge, while Alexandrian Jewry had avail-
able to it only a translated Judaism.

If the American community of the future is to prosper spiritually,
it must follow the pattern of Spanish Jewry of dedicating itself to
Jewish scholarship and the study of Torah on a distinct and undiluted
level.

Accordingly, the progress of Traditional Judaism is to be measured
essentially by our devotion to the study of Torah and the safeguarding
and the development of the well-springs of our faith. "Am haArazuth,"
Torah illiteracy, is the most serious impediment to the development of
Traditional Judaism. Without scholarship and knowledge of Torah
we cannot hope to achieve that synthesis that was once the glory of
Spanish Judaism. But knowledge of Halakhah requires more than
taking courses in Talmud. The technique of learning is also crucial.
The Yeshiva method is one of complete permeation with original

sources. One simply cannot take a course in the Talmud. One has to learn to inhale literally its spiritual aroma and to "swim" in the "Yam haTalmud."

The centrality of Torah thus constitutes the cornerstone of the Yeshiva University program. It is reflected in every area of expansion of the institution.

II

Now, because Yeshiva has pursued a course of keeping separate and undiluted our religious heritage, it has by the same token developed a process of integration with the general community through the advancement of the arts and sciences and secular wisdom.

Dr. Belkin has deepened the concept of "Synthesis" when he stated in one of his messages, "If we seek the blending of science and religion and the integration of secular knowledge into sacred wisdom, then it is not in the subject matter represented by these fields, but rather within the personality of the individual that we hope to achieve the synthesis."

The Jewish community has reflected three trends in its process of integrating itself into the culture of the general community. The first was one of abject surrender to the environment due to looking up to the majority culture as in Germany. The second trend may be characterized as an attempt to resist the environment by building an iron cultural wall around ourselves, shutting out any external influence. Such an attitude prevailed in Eastern Europe where the Jews looked down upon the surrounding cultures.

The Yeshiva has promulgated a third course of meeting up to the environment and enhancing it by our Biblical heritage, Rabbinic and Philosophic scholarship. For does not religion provide the highest moral sanctions for our behavior and in this respect is it not an inseparable part of our cultural and of our American tradition?

This was the basis that motivated Dr. Belkin to establish the nation's first College of Medicine under Jewish auspices. Dr. Belkin reasoned that if we are to make a distinct contribution to America, we must create an institution that will be permeated with the true spirit of our faith and at the same time highlight the basic doctrine of American freedom and equality. As a tercentenary gift by the Jewish community to the welfare of America, the Albert Einstein Medical College of Yeshiva University stands as a token of our enduring faith in the democratic way of life by the erection of a model, non-sectarian school where faculty and students are selected on the basis of merit without regard to race, color or creed. Moreover, the emphasis upon the principle that medicine is not only a physical science, but also a social science, helped to develop in each student a strong social motivation striving for health promotion and disease prevention.

By the same token, the infusion of our scientific system of education with a spiritual interpretation of history will succeed in utilizing our modern sciences and arts to the greater advantage of mankind, and at the same time fortify our religious knowledge with the valid insights of contemporary thought. For a sound educational system puts all of life into a total, unified perspective where value aspects blend with factual analysis; the secular is infused with the sacred, and the ritual with het doctrinal. A good school is one which does not simply have courses in religion but whose entire orientation is geared toward this organic unity of knowledge. Rationalism and scientific experimentation tend to fragmentize and analyze objective reality. Spiritual knowledge puts it into unified perspective by emphasizing its value aspects and wholeness. Moreover, the arts in general under such a system of synthesis are not merely a mirror reflecting contemporary events or values, but powerful forces which shape and mold the way in which people ought to live and behave.

III

Finally, Dr. Belkin has added a third ingredient to this program for a revitalized spiritual community life that will serve the nation and the Jewish community by a professional alumni and trained leaders. The first Jewish community in America was a Sephardic community. Its foundations were strong because at the heart of it were synagogues around which revolved the social and cultural agencies of the community. Yet after a century, the Sephardic community lost its hold upon the American scene. The reason for that was that the Sephardic community reared its religious and secular structures in a vacuum. Each synagogue constituted a unit by itself with no affiliation to a central fountainhead that helped to replenish its leadership and direct the currents of Jewish life.

The Sephardic Synagogue had no Academy of Learning whence it was able to draw renewed spiritual nourishment and recharge its cultural batteries.

The Yeshiva University, as the foremost institution of Jewish higher learning in America, constitutes the address of American traditional Judaism. It is anxious to forge a stronger bond between the traditional community and Yeshiva and create a Jewish community strong in its faith and loyal in its desires to serve God and humanity.

Dr. Belkin has often said, "We have no ambitions to become bigger merely for the sake of bigness, we rather consider it our duty to make our contribution in terms of service."

There are three kinds of leaders. One who emphasizes the civilization of the head and regards as the highest good the acquisition of knowledge. He, therefore, advances the cause of science, the inventive genius and general wisdom.

Then again there are leaders who emphasize the civilization of the hand. They strive after mechanical perfection and technological skills developed in scientific laboratories.

Finally there are leaders who espouse the civilization of the heart and the cultivation of the spirit of man. Their chief concern is the civilizing of the heart of man, the infusion of moral and spiritual values into our scientific skills and a sense of compassion and conscience into our relation with our fellow man.

As a penetrating scholar and dynamic architect of Yeshiva University, Dr. Belkin combines all three qualities in his personality and leadership.

In reverent gratitude for the three decades of dynamic leadership and consummate scholarship we are privileged to dedicate this volume to our highly esteemed President of Yeshiva University, as a mark of our recognition of his great achievement for the strengthening and

development of the Torah way of life in America. As we pay homage
to his inspiring leadership, we pray that the Almighty grant him long
years of consecrated service, that the light of Torah continue to burn
with increasing radiance and cast its glowing beams unto every corner
of the earth.

NOTES

[1] See also T.B. Hagigah, 12a where *reason* is only one of the ten instruments for Creation.

[2] Submission to the Will of God is the epitome of world wisdom. See Eccle. 9:1, 7; 6-10. Apparently the book's key concept, wisdom or Reason denotes practical wisdom. The wise man's superiority over the fool has nothing to do with theoretical, metaphysical knowledge, but a practical overview of life demonstrating its utilitarian consequences. Speculative thought is deprecated, and epigrammatically expressed in the phrase, "He that increaseth knowledge, increaseth sorrow" (*ibid.*, 1:18). In this notion it deviates from the Palestinian as well as the Greek tradition. For the affinity between the concept of Reason in Greek and in the Palestinian frame has been recognized by both sides at an early date. A student of Aristotle, Theophrastus, describes the Jews as a philosophic sect. Clearchus of Soli records a meeting of Aristotle with a Jewish philosopher. c/o H. Levy, "Aristotle and the Jewish Sage According to Clearchus of Soli," *Harvard Theological Review XXXI*, 206-235. Also J. Guttmann, "Theophrastus on the Knowledge of God in Israel," *Tarbiz*, XVIII, 157-165.

[3] The man theme of the Wisdom of Solomon is the praise of wisdom, and the exhortation to seek wisdom is delineated with all the attributes of the Stoic *pneuma* going even beyond it. The Book of Proverbs is replete with other philosophic concepts as well, such as Plato's four cardinal virtues. By the same token IV Maccabees with its central emphasis on the rule of reason over the emotions and will purports to follow the philosophic discourse in the Book of Proverbs.

The Book of Enoch, although consisting of four separate books, projects one experience of that mysterious Enoch referred to in Gen. 5:21, "And Enoch walked with God and vanished, for God took him." He thus became a mysterious being to whom all manner of experiences such as the spirit of Wisdom as the intermediary between God and man could be ascribed (Enoch 45:3-5).

[5] See Belkin's article in *Abraham Weiss Jubilee Vol.*, pp. 579-581.

[6] See essay in this anthology, S. Belkin's "Some Obscure Traditions Mutually Clarified in Philo and Rabbinic Literature."

17

BIBLIOGRAPHY
BOOKS AND ESSAYS BY DR. BELKIN

Philo and Oral Law (Vol. XI of the Hervard Semitic Series, 1940).
Essays in Traditional Jewish Thought (Philosophical Library, 1956).
In His Image (Abelard-Schuman, 1961).
The Philosophy of Purpose (Yeshiva University Press, 1958).

He has contributed to numerous learned publications, including *Journal of Biblical Literature, Jewish Quarterly Review, Hapardes, Talpioth, Horeb* and *Sura,* and served as associate editor of Rabbinics for the *Universal Jewish Encyclopedia.* Among his writings are: *The Alexandrian Halakhah in Apologetic Literature, The Midrash Tadshe and Its Hellenistic Sources, The Onomastic Midrash in Philo, The Munchen Edition of the Tractate Nedarim, The Midrash Hanaelam of the Zohar and Its Source in Alexandrian Midrashic Literature, The Philonic Exposition of the Law in Light of Ancient Rabbinic Midrashim, Questions and Answers in Genesis and Exodus — The Oldest Recorded Palestinian Midrash,* and *Philo and a Palestinian Midrashic Tradition.*

He has won wide acclaim for his papers and monographs, which include: *What Makes a Good Jew, Parent as Teacher and Teacher as Parent,* and *Man and His Creator.* His *The Four Dimensions of Higher Education* has been included in *Introduction to College Life, a Book of Readings* (Houghton Mifflin, 1962).

18

SOME OBSCURE TRADITIONS
MUTUALLY CLARIFIED IN PHILO
AND RABBINIC LITERATURE[1]

by SAMUEL BELKIN

This article is not primarily concerned with the problem of Philo's dependence upon ancient rabbinic traditions or with probing into his specific sources and primary texts. This subject has been discussed by me elsewhere.[2] The present paper limits itself to passages in Philo and rabbinic literature which, standing alone, are not sufficiently lucid or intelligible, but when placed side by side do shed light on one another. The approach is in the manner of the rabbinic evaluation of many Pentateuchal passages: "They are meager in their own area, but find abundance in some other place."[3] In the following discussion I dwell upon a number of instances illustrative of such relationships.

I. THE HORNS OF THE ALTAR

Concerning the characteristic structure of the altar, the Midrash Tadshe (ch. XI) states:[4]

ולמה יש קרנות למזבח אלא שכל החיות הטהורות בין הנקרבין למזבח
בין שאינן מתקרבין הכל מקרין ומפרים. ועוד למה הקב"ה גזר לעשות
קרנות למזבח אלא רצה הקב"ה ללמדנו אם מקריבין לו קרבנות
בצדקה הוא מהדף ומאבד ומכניע צריהם ואינו מניחו להזיק אותם שכן
כתיב וכל קרני רשעים אגדע תרוממנה קרנות צדיק (תהלים עה, יא)
ואם לאו הוא רודף ודוחף אותם מפניו שכן כתיב ונתתי את עריכם
חרבה וכו' ולא אריח בריח ניחחכם (ויקרא כו, לא) ואומר למה לי רוב
זבחיכם וכו' (ישעיה א, יא).

Editor's Note: We are indebted to Professor Solomon Zeitlin, editor of the *Jewish Quarterly Review,* and Dr. Sidney B. Hoenig, Dean of Bernard Revel Graduate School, Yeshiva University, for permitting us to print this scholarly essay.

Reprinted from *Seventy Fifth Anniversary Volume. Jewish Quarterly Review.* New Series. 1967.

"Why does the altar have horns? Because all the clean animals, whether these are brought as sacrifices or not, have horns and cleft hoofs. Once again, why did the Holy One, blessed be He, decree that horns be made for the altar? Because the Holy One, blessed be He, sought to teach us, that if we offered sacrifices to Him in righteousness, He would repel, destroy and subject their enemies and would not permit them to harm them (the Israelites). For it is written: 'And all the horns of the wicked I will cut off, but the horns of the righteous shall be lifted up' (Ps. 75:11). But, if not (i.e., should the Israelites become iniquitous), He would harass and repel them from before Him, as it is written: 'And I will make your cities a waste, (and will bring your sanctuaries unto desolation), and I will not smell the savor of your sweet odors' (Lev. 26:31); and it is also said: 'To what purpose is the multitude of your sacrifices unto me'" (Isa. 1:11).

We see that the Midrash Tadshe poses one question but gives two answers. The first answer is not clarified. Moreover, the question and the answers have no parallel in rabbinic literature. Upon examining Philo, however, we find not only a fuller exposition of this homily but a parallelism that is striking. As we have demonstrated elsewhere, the Tadshe is to a considerable extent a Hellenistic Midrash derived from or based upon the main structure of Philonic exposition.[5] The present instance proves this point beyond doubt.

Philo notes (*Qu. in Ex.,* II, 101, on Ex. 27:2): "Why does the altar have horns not attached from above but united (to it)? Because it is not proper to sacrifice any of those (animals) which do not have horns, neither those which are offerings nor anything else.[6] Accordingly, those which are to be offered as sacrifices are the following three (kinds): the sheep, the ox, and the goat. But besides these there are seven other (kinds permitted) for food: gazelle, deer, wild goat, buffalo, white-rumped antelope, oryx, and giraffe; each of these has horns. For He wishes to specify those (animals to be used) for food, for even though they are not to be offered as sacrifices, still they are similar to those which are to be sacrificed. Wherefore those who use them for need will not offer anything opposed to, or unworthy of, or alien to a sacrifice. In the second place, the horns (of the altar) incline and face toward the four sides of the world, toward the east, toward the west, toward the south, and toward the Dipper, for it is proper that those who are in all parts (of the world) should all bring their first-fruits and new (offerings) to this one altar, and sacrifice victims to God, the Father of the world. In the third place (this is said) symbolically, for in place of defensive weapons He has given a crop of horns to animals which grow horns. Just as the (animals) to be sacrificed, (namely) the ram, the ox, and the goat, repel their enemies with their horns, so also did He wish to rebuke the impious who presume to offer sacrifices, by teaching that the divine Logos opposes and repels the enemies of truth, goring every soul as if with horns, and showing up in their nakedness its unclean and unworthy deeds, which a little while before it had been concealing. For these reasons the horns are not to be placed upon (the altar) from outside, but by His command are to be united to the altar itself to extend it, since sacrificial animals have their horns growing out of themselves."

Philo here gives three answers to his question, whereas the Midrash gives only two. Also, Philo's first and third answers are similar to those of the Midrash not only in exposition but also in phraseology. But whereas the Midrash speaks briefly of "clean animals whether these are brought as sacrifices or not," Philo elaborates and enumerates the horned animals in their respective categories: those permitted to be offered as sacrifice, and those allowed only to be used as food. His summary also clarifies another aspect of the symbolism of "the horns of the altar," namely, the non-acceptance for the altar some of the clean animals: "Wherefore those who use them for need (i.e, for food, transportation, or ploughing for instance) will not offer anything opposed to, or unworthy of, or alien to a sacrifice." Thus, without this Philonic expatiation the first midrashic answer would remain incomplete and partially obscure.

II. ABRAHAM'S NAME

Philo states (*De Mut. Nom.*, 65-69):

"Such changes of name are signs of moral values, the signs small, sensible, obvious, the values great, intelligible, hidden. And these values are found in noble verities, in unerring and pure notions, and in soul-betterments. The proof of this is easy, starting from the change of name here before us, for Abram is interpreted as 'uplifted father,' Abraham as 'elect father of sound.' How the two differ we shall understand more clearly if we first discover the meaning of each. Resorting then to allegory, we say that 'uplifted' is one who, rising from earth to the heights, surveys the supraterrestrial, conversing with and studying the phenomena of the upper world, investigating the size of the sun and its courses, its regulation of the seasons of the year by its revolutions as it advances and retreats at the same rate of speed; one who considers also the different illuminations of the moon, its phases, its waning and waxing, and the movement of the other stars both in the fixed and the planetary order. To inquire into such matters bespeaks a soul not devoid of natural gifts or unproductive, but rather highly gifted, and capable of engendering offspring perfect and without blemish; and therefore he called the student of the upper world 'father' because he is not unproductive of wisdom. Such is our definition of the meanings conveyed under the symbol of the name Abram; those conveyed by Abraham are such as I proceed to describe. They are three in number: 'father,' 'elect,' and 'of sound.' We say that sound stands for the uttered word, for in living creatures the instrument of sound is the vocal power. Its father is the mind, since the stream of speech issues from the understanding as its fount. The elect mind is the mind of the wise, since it contains what is best."

Philo's explanation of the name "אברם" is concise and clear. אב-רם means "uplifted father." But how אברהם etymologically means "elect father of sound" is difficult to understand from the context.

Edmund Stein sought to explain the riddle on the basis of אב - בר - ר. אב meaning "father;" בר (ברר), "elect;" and רהם as a variation of רעם ("thunder"), meaning "sound."[7] Stein's surmise seems to me untenable, and especially so the meaning he ascribes to רהם. According to Philo, sound here stands "for the uttered word, for in living creatures the instrument of sound is the vocal power." It would be unwarranted, therefore, to convert this vocal power into a power of the elements ("thunder"), a metamorphosis which Philo did not intend.

and which would be preposterous for him to envisage for suporting his allegorical interpretation. Indeed המון, and not רעם, and certainly not the meaningless רהם, is at times the Hebrew equivalent for "vocal sound." Cf., for instance המון of המון שיריך, "the clamor of thy songs" (Amos 5:22). This significance of המון in אב המון would, as far as it goes, superbly fit Philo's "vocal power." What buttresses this supposition is the fact that the LXX translates המון שיריך as ἦχον ᾠδῶν θου; and ἠχοῦς (genitive of ἠχώ, "sound") is exactly the word which Philo uses in connection with "אברהם" in Gen. 17:5.[8]

Bearing this in mind, we proceed to clarify the remaining two Philonic etymologies.

To this end, we must first present the relevant testimony of Shab. 105a:

אמר רבי יוחנן משום רבי יוסי בן זימרא מניין ללשון נוטריקון מן
התורה שנאמר כי א"ב המו"ן גוים נתתיך (בראשית יז, ה) אב נתתיך
לאומות בחור נתתיך באומות המון חביב נתתיך באומות מלך נתתיׄך
לאומות ותיק נתתיך באומות נאמן נתתיך לאומות.

"R. Yoḥanan said in R. Yose b. Zimra's name: How do we know [that] abbreviated forms [are recognized] by the Torah? Because it is written, For AB [the father of] HaMWN [a multitude of] nations have I made thee: a father [Ab] of nations have I made thee; a chosen one [Baḥur] among nations have I made thee. HaMWN: beloved [Ḥabib], have I made thee among nations; a king [Melek] have I appointed thee for the nations; distinguished [Wathik] have I made thee among the nations; faithful [Ne'eman] have I made thee to the nations."[9]

The above statement of R. Yohanan patently contends with that of Stein. Did the rabbinic *notarikon* אב-בחור or the אב-בר configuration, as proposed by Stein, serve Philo as a pattern for his "father" and "elect"? I think there is little choice in the matter. True, אב-בר is by rabbinic definition also an admissible *notarikon*. However, not *it* but אב-בחור is attested to in rabbinic literature. In view of this, it is but natural to maintain that not an imaginary אב-בר, but an old vital Palestinian *notarikon*-tradition recorded in Shab. 105a also found its expression in Philo. And needless to add, the latter could hardly have happened to evolve a *notarikon* of his own that would be impregnated with an identical meaning. This would be a strange coincidence indeed.

But at this point, Philo had to part company with the tradition recorded in Shab. 105a. Evidently the מ, which spelled out in Shab. 105a "King have I appointed thee for the nations," prevented Philo from continuing with the rabbinic *notarikon* of המון. מלך had marked political overtones. It could be readily misunderstood by the non-Jews of Alexandria, or even wilfully misinterpreted by its anti-Semites of whom he bitterly complains in his *Flaccus* and *Embassy to Gaius*. He was therefore constrained to deviate at this juncture from the Palestinian pattern, and, in consonance with his method of abstract allegorization, define "sound" as the uttered word, "father" as the mind, i.e., the fountain of the stream of speech, and "elect" mind as the mind of the wise. Hence only in the light of the rabbinic *notarikon* can the origin of Philo's "father" and "elect" be best explained.

III. BRINGING THE FIRST-FRUITS

Pertaining to the offerings of Cain and Abel, Philo asks (*Qu. in Gen.* I, 60 on Gen. 4:3-4): "Why did Cain after some days bring first fruits as offerings, while Abel (brought an offering) from the first-born and fat ones, not after some days? Scripture manifests a distinction between the lover of self and the lover of God. For one of them took for himself the fruit of the first fruits and impiously thought God worthy (only) of the second fruits. For the words 'after some days' instead of 'immediately,' and 'from the offerings' instead of 'from the first fruits,' indicate great wickedness. But the other offered the first-born and elder animals without any delay at all or rejection by his Father."

Philo seeks to stress "after some days" (מקץ ימים) used in the verse telling of Cain's gift (Gen. 4:3). This phrase is not used in the next verse for Abel, but this verse contains the words מבכורות צאנו, "from the firstlings of his flock." Philo's answer is to show the superiority of Abel's gift: "But the other (Abel) offered the first born and elder animals without any delay at all."

Though one may think Philo speaks merely of Abel's promptness and generosity, "without delay at all" and "first-born" entail additional meanings that can be demonstrated only by adducing a Mishnah and a Midrashic text.

The Midrash comments:

ויהי מקץ ימים ר' אליעזר אומר בתשרי נברא העולם ר' יהושע אומר
בניסן מאן דאמר בתשרי עשה, הבל קיים מן החג ועד חנוכה (ב"ר,
כב, זר, הוצאת טהעאדאר, ע' 207).

. ."*After some days,* R. Eleazar said the world was created in Tishre; R. Joshua said (the world was created) in Nisan. He who maintains that He made (the world) in Tishre (implies) that Abel subsisted from the Festival (Sukkot) until Ḥanukkah."

The last statement in the Midrash is enigmatic, but the Mishnah that notes the laws of bringing the first-fruits clarifies it:

„מעצרת ועד החג מביא וקורא מן החג ועד חנוכה מביא ואינו קורא
רבי יהודה בן בתירא אומר מביא וקורא" (בכורים א. ו).

"A man may bring (the First-fruits) and make the Avowal (at any time) from Shabuot until the Feast (of Tabernacles); while from the Feast (of Tabernacles) until Ḥanukkah he may bring (them), but he may not make the Avowal. R. Judah ben Bathyra said: He may do both."

The duty, then, that Abel fulfilled in the interval between Sukkot and Ḥanukkah was that of offering the firstlings, whereas, by implication, Cain failed in that respect. But the latter fact is explicitly stated in the Philonic text quoted above. On the other hand, the rabbinic texts demarcate exactly the vague Philonic intimation, "without any delay at all."

IV. Heavenly Birds

We read in the Midrash *Tehillim* to Ch. 104:9-12:

„גבול שמת בל יעברון וכו' המשלח מעינים בנחלים וכו' עליהם עוף
השמים ישכון. ר' ישמעאל ור' עקיבא, ר' עקיבא אומר אלו מלאכי
השרת אמר לו ר' ישמעאל כלך מדברותיך ולך אצל נגעים ואהלות,
המשלח מעינים בנחלים, אלו מקוואות שטובלין בהם בעלי נגעים
המטמאים באהל המת".

" 'Thou hast set a bound that they may not pass over. . . . He sendeth the springs into the valleys. . . . Above them dwell the birds of the sky.' R. Ishmael and R. Akiba (differed). R. Akiba maintained that 'springs' referred to pools in which lepers, whose presence under a roof brings the same degree of uncleanness as a dead body, are required to immerse themselves (when they are healed); and 'the birds of the sky' are the ministering angels (hovering above, when the lepers are healed). But R. Ishmael said to R. Akiba: You ought to give up this kind of exegesis, and turn to the study of the treatises 'Signs of Leprosy' and 'Tents.' "

R. Akiba's interpretation of "the birds of the sky" as "the ministering angels" seems at first glance to be esoteric. Yet his interpretation, far-fetched though it appears, was founded on an earlier and well-established tradition.

Thus, Philo states in *De Gig.* 6-9: "It is Moses' custom to give the name of angels to those whom other philosophers call demons (or spirits), souls, that is, which fly and hover in the air.[10] And let no one suppose that what is said here is a myth. For the universe must needs be filled through and through with life . . . the air must needs be filled with living beings, though indeed they are invisible to us . . . yet the fact that our powers of vision are incapable of any perception of the forms of these souls is no reason why we should doubt that there are souls in the air; but they must be apprehended by the mind, that like may be discerned by like."

Philo's assertion that Moses calls the souls that fly in the air angels accords with R. Akiba's statement about ministering angels hovering above. And Philo's stressing that "what is said here is not a myth," and that "there is no reason why we should doubt that there are souls in the air," further proves that R. Akiba's opinion is not esoteric, but a widely held view.

Philo also notes that heaven consists of a "fifth element" which partakes of the nature of the divine, and that the birds which Abraham did not divide (see Gen. 15:10) symbolized this element which "is not of a nature to be divided." We thus read in *Qu. in Gen.*, III, 6:

"Why does (scripture) say, 'But the birds he did not divide'?

"It indicates the *fifth* and the *quintessence* of which the ancients said the heaven is made. For the four elements, as they are called, are mixtures rather than elements, and by them they divide those divided things into that of which they are mixed. . . . But only the fifth is made unmixed and pure, for which reason it is not of a nature to be divided. Wherefore it is well said that 'the birds he did not divide,' since, as in the case of birds, it is the nature of celestial bodies . . . to be elevated and to resemble both (kinds of) clean birds, the turtle-dove and the dove, which do not admit of cutting or division, since they belong to the simpler and unmixed fifth substance."

This accords with R. Akiba's designating "the birds of the sky" as "ministering angels."

Referring to the angels whom Jacob saw in his dream ascending and descending on the ladder, Philo says:

"Up and down throughout its whole extent are moving incessantly the 'Words' of God, drawing it (the soul) up with them when they ascend, and disconnecting it with what is mortal . . . and when they descend, not casting it down, for neither does God nor a divine Logos cause harm, but condescending out of love for man and compassion for our race to be helpers and comrades, so that with the healing of their breath they may quicken the soul into new life . . . *but in the understanding of those who are still undergoing cleansing and have not yet fully washed their life defiled and stained by the body's weight, there walk angels,* divine Words, making them bright and clean with the doctrines of all that is good and beautiful" (*De Somn.,* I, 147-148).

Here Philo speaks of the angels as healers of those who are undergoing cleansing. This brings him closer yet to R. Akiba, who speaks of ministering angels healing the lepers who immerse themselves in pools to remove their uncleanness.

But all this does not mean that R. Akiba's view is based upon Philo's. The tradition is doubtless much older than Philo. In the Book of Tobit God is said to have sent the angel Raphael to heal Tobit's blindness (3, 17). Since the very name of His angel is indicative of his ministerial function, there can be no doubt that his reputation as a worker of cures had been established long before the Book of Tobit was written.

V. HEAVENLY NOURISHMENT

The LXX translate מן הוא in Exod. 16:15 — τί ἐδτι τοῦτο ("what is this?"). The *Mekhilta* remarks on this verse:

ויראו בני ישראל ויאמרו איש אל אחיו וגו' (שמות טז, טו) כאדם
שאומר לחברו מה הוא, כך אמרו זה לזה מה הוא. דורשי רשומות אמרו
ישראל קראו את שמו מן (מכילתא שמות טז, טו).[11]

"And when the children of Israel saw it, they said one to another. . . . As a man says to his fellowman: 'What is it?' so the Israelites said to one another: 'What is it?' The Allegorists said: 'The Israelites rendered the name "Manna" (man).'"

Philo comments on Exod. 16:4-16 (*De Fuga*, 137-139):

"When they sought what it is that nourishes the soul (for, as Moses says, 'they knew not what it was,' Exod. XVI., 15), they became learners and found it to be a saying of God, that is the Divine Word (the Logos), from which all kinds of instruction and wisdom flow in perpetual stream. This is the heavenly nourishment, and it is indicated as such in the sacred records, when the First Cause in His Own Person says, 'Lo, it is I That am raining upon you bread out of the heaven' (*ibid.*, 4); for in very deed God drops from above the ethereal wisdom upon minds which are by nature apt and take delight in Contemplation; and they see it and taste it and are filled with pleasure, being fully aware of what they feel, but wholly ignorant of the cause which produced the feeling. So they inquire 'What is this' (*ibid.*, 15) which has a nature making it sweeter than honey and whiter than snow? And they will be taught by the seer that 'This is the bread, which the Lord hath given them to eat' (*ibid.*, 15). Tell me, then, of what kind the bread is. 'This saying,' he says, 'which the Lord ordained' (*ibid.*, 16). This Divine ordinance fills the soul that has vision alike with light and sweetness, flashing forth the radiancy of truth, and with the honied grace of persuasion imparting sweetness to those who hunger and thirst after nobility of character."

Although Philo allegorizes when he says that "God drops from above the ethereal wisdom upon minds," he does not ignore the literal meaning, and accordingly adds: "So they inquire what is this which has a nature making it sweeter than honey and whiter than snow?" As far, then, as the literal interpretation is concerned, Philo and the *Mekhilta* agree.

In the above passage Philo allegorizes the expression מן הוא, but in two other passages he allegorizes מן (τί) alone, imparting to it a different symbolic significance. Thus, he says in *Leg. Alleg.*, II, 86: "And when they have been given water to drink, they are filled also with the manna, the most generic of substances, for the manna is called 'somewhat,' and that suggests the *summum genus*. But the primal existence is God, and next to Him is the Word (logos) of God, but all other things subsist in word only, but in their active effects they are in some cases as good as non-subsisting." And in *Leg. Alleg.*, III, 175: "We have a proof of this in His feeding us with His own most 'generic' word; for 'manna' means 'something,' and this is the most generic of all terms. And the Word of God is above all the world, the eldest and most all-embracing of created things."

The word "somewhat" in Colson's and Whitaker's translation needs clarification. These translators add the following note on it: "Philo audaciously substitutes the indefinite for the interrogative pronoun ('something' for 'what'?)."

They add in the appendix to *Leg. Alleg.*, III, p. 483: ... "The Stoic phraseology . . . adopted τί, i.e., 'quiddity,' as the most generic and all-embracing of terms in place of the Platonic ἕν and the Aristotelian ." Wolfson too ascribes Philo's "something" to Stoic phraseology, but he goes further than Colson and Whitaker, ingeniously linking Philo's first allegorical interpretation of מן הוא to his second allegorical interpretation of מן. Professor Wolfson remarks:

"In still another place he says that God is 'the most generic' (τὸ γενικώτατον). . . . . Since God is the highest genus, He has no distinction of genus and species; that is, He belongs to no class, and hence we do not know What He is. . . . The proof-text is the verse in which it is said that when the children of Israel saw the manna, 'they said to one another, what is this (τί ἐϑτι τοῦτο)?—for they knew not what it was.' Drawing upon this explanation, he says that manna is 'the most generic' (τὸ γενικώτατον), for the manna is called 'what' (τί), and that suggests the primary genus of all things. . . . Undoubtedly this statement reflects the stoic teaching that 'the something' (τό τι) is the most generic (τὸ γενικώτατον) of all."[12]

These scholars have expertly and resourcefully uncovered the source and technique of Philo's interpretation. But what about the relationship, if any, of this Philonic exegesis to rabbinic tradition? The answer is found in the pivotal vocable מן, in the complex, מ-מין-מינין, as exemplified in Exod. Rab. 5, 9:

אמר ר"י ב"ר חנינא זמה המן שהיה מין אחד נהפך לכמה מינין בשביל צרך כל אחד ואחד הקול שהיה כח בו על אחת כמה וכמה שהיה משתנה לכל אחד ואחד.

"(Hence) did R. Yose b. Ḥanina say: If the manna, which is all of one kind, became converted into so many kinds to suit the capacity of each individual, was it not more possible for the Voice, which had power in it, to vary according to the capacity of each individual?"

It was through such word-play that the Alexandrian Jews, or for that matter Jews anywhere conversant with philosophy, sought to accomodate the homily to the Stoic "quiddity" as the most generic term. This is substantiated by the *Mekhilta* cited above, specifically in its last sentence:

דורשי רשומות אמרו ישראל קראו את שמו מן.

"The Allegorists said: "The Israelites called it manna *(man)*.' "[13]

This comment is strange indeed, for it adds nothing to the Scriptural verse, which already notes that the Israelites called it *man*.

Lauterbach, leaning on Philo, simply "guesses" that the *Doreshei Reshumot* understood "מן" here to refer to the "Word of God," but he does not explain their etymology.[14] The play on מ-מין-מינים, however, in light of the Stoic doctrine of "quiddity," turns his guess into a virtual certainty.

VI. ETERNAL DEATH

Twice Philo devotes attention to the repetition of the stem מות in the phrase מות תמות (Gen. 2:17).

(a) *Qu. in Gen.*, I, 16 (on Gen. 2:17):

"What is the meaning of the words, 'Ye shall die by the death'?

"The death of worthy men is the beginning of another life. For life is twofold: one is with corruptible body; the other is without body (and) incorruptible. So that the evil man dies by death even when he breathes, before he is buried, as though he preserved for himself no spark at all of the true life, which is excellence of character. The decent and worthy man, however, does not die by death, but after living long, passes away to eternity; that is, he is borne to eternal life."

(b) *Leg. Alleg.*, I, 105-107:

"'In the day that ye eat thereof, ye shall die by the death' (Gen. 2:17). And yet after they have eaten, not merely do they *not* die, but they beget children and become authors of life to others. What, then, is to be said to this? That death is of two kinds, one that of the man in general, the other that of the soul in particular. The death of the man is the separation of the soul from the body, but the death of the soul is the decay of virtue and the bringing in of wickedness. It is for this reason that God says not only "die" but "die by the death," indicating not the death common to us all, but that special death properly so called, which is that of the soul becoming entombed in passions and wickedness of all kinds. And this death is practically the antithesis of the death which awaits us all. The latter is a separation of combatants that had been pitted against each other, to wit, body and soul. The former, on the other hand, is a meeting of the two in conflict. And in this conflict the worse, the body, overcomes, and the better, the soul, is overcome. But observe that wherever Moses speaks of "dying by the death," he means the penalty-death, not that which takes place in the course of nature. That one is in the course of nature in which soul is parted from body; but the penalty-death takes place when the soul dies to the life of virtue, and is alive only to that of wickedness. That is an excellent saying of Heraclitus, who on this point followed Moses' teaching. 'We live,' he says, 'their death, and are dead to their life.' He means that now, when we are living, the soul is dead and has been entombed in the body as in a sepulchre; whereas, should we die, the soul lives forthwith its own proper life, and is released from the body, the baneful corpse to which it was tied."

In no rabbinic text do we find a similar explanation of the double wording of מות תמות, as referring to the eternal death of the soul. Though the Rabbis often use the phrase "he shall not have a portion in the world to come," they do not derive it from exegesis of מות תמות.

Philo, of course, will not deny that a heavenly sentence of death in the present world is expressed by מות תמות, or a court's sentence of capital punishment by מות יומת. (Num. 15:35), for instance, but his stressing that the punishment of everlasting death for the soul of the wicked is to be derived from the double use of the term "death" is unique.

Philo's concern about this doubling is obviously due to his belief that there are no superfluous words in the Pentateuch. We must admit, nevertheless, that he basically follows the literal interpretation of מות תמות, as rendered by the LXX —   , "Ye shall die by the death," which simply means that they will surely die the death common to all. His homily resulted, however, from a recognition that the phrase had also a deeper meaning than that which the text would ordinarily convey.

In only one instance in rabbinic literature is a similar exegesis evident, viz., in R. Akiba's interpretaton of הכרת תכרת (Num. 15:31), "shall utterly be cut off." This is the only biblical instance where the expression הכרת תכרת is employed, whereas the stem כרת is not doubled in such wise elsewhere. Quite possibly this unique expression in the Bible inspired R. Akiba's unique interpretation. We thus read in Sanh. 64b:

הכרת תכרת (במדבר טו, לא) הכרת בעולם הזה תכרת לעוה"ב דברי ר"ע.

" '(that the soul) shall utterly be cut off' (Numb. 15:31), הכרת (meaning destruction) in this world, תכרת-(destruction) in the world to come. This is the view of R. Akiba."

We thus see that this interpretation of הכרת תכרת closely resembles Philo's interpretation of מות תמות. Evidently both Philo and R. Akiba followed a tradition of interpreting in this way the double emphasis of words expressing destruction of human life. R. Akiba, like Philo, explained this double terminology as meaning that the soul of the wicked shall perish for ever. Philo further emphasizes this concept in *Qu. in Gen.*, I, 70 (on Gen. 4:10):

"What is the meaning of the words, 'The voice of thy brother calls to me from the earth'? This is most exemplary, for the Deity hears the deserving even though they are dead, knowing that they live an incorporeal life. But from the prayers of evil men He turns away His face even though they enjoy the prime of life, considering that they are dead to true life and bear their body with them like a tomb that they may bury their unhappy soul in it."

This tradition is similarly reiterated in Midrash ha-Gadol, on the very verse that Philo had commented. We read in the Midrash ha-Gadol:

כי ביום אכלך ממנו מות תמות (בראשית ב, יז) מות בעולם הזה תמות לעולם הבא.

"On the day that you eat of it ye shall surely die, ye shall die in this world; you shall meet death in the world to come."

The Midrash Tannaim (ed. Hoffmann, p. 101) also expounds this idea in its comment on Deut. 17:6:

יומת המת (דברים יז, ו) וכי המת מת אלא הרשעים שנקראו בחיים מתים.

" 'Let him that is to die be put to death' (literally, 'let the dead be put to death'). Do the dead die? It (means) that the wicked in their lifetime are called dead."

This brings home Philo's statement quoted above, namely:

". . . God says not only 'die' but 'die by the death,' indicating not the death common to us all, but that special death properly so called, which is that of the soul becoming entombed in passions and wickedness of all kinds."

VII. CAIN TO BE AVENGED

In connection with Gen. 4:23-24, Philo asks in *Qu. in Gen.*, I, 77:

"Why does Lamech after *five* generations condemn himself for his ancestor Cain's fratricide? For, says Scripture, he said to his wives Ada and Zillah, 'A man have I killed to my wound, and a young man to my hurt. If sevenfold punishment shall be exacted for Cain, then for Lamech seventy times seven.' "

Philo's "seventy times seven" is based on the LXX Text, reading, ὅτι ἑπτάκις ἐκδεδίκηται ἐκ καϊν, ἐκ δὲ λάμεχ ἑβδομήκον τάκις ἑπτά, i.e., "If sevenfold punishment shall be exacted from Cain, then for Lamech seventy times seven"; whereas the Hebrew text has: כי שבעתים יוקם קין ולמך שבעים ושבעה, i.e., "If Cain shall be avenged sevenfold, then Lamech seventy and sevenfold." But be that as it may, Philo's question has no bearing on either the Hebrew or the LXX text. It stands to reason, therefore, that Philo recorded a tradition that after *five* generations Cain will be avenged.

We read in Gen. Rab. 23:4:

ויאמר למך לנשיו עדה וצלה שמען קולי (בראשית ד, כג). רבי יוסי בר
חנינה אמר תבען לתשמיש אמרו לו למחר המבול בא נשמע לך ונהיה
פרות ורבות למארה אמר להן וכי איש הרגתי לפצעי שיבואו עלי
פצעים בשבילו וילד לחבורתי שיבואו עלי תבורות בשבילו, אתמהא,
קין הרג ונתלה לו ז' דורות ואני שלא הרגתי אינו דין שיתלה לי שבעים
ושבעה.

" 'And Lamech said unto his wives,' etc. R. Jose b. R. Ḥanina said: 'He summoned them to their marital duties.' Said they to him: 'Tomorrow a flood will come. Are we to obey thee and bear children for a curse?' He answered, 'For have I slain a man for my wounding— that wounds should come to me on his account? And a young man child for my bruising—that bruises should come upon me? Cain slew, yet judgment was suspended for him for *seven* generations; for me, who did not slay, surely judgment will wait seventy-seven generations."

In Targum Onkelos to Gen. 4:24:

ארי לשבעא דרין אתלין לקין הלא ללמך בריה שבעין ושבעא.

"If seven generations were suspended to Cain, will there not be (suspended) to Lamech, his descendant, seventy and seven?"

And in Pseudo-Jonathan to Gen. 4:24:

ארום קין דחב ותב בתיובתא עד שובעא דרין אתליו ליה ולמך בר בריה
דלא חב דינא הוא דיתלי ליה עד שויבעין ושבעא.

"For Cain, who sinned and repented, (protection) was extended to
him unto seven generations, and to Lamech, his descendant, who has
not sinned, it is (only) right that it shall be extended unto seventy
and seven."

This further indicates that Philo knew of a variant of this rabbinic
tradition. This variant must have counted only the five generations of,
חנוך, עירד, מהויאל, מתושאל, למך (Gen. 4:17-18), whereas the tradition recorded in the extant rabbinic literature must have added to these
five also the generations of Cain and the children of Lamech, making
seven.

VIII. MARITAL ABSTINENCE

The Talmud notes that cohabitation was interdicted to those in
Noah's ark. Thus we read in Sanh. 108b:

ומנלן דנאסרו דכתיב ובאת אל התבה אתה ובניך ואשתך ונשי בניך
אתך (בראשית ו, יח) וכתיב צא מן התבה אתה ואשתך ובניך ונשי
בניך אתך (בראשית ח, טז) וא"ר יוחנן מיכן אמרו שנאסרו בתשמיש
המטה.

"And whence do we know that they were forbidden? From the verse,
'And thou shalt enter into the ark, thou, and thy sons, and thy wife,
and the wives of thy sons with thee'; whilst further on it is written,
'Go forth from the ark, thou and thy wife, and thy sons, and thy sons'
wives with thee.' Whereon R. Yoḥanan observed: 'From this we deduce that cohabitation had been forbidden.'"

R. Yoḥanan's deduction is apparently based on the fact that the
first verse speaks separately of males and females, whereas the second
verse refers to them as mates, viz., "Noah and his wife," "his sons and
their wives." The deduction מיכן אמרו וכו' should not, however, be
regarded as made solely from the verse. The verse served only as a
support for an older tradition, not as the source of the tradition. Many
traditions related by the Tannaim of the Second Century or the
Amoraim of the Third Century may be traced back to traditions al-

ready known in the First Century. מיכן אמרו thus constitutes an ancient source, forgotten and restored. Indeed the tradition here of marital abstinence, first related by R. Yoḥanan, has its antecedence in
Philo's homily in *Qu. in Gen.*, II, 49 on Gen. 8:18:

"Why, when they entered the ark, was the order (of words) 'he
and his sons' and then 'and his sons' wives,' but when they went out, it
was changed? For (Scripture) says, 'Noah went out and his wife' and
then 'his sons and his sons'wives.' *(sic)*.[15] In the literal sense, by 'going
in' (Scripture) indicates the non-begetting of seed, but by 'going out'
it indicates generation. For when they went in, the sons are mentioned
together with their father, and the daughters-in-law together with
their mother-in-law. But when they went out, it was as married couples,
the father together with his wife, and then the several sons, each with
his wife. For He wishes through deeds rather than through words to
teach His disciples what is right for them to do. Accordingly, He said
nothing by way of verbal explanation to the effect that those who went
in should abstain from intercourse with their wives, and that when
they went out, they should sow seed in accordance with nature. This
(He indicated) by the order (of words) but not by exclaiming and
crying aloud, 'After so great a destruction of all those who were on
earth, do not indulge in luxury, for this is not fitting or lawful. It is
enough for you to receive the honour of life. But to go to bed with
your wives is the part of those seeking and desiring sensual satisfaction.' For these it was fitting to sympathize with wretched humanity,
as being kin to it. And at the same time they were watching for something unseen that might be impending, lest evil overtake them at some
time. But in addition to this, it would have been inept for them now,
while the living were perishing, to beget those who were not (yet) in
existence, and to be snared and surfeited at an unseasonable hour
with sensual pleasure. But after (the flood) had ceased and come to an
end, and they had been saved from the evil, He again instructed them
through the order (of their leaving the ark) to hasten to procreate, by
specifying not that men (should go out) with men, nor women with
women, but females with males."

As may be gathered from this Philonic passage, this old tradition must have sprung from a deep communal feeling, that when disaster overtakes mankind carnal pleasure is unseemly. This view is also expressed in Tanhuma, ed. Buber, Noah, 17:

ויבא נח ובניו (בראשית ז, ז) הזכרים לעצמן, ואשתו ונשי בניו (שם)
הנקבות לעצמן כך כל הימים שהיה נח בתבה היה נח ובניו וכל אשר
אתו אסוריםבתשמיש המטה אמר להם הקב"ה אפשר שאהא כועם
ומחריב את העולם ואתה בונה, אלא כשיעבור המבול אתם נזקקים
לפריה ורביה, שנאמר לאמר לאסירים צאו (ישעיה מט, ט).

" 'And Noah and his sons entered' (Gen. 7, 7), the males separately 'and his (Noah's) wife and the wives of his sons,' the females, separately. For all the time that Noah was in the ark, he and his sons and all that were with him were denied cohabitation. Said the Holy One, blessed be He, unto them: Will it be that while I destroy the world in my anger, you will be building it? (Not so), but only after the Flood shall have come to an end, will you be permitted to cohabit, as it is said: 'To say to the prisoners: Go forth!' " (Isa. 49:9).

IX. PREDESTINATION

Deut. 9:11-12 states that after Moses had remained on Mount Sinai forty days and forty nights, the Lord directed him to descend quickly from the mountain, because the people had turned aside from the way He had commanded them, and had made a molten image (*ibid.,* 5:18). Rabbinic tradition amplifies this account in *Ber.* 32a. But that before their backsliding God had *pointedly and ominously foretold Moses about it* is nowhere stated in rabbinic literature.

On the other hand, the Book of Jubilees tells us that at that time God did inform Moses about the imminent sins of his people, as well as of their misdeeds in the distant future and the punishments they are to incur on account of them. Thus, a long catalogue of national woes is prominently promulgated there:

"And Moses went up into the mount of God. . . . And He said: 'Incline thine heart to every word which I shall speak to thee on this mount, and write them in a book in order that their generations may see how I have not forsaken them, for all the evil which they have wrought in transgressing the covenant which I establish between Me and thee for their generations this day on Mount Sinai. . . . For they will forget all My commandments, (even) all that I commanded them, and they will walk after the Gentiles, and after their uncleanness, and after their shame, and will fall into the hands of the enemy, because they have forsaken My ordinances and My commandments". . . (I, 1-26).

Philo, on his part, has much to say on this subject in his *Qu. in Ex.,* II, 49 on Ex. 24:18:

"Why does Moses remain on the mountain forty days and the same number of nights? Concerning the number forty and its place in nature, a detailed account was given earlier, so that one need not speak further of this at length. Perhaps, however, it is necessary to add that the migrant generation was about to be condemned and waste away in corruption for forty years in all, after receiving many benefactions and showing ingratitude in many ways. And so, he remains there above for the same number of days as these years, reconciling the Father to the nation by prayers and intercessions, especially at the very time when the laws were given by God and there was constructed in words[16] the portable temple, which is called the Tent of Testimony. For whom, then, were the laws (given)? Was it indeed, for those who were to perish? And for whose sake were the oracles (given)? Was it for those who were to be destroyed a little later? It seems to me, however, that someone may say, 'Is it possible that he had foreknowledge of the judgment that was to come upon them?' But he who says this should bear in mind that every prophetic soul is divinely inspired, and prophesies many future things not so much by reflecting as through divine madness and certainty."

Philo, as we see, reports in substance the tradition so elaborately detailed in the Book of Jubilees, but at the same time we cannot fail to notice that he incorporated it into his homily with a good deal of hesitation. That his almost quizzical wavering and evident reluctance to be overly articulate about it is not a Philonic whim but the reflection of a studied rabbinic attitude to this phase of Moses' charge on the mountain, is evident from the following Talmudic passage:

In Sanh. 111a-b we read:

„כשעלה משה למרום מצאו להקב"ה שיושב וכותב ארך אפים אמר
לפניו רבונו של עולם ארך אפים לצדיקים אמר לו אף לרשעים א"ל
רשעים יאבדו א"ל השתא חזית דמיבעי לך. כשחטאו ישראל אמר לו
לא כך אמרת לי ארך אפים לצדיקים אמר לפניו רבש"ע ולא כך אמרת
לי אף לרשעים והיינו דכתיב ועתה יגדל נא כח ה' כאשר דברת לאמר:
(ה' ארך אפים)."(במדבר יד, יז-יח).

"When Moses ascended on high, he found the Holy One, blessed be
He, sitting and writing 'long-suffering.' Said he to Him: 'Sovereign of
the Universe! Long-suffering to the righteous?' He replied, 'Even to
the wicked.' He (Moses) urged, 'Let the wicked perish!' 'See now
what thou desirest,' was His answer. (That is to say, it is an ill-advised
request, which thou, Moses, wilt revoke at a future occasion, viz., at
the sin of the Golden Calf.)

"When Israel *sinned,* He (God) said to him, "Didst thou not urge
Me, (Let Thy) long-suffering be for the righteous (only)?' 'Sovereign
of the Universe!,' said he, 'but didst Thou not assure me, even to the
wicked!' Hence it is written, 'And now, I beseech Thee, let the power
of my Lord be great according as Thou has spoken, saying: The Lord
is long suffering" (Num. 14:17-18).

Why is there a persistent opposition to God's foretelling at this
juncture the woes that will befall Israel? And if indeed it was not
advisable to divulge the Jubilees' tradition, why not suppress it altogether? This is because we do find that the Bible attests to such fore-
warnings; cf., for instance, Abraham's vision of the plight of his
progeny in Egypt (see Gen. 15:12-14). Hence, undoubtedly, Philo's
cryptic remark, "That one should bear in mind that every prophetic
soul is divinely inspired and prophesies many future things," Philo—
and for that matter the Rabbis as well—somehow had to mention off-
hand, or only faintly allude to the Jubilees' tradition. The reason for
this cautious procedure is chiefly to be found in Philo's soul searching
questions: "For whom, then, were the laws (given)? Was it, indeed,
for those who were to perish? And for whose sake were the oracles
(given)? Was it for those who were to be destroyed a little later?"

In other words, it was psychologically unsound—and certainly not in the national interest—to give prominence to a tradition which stated that at the very moment the laws were given they were destined to be broken, and that at the very hour the nation was born under the Law it was consigned to perdition for transgressing it.

But, as already stated, in view of Gen. 15:12-14, the Jubilees' tradition could not be totally ignored. Therefore, in order to placate all questioners, some hint of it had to be given.

In sum, Philonic and rabbinic interpretations throw mutual light on each other; their purport and significance are enhanced and only fully understood when integrated.

NOTES

[1] With slight modifications here and there, the cited translations in the present article are those of Colson and Whitaker, Ralph Marcus, Herbert Danby, the Soncino Series, William G. Braude and Jacob Z. Lauterbach. These translations pertain respectively to the Greek texts of Philo, to the Armenian translation of Philo's Questions and Answers on Genesis and Exodus, to the Mishnah, to the Talmud and Midrash, to Midrash Tehillim and to the Mekhilta.

[2] *Horeb* (XII), N. Y., 1956, pp. 3-61: *Midrash ha-Shemot be-Philon*; ibid., (XIV-XV), 1960, pp. 1-74: *Midrash She'elot u'Teshubot al Bereshit u-Shemot le-Philon ha-Aleksandroni. Makor Kadum le-Midreshei Hazal.* Abraham Weiss Jubilee Volume, N. Y., 1964, pp. 579-633.

[3] Yer. R.H. 58d. דברי תורה עניים במקומן ועשירים במקום אחר

[4] 175 מדרש תדשא, בית המדרש של יעלינק, חדר ג', ,/. Cf. also *Midrash Tadsche,* ch. 11 (Warsaw ed.), 1876.

[5] See *Horeb,* (XI), N. Y., 1955, pp. 1-52: *Midrash Tadsche . . . Midrash Hellenisti Kadmon.*

[6] Cf. R. Marcus' note, *ad loc.*

[7] Edmund Stein, *Exegese des Philo aus Alexandria,* Giessen, 1929, p. 58.

[8] At times the LXX renders המון as πλήθους .

[9] Rabbi Samuel Edels in his commentary on Shabbat 105a well sensed the difficulty of this text by noting:

כי אב המון כו' דרשו כן מפני שנראה כי תיבת המון מיותר אשר לזה נתוספה ה"א דסגי ליה בהערה זה לכתוב אב לגוים וגו' דהיינו בתחלה אב לארם ועכשיו אב לגוים ומש"ה דרשו כן המון לנוטריקון ומדהא לדרשה אב נמי לדרשה נוטריקון וכולהו מפורשים במקרא א אב באומות דכתיב והיית לאב וגו' ב בחיר דכתיב ובחרת באברהם וגו' המון ה חביב ה מתחלף בה' בצורתה כדאמרי' ה' בח' ח' בה' ועוד שהם ממוצא א' וזמצינו באברהם שהיה אהוב וחביב דכתיב זרע אברהם אוהבי מ' מלך דכתיב נשיא אלקים אתה וגו'. (אגדות מהרש"א, דף ק"ה, ע"א)

Similar to the election of Abraham in Gen. 17:5 is the concept of Abraham's elevation recorded in Gen. 15:1: "He brought him forth outside." Rabbinic traditions here portray that Israel does not come under planetary influence (Shab. 156a, Ber. Rabbah 44:12, Tanhuma Hayye Sarah 6 and Midrash Hagadol on Genesis 15:5) and correspond to the following Philonic notices: *De Mut. Nom.,* 65-69; ibid., 76; *De Abr.,* 69, 71; *Heres* 280. See also H. A. Wolfson, *Philo* I, pp. 145-149.

10 Ψυχαὶ δ' εἰσὶ κατὰ τὸν ἀέρα πετομεναι.

11 Cf. J. Z. Lauterbach, Mekhilta III, 123. Horovitz-Rabin Edition has
ישראל קראוהו מן. The Mekhilta of R. Simon, 114, reads ישראל קראו
אותו מן.

12 See Wolfson, *Philo,* Vol. II, pp. 109-110.

13 See Commentary of Horovitz, *Mekhilta, ad loc.,* p. 166, indicating that
שמו refers to the "name of God"—שקראו להקב"ה מן כלומר המשפיע
מזון לכל חי. Cf. Dobschutz, Die Einfache Bibel Exegese der Tannaim.

14 Lauterbach, *The Ancient Jewish Allegorists in Talmud and Midrash,*
in *JQR,* ns. 1 (1911), pp. 324-326.

15 Philo's text, which is in agreement with LXX against the Hebrew
text, makes Noah's wife precede his sons in Gen. 8:18. See Marcus, *Qu. in
Gen.,* II, 49, n.b. The Massoretic text reads נה ובנין ואשתו ונשי בניו אתו.

16 I.e., at the Word of God.

Foreword

Rabbi Joseph B. Soloveitchick, Rosh Yeshiva at the Rabbi Isaac Elchanan Theological Seminary of Yeshiva University and Professor of Jewish Philosophy, is the acknowledged intellectual leader of Halakhic Judaism. Viewing all aspects of life from the framework of halakhah, he is recognized the world over as the authority in all halakhic matters. As an expositor of halakhah he attempts to interpret its welter of legal detail through the religious and philosophic principles inherent in the text. In his unusual ability to clearly formulate difficult technical propositions and expound upon sound supportable solutions, he is without a contemporary peer.

On the philosophical level he maintains that the most profound awareness comes at the point of experiential consciousness. His searching analysis of the nature of this existential consciousness constitutes the leitmotif of his speculative pursuits. Because of his unique position as "The Rav," the spoken and written words of Rabbi Soloveitchick have far-reaching impact on the nature of the Jewish religious experience and the development of Judaism.

We are deeply grateful that our revered mentor has permitted us to publish his essays which previously appeared in *Tradition* in honor of Dr. Belkin's anniversary.

Our appreciation also goes to Dr. Walter Wurzburger, editor of *Tradition,* for his kind cooperation in this matter.—LEON D. STITSKIN, .

43

CONFRONTATION

by JOSEPH B. SOLOVEITCHIK

I

1.

The Biblical account of the creation of man portrays him at three
progressive levels.

At the first level, he appears as a simple natural being. He is neither
cognizant of his unique station in the cosmos nor burdened by the
awareness of his paradoxical capability of being concurrently free and
obedient, creative to the point of self-transcendence and submissive in
a manner bordering on self-effacement. At this stage, natural man is
irresponsive to the pressure of both the imperative from without and
the "ought" from within—the inner call of his humanity surging
de profundis—מִמַּעֲמַקִּים. For the norm either from within or from
without addresses itself only to man who is sensitive to his own incongruity and tragic dilemma. The illusory happy-mindedness of natural
man stands between him and the norm. Natural man, unaware of the
element of tension prevailing between the human being and the environment of which he is an integral part, has no need to live a
normative life and to find redemption in surrender to a higher moral
will. His existence is unbounded, merging harmoniously with the general order of things and events. He is united with nature, moving
straightforward, with the beast and the fowl of the field, along an
unbroken line of mechanical life-activities, never turning around, never
glancing backwards, leading an existence which is neither fraught with

Reprinted from *Tradition*. Volume 6, 1964.

contradiction nor perplexed by paradoxes, nor marred by fright.

וכל שיח השדה טרם יהיה בארץ וכל עשב השדה טרם יצמח . . .
ואדם אין לעבד את האדמה. ואד יעלה מן הארץ והשקה את כל פני
האדמה. וייצר ה' א' את האדם עפר מן האדמה ויפח באפיו נשמת חיים
ויהי האדם לנפש חיה.

"And every plant of the field was not yet in the earth and every herb of the field had not yet grown, . . . and there was no man to till the ground. And the Lord God formed the man of the dust of the ground and breathed into his nostrils the breath of life and the man became a living soul" (Genesis 2:5-7).[1]

Man who was created out of the dust of the ground, enveloped in a mist rising from the jungle, determined by biological immediacy and mechanical necessity, knows of no responsibility, no opposition, no fear, and no dichotomy, and hence he is free from carrying the load of humanity.

In a word, this man is a non-confronted being. He is neither conscious of his assignment vis-a-vis something which is outside of himself nor is he aware of his existential otherness as a being summoned by his Maker to rise to tragic greatness.

2.

When I refer to man at the level of naturalness, I have in mind not the *Urmensch* of bygone times but modern man. I am speaking not in anthropological but typological categories. For non-confronted man is to be found not only in the cave or the jungle but also in the seats of learning and the halls of philosophers and artists. Non-confrontation is not necessarily restricted to a primitive existence but applies to human existence at all times, no matter how cultured and sophisticated. The *hédoné*-oriented, egocentric person, the beauty-worshipper, committed to the goods of sense and craving exclusively for boundless aesthetic experience, the voluptuary, inventing needs in order to give himself the opportunity of continual gratification, the sybarite, constantly discovering new areas where pleasure is pursued and happiness found and lost, leads a non-confronted existence. At this stage, the intellectual gesture is not the ultimate goal but a means to another end—the attainment of unlimited aesthetic experience. Hence, non-confronted man is prevented from finding himself and bounding his existence as distinct and singular. He fails to realize his great capacity for winning freedom from an unalterable natural order and offering this very freedom as the great sacrifice to God, who wills man to be free in order that he may commit himself unreservedly and forfeit his freedom.

Beauty, uncouth and unrefined but irresistible, seducing man and contributing to his downfall, emerges in the Biblical arena for the first time—according to the Midrash quoted by Nachmanides (Genesis 4:22)—in the person of Naamah (the name signifies pleasantness), the sister of Tubal-Cain.

ומדרש אחר לרבותינו שהיא האשה היפה היא מאד שממנה טעו בני האלהים והיא והנרמזת בפסוק ויראו בני האלהים את בנות האדם.

"Our sages offered another Midrashic interpretation, that Naamah was the fairest of all women, who seduced the sons of the mighty, and it is she who is referred to in the verse: 'and the sons of the mighty saw the daughters of man that they were fair.' " Her seductive charms captivated the sons of the mighty and led to their appalling disregard for the central divine norm enjoining man from reaching out for the fascinating and beautiful that does not belong to him. The sons of the mighty yielded to the hedonic urge and were unable to discipline their actions. They were a non-confronted, non-normative group. They worshipped beauty and succumbed to its overwhelming impact.

Naamah, the incarnation of unhallowed and unsublimated beauty, is, for the Midrash, not so much an individual as an idea, not only a real person but a symbol of unredeemed beauty. As such, she appears in the Biblical drama in many disguises. At times her name is Delilah, seducing Samson; at other times she is called Tamar, corrupting a prince. She is cast in the role of a princess or queen, inflicting untold harm upon a holy nation and kingdom · of priests whose king, the wisest of all men, abandoned his wisdom when he encountered overpowering beauty. The Book of Wisdom (Proverbs) portrays her as the anonymous woman with an "impudent face" who "lieth in wait at every corner" and the Aggadah—also cited here by Nachmanides—as the beautiful queen of the demons tempting man and making him restless.

No less than their seductress, the sons of the mighty also represent a universal type. Non-confronted man—whether he be a primitive caveman, the king depicted in Ecclesiastes, or a modern counterpart— is dominated by two characteristics: he can deny himself nothing, and he is aware of neither the indomitable opposition he is bound to meet in the form of a restrictive outside, nor of the absurdity implied in man's faith that the beautiful is a source of pleasure rather than one of frustration and disillusionment. The aesthete of today, like the aesthete of old, is prisoner of—no matter what her name—beauty unethicized and unreclaimed from aboriginal immediacy. He enjoys a sense of oneness with the natural scheme of events and occurrences and his transient successful performance encourages him to strive for the absurd—an unopposed and uncontradicted hedonic *modus existentiae*.

ויטע ה' א' גן בעדן מקדם וישם שם את האדם אשר יצר. ויצמח ה' א'
מן האדמה כל עץ נחמד למראה וטוב למאכל ועץ החיים בתוך הגן ועץ
הדעת טוב ורע.

"And the Lord God planted a garden eastward in Eden and there He put the man whom He had formed. And out of the ground the Lord God caused to grow every tree that is desirable to the sight and good for food; the tree of life in the midst of the garden and the tree of knowledge of good and evil" (Genesis 2:8-9).[2]

Man depicted in these verses is hedonically-minded and pleasure-seeking, having at his disposal a multitude of possibilities of sense-gratification. Before him stretches a vast garden with an almost endless variety of trees desirable and good, tempting, fascinating, and exciting the boundless fantasy with their glamorous colors.

3.

At the second level, natural man, moving straightforward, comes suddenly to a stop, turns around, and casts, as an outsider, a contemplative gaze upon his environment. Even the most abandoned voluptuary becomes disillusioned like the king of Ecclesiastes and finds himself encountering something wholly other than his own self, an outside that defies and challenges him. At this very moment, the separation of man from cosmic immediacy, from the uniformity and simplicity which he had shared with nature, takes place. He discovers an awesome and mysterious domain of things and events which is independent of and disobedient to him, an objective order limiting the exercise of his power and offering opposition to him. In the wake of this discovery, he discovers himself. Once self-discovery is accomplished, and a new I-awareness of an existence which is limited and opposed by a non-I outside emerges, something new is born—namely, the divine norm. "ויצו ה' א' על האדם"—"And the Lord God commanded the man." With the birth of the norm, man becomes aware of his singularly human existence which expresses itself in the dichotomous experience of being unfree, restricted, imperfect and unredeemed, and, at the same time, being potentially powerful, great, and exalted, uniquely endowed, capable of rising far above his environment in response to the divine moral challenge. Man attains his unique identity when, after having been enlightened by God that he is not only a committed but also a free person, endowed with power to implement his commitment, he grasps the incommensurability of what he is and what he is destined to be, of the ויהי and יהי.

God, in answer to Moses' inquiry, gave His Name as אהי' אשר אהי' —I am what I am. God is free from the contradiction between potentiality and actuality, ideal and reality. He is pure actuality, existence par excellence.[3] Man, however, is unable to state of himself אהיה אשר אהיה since his real existence always falls short of the ideal which his Maker set up for him as the great objective. This tragic schism reflects, in a paradoxical fashion, human distinctiveness and grandeur.

Simultaneously with man's realization of his inner incongruity and complete alienation from his environment, the human tragic destiny begins to unfold. Man, in his encounter with an objective world and in his assumption of the role of a subject who asks questions about something hitherto simple, forfeits his sense of serenity and peace. He is no longer happy, he begins to examine his station in this world and he finds himself suddenly assailed by perplexity and fear, and especially loneliness: ויאמר ה' א' לא טוב היות האדם לבדו "And the Lord God said: 'It is not good that the man should be alone'." The I-experience is a passional one and real man is born amid the pains of confrontation with an "angry" environment of which he had previously been an integral part.

Confronted man is called upon to choose either of two alternatives:

1) To play an active role as a subject-knower, utilizing his great endowment, the intellect, and trying to gain supremacy over the objective order. However, this performance is fraught with difficulty because knowledge is gained only through conflict and the intellectual performance is an act of conquest.[4] The order of things and events, in spite of its intrinsic knowability and rationality, does not always respond to human inquiry and quite often rejects all pleas for a cooperative relationship. The subject-knower must contest a knowable object, subdue it and make it yield its cognitive contents.[5]

2) Man may despair, succumb to the overpowering pressure of the objective outside and end in mute resignation, failing to discharge his duty as an intellectual being, and thus dissolving an intelligent existence into an absurd nightmare.

Of course, the Torah commanded man to choose the first alternative, to exercise his authority as an intelligent being whose task consists in engaging the objective order in a cognitive contest. We have always rejected the nirvana of inaction because the flight from confrontation is an admission of the bankruptcy of man. When man became alienated from nature and found himself alone, confronted by everything outside of him, God brought the "animal of the field and every fowl of the heaven unto the man to see what he would call it . . . and the man gave name to all the beasts and the fowl of the heaven and to every animal of the field."

ויצר ה' א' מן האדמה כל חית השדה ואת כל עוף השמים ויבא אל האדם לראות מה יקרא לו . . . ויקרא האדם שמות לכל הבהמה ולעוף השמים ולכל חית השדה.

Man no longer marched straightforward with the brutes of the field and the forest. He made an about-face and confronted them as an intelligent being remote from and eager to examine and classify them.

God encouraged him to engage in the most miraculous of all human gestures—the cognitive. Confronted Adam responded gladly because he already realized that he was no longer a part of nature but an outsider, a singular being, endowed with intelligence. In his new role, he became aware of his loneliness and isolation from the entire creation. ולאדם לא מצא עזר כנגדו. "And for the man [God] had not found a helpmeet opposite him." As a lonely being, Adam discovered his great capacity for facing and dominating the non-human order.[6]

4.

The Book of Genesis, after describing the four rivers which flow from the Garden of Eden, offers us a new account of the placing of Adam in this garden.

ויקח ה' א' את האדם וינחהו בגן עדן לעבדה ולשמרה.
"And the Lord God took the man and placed him in the Garden of Eden to cultivate it and to keep it." This sentence in Genesis 2:15 is almost a verbatim repetition of Genesis 2:8, yet the accounts differ in two respects.

First, in the second account, the Bible uses a verb denoting action preceding the placing of man in the Garden of Eden —"And God took (ויקח) the man and placed him"— whereas in the previous account, the verb "he placed," וישם, is not accompanied by any preliminary action on the part of the Almighty. The expression ויקח does not occur in the first account. Second, there is no mention in the previous account of any assignment given to man while this account does specify that man was charged with the task of cultivating and keeping the garden.

The reason for these variations lies in the fact that the two accounts are related to two different men. The first story, as we have previously indicated, is of non-confronted man carried by the mighty tide of a uniform, simple, non-reflective life, who was placed in the Garden of Eden for one purpose only—to pursue pleasure, to enjoy the fruit of the trees without toil, to live in ignorance of his human destiny, to encounter no problem and to be concerned with no obligation. As we stated previously, non-confronted man is a non-normative being. The second story is of confronted man who began to appraise critically his position vis-a-vis his environment and found his existential experience too complex to be equated with the simplicity and non-directedness of the natural life-stream. This man, as a subject-knower facing an almost impenetrable objective order, was dislocated by God from his position of naturalness and harmonious being and placed in a new existential realm, that of confronted existence. Confronted man is a displaced person. Having been taken out of a state of complacency and optimistic naivete, he finds the intimate relationship between him and the order of facticity ending in tension and conflict. The verb ויקח signifies that God removed man from one dimension and thrust him into another—that of confronted existence. At this phase, man, estranged from nature, fully aware of his grand and tragic destiny, became the recipient of the first norm—"ויצו ה' א' על האדם." "And the Lord God commanded the man." The divine imperative burst forth out of infinity and overpowered finite man.

Alas, not always does creative man respond readily to the divine normative summons which forms the very core of his new existential status as a confronted being. All too often, the motivating force in creative man is not the divine mandate entrusted to him and which must be implemented in full at both levels, the cognitive and the normative, but a demonic urge for power. By fulfilling an incomplete task, modern creative man falls back to a non-confronted, natural existence to which normative pressure is alien. The reason for the failure of confronted man to play his role fully lies in the fact that, while the cognitive gesture gives man mastery and a sense of success, the normative gesture requires of man surrender. At this juncture, man of today commits the error which his ancestor, Adam of old, committed by lending an attentive ear to the demonic whisper "Ye shall be as God, knowing good and evil."

5.

There is, however, a third level which man, if he is longing for self-fulfillment, must ascend. At this level, man finds himself confronted again. Only this time it is not the confrontation of a subject who gazes, with a sense of superiority, at the object beneath him, but of two equal subjects, both lonely in their otherness and uniqueness, both opposed and rejected by an objective order, both craving for companionship. This confrontation is reciprocal, not unilateral. This time the two confronters stand alongside each other, each admitting the existence of the other. An aloof existence is transformed into a together-existence.

ויאמר ה' א' לא טוב היות האדם לבדו אעשה לו עזר כנגדו . . . ויבן
ה' א' את הצלע אשר לקח מן האדם לאשה ויבאה אל האדם.

"And the Lord God said, It is not good that the man should be alone. I will make a helpmeet opposite him.... And the Lord God made the rib which He had taken from the man into a woman and brought her unto man" (Genesis 2:18, 22). God created Eve, another human being. Two individuals, lonely and helpless in their solitude, meet, and the first community is formed.

The community can only be born, however, through an act of communication. After gazing at each other in silence and defiance, the two individuals involved in a unique encounter begin to communicate with each other. Out of the mist of muteness the miraculous word rises and shines forth. Adam suddenly begins to talk—ויאמר האדם—"And the man said." He addresses himself to Eve, and with his opening remark, two fenced-in and isolated human existences open up, and they both ecstatically break through to each other.

The word is a paradoxical instrument of communication and contains an inner contradiction. On the one hand, the word is the medium of expressing agreement and concurrence, of reaching mutual understanding, organizing cooperative effort, and uniting action. On the other hand, the word is also the means of manifesting distinctness, emphasizing incongruity, and underlining separateness. The word brings out not only what is common in two existences but the singularity and uniqueness of each existence as well. It emphasizes not only common problems, aspirations and concerns, but also uniquely individual questions, cares and anxieties which assail each person. Our sages, in explaining the graphic difference between the open and closed *mem,* spoke of מאמר סתום and מאמר פתוח—the enigmatic and the clear or distinct phrase. They felt that the word at times enlightens, at times, confounds; at times, elucidates, and at other times, emphasizes the unintelligible and unknowable.

When Adam addressed himself to Eve, employing the word as the means of communication, he certainly told her not only what united them but also what separated them. Eve was both enlightened and perplexed, assured and troubled by his word. For, in all personal unions such as marriage, friendship, or comradeship, however strong the bonds uniting two individuals, the *modi existentiae* remain totally unique and hence, incongruous, at both levels, the ontological and the experiential. The hope of finding a personal existential equation of two human beings is rooted in the dangerous and false notion that human existences are abstract magnitudes subject to the simple mathematical processes. This error lies at the root of the philosophies of the corporate state and of mechanistic behaviorism. In fact, the closer two individuals get to know each other, the more aware they become of the metaphysical distance separating them. Each one exists in a singular manner, completely absorbed in his individual awareness which is egocentric and exclusive. The sun of existence rises with the birth of one's self-awareness and sets with its termination. It is beyond the experiential power of an individual to visualize an existence preceding or following his.

It is paradoxical yet nonetheless true that each human being lives both in an existential community, surrounded by friends, and in a state of existential loneliness and tension, confronted by strangers. In each to whom I relate as a human being, I find a friend, for we have many things in common, as well as a stranger, for each of us is unique and wholly other. This otherness stands in the way of complete mutual understanding. The gap of uniqueness is too wide to be bridged. Indeed, it is not a gap, it is an abyss. Of course, there prevails, quite often, a harmony of interests—economic, political, social—upon which two individuals focus their attention. However, two people glancing at the same object may continue to lead isolated, closed-in existences. Coordination of interests does not spell an existential union. We frequently engage in common enterprise and we prudently pursue common goals, travelling temporarily along parallel roads, yet our destinations are not the same. We are, in the words of the Torah, an עֵזֶר—a helpmeet to each other, yet at the same time, we experience the state of כְּנֶגְדּוֹ—we remain different and opposed to each other.[7] We think, feel and respond to events not in unison but singly, each one in his individual fashion. Man is a social being, yearning for a together-existence in which services are exchanged and experiences shared, and a lonely creature, shy and reticent, fearful of the intruding cynical glance of his next-door neighbor. In spite of our sociability and outer-directed nature, we remain strangers to each other. Our feelings of sympathy and love for our confronter are rooted in the surface personality and they do not reach into the inner recesses of our depth personality which never leaves its ontological seclusion and never becomes involved in a communal existence.

In a word, the greatness of man manifests itself in his dialectical approach to his confronter, in ambivalent acting toward his fellow-man, in giving friendship and hurling defiance, in relating himself to, and at the same time, retreating from him. In the dichotomy of עֵזֶר and כְּנֶגְדּוֹ we find our triumph as well as our defeat.

Modern man, who did not meet to the fullest the challenge of confrontation on the second level, does not perform well at the level of personal confrontation either. He has forgotten how to master the difficult dialectical art of עֵזֶר כְּנֶגְדּוֹ—of being one with and, at the same time, different from, his human confronter, of living in community and simultaneously in solitude. He has developed the habit of confronting his fellow man in a fashion similar to that which prevails at the level of subject-object relationship, seeking to dominate and subordinate him instead of communicating and communing with him. The wondrous personal confrontation of Adam and Eve is thus turned into an ugly attempt at depersonalization. Adam of today wants to appear as master-hero and to subject Eve to his rule and dominion, be it ideological, religious, economic, or political. As a matter of fact, the divine curse addressed to Eve after she sinned, וְהוּא יִמְשָׁל בָּךְ—"and he shall rule over thee," has found its fulfillment in our modern society. The warm personal relationship between two individuals has been supplanted by a formal subject-object relationship which manifests itself in a quest for power and supremacy.

II

1.

We Jews have been burdened with a twofold task; we have to cope with the problem of a double confrontation. We think of ourselves as human beings, sharing the destiny of Adam in his general encounter with nature, and as members of a covenantal community which has preserved its identity under most unfavorable conditions, confronted by another faith community. We believe we are the bearers of a double charismatic load, that of the dignity of man, and that of the sanctity of the covenantal community. In this difficult role, we are summoned by God, who revealed Himself at both the level of universal creation and that of the private covenant, to undertake a double mission—the universal human and the exclusive covenantal confrontation.

Like his forefather, Jacob—whose bitter nocturnal struggle with a mysterious antagonist is so dramatically portrayed in the Bible—the Jew of old was a doubly confronted being. The emancipated modern Jew, however, has been trying, for a long time, to do away with this twofold responsibility which weighs heavily upon him. The Westernized Jew maintains that it is impossible to engage in both confrontations, the universal and the covenantal, which, in his opinion, are mutually exclusive. It is, he argues, absurd to stand shoulder to shoulder with mankind preoccupied with the cognitive-technological gesture for the welfare of all, implementing the mandate granted to us by the Creator, and to make an about-face the next instant in order to confront our comrades as a distinct and separate community. Hence, the Western Jew concludes, we have to choose between these two encounters. We are either confronted human beings or confronted Jews. A double confrontation contains an inner contradiction.

What is characteristic of these single-confrontation philosophers is their optimistic and carefree disposition. Like natural Adam of old, who saw himself as part of his environment and was never assailed by a feeling of being existentially different, they see themselves as secure and fully integrated within general society. They do not raise any questions about the reasonableness and justification of such an optimistic attitude, nor do they try to discover in the deep recesses of their personality commitments which transcend mundane obligations to society.

The proponents of the single-confrontation philosophy (with the exception of some fringe groups) do not preach complete de-Judaization and unqualified assimilation. They also speak of Jewish identity (at least in a religious sense), of Jewish selfhood and the natural will for preservation of the Jewish community as a separate identity. As a matter of fact, quite often they speak with great zeal and warmth about the past and future role of Judaism in the advancement of mankind and its institutions. However, they completely fail to grasp the real nature and the full implications of a meaningful Jewish identity.

2.

This failure rests upon two misconceptions of the nature of the faith community. First, the single-confrontation philosophy continues to speak of Jewish identity without realizing that this term can only be understood under the aspect of singularity and otherness. There is no identity without uniqueness. As there cannot be an equation between two individuals unless they are converted into abstractions, it is likewise absurd to speak of the commensurability of two faith communities which are individual entities.

The individuality of a faith community expresses itself in a three-fold way. First, the divine imperatives and commandments to which a faith community is unreservedly committed must not be equated with the ritual and ethos of another community. Each faith community is engaged in a singular normative gesture reflecting the numinous nature of the act of faith itself, and it is futile to try to find common denominators. Particularly when we speak of the Jewish faith community, whose very essence is expressed in the halakhic performance which is a most individuating factor, any attempt to equate our identity with another is sheer absurdity. Second, the axiological awareness of each faith community is an exclusive one, for it believes—and this belief is indispensable to the survival of the community—that its system of dogmas, doctrines and values is best fitted for the attainment of the ultimate good. Third, each faith community is unyielding in its eschatological expectations. It perceives the events at the end of time with exultant certainty, and expects man, by surrender of selfish pettiness and by consecration to the great destiny of life, to embrace the faith that this community has been preaching throughout the millenia. Standardization of practices, equalization of dogmatic certitudes, and the waiving of eschatological claims spell the end of the vibrant and great faith experience of any religious community. It is as unique and enigmatic as the individual himself.

The second misconception of the single-confrontation philosophy consists in not realizing the compatibility of the two roles. If the relationship of the non-Jewish to the Jewish world had conformed to the divine arrangement for one human being to meet the other on the basis of equality, friendship and sympathy, the Jew would have been able to become fully involved together with the rest of humanity in the cosmic confrontation. His covenantal uniqueness and his additional mandate to face another faith community as a member of a different community of the committed would not have interfered in the least with his readiness to and capability of joining the cultural enterprise of the rest of humanity. There is no contradiction between coordinating our cultural activity with all men and at the same time confronting them as members of another faith community. As a matter of fact even within the non-Jewish society, each individual sees himself under a double aspect: first, as a member of a cultural-creative community in which all are committed to a common goal and, at the same time, as an individual living in seclusion and loneliness.

Unfortunately, however, non-Jewish society has confronted us throughout the ages in a mood of defiance, as if we were part of the subhuman objective order separated by an abyss from the human, as if we had no capacity for thinking logically, loving passionately,

yearning deeply, aspiring and hoping. Of course, as long as we were
exposed to such a soulless, impersonal confrontation on the part of
non-Jewish society, it was impossible for us to participate to the fullest
extent in the great universal creative confrontation between man and
the cosmic order. The limited role we played until modern times in
the great cosmic confrontation was not of our choosing. Heaven knows
that we never encouraged the cruel relationship which the world displayed toward us. We have always considered ourselves an inseparable
part of humanity and we were ever ready to accept the divine challenge,
מלאו את הארץ וכבשה "Fill the earth and subdue it," and the responsibility implicit in human existence. We have never proclaimed the
philosophy of *contemptus* or *odium seculi*. We have steadily maintained that involvement in the creative scheme of things is mandatory.

Involvement with the rest of mankind in the cosmic confrontation
does not, we must repeat, rule out the second personal confrontation
of two faith communities, each aware of both what it shares with the
other and what is singularly its own. In the same manner as Adam
and Eve confronted and attempted to subdue a malicious scoffing
nature and yet nevertheless encountered each other as two separate
individuals cognizant of their incommensurability and uniqueness, so
also two faith communities which coordinate their efforts when confronted by the cosmic order may face each other in the full knowledge
of their distinctness and individuality.

We reject the theory of a single confrontation and instead insist
upon the indispensability of the double confrontation. First, as we have
mentioned previously, we, created in the image of God, are charged
with responsibility for the great confrontation of man and the cosmos.
We stand with civilized society shoulder to shoulder over against an
order which defies us all. Second, as a charismatic faith community,
we have to meet the challenge of confronting the general non-Jewish
faith community. We are called upon to tell this community not only
the story it already knows—that we are human beings, committed to
the general welfare and progress of mankind, that we are interested in
combatting disease, in alleviating human suffering, in protecting man's

rights, in helping the needy, *et cetera*—but also what is still unknown to it, namely, our otherness as a metaphysical covenantal community.

3.

It is self-evident that a confrontation of two faith communities is possible only if it is accompanied by a clear assurance that both parties will enjoy equal rights and full religious freedom. We shall resent any attempt on the part of the community of the many to engage us in a peculiar encounter in which our confronter will command us to take a position beneath him while placing himself not alongside of but above us. A democratic confrontation certainly does not demand that we submit to an attitude of self-righteousness taken by the community of the many which, while debating whether or not to "absolve" the community of the few of some mythical guilt, completely ignores its own historical responsibility for the suffering and martyrdom so frequently recorded in the annals of the history of the few, the weak, and the persecuted.

We are not ready for a meeting with another faith community in which we shall become an object of observation, judgment and evaluation, even though the community of the many may then condescendingly display a sense of compassion with the community of the few and advise the many not to harm or persecute the few. Such an encounter would convert the personal Adam-Eve meeting into a hostile confrontation between a subject-knower and a knowable object. We do not intend to play the part of the object encountered by dominating man. Soliciting commiseration is incongruous with the character of a democratic confrontation. There should rather be insistence upon one's inalienable rights as a human being, created by God.

In light of this analysis, it would be reasonable to state that in any confrontation we must insist upon four basic conditions in order to safeguard our individuality and freedom of action.

First, we must state, in unequivocal terms, the following. We are a totally independent faith community. We do not revolve as a satellite in any orbit. Nor are we related to any other faith community as "brethren" even though "separated." People confuse two concepts when they speak of a common tradition uniting two faith communities such as the Christian and the Judaic. This term may have relevance if one looks upon a faith community under an historico-cultural aspect and interprets its relationship to another faith community in sociological, human, categories describing the unfolding of the creative consciousness of man. Let us not forget that religious awareness manifests itself not only in a singular apocalyptic faith experience but in a mundane cultural experience as well. Religion is both a divine imperative which was foisted upon man from without and a new dimension of personal being which man discovers within himself. In a word, there is a cultural aspect to the faith experience which is, from a psychological viewpoint, the most integrating, inspiring and uplifting spiritual force. Religious values, doctrines and concepts may be and have been translated into cultural categories enjoyed and cherished even by secular man. All the references throughtout the ages to universal religion, philosophical religion, *et cetera,* are related to the cultural aspect of the faith experience of which not only the community of believers but a pragmatic, utilitarian society avails itself as well. The cultural religious experience gives meaning and directedness to human existence and relates it to great ultimates, thus enhancing human dignity and worth even at a mundane level.

Viewing the relationship between Judaism and Christianity under this aspect, it is quite legitimate to speak of a cultural Judeo-Christian tradition for two reasons: First, Judaism as a culture has influenced, indeed, molded the ethico-philosophical Christian world-formula. The basic categories and premises of the latter were evolved in the cultural Judaic orbit. Second, our Western civilization has absorbed both Judaic and Christian elements. As a matter of fact, our Western heritage was shaped by a combination of three factors, the classical, Judaic, and Christian, and we could readily speak of a Judeo-Hellenistic-Christian tradition within the framework of our Western civilization. However, when we shift the focus from the dimension of culture to that of faith—where total unconditional commitment and involvement are necessary—the whole idea of a tradition of faiths and the continuum of revealed doctrines which are by their very nature incommensurate and related to different frames of reference is utterly absurd, unless one is ready to acquiesce in the Christian theological claim that Christianity has superseded Judaism.

As a faith individuality, the community of the few is endowed with intrinsic worth which must be viewed against its own meta-historical backdrop without relating to the framework of another faith community. For the mere appraisal of the worth of one community in terms of the service it has rendered to another community, no matter how great and important this service was, constitutes an infringement of the sovereignty and dignity of even the smallest of faith communities. When God created man and endowed him with individual dignity, He decreed that the ontological legitimacy and relevance of the individual human being is to be discovered not without but within the individual. He was created because God approved of him as an autonomous human being and not as an auxiliary being in the service of someone else. The ontological purposiveness of his existence is immanent in him. The same is true of a religious community, whose worth is not to be measured by external standards.

Therefore, any intimation, overt or covert, on the part of the community of the many that it is expected of the community of the few that it shed its uniqueness and cease existing because it has fulfilled its mission by paving the way for the community of the many, must be rejected as undemocratic and contravening the very idea of religious freedom. The small community has as much right to profess its faith in the ultimate certitude concerning the doctrinal worth of its world formula and to behold its own eschatological vision as does the community of the many. I do not deny the right of the community of the many to address itself to the community of the few in its own eschatological terms. However, building a practical program upon this right is hardly consonant with religious democracy and liberalism.

Second, the *logos,* the word, in which the multifarious religious experience is expressed, does not lend itself to standardization or universalization. The word of faith reflects the intimate, the private, the paradoxically inexpressible cravings of the individual for and his linking up with his Maker. It reflects the numinous character and the strangeness of the act of faith of a particular community which is totally incomprehensible to the man of a different faith community. Hence, it is important that the religious or theological *logos* should not be employed as the medium of communication between two faith communities whose modes of expression are as unique as their apocalyptic experiences. The confrontation should occur not at a theological, but at a mundane human level. There, all of us speak the universal language of modern man. As a matter of fact, our common interests lie not in the realm of faith, but in that of the secular orders.[8] There, we all face a powerful antagonist, we all have to contend with a considerable number of matters of great concern. The relationship between two communities must be outer-directed and related to the secular orders with which men of faith come face to face. In the secular sphere, we may discuss positions to be taken, ideas to be evolved, and plans to be formulated. In these matters, religious communities may together recommend action to be developed and may seize the initiative to be implemented later by general society. However, our joint engagement in this kind of enterprise must not dull our sense of identity as a faith community. We must always remember that our singular commitment to God and our hope and indomitable will for survival are non-negotiable and non-rationalizable and are not subject to debate and argumentation. The great encounter between God and man is a wholly personal private affair incomprehensible to the outsider—even to a brother of the same faith community. The divine message is incommunicable since it defies all standardized media of information and all objective categories. If the powerful community of the many feels like remedying an embarrassing human situation or redressing an historic wrong, it should do so at the human ethical level. However, if the debate should revolve around matters of faith, then one of the confronters will be impelled to avail himself of the language of his opponent. This in itself would mean surrender of individuality and distinctiveness.

Third, we members of the community of the few should always act with tact and understanding and refrain from suggesting to the community of the many, which is both proud and prudent, changes in its ritual or emendations of its texts. If the genuinely liberal dignitaries of the faith community of the many deem some changes advisable, they will act in accordance with their convictions without any prompting on our part. It is not within our purview to advise or solicit. For it would be both impertinent and unwise for an outsider to intrude upon the most private sector of the human existential experience, namely, the way in which a faith community expresses its relationship to God. Non-interference with and non-involvement in something which is totally alien to us is a *conditio sine qua non* for the furtherance of good-will and mutual respect.

Fourth, we certainly have not been authorized by our history, sanctified by the martyrdom of millions, to even hint to another faith community that we are mentally ready to revise historical attitudes, to trade favors pertaining to fundamental matters of faith, and to reconcile "some" differences. Such a suggestion would be nothing but a betrayal of our great tradition and heritage and would, furthermore, produce no practical benefits. Let us not forget that the community of the man will not be satisfied with half measures and compromises which are only indicative of a feeling of insecurity and inner emptiness. We cannot command the respect of our confronters by displaying a servile attitude. Only a candid, frank and unequivocal policy reflecting unconditional commitment to our God, a sense of dignity, pride and inner joy in being what we are, believing with great passion in the ultimate truthfulness of our views, praying fervently for and expecting confidently the fulfillment of our eschatological vision when our faith will rise from particularity to universality, will impress the peers of the other faith community among whom we have both adversaries and friends. I hope and pray that our friends in the community of the many will sustain their liberal convictions and humanitarian ideals by articulating their position on the right of the community of the few to live, create, and worship God in its own way, in freedom and with dignity.

4.

Our representatives who meet with the spokesmen of the community of the many should be given instructions similar to those

enunciated by our patriarch Jacob when he sent his agents to meet
his brother Esau.

ויצו את הראשון לאמר כי יפגשך עשו אחי ושאלך לאמר למי אתה
ואנה תלך ולמי אלה לפניך ואמרת לעבדך ליעקב מנחה היא שלוחה
לאדני לעשו והנה גם הוא אחרינו ויצו גם את השני גם את השלישי
גם את כל ההלכים אחרי העדרים לאמר כדבר הזה תדברון אל עשו
במצאכם אתו.

"And he commanded the foremost, saying, when Esau my brother,
meeteth thee and asketh thee, saying: whose art thou and whither
goest thou? And whose are these before thee? Then thou shalt say
they are thy servant Jacob's; it is a present sent unto my lord Esau,
and behold he also is behind us. And he commanded also the second,
and the third and all that followed the droves, saying in this manner
shall ye speak unto Esau when ye find him" (Genesis 32:18-20).

What was the nature of these instructions? Our approach to and
relationship with the outside world has always been of an ambivalent
character, intrinsically authentic, bordering at times on the paradoxical. We relate ourselves to and at the same time withdraw from, we
come close to and simultaneously retreat from the world of Esau.
When the process of coming nearer and nearer is almost consummated,
we immediately begin to retreat quickly into seclusion. We cooperate
with the members of other faith communities in all fields of constructive human endeavor, but, simultaneously with our integration into
the general social framework, we engage in a movement of recoil and
retrace our steps. In a word, we belong to the human society and, at
the same time, we feel as strangers and outsiders. We are rooted in
the here and now reality as inhabitants of our globe, and yet we experience a sense of homelessness and loneliness as if we belonged
somewhere else. We are both realists and dreamers, prudent and practical on the one hand, and visionaries and idealists on the other. We
are indeed involved in the cultural endeavor and yet we are committed
to another dimension of experience. Our first patriarch, Abraham, already introduced himself in the following words: "I am a stranger
and sojourner with you"—"גר ותושב אנכי עמכם." Is it possible to be
both—גר ותושב—at the same time? Is not this definition absurd since

it contravenes the central principle of classical logic that no cognitive judgment may contain two mutually exclusive terms? And yet, the Jew of old defied this time-honored principle and did think of himself in contradictory terms. He knew well in what areas he could extend his full cooperation to his neighbors and act as a תושב, a resident, a sojourner, and at what point this gesture of cooperation and goodwill should terminate, and he must disengage as if he were a גר, a stranger. He knew in what enterprise to participate to the best of his ability and what offers and suggestions, however attractive and tempting, to reject resolutely. He was aware of the issues on which he could compromise, of the nature of the goods he could surrender, and vice versa, of the principles which were not negotiable and the spiritual goods which had to be defended at no matter what cost. The boundary line between a finite idea and a principle nurtured by infinity, transient possessions and eternal treasures, was clear and precise. Jacob, in his instructions to his agents, laid down the rule:

כי יפגשך עשו אחי ושאלך למי אתה ואנה תלך ולמי אלה אלה לפניך ?

"When Esau my brother meeteth thee and asketh thee, saying: whose art thou, and whither goest thou and whose are these before thee?" My brother Esau, Jacob told his agents, will address to you three questions. "Whose art thou?" "To whom do you as a metaphysical being, as a soul, as a spiritual personality belong?" "And whither goest thou?" To whom is your historical destiny committed? To whom have you consecrated your future? What is your ultimate goal, your final objective? Who is your God and what is your way of life? These two inquiries are related to your identity as members of a covenantal community. However, Jacob continued, my brother Esau will also ask a third question: "And whose are these before thee?" Are you ready to contribute your talents, capabilities and efforts toward the material and cultural welfare of general society? Are you ready to present me with gifts, oxen, goats, camels and bulls? Are you willing to pay taxes, to develop and industrialize the country? This third inquiry is focused on temporal aspects of life. As regards the third question, Jacob told his agents to answer in the positive. "It is a present unto my lord, even unto Esau." Yes, we are determined to participate in every civic, scientific, and political enterprise. We feel obligated to enrich society with our creative talents and to be constructive and useful citizens. Yet, pertaining to the first two questions—whose art thou and whither goest thou—Jacob commanded his representatives to reply in the negative, clearly and precisely, boldly and courageously. He commanded them to tell Esau that their soul, their personality, their metaphysical destiny, their spiritual future and sacred commitments, belong exclusively to God and His servant Jacob. "They are Thy servant Jacob's," and no human power can succeed in severing the eternal bond between them and God.

This testament handed down to us by Jacob has become very relevant now in the year 1964. We find ourselves confronted again like Jacob of old, and our confronters are ready to address to us the identical three questions: "Whose are thou? Whither goest thou? Whose are these before thee?" A millenia-old history demands from us that we meet the challenge courageously and give the same answers with which Jacob entrusted his messengers several thousand years ago.

NOTES

[1] While the Biblical phrase נפש חיה refers to natural man, Onkelos' רוח ממללא is related to a typologically more advanced stage.

[2] Maimonides translated טוב ורע into aesthetic terms as "pleasing and displeasing." Paradisical man, violating the divine commandment by eating from the tree of knowledge, suspended the ethical and replaced it wih the aesthetic experience (*Guide of the Perplexed*, I, 2).

[3] See *Guide of the Perplexed*, I, 63.

[4] The Latin *objectus* derived from *objicere*, to oppose, the German *Gegenstand*, denoting something standing opposite, the Hebrew חפץ having the connotation of something intensely desired but not always attainable, are quite indicative of the element of tension which is interwoven into the logical subject-knower knowable-object relationship.

[5] The element of tension in the subject-object relationship is a result not of sin but of the incongruity of "attitudes" on the part of the confronters. The attitude of man is one of dominion while the "attitude" on the part of the objective order is one of irresponsiveness. The knowable object refuses to surrender to the subject-knower. The result of man's sin was not the emergence of tension and resistance—since this state of affairs prevailed even before man's expulsion from Paradise—but the change from tension to frustration, from a creative, successful performance to defeat. In imposing this metaphysical curse upon man, God decreed that the latter, in spite of all his glorious achievements, be finally defeated by death and ignorance. Judaism does not believe that man will ever succeed in his bold attempt to unravel the *mysterium magnum* of being and to control nature as a whole. The human cognitive and technological gestures, Judaism maintains, have a chance to succeed only in small sectors of reality. וקוץ ודרדר תצמיה לך—"Thorns and thistles shall it bring forth to thee."

[6] See Nachmanides (Genesis 2:9).

[7] The interpretation of כנגדו as "opposing" was accepted by our Talmudic sages. See *Yebamot*, 63a.

[8] The term "secular orders" is used here in accordance with its popular semantics. For the man of faith, this term is a misnomer. God claims the whole, not a part of man, and whatever He established as an order within the scheme of creation is sacred.

THE LONELY MAN OF FAITH

by JOSEPH B. SOLOVEITCHIK

It is not the plan of this paper[1] to discuss the millennium-old problem of faith and reason. Theory is not my concern at the moment. I want instead to focus attention on a human life situation in which the man of faith as an individual concrete being, with his cares and hopes, concerns and needs, joys and sad moments, is entangled. Therefore, whatever I am going to say here has been derived not from philosophical dialectics, abstract speculation, or detached impersonal reflections, but from actual situations and experiences with which I have been confronted. Indeed, the term lecture is, in this context, a misnomer. It is rather a tale of a personal dilemma. Instead of talking theology, in the didactic sense, eloquently and in balanced sentences, I would like, hesitantly and haltingly, to confide in you, and to share with you some concerns which weigh heavily on my mind and which frequently assume the proportions of an awareness of crisis.

I have no problem-solving thoughts. I do not intend to suggest a new method of remedying the human situation which I am about to describe; neither do I believe that it can be remedied at all. The role of the man of faith, whose religious experience is fraught with inner conflicts and incongruities, who oscillates between ecstasy in God's companionship and despair when he feels abandoned by God, and who is torn asunder by the heightened contrast between self-appreciation and abnegation, has been a difficult one since the times of Abraham and Moses. It would be presumptuous of me to attempt to convert the passional antinomic faith-experience into a eudaemonic-harmonious one, while the Biblical knights of faith lived heroically with this very tragic and paradoxical experience.

Reprinted from *Tradition*, Volume 7, 1965.

All I want is to follow the advice given by Elihu the son of Berachel of old who said, "I will speak that I may find relief"; for there is a redemptive quality for an agitated mind in the spoken word and a tormented soul finds peace in confessing.

I

A.

The nature of the dilemma can be stated in a three-word sentence. I am lonely. Let me emphasize, however, that by stating "I am lonely" I do not intend to convey to you the impression that I am alone. I, thank God, do enjoy the love and friendship of many. I meet people, talk, preach, argue, reason; I am surrounded by comrades and acquaintances. And yet, companionship and friendship do not alleviate the passional experience of loneliness which trails me constantly. I am lonely because at times I feel rejected and thrust away by everybody, not excluding my most intimate friends, and the words of the Psalmist, "My father and my mother have forsaken me," ring quite often in my ears like the plaintive cooing of the turtledove It is a strange, alas, absurd experience engendering sharp, enervating pain as well as a stimuating, cathartic feeling. I despair because I am lonely and, hence, feel frustrated. On the other hand, I also feel invigorated because this very experience of loneliness presses everything in me into the service of God. In my "desolate, howling solitude" I experience a growing awareness that, to paraphrase Plotinus' apothegm about prayer, this service to which I, a lonely and solitary individual, am committed is wanted and gracefully accepted by God in His transcendental loneliness and numinous solitude.

I must address myself to the obvious question: why am I beset by this feeling of loneliness and being unwanted? Is it the Kierkegaardian anguish—an ontological fear nurtured by the awareness of non-being threatening one's existence—that assails me, or is this feeling of loneliness solely due to my own personal stresses, cares and frustrations? Or is it perhaps the result of the pervasive state of mind of Western man who has become estranged from himself, a state with which all of us as Westerners are acquainted?

I believe that even though all three explanations might be true to some extent, the genuine and central cause of the feeling of loneliness from which I cannot free myself is to be found in a different dimension, namely, in the experience of faith itself. I am lonely because, in my humble, inadequate way, I am a man of faith for whom to be means to believe, and who substituted "credo" for "cogito" in the time-honored Cartesian maxim.[2] Apparently, in this role, as a man of faith, I must experience a sense of loneliness which is of a compound nature. It is a blend of that which is inseparably interwoven into the very texture of the faith gesture, characterizing the unfluctuating metaphysical destiny of the man of faith, and of that which is extraneous to the act of believing and stems from the ever-changing human-historical situation with all its whimsicality. On the one hand, the man of faith has been a solitary figure throughout the ages, indeed millennia, and no one has succeeded in escaping this unalterable destiny which is an "objective" awareness rather than a subjective feeling. On the other hand, it is undeniably true that this basic awareness expresses itself in a variety of ways, utilizing the whole gamut of one's affective emotional life which is extremely responsive to outward challenges and moves along with the tide of cultural-historical change. Therefore, it is my intent to analyze this experience at both levels: at the ontological, at which it is a root awareness, and at the historical, at which a highly sensitized and agitated heart, overwhelmed by the impact of social and cultural forces, filters this root awareness through the medium of painful, frustrating emotions.

As a matter of fact, the investigation at the second level is my prime concern since I am mainly interested in contemporary man of faith who is, due to his peculiar position in our secular society, lonely in a special way. No matter how time-honored and time-hallowed the interpenetration of faith and loneliness is, and it certainly goes back to the dawn of the Judaic covenant, contemporary man of faith lives through a particularly difficult and agonizing crisis.

Let me spell out this passional experience of contemporary man of faith.

He looks upon himself as a stranger in modern society which is technically minded, self-centered, and self-loving, almost in a sickly narcissistic fashion, scoring honor upon honor, piling up victory upon victory, reaching for the distant galaxies, and seeing in the here-and-now sensible world the only manifestation of being. What can a man of faith like myself, living by a doctrine which has no technical potential, by a law which cannot be tested in the laboratory, steadfast in his loyalty to an eschatological vision whose fulfillment cannot be predicted with any degree of probability, let alone certainty, even by the most complex, advanced mathematical calculations—what can such a man say to a functional utilitarian society which is *saeculum*-oriented and whose practical reasons of the mind have long ago supplanted the sensitive reasons of the heart?

It would be worthwhile to add the following in order to place the dilemma in the proper focus. I have never been seriously troubled by the problem of the Biblical doctrine of creation vis-à-vis the scientific story of evolution at both the cosmic and the organic levels, nor have I been perturbed by the confrontation of the mechanistic interpretation of the human mind with the Biblical spiritual concept of man. I have not been perplexed by the impossibility of fitting the mystery of revelation into the framework of historical empiricism. Moreover, I have not even been troubled by the theories of Biblical criticism which contradict the very foundations upon which the sanctity and integrity of the Scriptures rest. However, while theoretical oppositions and dichotomies have never tormented my thoughts, I could not shake off the disquieting feeling that the practical role of the man of faith within modern society is a very difficult, indeed, a paradoxical one.

The purpose of this paper, then, is to define the great dilemma confronting contemporary man of faith. Of course, as I already remarked, by defining the dilemma we do not expect to find its solution, for the dilemma is insoluble. However, the defining itself is a worthwhile cognitive gesture which, I hope, will yield a better understanding of ourselves and our commitment. Knowledge in general and self-knowledge in particular are gained not only from discovering logical answers but also from formulating logical, even though unanswerable, questions. The human logos is as concerned with an honest inquiry into an insoluble antinomy which leads to intellectual despair and humility as it is with an unprejudiced true solution of a complex problem arousing joy and enhancing one's intellectual determination and boldness.

Before beginning the analysis, we must determine within which frame of reference, psychologico-empirical or theologico-Biblical, should our dilemma be described. I believe you will agree with me that we do not have much choice in the matter; for, to the man of faith, self-knowledge has one connotation only—to understand one's place and role within the scheme of events and things willed and approved by God, when He ordered finitude to emerge out of infinity and the Universe, including man, to unfold itself. This kind of self-knowledge may not always be pleasant or comforting. On the contrary, it might from time to time express itself in a painful appraisal of the difficulties which man of faith, caught in his paradoxical destiny, has to encounter, for knowledge at both planes, the objective-natural and subjective-personal, is not always a eudaemonic experience. However, this unpleasant prospect should not deter us from our undertaking.

Before I go any further, I want to make the following reservation. Whatever I am about to say is to be seen only as a modest attempt on the part of a man of faith to interpret his spiritual perceptions and emotions in modern theologico-philosophical categories. My interpretive gesture is completely subjective and lays no claim to representing a definitive halakhic philosophy. If my audience will feel that these interpretations are also relevant to their perceptions and emotions, I shall feel amply rewarded. However, I shall not feel hurt if my thoughts will find no response in the hearts of my listeners.

B.

We all know that the Bible offers two accounts of the creation of man. We are also aware of the theory suggested by Bible critics attributing these two accounts to two different traditions and sources. Of course, since we do unreservedly accept the unity and integrity of the Scriptures and their divine character, we reject this hypothesis which is based, like many other Biblico-critical theories, on literary categories invented by modern man, ignoring completely the eidetic-noetic content of the Biblical story. It is, of course, true that the two accounts of the creation of man differ considerably. This incongruity was not discovered by the Bible critics. Our sages of old were aware of it.[3] However, the answer lies not in an alleged dual tradition but in dual man, not in an imaginary contradiction between two versions but in a real contradiction in the nature of man. The two accounts deal with two Adams, two men, two fathers of mankind, two types, two representatives of humanity, and it is no wonder that they are not identical. Let us just read these two accounts.

In Genesis I we read: "So God created man in His own image, in the image of God created He him, male and female created He them. And God blessed them and God said unto them, be fruitful and multiply, and fill the earth and subdue it, and have dominion over the fish of the sea, over the fowl of the heaven, and over the beasts, and all over the earth."

In Genesis II, the account differs substantially from the one we just read: "And the eternal God formed the man of the dust of the ground and breathed into his nostrils the breath of life and man became a living soul. And the eternal God planted a garden eastward in Eden. . . . And the eternal God took the man and placed him in the Garden of Eden to serve it and to keep it."

I want to point out four major discrepancies between these two accounts.

1) In the story of the creation of Adam the first, it is told that the latter was created in the image of God, בצלם א-לקים, while nothing is said about how his body was formed. In the account of the creation of Adam the second, it is stated that he was fashioned from the dust of the ground and God breathed into his nostrils the breath of life.

2) Adam the first received the mandate from the Almighty to fill the earth and subdue it, מלאו את הארץ וכבשה. Adam the second was

charged with the duty to cultivate the garden and to keep it, לעבדה
ולשמרה.

3) In the story of Adam the first, both male and female were created concurrently, while Adam the second emerged alone, with Eve
appearing subsequently as his helpmate and complement.

4) Finally, and this is a discrepancy of which Biblical criticism has
made so much, while in the first account only the name of E-lohim
appears, in the second, E-lohim is used in conjunction with the
Tetragrammaton.

C.

Let us portray these two men, Adam the first and Adam the second,
in typological categories.

There is no doubt that the term "image of God" in the first account
refers to man's inner charismatic endowment as a creative being. Man's
likeness to God expresses itself in man's striving and ability to become
a creator. Adam the first who was fashioned in the image of God was
blessed with great drive for creative activity and immeasurable resources for the realization of this goal, the most outstanding of which
is the intelligence, the human mind, capable of confronting the outside world and inquiring into its complex workings.[4] In spite of the
boundless divine generosity providing man with many intellectual ca-
pacities and interpretive perspectives in his approach to reality, God,
in imparting the blessing to Adam the first and giving him the mandate to subdue nature, directed Adam's attention to the functional and
practical aspects of his intellect through which man is able to gain
control of nature. Other intellectual inquiries, such as the metaphysical
or axiologico-qualitative, no matter how incisive and penetrating, have
never granted man dominion over his environment. The Greeks who
excelled in philosophical noesis were less skillful in technological
achievements. Modern science has emerged victorious from its encounter with nature because it has sacrificed qualitative-metaphysical speculation for the sake of a functional duplication of reality and substituted
the *quantus* for the *qualis* question. Therefore, Adam the first is interested in just a single aspect of reality and asks one question only—

"How does the cosmos function?" He is not fascinated by the question, "Why does the cosmos function at all?" nor is he interested in the question, "What is its essence?" He is only curious to know how it works. In fact, even this "how"-question with which Adam the first is preoccupied is limited in scope. He is concerned not with the question per se, but with its practical implications. He raises not a metaphysical but a practical, technical "how"-question. To be precise, his question is related not to the genuine functioning of the cosmos in itself but to the possibility of reproducing the dynamics of the cosmos by employing quantified-mathematized media which man evolves through postulation and creative thinking. The conative movement of attraction which Adam the first experiences toward the world is not of an exploratory-cognitive nature. It is rather nurtured by the selfish desire on the part of Adam to better his own position in relation to his environment. Adam the first is overwhelmed by one quest, namely, to harness and dominate the elemental natural forces and to put them at his disposal. This practical interest arouses his will to learn the secrets of nature. He is completely utilitarian as far as motivation, teleology, design and methodology are concerned.

D.

What is Adam the first out to achieve? What is the objective toward which he incessantly drives himself with enormous speed? The objective, it is self-evident, can be only one, namely, that which God put up before him: to be "man," to be himself. Adam the first wants to be human, to discover his identity which is bound up with his humanity. How does Adam find himself? He works with a simple equation introduced by the Psalmist who proclaimed the singularity and unique station of man in nature:

"For thou made him a little lower than the angels and hast crowned him with glory and honor (dignity)."[5] Man is an honorable being. In other words, man is a dignified being and to be human means to live with dignity. However, this equation of two unknown qualities requires further elaboration. We must be ready to answer the question: what is dignity and how can it be realized? The answer we find again in the words of the Psalmist who addressed himself to this obvious question, and who termed man not only an honorable but also a glorious being, spelling out the essence of glory in unmistakable terms:

"Thou hast made him to have dominion over the works of Thy hands. Thou hast put all things under his feet."

In other words, dignity was equated by the Psalmist with man's capability of dominating his environment and exercising control over it. Man acquires dignity through glory, through his *majestic* posture vis-à-vis his environment.[6]

The brute's existence is an undignified one because it is a helpless existence. Human existence is a dignified one because it is a glorious, majestic, powerful existence. Hence, dignity is unobtainable as long as man has not reclaimed himself from co-existence with nature and has not risen from a non-reflective, degradingly helpless instinctive life to an intelligent, planned, and majestic one. For the sake of clarification of the double equation humanity = dignity and dignity = glory-majesty, it is necessary to add another thought. There is no dignity without responsibility, and one cannot assume responsibility as long as he is not capable of living up to his commitments. Only when man rises to the heights of freedom of action and creativity of mind does he begin to implement the mandate of dignified responsibility entrusted to him by his Maker. Dignity of man expressing itself in the awareness of being responsible and of being capable of discharging his responsibility cannot be realized as long as he has not gained mastery over his environment. For life in bondage to insensate elemental forces is a non-responsible and hence an undignified affair.[7]

Man of old who could not fight disease and succumbed in multitudes to yellow fever or any other plague with degrading helplessness could not lay claim to dignity. Only the man who builds hospitals, discovers therapeutic techniques and saves lives is blessed with dignity. Man of the 17th and 18th centuries who needed several days to travel from Boston to New York was less dignified than modern man who attempts to conquer space, boards a plane at the New York Airport at midnight and takes several hours later a leisurely walk along the streets of London.[8] The brute is helpless, and, therefore, not dignified.

Civilized man has gained limited control of nature and has become, in certain respects, her master, and with his mastery, he has attained dignity, as well. His mastery has made it possible for him to act in accordance with his responsibility.

Hence, Adam the first is aggressive, bold, and victory-minded. His motto is success, triumph over the cosmic forces. He engages in creative work, trying to imitate his Maker (*imitatio Dei*). The most characteristic representative of Adam the first is the mathematical scientist who whisks us away from the array of tangible things, from color and sound, from heat, touch, and smell which are the only phenomena accessible to our senses, into a formal relational world of thought constructs, the product of his "arbitrary" postulating and spontaneous positing and deducing. This world, woven out of human thought processes, functions with amazing precision and runs parallel to the workings of the real multifarious world of our senses. The modern scientist does not try to explain nature. He only duplicates it. In his full resplendent glory as a creative agent of God, he constructs his own world and in mysterious fashion succeeds in controlling his environment through manipulating his own mathematical constructs and creations.

Adam the first is not only a creative theoretician. He is also a creative esthete. He fashions ideas with his mind, and beauty with his heart. He enjoys both his intellectual and esthetic creativity and takes pride in it. He also displays creativity in the world of the norm: he legislates for himself norms and laws because a dignified existence is an orderly one. Anarchy and dignity are mutually exclusive. He is this-worldly-minded, finitude-oriented, beauty-centered. Adam the first is always an esthete, whether engaged in an intellectual or ethical performance. His conscience is energized not by the idea of the good, but by that of the beautiful. His mind is questing not for the true, but for the pleasant and functional, which are rooted in the esthetical, not the noetic-ethical, sphere.[9]

In doing all this, Adam the first is trying to carry out the mandate entrusted to him by his Maker who, at dawn of the sixth mysterious day of creation, addressed Himself to man and summoned him to "fill the earth and subdue it." It is God who decreed that the story of Adam the first be the great saga of freedom of man-slave who gradually transforms himself into man-master. While pursuing this goal, driven by an urge which he cannot but obey, Adam the first transcends the limits of the reasonable and probable and ventures into the open spaces of a boundless universe. Even this longing for vastness, no matter how adventurous and fantastic, is legitimate. Man reaching for the distant stars is acting in harmony with his nature which was created, willed, and directed by his Maker. It is a manifestation of obedience to rather than rebellion against God. Thus, in sum, we have obtained the following triple equation: humanity = dignity = responsibility = majesty.

III

A.

Adam the second is, like Adam the first, also intrigued by the cosmos. Intellectual curiosity drives them both to confront courageously the *mysterium magnum* of Being. However, while the cosmos provokes Adam the first to quest for power and control, thus making him ask the functional "how"-question, Adam the second responds to the call of the cosmos by engaging in a different kind of cognitive gesture. He does not ask a single functional question. Instead his inquiry is of a metaphysical nature and a threefold one. He wants to know: "Why is it?" "What is it?" "Who is it?" (1) He wonders: "Why did the world in its totality come into existence? Why is man confronted by this stupendous and indifferent order of things and events?" (2) He asks: "What is the purpose of all this? What is the message that is embedded in organic and inorganic matter, and what does the great challenge reaching me from beyond the fringes of the universe as well as from the depths of my tormented soul mean?" (3) Adam the second keeps on wondering: "Who is He who trails me steadily, uninvited and unwanted, like an everlasting shadow, and vanishes into the recesses of transcendence the very instant I turn around to confront this numinous, awesome and mysterious 'He'?

Who is He who fills Adam with awe and bliss, humility and a sense of greatness, concurrently? Who is He to whom Adam clings in passionate, all-consuming love and from whom he flees in mortal fear and dread? Who is He who fascinates Adam irresistibly and at the same time rejects him irrevocably? Who is He whom Adam experiences both as the *mysterium tremendum* and as the most elementary, most obvious, and most understandable truth? Who is He who is *deus revelatus* and *deus absconditus* simultaneously? Who is He whose life-giving and life-warming breath Adam feels constantly and who at the same time remains distant and remote from all?"

In order to answer this triple question, Adam the second does not apply the functional method invented by Adam the first. He does not create a world of his own. Instead, he wants to understand the living, "given" world into which he has been cast. Therefore, he does not mathematize phenomena or conceptualize things. He encounters the universe in all its colorfulness, splendor, and grandeur, and studies it with the naivete, awe and admiration of the child who seeks the unusual and wonderful in every ordinary thing and event. While Adam the first is dynamic and creative, transforming sense data into thought constructs, Adam the second is receptive and beholds the world in its original dimensions. He looks for the image of God not in the mathematical formula or the natural relational law but in every beam of light, in every bud and blossom, in the morning breeze and the stillness of a starlit evening. In a word, Adam the second explores not the scientific abstract universe but the irresistibly fascinating qualitative world where he establishes an intimate relation with God. The Biblical metaphor referring to God breathing life into Adam alludes to the actual preoccupation of the latter with God, to his genuine living experience of God rather than to some divine potential or endowment in Adam symbolized by *imago Dei*.[10] Adam the second lives in close union with God. His existential "I" experience is interwoven in the awareness of communing with the Great Self whose footprints he discovers along the many tortuous paths of creation.

B.

I stated previously that both Adams are equally provoked by the mystery of Being even though the methods they employ in their heroic attempt to come to terms and to arrange a *modus vivendi* with the *mysterium magnum* are incongruous. Let me add now that not only the etiological impulse and drive but also the objective and hence the motivation are identical. Both Adams want to be human. Both strive to be themselves, to be what God commanded them to be, namely, man. They certainly could not reach for some other objective since this urge, as I noted, lies in accordance with God's scheme of creation, at the root of all human strivings and any rebellious effort on the part of man to substitute something else for this urge would be in distinct opposition to God's will which is embedded in man's nature. The incongruity of methods is, therefore, a result not of diverse objectives but of diverse interpretive approaches to the one objective they both pursue. The two Adams do not concur in their interpretations of this objective. The idea of humanity, the great challenge summoning man to action and movement, is placed by them in two incommensurate perspectives.

While Adam the first wants to reclaim himself from a closed-in, non-reflective, natural existence by setting himself up as a dignified majestic being capable of ruling his environment, Adam the second sees his *separateness* from nature and his existential uniqueness not in dignity or majesty but in something else. There is, in his opinion, another mode of existence through which man can find his own self, namely, the redemptive, which is not necessarily identical with the dignified. Quite often, an existence might be replete with dignity and mastery, and yet remain unredeemed. An atheist cosmonaut circling the earth, advising his superiors who placed him in orbit that he did not encounter any angels, might lay claim to dignity because he courageously mastered space; he is, however, very far from experiencing a redeemed existence.

In order to delineate more sharply the contours of Adam the second, who rejected dignity as the sole objective of human questing, let us add the following observation. Dignity is a social and behavioral category, expressing not an intrinsic existential quality, but a technique of living, a way of impressing society, the know-how of commanding respect and attention of the other fellow, a capacity to make one's presence felt. In Hebrew, the noun *kavod*, dignity, and the noun *koved*, weight, *gravitas*, stem from the same root. The man of dignity is a weighty person. The people who surround him feel his impact. Hence, dignity is measured not by the inner worth of the in-depth-personality, but by the accomplishments of the surface-personality. No matter how fine, noble, and gifted one may be, he cannot command respect or be appreciated by others if he has not succeeded in realizing his talents and communicating his message to society through the medium of the creative majestic gesture. In light of the aforementioned, dignity as a behavioral category can find realization only in the outward gesture which helps the inner personality to objectify itself and to explain and interpret itself to the external world. Hence, dignity can only be predicated of *kerygmatic* man who has the capability of establishing lines of communication with neighbors, acquaintances and friends, and engaging them in a dialogue, not of words, but of action. Dignity is linked with fame. There is no dignity in anonymity. If one succeeds in putting his message (*kerygma*) across he may lay claim to dignity. The mute person, whose message remains hidden and suppressed in the silence of the in-depth-personality, cannot be considered dignified.

Therefore, Adam the first was created not alone, but together with Eve—male and female emerged simultaneously. Adam the first exists in society, in community with others. He is a social being, gregarious, communicative, emphasizing the artistic aspect in life and giving priority to form over content, to literary expression over the eidos, to practical accomplishments over inner motivation. He is blessed with the gift of rhetoric, with the faculty of communication, be it the beautiful word, the efficacious machine, the socially acceptable ethic-etiquette, or the hush of the solemn memorial assembly. The visible, perceptible public image of the personality is fraught with majesty and dignity. Adam the first is never alone. Man in solitude has no opportunity to display his dignity and majesty, since both are behavioral social traits. Adam the first was not left alone even on the day of creation. He emerged into the world together with Eve, and God addressed Himself to both of them as inseparable members of one community.

IV

The community of which Adam the first, majestic man, is a member, is a natural one, a product of the creative, social gesture in which Adam engages whenever he thinks that collective living and acting will promote his interests.[11] I term this community a natural one, because the urge for organized activity at this level is not nurtured by the singular needs and experiences of spiritual man created in God's image but by biological instinctual pressures. It is a natural reaction on the part of man, as a biological being bent on survival, to the menacing challenge of the outside world. In fact, the root of the instinct of gregariousness which is the very foundation of the natural community is to be found already in the animal kingdom. Let cattle grazing quietly along a wide area of green pastures sense suddenly that danger is lurking somewhere, they, overcome by instinctive panic, will begin to herd together and to cling to each other as if mere physical contiguity could avert the impending catastrophe. The difference between man associating with others and animals flocking together consists, of course, in the fact that while the mute creatures *react* in a mechanical, spurious, and purposeless way, eloquent and wise man *acts* intelligently and teleologically. Yet this discrepancy does not contradict our premise that the primordial urge to come together in face of opposition is shared by both animal and biological man.

Adam the first is challenged by a hostile environment and hence summoned to perform many tasks which he alone cannot master. Consequently, he is impelled to take joint action. Helpless individuals, cognizant of the difficulties they encounter when they act separately, congregate, make arrangements, enter into treaties of mutual assistance, sign contracts, form partnerships, etc.[12] The natural community is born of a feeling of individual helplessness. Whenever Adam the first wants to work, to produce and to succeed in his undertakings, he must unite with others. The whole theory of the social contract brought to perfection by the philosophers of the age of reason, reflects the thinking of Adam the first, identifying man with his intellectual nature and creative technological will and finding in human existence coherence, legitimacy, and reasonableness exclusively. To the thinkers of the Age of Reason man posed no problem. He was for them an understandable, simple affair. Their admiration, alas adoration, of the human mind hindered them from realizing the metaphysical dilemma and existential paradoxicality, indeed absurdity, embedded in the human "I" awareness. They saw man in his glory but failed to see him in his tragic plight. They considered the individual ontologically perfect and existentially adequate.[13] They admitted only that he was functionally handicapped even though he could, like Robinson Crusoe, surmount this difficulty, too. If the individual is ontologically complete, even perfect, then the experience of loneliness must be alien to him, since loneliness is nothing but the act of questioning one's own ontological legitimacy, worth and reasonableness. In fact, according to the Biblical story, God was not concerned with the loneliness of Adam the first. Neither was Adam aware of the pronouncement לא טוב היות האדם לבדו. "It is not good for man to be lonely." Moreover, the connotation of these words in the context of the world-view of Adam the first, even if they had been addressed to him, would have been related not to loneliness, an existential in-depth-experience, but to aloneness, a practical surface-experience. Adam the first, representing the natural community, would translate this pronouncement into pragmatic categories, referring not to existence as such, but to productive work. If pressed for an interpretation of the pronouncement, he would paraphrase it: "It is not good for man to work (not to be) alone." לא טוב עשות האדם מלאכה לבדו. The words "I shall make him a helpmate" would refer, in accordance with his social philosophy, to a functional partner to whom it would be assigned to collaborate with and assist Adam the first in his undertakings, schemes, and projects. Eve vis-à-vis Adam the first would be a work partner, not an existential co-participant. Man alone cannot succeed, says Adam the first, because a successful life is possible only within a communal framework. Robinson Crusoe may be self-sufficient as far as mere survival is concerned, but he cannot make a success of his life. Distribution of labor, the coordinated efforts of the many, the accumulated experiences of the multitude, the cooperative spirit of countless individuals, raise man above the primitive level of a natural existence and grant him limited dominion over his environment. What we call civilization is the sum total of a community effort through the millennia. Thus, the natural community fashioned by Adam the first is a work community, committed to the successful production, distribution, and consumption of goods, material as well as cultural.

Ecclesiastes (Kohelet) has portrayed the act of grouping and coalescing as envisioned by Adam the first in unmistakable categories: "The two are better than the one because they have a good reward for their labor. For if they fall, the one will lift up his fellow; but woe to him that is alone when he falleth, and hath not another to help him out." The natural community of Adam the first enhances man's chances for successful survival, yet does not elevate or enhance his existential experience, since the latter is in no need of redemption or catharsis. Adam the first feels safer and more comfortable in the company of Eve in a practical, not ontological, way. He will never admit that he cannot, ontologically, see himself without Eve. They, Adam and Eve, act together, work together, pursue common objectives together; yet they do not exist together. Ontologically, they do not belong to each other; each is provided with an "I" awareness and knows nothing of a "We" awareness. Of course, they communicate with each other. But the communication lines are open between two surface-personalities engaged in work, dedicated to success, and speaking in cliches and stereotypes, and not between two souls bound together in an indissoluble relation, each one speaking in unique *logoi*. The in-depth-personalities do not communicate, let alone commune, with each other. "And God blessed them and God said unto them be fruitful and multiply and replenish the earth and subdue it and have dominion over the fish of the sea, and over the fowl of the air, and over everything that creepeth over the earth."

Male and female were summoned by their Creator to act in unison in order to act successfully. Yet, they were not charged with the task of existing in unison, in order to cleanse, redeem and hallow their existence.

V

A.

Having described majestic Adam both as an individual and as a member of a work community, let us return to Adam the second in his dual role as a lonely individual and as one committed to a peculiar community idea.

There are two basic distinctions between dignity and cathartic redemptiveness:

1) Being redeemed is, unlike being dignified, an ontological awareness. It is not just an extraneous, accidental attribute—among other attributes—of being, but a definitive mode of being itself. A redeemed existence is intrinsically different from an unredeemed. Redemptiveness does not have to be acted out vis-à-vis the outside world.[14] Even a hermit, while not having the opportunity to manifest dignity, can live a redeemed life. Cathartic redemptiveness is experienced in the privacy of one's in-depth-personality and it cuts below the relationship between the "I" and the "thou" (to use an existential term) and reaches into the very hidden strata of the isolated "I" who knows himself as a singular being. When objectified in personal affective-emotional categories, cathartic redemptiveness expresses itself in the feeling of axiological security. The individual intuits his existence as worthwhile, legitimate and adequate, anchored in something stable and unchangeable.

2) Cathartic redemptiveness, in contrast with dignity, cannot be attained through man's acquisition of control of his environment, but through man's exercise of control over himself. A redeemed life is *ipso facto* a disciplined life. While a dignified existence is attained by majestic man who courageously surges forward and confronts mute nature—a lower form of being—in a mood of defiance, redemption

is achieved when humble man makes a movement of recoil, and lets himself be confronted and defeated by a Higher and Truer Being. God summoned Adam the first to advance steadily, Adam the second to retreat. Adam the first He told to exercise mastery and to "fill the earth and subdue it," Adam the second, to serve. He was placed in the Garden of Eden "to cultivate it and to keep it."

Dignity is acquired by man whenever he triumphs over nature. Man finds redemption whenever he is overpowered by the Creator of nature. Dignity is discovered at the summit of success; redemption in the depth of crisis and failure. ממעמקים קראתיך ה׳, "Out of the depths have I called Thee, Oh God." The Bible has stated explicitly that Adam the second was formed from the dust of the ground because the knowledge of the humble origin of man is an integral part of Adam's "I"-experience. Adam the second has never forgotten that he is just a handful of dust.[15]

B.

And defeated must Adam the second feel the very instant he scores his greatest success: the discovery of his humanity, his "I" identity. The "I" awareness which he attains as the result of his untiring search for a redeemed, secure existence brings its own antithesis to the fore: the awareness of his exclusiveness and ontological incompatibility with any other being. Adam the second suddenly finds out that he is alone, that he has alienated himself from the world of the brute and the instinctual mechanical state of an outward existence, while he has failed to ally himself with the intelligent, purposive inward beings who inhabit the new world into which he has entered. Each great redemptive step forward in man's quest for humanity entails the ever-growing tragic awareness of his aloneness and only-ness and consequently of his loneliness and insecurity. He struggles for the discovery of his identity because he suffers from the insecurity implied in seeing the icy darkness of uniformity and irresponsiveness, in gazing into that senseless something without being awarded a reciprocal gaze, in being always a silent watcher without in turn being watched. With the redeeming daybreak of a new "I" identity, Adam the second is ushered into a world of diversity and change where the feeling of insecurity expresses itself in the fact that the term "man" clothes a wondrous, unique and incommunicable reality, in the gazing into somebody who returns one's gaze suspiciously, in watching and being watched in bewilderment. Who knows what kind of loneliness is more agonizing: the one which befalls man when he casts his glance at the mute cosmos, at its dark spaces and monotonous drama, or the one that besets man exchanging glances with his fellow man in silence? Who knows whether the first astronaut who landed on the moon, confronted with a strange, weird, and grisly panorama, felt a greater loneliness than Mr. X, moving along jubilantly with the crowd and exchanging greetings on New Year's Eve at a public square?

Adam the second is still lonely. He separated himself from his environment which became the object of his intellectual gaze. "And the man gave names to all the beasts and to the fowl of the heaven and to every animal of the field." He is a citizen of a new world, the world of man, but he has no companion with whom to communicate and therefore he is existentially insecure. Neither would the availability of the female, who was created with Adam the first, have changed this human situation if not for the emergence of a new kind of companionship. At this crucial point, if Adam is to bring his quest for redemption to full realization, he must initiate action leading to the discovery of a companion who, even though as unique and singular as he, will master the art of communicating and, with him, form a community. However, this action, since it is part of the redemptive gesture, must also be sacrificial. The medium of attaining full redemption is, again, defeat. This new companionship is not attained through conquest, but through surrender and retreat. "And the eternal God caused an overpowering sleep to fall upon the man." Adam was overpowered and defeated— and in defeat he found his companion.

Again, the contrast between the two Adams comes into focus. Adam the first was not called to sacrifice in order that his female companion come into being, while it was indispensable for Adam the second to give away part of himself in order to find a companion. The community-fashioning gesture of Adam the first is, as I indicated before, purely utilitarian and intrinsically egotistic and, as such, rules out sacrificial action. For Adam the second, communicating and communing are redemptive sacrificial gestures. Thus, in crisis and distress there was planted the seed of a new type of community—the faith community which reached full fruition in the covenant between God and Abraham.[16]

C.

The covenantal faith community, in contradistinction to the natural work community, interprets the divine pronouncement "It is not good for man to be alone" לא טוב היות האדם לבדו, not in utilitarian but in ontological terms: it is not good for man to be lonely (not alone) with emphasis placed upon "to be." Being at the level of the faith community does not lend itself to any equation. "To be" is not to be equated with "to work and produce goods" (as historical materialism wants us to believe). "To be" is not identical with "to think" (as the classical tradition of philosophical rationalism throughout the ages culminating in Descartes and later in Kant tried to convince us). "To be" does not exhaust itself either in suffering (as Schopenhauer preached) or in enjoying the world of sense (in accordance with ethical hedonism). "To be" is a unique in-depth-experience of which only Adam the second is aware and it is unrelated to any function or performance. "To be" means to be the only one, singular and different, and consequently lonely. For what causes man to be lonely and feel insecure if not the awareness of his uniqueness and exclusiveness. The "I" is lonely, experiencing ontological incompleteness and casualness, because there is no one who exists like the "I" and because the *modus existentiae* of the "I" cannot be repeated, imitated, or experienced by others.

Since loneliness reflects the very core of the "I" experience and is not an accidental modus, no accidental activity or external achievement—such as belonging to a natural work community and achieving cooperative success—can reclaim Adam the second from this state. Therefore, I repeat, Adam the second must quest for a different kind of community. The companionship which Adam the second is searching is not to be found in the depersonalized regimentation of the army, in the automatic coordination of the assembly line, or in the activity of the institutionalized soulless political community. His quest is for a new kind of fellowship which one finds in the existential community. There, not only hands are joined, but experiences as well; there, one hears not only the rhythmic sound of the production line, but also the rhythmic beat of hearts starved for existential companionship and all-embracing sympathy and experiencing the grandeur of the faith commitment; there, one lonely soul finds another soul tormented by loneliness and solitude yet unqualifiedly committed.

VI

At this point, the main distinction between the natural community of Adam the first and the covenantal faith community of Adam the second becomes clear. The first is a community of interests, forged by the indomitable desire for success and triumph and consisting at all times of two grammatical *personae,* the "I" and the "thou" who collaborate in order to further their interests. A newcomer, upon joining the community, ceases to be the anonymous "he" and turns into a knowable, communicative "thou." The second is a community of commitments born in distress and defeat and comprises three participants: "I, thou, and He," the He in whom all being is rooted and in whom everything finds its rehabilitation and, consequently, redemption. Adam the first met the female all by himself, while Adam the second was introduced to Eve by God, who summoned Adam to join Eve in an existential community molded by sacrificial action and suffering, and who Himself became a partner in this community. God is never outside of the covenantal community. He joins man and shares in his covenantal existence. Finitude and infinity, temporality and eternity, creature and creator become involved in the same community. They bind themselves together and participate in a unitive existence.[17]

The element of togetherness of God and man is indispensable for the covenantal community for the very validity of the covenant rests upon the juridic-Halakhic principle of free negotiation, mutual assumption of duties, and full recognition of the equal rights of both parties concerned with the covenant.[18] Both parties entering a covenantal relationship possess inalienable rights which may only be surrendered by mutual consent. The paradoxical experience of freedom, reciprocity, and "equality" in one's personal confrontation with God is basic for the understanding of the covenantal faith community.[19] We meet God in the covenantal community as a comrade and fellow member. Of course, even within the framework of this community, God appears as the leader, teacher, and shepherd. Yet the leader is an integral part of the community, the teacher is inseparable from his pupils, and the shepherd never leaves his flock. They all belong to one group. The covenant draws God into the society of men of faith. "The God before whom my fathers did walk—the God who has been my shepherd all my life." God was Jacob's shepherd and companion. The covenantal faith community manifests itself in a three-fold personal union: I, thou and He.[20]

VII

Even though, as we said before, the man of faith is provoked, like Adam the first, by the cosmos about which he is inquisitive, the covenant, not the cosmos, provides him with an answer to his questions. The covenantal confrontation is indispensable for the man of faith. In his longing for God, he is many a time disenchanted with the cosmic revelation and lives through moments of despair. Naturally, he is inspired by the great joy experienced when he gets a glimpse of the Truly Real hiding behind the magnificent cosmic facade. However, he is also tormented by the stress and exasperation felt when the Truly Real seems to disappear from the cosmic scene. Of course, God speaks through His works: השמים מספרים כבוד א-ל וגו' "The heavens declare the glory of God and the firmament showeth His handiwork." Yet, let me ask, what kind of a tale do the heavens tell? Is it a personal tale addressed to someone, or is it a tale which is not intended for any audience? Do the heavens sing the glory of the Creator without troubling themselves to find out whether or not someone is listening to this great song or are they really interested in man, the listener?

I believe that the answer to this question is obvious. If the tale of the heavens were a personal one, addressed to man, then there would be no need for another encounter with God. Since God in His infinite wisdom arranged for the apocalyptic-covenantal meeting with man, we may conclude that the message of the heavens is at best an equivocal one.

As a matter of fact, at the level of his cosmic confrontation with God, man is faced with an exasperating paradox. On the one hand, he beholds God in every nook and corner of creation, in the flowering of the plant, in the rushing of the tide, and in the movement of his own muscle, as if God were at hand close to and beside man, engaging him in a friendly dialogue. And yet the very moment man turns his face to God, he finds Him remote, unapproachable, enveloped in transcendence and mystery. Did not Isaiah behold God רם ונשא, exalted and enthroned above creation, and at the same time ושוליו מלאים את ההיכל, the train of his skirts filling the Temple, the great universe, from the flying nebulae to one's most intimate heartbeat? Did not the angels sing קדוש קדוש קדוש holy, holy, holy, transcendent, transcendent, transcendent, yet ה' צב' מלא כל הארץ כבודו, He is the Lord of the hosts, Who resides in every infinitesimal particle of creation and the whole universe is replete with His glory? In short, the cosmic experience is antithetic and tantalizing. It exhausts itself in the awesome dichotomy of God's involvement in the drama of creation, and His exaltedness above and remoteness from this very drama. This dichotomy cancels the intimacy and immediacy from one's relationship with God and renders the personal approach to God complicated and difficult. God, as the cosmic ruler, is beheld in His boundless majesty reigning supreme over creation, His will crystallized in the natural law, His word determining the behavioral patterns of nature. He is everywhere but at the same time above and outside of everything. When man who just beheld God's presence turns around to address himself to the Master of creation in the intimate accents of the "Thou," he finds the Master and Creator gone, enveloped in the cloud of mystery, winking to him from the awesome "beyond." Therefore, the man of faith, in order to redeem himself from his loneliness and misery, must meet God at a personal covenantal level, where he can be near Him and feel free in His presence. Abraham, the knight of faith, according to our tradition, searched and discovered God in the star-lit heavens of Mesopotamia. Yet, he felt an intense loneliness and could not find solace in the silent companionship of God whose image was reflected in the boundless stretches of the cosmos. Only when he met God on earth as Father, Brother and Friend—not only along the uncharted astral routes—did he feel redeemed. Our sages said that before Abraham appeared *majestas dei* was reflected only by the distant heavens and it was a mute nature which "spoke" of the glory of God. It was Abraham who "crowned" Him the God of earth, i.e., the God of men.[21]

Majestic man, even when he belongs to the group of *homines religiosi* and feels a distinct need for transcendental experiences, is gratified by his encounter with God within the framework of the cosmic drama. Since majestic man is incapable of breaking out of the cosmic cycle, he cannot interpret his transcendental adventure in anything but cosmic categories. Therefore, the divine name of E-lohim which denotes God being the source of the cosmic dynamics sufficed to characterize the relationship prevailing between majestic man and his Creator addressing Himself to him through the cosmic occurrence.

However, covenantal man of faith craving for a personal and intimate relation with God could not find it in the cosmic E-lohim encounter and had to shift his transcendental experience to a different level at which the finite "I" meets the infinite He "face to face." This strange communal relation between man and God is symbolized by the Tetragrammaton[22] which therefore appears in the Biblical account of Adam the second.

VIII

A.

I mentioned previously that only the covenantal community consisting of all three grammatical personae—I, thou, and He—can and does alleviate the passional experience of Adam the second by offering him the opportunity to communicate, indeed to commune with, and to enjoy the genuine friendship of Eve. Within the covenantal community, we said, Adam and Eve participate in the existential experience of being, not merely working, together. The change from a technical utilitarian relationship to a covenantal existential one occurs in the following manner. When God joins the community of man the miracle of revelation takes place in two dimensions: in the transcendental—*Deus absconditus* emerges suddenly as *Deu revelatus*—and in the human—*homo absconditus* sheds his mask and turns into *homo revelatus*. With the sound of the divine voice addressing man by his name, be it Abraham, Moses, or Samuel, God, whom man has searched along the endless trails of the universe, is discovered suddenly as being close to and intimate with man, standing just opposite or beside him. At this meeting—initiated by God—of God and man, the covenantal-prophetic community is established. When man addresses himself to God, calling Him in the informal, friendly tones of "Thou," the same miracle happens again: God joins man and at this meeting, initiated by man, a new covenantal community is born—the prayer community.

I have termed both communities, the prophetic and the prayerful, covenantal because of a three-fold reason. (1) In both communities, a confrontation of God and man takes place. It is quite obvious that the prophecy awareness which is *toto genere* different from the mystical experience, can only be interpreted in the unique categories of the covenantal event. The whole idea of prophecy would be fraught with an inner contradiction if man's approach to God remained indirect and impersonal, expecting nature to mediate between him and his Creator. Only within the covenantal community which is formed by God descending upon the mount[23] and man, upon the call of the Lord, ascending the mount,[24] is a direct and personal relationship expressing itself in the prophetic "face to face" colloquy established. "And the Lord spake unto Moses face to face as man speaketh unto his friend."[25]

Prayer likewise is unimaginable without having man stand before and address himself to God in a manner reminiscent of the prophet's dialogue with God. The cosmic drama, notwithstanding its grandeur and splendor, no matter how distinctly it reflects the image of the

Creator and no matter how beautifully it tells His glory, cannot provoke man to prayer. Of course, it may arouse an adoring-ecstatic mood in man; it may even inspire man to raise his voice in a song of praise and thanksgiving. Nevertheless, ecstatic adoration, even if expressed in a hymn, is not prayer. The latter transcends the bounds of liturgical worship and must not be reduced to its external-technical aspects such as praise, thanksgiving or even petition. Prayer is basically an awareness of man finding himself in the presence of and addressing himself to his Maker, and to pray has one connotation only: to stand before God.[26] To be sure, this awareness has been objectified and crystallized in standardized, definitive texts whose recitation is obligatory. The total faith commitment tends always to transcend the frontiers of fleeting, amorphous subjectivity and to venture into the outside world of the well-formed, objective gesture. However, no matter how important this tendency on the part of the faith commitment is—and it is of enormous significance in the Halakhah which constantly demands from man that he translate his inner life into external facticity—it remains unalterably true that the very essence of prayer is the covenantal experience of being together with and talking to God and that the concrete performance such as the recitation of texts represents the technique of implementation of prayer and not prayer itself.[27] In short, prayer and prophecy are two synonymous designations of the covenantal God-man colloquy. Indeed, the prayer community was born the very instant the prophetic community expired and, when it did come into the spiritual world of the Jew of old, it did not supersede the prophetic community but rather perpetuated it. Prayer is the continuation of prophecy and the fellowship of prayerful men is *ipso facto* the fellowship of prophets. The difference between prayer and prophecy is, as I have already mentioned, related not to the substance of the dialogue but rather to the order in which it is conducted. While within the prophetic community God takes the initiative—He speaks and man listens—in the prayer community the initiative belongs to man: he does the speaking and God, the listening. The word of prophecy is God's and is accepted by man. The word of prayer is man's and God accepts it. The two Halakhic traditions tracing the origin of

prayer to Abraham and the other Patriarchs and attributing the authorship of statutory prayer to the men of the Great Assembly reveal the
Judaic view of the sameness of the prophecy and prayer communities.[28]
Covenantal prophecy and prayer blossomed forth the very instant
Abraham met God and became involved in a strange colloquy. At a
later date, when the mysterious men of this wondrous assembly witnessed the bright summer day of the prophetic community full of
color and sound turning to a bleak autumnal night of dreadful silence
unillumined by the vision of God or made homely by His voice, they
refused to acquiesce in this cruel historical reality and would not let
the ancient dialogue between God and men come to an end. For the
men of the Great Assembly knew that with the withdrawal of the
colloquy from the field of consciousness of the Judaic community, the
latter would lose the intimate companionship of God and consequently
its covenantal status. In prayer they found the salvation of the colloquy, which, they insisted, must go on forever. If God had stopped
calling man, they urged, let man call God. And so the covenantal
colloquy was shifted from the level of prophecy to that of prayer.

(2) Both the prophetic and the prayerful community are three-fold
structures, consisting of all three grammatical personae—I, thou, and
He. The prophet in whom God confides and to whom He entrusts His
eternal word must always remember that he is the representative of
the many anonymous "they" for whom the message is earmarked. No
man, however great and noble, is worthy of God's word if he fancies
that the word is his private property not to be shared by others.[29]

The prayerful community must not, likewise, remain a two-fold
affair: a transient "I" addressing himself to the eternal "He." The inclusion of others is indispensable. Man should avoid praying for himself alone. The plural form of prayer is of central Halakhic significance.[30] When disaster strikes, one must not be immersed completely
in his own passional destiny, thinking exclusively of himself, being
concerned only with himself, and petitioning God merely for himself.
The foundation of efficacious and noble prayer is human solidarity and
sympathy or the covenantal awareness of existential togetherness, of
sharing and experiencing the travail and suffering of those for whom

majestic Adam the first has no concern. Only Adam the second knows the art of praying since he confronts God with the petition of the many. The fenced-in egocentric and ego-oriented Adam the first is ineligible to join the covenantal prayer community of which God is a fellow member. If God abandones His transcendental numinous solitude, He wills man to do likewise and to step out of his isolation and aloneness.[31] Job did not understand this simple postulate. "And it was so, when the days of their feasting were gone about, that Job sent and sanctified them, and rose up early in the morning, and offered burnt offerings according to the *"number of them all."*[32]He did pray, he did offer sacrifices, but only for his household. Job failed to understand the covenantal nature of the prayer community in which destinies are dovetailed, suffering or joy is shared and prayers merge into one petition on behalf of all. As we all know, Job's sacrifices were not accepted, Job's prayers remained unheard, and Job—pragmatic Adam the first—met with catastrophe and the whirlwind uprooted him and his household. Only then did he discover the great covenantal experience of being together, praying together and for one another. "And the Lord turned the captivity of Job, when he prayed for his friends; also the Lord gave Job twice as much as he had before." Not only was Job rewarded with a double measure in material goods, but he also attained a new dimension of existence—the covenantal one.

(3) Both communities sprang into existence not only because of a singular experience of having met God, but also and perhaps mainly, because of the discovery of the normative *kerygma* entailed in this very experience. Any encounter with God, if it is to redeem man, must be crystallized and objectified in a normative ethico-moral message. If, however, the encounter is reduced to its non-kerygmatic and non-imperative aspects, no matter how great and magnificent an experience it is, it cannot be classified as a covenantal encounter since the very semantics of the term covenant implies freely assumed obligations and commitments. In contradistinction to the mystical experience of intuition, illumination, or union which rarely results in the formulation of a practical message, prophecy, which, as I emphasized before, has very little in common with the mystical experience, is inseparable from its

normative content. Isaiah, Ezekiel, or other prophets were not led through the habitations of heaven, past the seraphim and angels, to the hidden recesses where God is enthroned above and beyond everything in order to get the overpowering glimpse of the Absolute, True and Real, and to bring their individual lives to complete fulfillment. The prophetic pilgrimage to God pursues a practical goal in whose realization the whole covenantal community shares. When confronted with God, the prophet receives an ethico-moral message to be handed down to and realized by the members of the covenantal community which is mainly a community in action. What did Isaiah hear when he beheld God sitting on the throne, high and exalted? "Also I heard the voice of the Lord saying, 'Whom shall I send and who will go for us . . .?'" What did Ezekiel hear when he completed his journey through the heavenly hierarchy to the mysterious sanctuary of God? "And He said unto me: son of man, I send thee to the children of Israel, to a rebellious nation that hath rebelled against Me . . ." The prophet is a messenger carrying the great divine imperative addressed to the covenantal community. "So I turned and came down from the mount. . . . And the two tablets of the covenant were on my two hands." This terse description by Moses of his noble role as the carrier of the two tablets of stone on which the divine norm was engraved has universal significance applicable to all prophets.[33] "I will raise them up a prophet . . . and will put my words into his mouth. . . . Whosoever will not hear unto my words which he shall speak in my name, I will require of him."

The above-said, which is true of the universal faith community in general, has particular validity for the Halakhic community. The prime purpose of revelation in the opinion of the Halakhah is related to the giving of the Law. The God-man confrontation serves a didactic goal. God involves Himself in the covenantal community through the medium of teaching and instructing. The Halakhah has looked upon God since time immemorial as the teacher par excellence.[34] This educational task was in turn entrusted to the prophet whose greatest ambition is to teach the covenantal community. In short, God's word is *ipso facto* God's law and norm.

Let me add that for Judaism the reverse would be not only unthinkable, but immoral, as well. If we were to eliminate the norm from the prophetic God-man encounter, confining the latter to its apocalyptic aspects, then the whole prophetic drama would be acted out by a limited number of privileged individuals to the exclusion of the rest of the people.[35] Such a prospect, turning the prophetic colloquy into an esoteric-egotistic affair, would be immoral from the viewpoint of Halakhic Judaism which is exoterically-minded and democratic to its every core. The democratization of the God-man confrontation was made possible by the centrality of the normative element in prophecy. Only the norm engraved upon the two tablets of stone, visible and accessible to all, draws the people into this confrontation "Ye are placed this day, all of you, before the Eternal, your God; your heads of your tribes, your elders and your bailiffs, with all the men of Israel . . . from the hewer of thy wood unto the drawer of thy water." And how can the woodchopper and the water drawer participate in this adventurous meeting of God and man, if not through helping in a humble way to realize the covenantal norm?

Prayer likewise consists not only of an awareness of the presence of God, but of an act of committing oneself to God and accepting His ethico-moral authority.[36]

Who is qualified to engage God in the prayer colloquy? Clearly, the person who is ready to cleanse himself of imperfection and evil. Any kind of injustice, corruption, cruelty, etc., desecrates the very essence of the prayer adventure, since it encases man in an ugly little world into which God is unwilling to enter. If man craves to meet God in prayer, then he must purge himself of all that separates him from God. The Halakhah has never looked upon prayer as a separate magical gesture in which man may engage without integrating it into the total pattern of his life. God hearkens to prayer if its rises from a heart contrite over a muddled and faulty life and from a resolute mind ready to redeem this life. In short, only the committed person is qualified to pray and to meet God. Prayer is always the harbinger of moral reformation.[37]

This is the reason why prayer per se does not occupy as prominent a place in the Halakhic community as it does in other faith communities and why prayer is not the great religious activity claiming, if not exclusiveness, at least centrality. Prayer must always be related to a prayerful life which is consecrated to the realization of the divine imperative and, as such, it is not a separate entity, but the sublime prologue to Halakhic action.

B.

If the prophecy and prayer colloquy is based upon friendship and solidarity nurtured by the "we"-consciousness at the experiential as well as the normative level, as a consciousness of both mutual concern and sympathy and of common commitment and determination to bring the divine imperative to full realization, the reverse is alo true—that *homo absconditus* cannot reveal himself to his fellow man without joining him in covenantal prayer and moral action. In the natural community which knows no prayer, majestic Adam can offer only his accomplishments, not himself. There is certainly even within the framework of the natural community, as the existentialists are wont to say, a dialogue between the "I" and the "thou." However, this dialogue may only gratify the necessity for communication which urges Adam the first to relate himself to others, since communication for him means information about the surface activity of practical man. Such a dialogue certainly cannot quench the burning thirst for communication in depth of Adam the second, who always will remain a *homo absconditus* if the majestic *logoi* of Adam the first should serve as the only medium of expression. What really can this dialogue reveal of the numinous in-depth-personality? Nothing! Yes, words are spoken, but these words reflect not the unique and intimate, but the universal and public in man. As a *homo absconditus,* Adam the second is not capable of telling his personal experiential story in majestic formal terms. His emotional life is inseparable from his unique *modus existentiae* and therefore, if communicated to the "thou" only as a piece of surface information, unintelligible. They belong exclusively to Adam the second, they are his and only his, and they would make no sense if disclosed to others. Can a sick person afflicted with a fatal disease tell the "thou," who happens to be a very dear and close friend, the tale of a horror-stricken mind confronted with the dreadful prospect of death? Can a parent explain to a rebellious child, who rejects everything the parent stands for, his deep-seated love for him? Distress and bliss, joys and frustrations are incommunicable within the framework of the natural dialogue consisting of common words. By the time *homo absconditus* manages to deliver the message, the personal and intimate content of the latter is already recast in the lingual matrix, which standardizes the unique and universalizes the individual.

If God had not joined the community of Adam and Eve, they would have never been able and would have never cared to make the paradoxical leap over the gap, indeed abyss, separating two individuals whose personal experiential messages are written in a private code undecipherable by anyone else. Without the covenantal experience of the prophetic or prayerful colloquy, Adam *absconditus* would have persisted in his he-role and Eve *abscondita* in her she-role, unknown to and distant from each other. Only when God emerged from the transcendent darkness of He-anonymity into the illumined spaces of community-knowability and charged man with an ethico-moral mission, did Adam *absconditus* and Eve *abscondita*, while revealing themselves to God in prayer and in unqualified commitment—also reveal themselves to each other in sympathy and love on the one hand and common action on the other. Thus, the final objective of human quest for redemption was attained; the individual felt relieved from loneliness and isolation. The community of the committed became, *ipso facto,* a community of friends—not of neighbors or acquaintances. Friendship—not as a social surface-relation but as an existential in-depth-relation between two individuals—is realizable only within the framework of the covenantal community where in-depth-personalities relate themselves to each other ontologically and total commitment to God and fellow-man is the order of the day. In the majestic community, in which surface-personalities meet and commitment never exceeds the bounds of the utilitarian, we may find collegiality, neighborliness, civility, or courtesy—but not friendship, which is the exclusive experience awarded by God to covenantal man who is thus redeemed from his agonizing solitude.

C.

Let us go further. The existential insecurity of Adam the second stems, to a great extent, also from his tragic role as a temporal being. He simply cannot pinpoint his position within the rushing stream of time. He knows of an endless past which rolled on without him. He is aware also of an endless future which will rush on with no less force long after he will cease to exist. The link between the "before" in which he was not involved and the "after" from which he will be excluded is the present moment which vanishes before it is experienced. In fact, the whole accidental character of his being is tied up with this frightening time-consciousness. He began to exist at a certain point— the significance of which he cannot grasp—and his existence will end at another equally arbitrary point. Adam the second experiences the transience and evanescence of a "now"-existence which is not warranted either by the "before" or the "after."

Majestic man is not confronted with this time dilemma. The time with which he works and which he knows is quantified, spatialized, and measured, belonging to a cosmic coordinate system. Past and future are not two experiential realities. They just represent two horizontal directions. "Before" and "after" are understandable only within the framework of the causal sequence of events.[38] Majestic man lives in micro-units of clock time, moving with ease from "now" to "now," completely unaware of a "before" or an "after." Only Adam the second, to whom time is an all-enveloping personal experience, has to cope with the tragic and paradoxical implied in it.

In the covenantal community man of faith finds deliverance from his isolation in the "now," for the latter contains both the "before" and the "after." Every covenantal time experience is both retrospective, reconstructing and reliving the bygone, as well as prospective, anticipating the "about to be." In retrospect, covenantal man re-experiences the rendezvous with God in which the covenant, as a promise, hope, and vision, originated. In prospect, he beholds the full eschatological realization of this covenant, its promise, hope, and vision. Let us not forget that the covenantal community includes the "He" who addresses Himself to man not only from the "now" dimension but also from the supposedly already vanished past, from the ashes of a dead "before"-facticity as well as from the as yet unborn future, for all boundaries establishing "before," "now," and "after" disappear when God the Eternal speaks. Within the covenantal community not only contemporary individuals but generations are engaged in a colloquy and each single experience of time is three-dimensional, manifesting itself in memory, actuality and anticipatory tension. This experiential triad, translated into moral categories, results in an awesome awareness of responsibility to a great past which handed down the divine imperative to the present generation in trust and confidence and to a mute future expecting this generation to discharge its covenantal duty conscientiously and honorably. The best illustration of such a paradoxical time awareness which involves the individual in the historic performances of the past and makes him also participate in the dramatic action of an unknown future can be found in the Judaic *masorah* community. The latter represents not only a formal succession within the framework of calendaric time but the union of the three grammatical tenses in an all-embracing time experience. The *masorah* community cuts across the centuries, indeed millenia, of calendaric time and unites those who already played their part, delivered their message, acquired fame, and withdrew from the covenantal stage quietly and humbly with those who have not yet been given the opportunity to appear on the covenantal stage and who wait for their turn in the anonymity of the "about to be."

Thus, the individual member of the covenantal faith community feels rooted in the past and related to the future. The "before" and the "after" are interwoven in his time experience. He is not a hitchhiker suddenly invited to get into a swiftly travelling vehicle which emerged from nowhere and from which he will be dropped into the abyss of timelessness while the vehicle will rush on into parts unknown, continually taking on new passengers and dropping the old ones. Covenantal man begins to find redemption from insecurity and to feel at home in the continuum of time and responsibility which is experienced by him in its endless totality[39]— מֵעוֹלָם וְעַד עוֹלָם, from everlasting even to everlasting. He is no longer an evanescent being. He is rooted in everlasting time, in eternity itself. And so covenantal man confronts not only a transient contemporary "thou" but countless "thou"-generations which advance toward him from all sides and engage him in the great colloquy in which God Himself participates with love and joy.

This act of revelation does not avail itself of universal speech, objective logical symbols, or metaphors. The message communicated from Adam to Eve certainly consists of words. However, words do not always have to be identified with sound.[40] It is rather a soundless revelation accomplished in muteness and in the stillness of the covenantal community when God responds to the prayerful outcry of lonely man and agrees to meet him as brother and friend, while man, in turn, assumes the great burden which is the price he pays for his encounter with God.

IX

A.

Having arrived at this point, we begin to see the lines of the destiny of the man of faith converge. The man of faith, as we explained previously, is lonely because of his being himself exclusively and not having a comrade, a "duplicate I." The man of faith, we further brought out, finds redemption in the covenantal faith community by dovetailing his accidental existence with the necessary infinite existence of the Great True Real Self. There, we pointed out, *homo absconditus* turns into *homo revelatus* vis-à-vis God and man as well.

However, the element of the tragic is not fully eliminated from the destiny of the man of faith even after joining the covenantal community. We said at the very beginning of this lecture that the loneliness of the man of faith is an integral part of his destiny from which he can never be completely liberated. The dialectical awareness, the steady oscillating between the majestic natural community and the covenantal faith community renders the act of complete redemption unrealizable. The man of faith, in his continuous movement between the pole of natural majesty and that of covenantal humility, is prevented from totally immersing in the immediate covenantal awareness of the redeeming presence, knowability, and involvement of God in the community of man. From time to time the man of faith is thrown into the majestic community where the colloquy as well as the covenantal consciousness are swept away. He suddenly finds himself revolving around the cosmic center, now and then catching a glimpse of the Creator who hides behind the boundless drama of creation. To be sure, this alternation of cosmic and covenantal involvement is not one of "light and shade," enhanced activity and fatigue as the mystics are accustomed to call their alternating experiences, but represents two kinds of creative and spontaneous activity both willed and sanctioned by God.[41] Let us not forget that the majestic community is willed by God as much as the covenantal faith community. He wants man to engage in the pursuit of majesty-dignity as well as redemptiveness. He summoned man to retreat from peripheral, hard-won positions of vantage and power to the center of the faith experience. He also commanded man to advance from the covenantal center to the cosmic periphery and recapture the positions he gave up a while ago. He authorized man to quest for "sovereignty"; he also told man to surrender and be totally committed. He enabled man to interpret the world in functional, empirical "how"-categories to explain, for instance, the sequence of phenomena in terms of transeunt, mechanical causality and a quantified-spatialized, basically (if not for the law of entropy) reversible time, suitable to the human majestic role. Simultaneously, He also requires of man to forget his functional and bold approach, to stand in humility and dread before the *mysterium magnum* surrounding him, to interpret the world in categories of purposive activity instead of those of mechanical facticity, and to substitute time, wedded to eternity, stretching from *archē* to *eschatos,* for uniform, measured clock time.

On the one hand, the Bible commands man, "And thou shalt love the Lord thy God with all thy heart and with all thy soul and with all they might," a performance of which only covenantal man is capable since he alone possesses the talent for complete concentration upon and immersion in the focus without being distracted by peripheral interests, anxieties, and problems. On the other hand, the same Bible which just enjoined man to withdraw from the periphery to the center commands him to return to the majestic community which, preoccupied with peripheral interests, anxieties, and problems, builds, plants, harvests, regulates rivers, heals the sick, participates in state affairs, is imaginative in dreaming, bold in planning, daring in undertaking and is out to "conquer" the world. With what simplicity, not paying the least attention to the staggering dialectic implied in such an approach, the Bible speaks of an existence this-worldly centered — "When thou buildest a new home; when thou cuttest down thine harvest; when thou comest into thy neighbor's vineyard"— yet theo-oriented and unqualified committed to an eternal purpose! If one would inquire of me about the teleology of the Halakhah, I would tell him that it manifests itself exactly in the paradoxical yet magnificent dialectic which underlines the halakhic gesture. When man gives himself to the covenantal community the Halakhah reminds him that he is also wanted and needed in another community, the cosmic-majestic, and when it comes across man while he is involved in the creative enterprise of the majestic community, it does not let him forget that he is a covenantal being who will never find self-fulfillment outside of the covenant and that God awaits his return to the covenantal community.[42] I would also add, in reply to such a question, that many a time I have the distinct impression as if the Halakhah considered the steady oscillating of the man of faith between majesty and covenant not as a dialectical but rather as a complementary movement. The majestic gesture of the man of faith, I am inclined to think, is looked upon by the Halakhah not as contradictory to the covenantal encounter but rather as the reflex action which is caused by this encounter when man feels the gentle touch of God's hand upon his shoulder and the covenantal invitation to join God is extended to him. I am prompted to draw this remarkable inference from the fact that the Halakhah has a monastic approach to reality and has unreservedly rejected any kind of dualism.

The Halakhah believes that there is only one world—not divisible into secular and hallowed sectors—which can either plunge into ugliness and hatefulness, or be roused to meaningful, redeeming activity, gathering up all latent powers into a state of holiness. Accordingly, the task of covenantal man is to be engaged not in dialectical surging forward and retreating, but in uniting the two communities into one community where man is both the creative, free agent and the obedient servant of God. Notwithstanding the huge disparity between these two communities which expresses itself in the typological oppositions and conflicts described previously, the Halakhah sees in the ethicomoral norm a uniting force. The norm which originates in the covenantal community addresses itself almost exclusively to the majestic community where its realization takes place. To use a metaphor, I would say that the norm in the opinion of the Halakhah is the tentacle by which the covenant, like the ivy, attaches itself to and spreads over the world of majesty.[43]

B.

The Biblical dialectic stems from the fact that Adam the first, majestic man of dominion and success, and Adam the second, the lonely man of faith, obedience and defeat, are not two different people locked in an external confrontation as an "I" opposite a "thou," but one person who is involved in self-confrontation. "I," Adam the first, confront the "I," Adam the second. In every one of us abide two personae—the creative majestic Adam the first, and the submissive, humble Adam the second. As we portrayed them typologically, their views are not commensurate; their methods are different, their modes of thinking, distinct, the categories in which they interpret themselves and their environment, incongruous. Yet, no matter how far-reaching the cleavage, each of us must willy-nilly identify himself with the whole of an all-inclusive human personality, charged with responsibility as both a majestic and covenantal being. God created two Adams and sanctioned both. Rejection of either aspect of humanity would be tantamount to an act of disapproval of the divine scheme of creation which was approved by God as being very good. As a matter of fact, men of faith have accepted Adam the first a long time ago. Notwithstanding the fact that Adam the second is the bearer of a unique commitment, he remains also a man of majesty who is inspired by the joyous spirit of creativity and constructive adventure.[44]

C.

Since the dialectical role has been assigned to man by God, it is God who wants the man of faith to oscillate between the faith community and the community of majesty, between being confronted by God in the cosmos and the intimate, immediate apprehension of God through the covenant, and who therefore willed that complete human redemption be unattainable.

Had God placed Adam in the majestic community only, then Adam would, as it was stated before, never be aware of existential loneliness. The sole problem would then be that of aloneness—one that majestic Adam could resolve. Had God, vice versa, thrust Adam into the covenantal community exclusively, then he would be beset by the passional experience of existential loneliness and also provided with the means of finding redemption from this experience through his covenantal relation to God and to his fellow man. However, God, in His inscrutable wisdom, has decreed differently. Man discovers his loneliness in the covenantal community and before he is given a chance to climb up to the high level of a complete covenantal, revealed existence, dedicated in faith to God and in sympathy to man, man of faith is pushed into a new community where he is told to lead an expanded surface existence rather than a covenantal, concentrated in-depth-existence. Because of this onward movement from center to center, man does not feel at home in any community. He is commanded to move on before he manages to strike roots in either of these communities and so the ontological loneliness of man of faith persists. Verily, "A straying Aramean was my father."[45]

X

A.

While the ontological loneliness of the man of faith is due to a God-made and willed situation and is, as part of his destiny, a wholesome and integrating experience, the special kind of loneliness of contemporary man of faith referred to at the beginning of this paper is of a social nature due to a man-made historical situation and is, hence, an unwholesome and frustrating experience.

Let me diagnose the situation in a few terse sentences. Contemporary Adam the first, extremely successful in his cosmic-majestic enterprise, refuses to pay earnest heed to the duality in man and tries to deny the undeniable, that another Adam exists beside or, rather, in him. By rejecting Adam the second, contemporary man, *eo ipso*, dismisses the covenantal faith community as something superfluous and obsolete. To clear up any misunderstanding on the part of my audience, I wish to note that I am not concerned in this paper with the vulgar and illiterate atheism professed and propagated in the most ugly fashion by a natural-political community which denies the unique transcendental worth of the human personality. I am referring rather to Western man who is affiliated with organized religion and is a generous supporter of its institutions. He stands today in danger of losing his dialectical awareness and of abandoning completely the metaphysical polarity implanted in man as a member of both the majestic and covenantal community. Somehow, man of majesty considers the dialectical awareness too great a burden, interfering with his pursuit of happiness and success, and is, therefore, ready to cast it off.

B.

Let us try to describe in brief the philosophy by which successful Western man is guided in his appraisal of this transcendental commitment.

I said a while ago that I am speaking of Western man who belongs and extends help to some religious establishment. Nevertheless, no matter how conscientious and devoted a fellow member he is, he belongs not to a covenantal faith community but to a religious community. The two communities are as far apart as the two Adams. While the covenantal faith community is governed, as I emphasized, by a desire for a redeemed existence, the religious community is dedicated to the attainment of dignity and success and is, along with the whole gamut of communities such as the political, the scientific, the artistic, a creation of Adam the first, all conforming to the some sociological structural patterns. The religious community is, therefore, also a work community consisting of two grammatical *personae* not including the Third Person. The prime purpose is the successful furtherance of the interests, not the deepening and enhancing of the commitments, of man who values religion in terms of its usefulness to him and considers the religious act a medium through which he may increase his happiness. This assumption on the part of majestic man about the role of religion is not completely wrong, if only, as I shall explain, he would recognize also the non-pragmatic aspects of religion. Faith is indeed relevant to man not only metaphysically but also practically. It gives his life, even at the secular mundane level, a new existential dimension. Certain aspects of the doctrinal and normative covenantal *kerygma* of faith are of utmost importance to majestic man and are, in a paradoxical way, translatable into the latter's vernacular. It is very certain and self-evident that Adam the first cannot succeed completely in his efforts to attain majesty-dignity without having the man of faith contribute his share. The cultural edifice whose great architect Adam the first is would be built on shifting sands if he sought to conceal from himself and from others the fact that he alone cannot implement the mandate of majesty-dignity entrusted to him by God and that he must petition Adam the second for help. To be sure, man can build space ships capable of reaching other planets without addressing himself to the mystery of faith and without being awakened to an enhanced inspired life which reflects the covenantal truth. He certainly can triumph to a limited degree over the elemental forces of nature without crossing the frontiers of here-and-now sense-facticity. The Tower of Babel can be built high and mighty without beholding and acknowledging the great verity that Heaven is yet higher. However, the idea of majesty which Adam the first is striving to realize embraces much more than the mere building of machines no matter how complex and efficacious. Successful man wants to be a sovereign not only in the physical but also in the spiritual world. He is questing not only for material success, but for ideologico-axiological achievements as well. He is concerned with a philosophy of nature and man, of matter and mind, of things and ideas.

Adam the first is not only a creative mind, incessantly looking and pressing forward, but also a meditating mind, casting a backward glance and appraising his handiwork, thereby imitating his Maker who, at the end of each stage of creation, inspected and appraised it. Adam frequently interrupts his forward march, turns around, views and evaluates his creative accomplishments, making an effort to place them in some philosophico-axiological perspective.

Furthermore, as I commented previously, Adam distinguishes himself not only in the realm of scientific theory but in that of the ethico-moral and aesthetic gestures as well. He legislates norms which he invests with validity and great worth. He fashions beautiful forms and considers the encounter with them ennobling and cleansing, exhilarating and enriching. All this Adam the first seeks yet he is not always lucky to find it. For the retrospective appraisal and appreciation of the cognitive drama as well as the successful performance at the ethico-moral and aesthetic levels are unattainable as long as man moves continuously within the closed, vicious cycle of the insensate natural occurrence and never reaches for the "beyond." To take an illustration, the parallelism between *cogitatio* and *existentia,* between the pure logical constructs of the mind and the real dynamics of nature, on which modern science rests and which troubles the meditating mind of Adam the first, will remain a mystery as long as he will not admit that these two parallel lines of thought and facticity converge in infinity within the True, Real Self. In like manner, the worth and validity of the ethical norm, if it is born of the finite creative-social gesture of Adam the first, cannot be upheld. Only the sanctioning by a higher moral will is capable of lending to the norm fixity, permanence, and worth. Likewise, majestic man is quite often in need of the redemptive and therapeutic powers inherent in the act of believing which, in times of crisis, may give aid and comfort to the distressed mind. In similar fashion, the aesthetic experience to which contemporary man abandons himself with almost mystical ecstasy remain incomplete as long as beauty does not rise to sublimity and remains unredeemed. However, redemption is a covenantal category and the sublime is inseparable from the exalted. And how can majestic man be confronted with redeemed beauty in which the exalted is reflected if he is enclosed in a dreary mechanical world from which he has neither strength nor courage to free himself. In short, the message of faith, if translated into cultural categories, fits into the axiologico-philosophical frame of reference of the creative cultural consciousness and is pertinent even to secular man.

For good reason did the thinkers throughout the centuries speak of philosophical religion which emanates from the deep recesses of the human personality. They knew very well that the human, creative, cultural gesture is incomplete if it does not relate itself to a higher *modus existentiae*. No wonder that the Kantian and neo-Kantian philosophies, scientific and empirical as they are, let the creative cultural consciousness pick out from the flow of transient impressions, abstract constructs and ideas those bits that point toward the infinite and eternal. From these elements they tried to construct a pure rational religious awareness in order to endow the whole creative gesture with intrinsic worth and with ultimate and unconditioned validity.[46] Since majestic man is in need of a transcendental experience in order to strengthen his cultural edifice, it is the duty of the man of faith to provide him with some component parts of this experience. God would not have implanted the necessity in majestic man for such spiritual perceptions and ideas if He had not at the same time endowed the man of faith with the skill of converting some of his apocalyptic experiences—which are meta-logical and non-hedonic—into a system of values and verities comprehensible to majestic man, the experimenter, esthete, and, above all, the creative mind.

C.

At this point, however, the crisis in the relations between man of faith and majestic man begins to develop. If the job of translating faith mysteries into cultural aspects could be fully accomplished, then contemporary man of faith could free himself, if not from the onto-logical awareness which is perennial, then, at least, from the peculiar feeling of psychological loneliness and anguish which is due to his historical confrontation with the man of culture. The man of faith would, if this illusion came true, be at peace with the man of culture so that the latter would fully understand the significance of human dialectics and a perfect harmonious relationship would prevail between both Adams.[47]

However, this harmony can never be attained since the man of faith is not the compromising type and his covenantal commitment eludes cognitive analysis by the *logos* and hence does not lend itself com-pletely to the act of cultural translation. There are simply no cognitive categories in which the total commitment of the man of faith could be spelled out. This commitment is rooted not in one dimension, such as the rational one, but in the whole personality of the man of faith. The whole of the human being, the rational as well as the non-rational aspects, are committed to God. Hence, the magnitude of the commit-ment is beyond the comprehension of the *logos* and the *ethos*. The act of faith is aboriginal, exploding with elemental force as an all-consum-ing and all-pervading eudaemonic-passional experience in which our most secret urges, aspirations, fears and passions, at times even unsus-pected by us, manifest themselves. The commitment of the man of faith is thrown into the mold of the in-depth-personality and immedi-ately accepted before the mind is given a chance to investigate the reasonableness of this unqualified commitment. The intellect does not chart the course of the man of faith; its role is an *a posteriori* one. It attempts, *ex post facto*, to retrace the footsteps of the man of faith, and even in this modest attempt the intellect is not completely suc-cessful. Of course, as long as the path of the man of faith cuts across the territory of the reasonable, the intellect may follow him and iden-tify his footsteps. The very instant, however, the man of faith transcends the frontiers of the reasonable and enters into the realm of the unreasonable, the intellect is left behind and must terminate its search for understanding. The man of faith animated by his great experience is able to reach the point at which not only his logic of the mind but even his logic of the heart and of the will, everything—even his own "I" awareness—has to give in to an "absurd" commitment. The man of faith is "insanely" committed to and "madly" in love with God.[48]

"Stay ye me with dainties, refresh me with apples, for I am love-sick."[49]

D.

The untranslatability of the complete faith experience is due not to the weakness, but to the greatness of the latter.

If an all-embracing translation of the great mystery of revelation and its *kerygma* were possible, then the uniqueness of the faith-experience and its commitments would be lost. Only peripheral elements of the act of faith can be projected on a cognitive pragmatic background. Prayer, for instance, might appeal to majestic man as the most uplifting, integrating and purifying act, arousing the finest and noblest emotions, yet these characteristics, however essential to Adam the first, are of marginal interest to Adam the second, who experiences prayer as the awesome confrontation of God and man, as the great paradox of man conversing with God as an equal fellow member of the covenantal society, and at the same time being aware that he fully belongs to God and that God demands complete surrender and self-sacrifice.

There is, of course, an amazing parallelism between the cultural experience and the apocalyptic one. Yet, I repeat, no matter how impressive the similarities are, the act of faith is unique and cannot be fully translated into cultural categories.

In a word, the message of translated religion is not the only one which the man of faith must address to majestic man of culture. Besides this message, man of faith must bring to the attention of man of culture the *kerygma* of original faith in all its singularity and pristine purity in spite of the incompatability of this message with the fundamental credo of a utilitarian society. How staggering this incompatibility is! This unique message speaks of defeat instead of success, of accepting a higher will instead of commanding, of giving instead of conquering, of retreating instead of advancing, of acting "irrationally" instead of being always reasonable. Here the tragic event occurs. Contemporary majestic man rejects his dialectical assignment and, with it, the man of faith.

The situation has deteriorated considerably in this century which has witnessed the greatest triumphs of majestic man in his drive for conquest. Majestic Adam has developed a demonic quality: laying claim to unlimited power—alas, to infinity itself. His pride is almost boundless, his imagination arrogant, and he aspires to complete and absolute control of everything. Indeed, like the men of old, he is engaged in constructing a tower whose apex should pierce Heaven. He is intoxicated with his own adventures and victories and is bidding for unrestricted dominion. In order to avoid misinterpretation, let me say that I am not referring here to man's daring experiments in space. From a religious point of view, as I said before, they are quite legitimate and in compliance with the divine testament given to Adam the first that he should rule nature. When I say that modern man is projecting a demonic image, I am thinking of man's attempt to dominate himself, or, to be more precise, of Adam the first's desire to identify himself with the total human personality, declaring his creative talents as ultimate, ignoring completely Adam the second and his preoccupation with the unique and strange transcendental experience which resists subservience to the cultural interests of majestic man. Notwithstanding the fact that Western man is in a nostalgic mood, he is determined not to accept the dialectical burden of humanity. He certainly feels spiritually uprooted, emotionally disillusioned, and, like the old king of Ecclesiastes, is aware of his own tragedy. Yet this pensive mood does not arouse him to heroic action. He, of course, comes to a place of worship. He attends lectures on religion and appreciates the ceremonial, yet he is searching not for a faith in all its singularity and otherness, but for religious culture. He seeks not the greatness found in sacrificial action but the convenience one discovers in a comfortable, serene state of mind. He is desirous of an aesthetic experience rather than a covenantal one, of a social ethos rather than a divine imperative. In a word, he wants to find in faith that which he cannot find in his laboratory, or in the privacy of his luxurious home. His efforts are noble, yet he is not ready for a genuine faith experience which requires the giving of one's self unreservedly to God, who demands unconditional commitment, sacrificial action, and retreat. Western man diabolically insists on being successful. Alas, he wants to be successful even in his adventure with God. If he gives of himself to God, he expects reciprocity. He also reaches a covenant with God but this covenant is a mercantile one. In a primitive manner, he wants to trade "favors" and exchange goods. The gesture of faith for him is a give-and-take affair and reflects the philosophy of Job which led to catastrophe—a philosophy which sees faith as a *quid pro quo* arrangement and expects compensation for each sacrifice one offers. Therefore, modern man puts up demands that faith adapt itself to the mood and temper of modern times. He does not discriminate between translated religion formulated in cultural categories—which are certainly fluid since they have been evolved by the human creative consciousness—and the pure faith commitment which is as unchangeable as eternity itself. Certainly, when the man of faith interprets his transcendental awareness in cultural categories, he takes advantage of modern interpretive methods and is selective in picking his categories. The cultural message of faith changes, indeed, constantly, with the flow of time, the shifting of the spiritual climate, the fluctuations of axiological moods, and the rise of social needs. However, the act of faith itself is unchangeable, for it transcends the bounds of time and space. Faith is born of the intrusion of eternity upon temporality. Its essence is characterized by fixity and enduring identity. Faith is experienced not as a product of some emergent evolutionary process, or as something which has been brought into existence by man's creative cultural gesture, but as something which was given to man when the latter was overpowered by God. Its prime goal is redemption from the inadequacies of finitude and, mainly, from the flux of temporality. Unfortunately, modern Adam the first refuses to accept this unique message which would cause him to become involved in the dialectical movement and he clings instead zealously to his role as majestic man exclusively, demanding the surrender of faith to his transient interests. In his demonic quest for dominion, he forgets that relativization of faith, doctrine and norm, will inflict untold harm upon him and his majestic interests. He fails to realize that the reality of the power of faith which may set modern man free from anxiety and neurotic complexes and help him plan the strategy of invincible majestic living can only be experienced if the faith gesture is left alone, outside of the fleeting stream of socio-cultural metamorphoses and tolerated as something stable and immutable. If the faith gesture should be cut loose from its own absolute moorings and allowed to float upon the mighty waters of historical change, then it will forfeit its redemptive and therapeutic qualities.

It is here that the dialogue between the man of faith and the man of culture comes to an end. Modern Adam the second, as soon as he finishes translating religion into the cultural vernacular, and begins to talk the "foreign" language of faith, finds himself lonely, forsaken, misunderstood, at times even ridiculed by Adam the first, by himself. When the hour of estrangement strikes, the ordeal of man of faith begins and he starts his withdrawal from society, from the Adam the first—be he an outsider, be he himself. He returns, like Moses of old, to his solitary hiding and to the abode of loneliness. Yes, the loneliness of contemporary man of faith is of a special kind. He experiences not only ontological loneliness but also social isolaltion, whenever he dares to deliver the genuine faith-*kerygma*. This is both the destiny and the human historical situation of the man who keeps a rendezvous with eternity, and who, in spite of everything, continues tenaciously to bring the message of faith to majestic man.

XI

So he departed thence, and found Elisha, the son of Shafat, who was ploughing with twelve yoke of oxen before him and he with the twelfth; and Elijah passed by him and cast his mantle upon him. And he left the oxen and ran after Elijah, and said, "let me I pray thee kiss my father and my mother and then I will follow thee," and he said unto him, "go back again for what have I done to thee." And he returned back from him and took a yoke of oxen and slew them, and boiled their flesh with the instruments of the oxen and gave unto the people and they did eat. Then he arose and went after Elijah and ministered unto him (I Kings, 19:19-21).

Elisha was a typical representative of the majestic community. He was the son of a prosperous farmer, a man of property, whose interests were centered around this-worldly, material goods such as crops, livestock, and market prices. His objective was economic success, his aspiration—material wealth. The Bible portrays him as efficient, capable, and practical, remindful of a modern business executive. When Elijah met him, we are told, he was supervising the work done by the slaves. He was with the twelfth yoke in order not to lose sight of the slave-laborers. What did this man of majesty have in common with Elijah, the solitary covenantal prophet, the champion of God, the adversary of kings, who walked as a stranger through the bustling cities of Shomron, past royal pomp and grandeur, negating the worth of all goods to which his contemporaries were committed, reproaching the sinners, preaching the law of God and portending His wrath? What bond could exist between a complacent farmer who enjoyed his homestead and the man in the hairy dress who came from nowhere and who finally disappeared under a veil of mystery? Yet unexpectedly, the call came through to this unimaginative, self-centered farmer. Suddenly the mantle of Elijah was cast upon him. While he was engaged in the most ordinary, everyday activity, in toiling the soil, he encountered God and felt the transforming touch of God's hand. The strangest metamorphosis occurred. Within seconds, the old Elisha disappeared and a new Elisha emerged. Majestic man was replaced by covenantal man. He was initiated into a new spiritual universe in which clumsy social class distinctions had little meaning, wealth played no role and a serene illuminated universal "we"-consciousness supplanted the small, limited, and selfish "I"-consciousness. Old concerns changed, past commitments vanished, cherished hopes faded, and a new vision of a redemptive-covenantal reality incommensurate with the old vision of an enjoyable-majestic reality beckoned to him. No more did the "farmer" care for the oxen, the means of making the soil yield its abundance, which were so precious to him a while ago. No more was he concerned with anything which was so dear to him before. He slew the oxen and fed the meat to the slaves who, half-starved, toiled the soil for him and whom he, until that meeting with Elijah, had treated with contempt. Moreover, covenantal man renounced his family relationships. He bade farewell to father and mother and departed from their home for good. Like his master, he became homeless. Like his ancestor Jacob he became a "straying Aramean" who took defeat and humiliation with charity and gratitude. However, Elisha's withdrawal from majesty was not final. He followed the dialectical course of all our prophets. Later, when he achieved the pinnacle of faith and arrived at the outer boundaries of human commitment, he came back to society as a participant in state affairs, as an adviser of kings and a teacher of the majestic community. God ordered him to return to the people, to offer them a share in the covenantal drama and to involve them in the great and solemn colloquy. He was God's messenger carrying, like Moses, two tablets of stone containing the covenantal *kerygma*. Many a time he felt disenchanted and frustrated because his words were scornfully rejected. However, Elisha never despaired or resigned. Despair and resignation were unknown to the man of the covenant who found triumph in defeat, hope in failure, and who could not conceal God's Word that was, to paraphrase Jeremiah, deeply implanted in his bones and burning in his heart like an all-consuming fire. Elisha was indeed lonely but in his loneliness he met the Lonely One and discovered the singular covenantal confrontation of solitary man and God who abides in the recesses of transcendental solitude.

Is modern man of faith entitled to a more privileged position and a less exacting and sacrificial role?

NOTES

¹ The basic ideas of this paper were formulated in my lectures to the students of the program "Marriage and Family — National Institute of Mental Health Project, Yeshiva University, New York."

² This is, of course, a rhetorical phrase, since all emotional and volitional activity was included in the Cartesian *cogitatio* as *modi cogitandi*. In fact, faith in the existence of an intelligent *causa prima* was for Descartes an integral part of his logical postulate system, by which he proves the existence of the external world.

³ *Vide Berakhot*, 61a; *Ketuvot*, 8a; Nachmanides Genesis 2:7; *Cuzari*, IV.

⁴ *Vide Yesode Ha-Torah*, IV, 8-9; *Moreh Nevukhim*, I, 1.

⁵ As a matter of fact, the term *kavod* has a dual meaning in Hebrew: (1) majesty, as in the phrase כבוד מלכותו, (2) dignity as in the Halakhic phrase כבוד הבריות. That dignity is a criterion by which the worth of an individual is measured can be demonstrated by the Halakhah that בזויים, self-abased persons, are disqualified from giving testimony. In particular, the phrase: האוכל בשוק דומה לכלב "whoever eats in the street or at any public place acts like a dog" used by both the Talmud (*Kiddushin* 40b) and Maimonides (*Mishneh Torah, Edut* XI, 5) is characteristic of the attitude of the Halakhah toward a man who has lost his sense of dignity.

Likewise, I wish to point out the law that the principle of human dignity overrides certain Halakhic injunctions; *vide Berakhot* 19b. See also Nachmanides, Leviticus 19:1 (the description of the quality of sanctity).

⁶ It might be pointed out that in the Septuagint the word is here given an intellectualistic coloring, being rendered as *doxe*. The Vulgate has the more literal *gloria*. In other contexts in which the term כבוד signifies the human personality rather than honor, it is variously translated. See e.g. Psalms 16:9, לכן שמח לבי ויגל כבודי, where כבודי is rendered *he glossa mou* and *lingua mea*, respectively; and Psalms 30:13, למען יזמרך כבוד, where כבוד is translated as *he doxa mou* and *gloria mea*.

⁷ *Vide* Nachmanides, Genesis 1:24: כדכתיב וכבוד והדר תעטרהו והוא מגמת פניו בחכמה ובדעת וכשרון המעשה "As it is written, 'and (Thou) hast crowned him with honor and glory,' which refers to his (i.e. man's) intelligent, wise, and technically resourceful striving."

120

[8] It is obvious that this paper refers to Adam the first as a type representing the collective human technological genius, and not to individual members of the human race.

[9] It is worthwhile to note that Maimonides interpreted the story of the fall of man in terms of the betrayal of the intellectual and the ethical for the sake of the esthetic. The Hebrew phrase ועץ הדעת טוב ורע was translated by Maimonides as "And the tree of experiencing the pleasant and unpleasant."

[10] *Vide* Nachmanides, Genesis 2:7: ואמר כי הוא נפח באפיו נשמת חיים להודיע כי לא באה מן היסודות...גם לא כהשתלשלות מן השכלים הנבדלים אבל היא רוח השם הגדול "And it is stated that He (i.e. God) breathed into his (i.e. man's) nostrils the breath of life because it (i.e. the soul) was not formed of the elements .. nor did it emanate from the Separate Intelligences but it was God's own breath."

[11] The social contract theory is not to be interpreted in chronological terms. It never claimed that individuals ever existed outside of society. The precedence of the individual over society is to be interpreted in conceptual terms: a Robinson Crusoe existence is thinkable and morally justified. The most important practical inference to be drawn from this theory is the moral right of the individual or individuals to secede from an existing society and form a new one. This kind of thinking, as we know, played an enormous role in the American as well as in the French Revolution. Therefore, there is no contradiction between the Biblical story of Adam the first and the social contract theory.

[12] I am using the social contract theory as an illustration of the functional character of the community formed by Adam the first. However, I could also demonstrate this idea by introducing organic theories of society which emphasize the primacy of society over the individual. Even, and perhaps primarily, the corporate state is of a functional character.

[13] The same naivete in evaluating the role of man is to be found in the Marxist philosophical anthropology.

[14] The Halakhic requirement of dignified behavior, כבוד הבריות, applies in some cases to public actions while in other cases even to one's private actions. The problem of כבוד הבריות with which the Talmud, *Berakhot* 19b, deals is related to public offensive actions, such as disrobing, while in *Shabbat* 81a, and *Eruvin* 41b, the Talmud is concerned with undignified action even in private. Apparently, the determining factor in these cases is the nature of the act itself. A certain act, such as disrobing, is unworthy only if exposed to public view, whereas another, such as the lack of bodily hygiene, is always disgraceful. This Halakhic approach does not contradict our viewpoint that dignity is a social behavioral category and that the hermit cannot realize it in full.

[15] The Halakhah has linked human distress with the human capability of renewal and self-transformation. Man's confrontation with evil and suffering must result, according to the Halakhah, in the great act of *teshuvah* (repentance). "In thy distress when all these things are come upon thee . . . thou wilt return to the Lord thy God and hearken unto His voice." (Deut. 4:30).

[16] The Biblical account of the original sin is the story of man of faith who realizes suddenly that faith can be utilized for the acquisition of majesty and glory and who, instead of fostering a covenantal community, prefers to organize a political utilitarian community exploiting the sincerity and unqualified commitment of the crowd for non-covenantal, worldly purposes. The history of organized religion is replete with instances of desecration of the covenant.

[17] The whole concept of עמו אנכי בצרה "I shall be with him in trouble" can only be understood within the perspective of the covenantal community which involves God in the destiny of His fellow members. *Vide Sanhedrin*, 46a; *Yerushalmi, Sukkah*, 4, 3.

[18] The giving of the law on Mt. Sinai was a result of free negotiation between Moses and the people who consented to submit themselves to the Divine Will. The Halakhah treats the Sinai and Moab covenants in categories and terms governing any civil agreement. The Talmudic opinion (*Shabbat* 88a) כפה עליהם הר כגיגית, that there was coercive action on the part of God during the Sinai revelation, does not refute our thesis. The action to which the Talmud refers was taken after the covenant had been voluntarily transacted on the preceding day (the fifth of Sivan) according to the chronology elaborated by Rashi (based on the *Mekhilta*). Even Nachmanides, who disagreed with Rashi and accepted the opposite view of the *Mekhilta*, placing the transaction on the seventh of Sivan after the ultimatum had been issued to the community, must admit that the latter obligated itself to abide by God's will prior to the revelation, as it is distinctly stated in Exodus 19:8. Nachmanides differs with Rashi only with reference to the solemn formalization of the covenant as told in Exodus 24:3-8.

In light of this, the Talmudic saying (*loc. cit.*) מכאן מודעא רבה לאורייתא is puzzling inasmuch as coercion was applied only to the implementation and not to the assumption of the covenantal obligation. To be sure, this phrase is not to be construed in its literal meaning, since no scholar has ever questioned the validity of the Sinai covenant even prior to its reaffirmation in the days of Mordecai and the other men of the Great Assembly to which the Talmud (*loc. cit.*) refers. The idea underlying this phrase is to be understood as referring to a moral mitigating circumstance rather than a juridic-Halakhic defense. See *Chiddushei Ha-ramban ad locum.*

It appears that God required two commitments on the part of the community: a general one to abide by the will of God while the community was still unaware of the nature of the commitment and a specific one concerning each individual law. The second commitment was assumed under constraint. *Vide Mekhilta* quoted by Rashi, Exodus, 20:1; Rashi and Nachmanides, Exodus, 24:1. See *Tosafot, Shabbat* 88a, sub   and *Kiddushin,* 61b.

The reason for introducing an element of coercion into the great Sinai covenant in contradistinction, prima facie, to the Biblical story, lies in the idea that covenantal man feels overpowered and defeated by God even when he appears to be a free agent of his own will.

19 The strange Aggadic stories about a theoretical Halakhic "controversy" between the Almighty and Heavenly Academy (מתיבתא דרקיעא) and about R. Joshua b. Chanania's rejecting a Divine decision which favored a minority opinion over that of the majority are characteristic of the intimate Halakhic-covenantal relationship prevailing between man and God. *Vide Bava Mezi'a* 59b and 86a.

20 *Vide* Leviticus 26:12, *Sifra* and Rashi.

21 *Bereshit Rabbah*, 59; Rashi, Genesis 24:7. I intentionally used the term "cosmic" instead of "cosmological." While one may speak of the cosmic confrontation of man and God as an experiential reality, it is hard to speak of a cosmological experience. When God is apprehended *in* reality it is an experience; when God is comprehended *through* reality it is just an intellectual performance. Therefore, one must not equate the cosmic experience, no matter how inadequate it is, with Judah Halevi's "God of Aristotle." As we mentioned in the text, the cosmic experience is part of the patriarchial tradition. The Halakhah has granted full recognition to this experience, which is reflected in many of our benedictions.

The trouble with all rational demonstrations of the existence of God, with which the history of philosophy abounds, consists in their being exactly what they were meant to be by those who formulated them: abstract logical demonstrations divorced from the living primal experiences in which these demonstrations are rooted. For instance, the cosmic experience was transformed into a cosmological proof, the ontic experience into an ontological proof, et cetera. Instead of stating that the most elementary existential awareness as a subjective "I exist" and an objective "the world around me exists" awareness is unattainable as long as the ultimate reality of God is not part of this awareness, the theologians engaged in formal postulating and deducing in an experiential vacuum. Because of this, they exposed themselves to Hume's and Kant's biting criticism that logical categories are applicable only within the limits of the human scientific experience.

Does the loving bride in the embrace of her beloved ask for proof that he is alive and real? Must the prayerful soul clinging in passionate love and ecstasy to her Beloved demonstrate that He exists? So asked Soren Kierkegaard sarcastically when told that Anselm of Canterbury, the father of the very abstract and complex ontological proof, spent many days in prayer and supplication that he be presented with rational evidence of the existence of God.

Maimonides' term לידע (*Yesode ha-Torah,* 1:1) transcends the bounds of the abstract *logos* and passes over into the realm of the boundless intimate and impassioned experience where postulate and deduction, discursive knowledge and intuitive thinking, conception and perception, subject and object, are one. Only in paragraph five, after the aboriginal experience of God had been established by him as a firm reality (in paragraph one), does he introduce the Aristotelian cosmological proof of the unmoved mover.

[22] This distinction between E-lohim and the Tetragrammaton was developed in detail by Judah Halevi.

[23] "וירד ה' על הר סיני": And the Lord came down upon Mt. Sinai."

[24] "ויקרא ה' למשה אל ראש ההר ויעל משה": And the Lord called Moses up to the top of the mount, and Moses went up."

[25] This verse telling us about the prophetic encounter of Moses with God describes the ideal state of prophecy as it was attained by Moses. The Bible itself in another passage contrasts the Mosaic confrontation with God with that of other prophets who failed to reach the same heights and hence experienced the numinous apocalyptic dread and awe. *Vide* Exodus 33:17; Numbers 12:6-8; *Yesode ha-Torah,* VII:6.

[26] The fact that we commence the recital of the "Eighteen Benedictions" by addressing ourselves to the God of Abraham, Isaac, and Jacob, is indicative of the covenantal relationship which, in the opinion of our sages, lies at the very root of prayer.

The fact that prayer is founded upon the covenantal relationship is responsible for the omission of *Malkhut* (God's *cosmic* kingship or sovereignty) from the "Eighteen Benedictions." In order to avoid misunderstanding, I wish to add that only the phrase *melekh ha-olam* was eliminated from the basic benediction formula while the term *melekh* does appear in several places; *vide Tosafot, Berakhot* 40b sub אמר.

[27] The popular Biblical term *tefillah* and the esoteric Halakhic term *avodah shebelev* refer to an inner activity, to a state of mind. *Kavvanah,*

related to prayer, is, unlike the *kavvanah* concerning other *mitzvah* performances, not an extraneous addendum but the very core of prayer. The whole Halakhic controversy about *kavvanah* vis-à-vis other *mitzvot* has no relevance to prayer. There is not a single opinion that the latter can be divorced from *kavvanah*. Moreover, the substance of the *kavvanah* as far as prayer is concerned differs fundamentally from that which some require during the performance of other *mitzvot*. While the former denotes a state of mind, an all-embracing awareness of standing before the Almighty, the latter manifests itself only in the normative intention on the part of the *mitzvah*-doer to act in accordance with the will of God. *Kavvanah* in both cases, of course, expresses direction or aiming. However, in prayer one must direct his whole self toward God whereas in the case of other *mitzvot* the directing is confined to a single act. *Vide Berakhot* 28b, 30a-b, 32b, 33a; *Sanhedrin* 22a; Maimonides, *Hilkhot Tefillah*, IV, 16; V, 4. The fact that *kavvanah* is indispensable only for the first benediction of the Silent Prayer does not contradict our premise. The Halakhah simply took into consideration human weakness and inability to immerse in the covenantal awareness for a long time and, in sympathy with the worshipper who is incapable of sustaining a continuous contemplate mood, related the initial *kavvanah* to the entire *Tefillah*. *Vide Berakhot* 34b and *Chidushe R. Hayyim Halevi, Tefillah*, IV, 1.

[28] *Vide Berakhot* 26b, 33a; *Megillah* 18a. It is not my intention here to investigate the controversy between Maimonides and Nachmanides as to whether the precept of prayer is of Pentateuchic or Rabbinic origin. All agree that statutory standardized prayer was introduced by the men of the Great Assembly.

[29] The strict Halakhic censure of the prophet who fails to deliver the divine message underscores the public character of prophecy. *Vide Sanhedrin* 89a. It should be noted that Maimonides speaks also of prophecy confined to the individual; see *Yesode ha-Torah*, VII, 7 and *Moreh Nevukhim*, II, 37. However, such individual illumination cannot be termed covenantal prophecy.

[30] *Vide Berakhot* 12b; *Bava Kamma* 92a; *Shabbat* 12b.

[31] This is the reason underlying the institution of תפלת הצבור, the recital of prayers with the congregation, which occupies such a prominent position in the Halakhah.

[32] Job 1:5. See *Bava Kamma* 92a.

[33] That every prophecy is normative does not contradict the statement of our sages אלה המצות שאין נביא רשאי לחדש דבר מעתה that no prophet is allowed to change even the smallest detail of the law. (*Torat Kohanim* 120; *Temurah* 16a; *Shabbat* 104a; *Megillah* 3a; *Yoma* 80a). The

adjective "normative" has a dual connotation: first, legislative action; second, exhortatory action. While Moses' prophecy established a new covenant entailing a new moral code, the prophecies of his followers addressed themselves to the commitment taken on by the covenantal community to realize the covenant in full. *Vide Chagigah* 10b; *Bava Kamma* 2b; *Niddah* 23a; *Yesode ha-Torah*, IX, 1-4.

[34] There are many allusions in our Aggadah and liturgy to the teaching of Torah as part of God's "routine."

[35] According to our tradition, the entire community, even at the revelation at Sinai, heard only the first two, not all ten, commandments. *Vide Makkot* 24a.

[36] The Halakhic requirement of סמיכת גאולה לתפלה, that the recitation of *Shema* with its benedictions be joined to the recital of *Tefillah*, the "Eighteen Benedictions," is indicative of this idea. One has no right to appear before the Almighty without accepting previously all the covenantal commitments implied in the three sections of *Shema*. *Vide Berakhot* 9b and 29b. Both explanations in Rashi, *Berakhot* 4b, actually express the same idea. *Vide Berakhot* 14b and 15a, where it is stated that the reading of *Shema* and the prayers is an integrated act of accepting the Kingdom of Heaven in the most complete manner. It should nevertheless be pointed out, that the awareness required by the Halakhah during the recital of the first verse of *Shema* and that which accompanies the act of praying (the recital of the first benediction) are related to two different ideas. During the recital of *Shema* man ideally feels totally committed to God and his awareness is related to a normative end, assigning to man ontological legitimacy and worth as an ethical being whom God charged with a great mission and who is conscious of his freedom either to succeed or to fail in that mission. On the other hand, the awareness which comes with prayer is rooted in man's experiencing his "creatureliness" (to use a term coined by Rudolf Otto) and the absurdity embedded in his own existence. In contrast with the *Shema* awareness, the *Tefillah* awareness negates the legitimacy and worth of human existence. Man, as a slave of God, is completely dependent upon Him. Man enjoys no freedom. "Behold, as the eyes of servants unto the hand of their master, as the eyes of a maiden unto the hand of her mistress, so our eyes look unto the Lord our God until He be gracious unto us."

When the Talmud (*Berakhot*, 14b and 15a) speaks of קבלת מלכות שמים שלמה, the unitary acceptance of the Kingdom of God, it refers to the two awarenesses which, notwithstanding their antithetic character, merge into one comprehensive awareness of man who is at the same time the free messenger of God and His captive as well.

However, whether the awareness of prayer *per se* is, from a Halakhic viewpoint, to be construed as קבלת מלכות שמים, as an act of acceptance of the Kingdom of Heaven, is discussed in another passage; see *Berakhot* 21a and Rashi there.

[37] The interrelatedness of prayer, moral life, and repentance was emphasized already in Solomon's prayer, I Kings 8:34-51; II Chronicles 7:36-40. See also *Exodus Rabbah*, XXII:3: "Just as they purified their hearts and uttered Song . . . so must a man purify his heart and then pray. . . . This is what Job said. 'Although there is no violence in my hands and my prayer is pure' (15:7). Rabbi Joshua the priest the son of R. Nechemiah said: 'Is there, then, an impure prayer? No; but he who prays unto God with hands soiled from violence is not anwered . . .' Rabbi Chama b. Chanina said 'whence do we know that the prayer of one who has committed violence is impure? Because it says, "And when you spread forth your hands . . . I will not hear because your hands are full of blood." Whence do we know that the prayer of him who removes himself from violence is pure? Because it says . . .'"; Saadya, *Emunot Ve-Deot*, V:6. Also Maimonides, discussing the precept of prayer during times of crisis, says in unequivocal terms that prayer is only the medium through which man may normally rehabilitate himself, although with regard to daily prayer he omitted mention of this relationship. *Vide Ta'anit* I, 1-3; *Tefillah*, IV. It is worthy of note that there is a double discrepancy between the Talmud (*Berakhot* 32b) and the above-quoted Midrash. The Talmud confined the verse of Isaiah 1:15 to the sin of murder which disqualifies the priest from imparting the priestly blessing. The Midrash extended it to all kinds of violence (embezzlement or other corrupt practices) and barred not only priests from blessing the community but all people from prayer.

In my opinion, the discrepancy is only a single one, pertaining to the meaning of the phrase "your hands are full of blood," whether it be limited to murder or extended to all acts of dishonesty and corruption. However, there is no contradiction between the two interpretations as far as extending the applicability of the verse to *Tefillah;* nor could there be, since, in the latter part of the verse, Isaiah himself explicitly mentions *Tefillah* — גם כי תרבו תפלה אינני שומע, "Yea, when ye make prayers, I will not hear." However, the Talmud and the Midrash treated the verse of Isaiah at two defferent levels. While the Talmud speaks in formal Halakhic categories, the Midrash places it in a metaphysico-moral perspective. The Talmud treats the problem of disqualification; whoever committed murder forfeits the priestly prerogative and right to bless the people. In Halakhic terms, I would say that murder results in a פסול גברא, in the emergence of a personal inadequacy. Indeed, in Maimonides' view, it is not the moral culpability for the sin of murder but the bare fact of being the agent and instrument of murder which causes this disqualification. Hence, the disqualification persists even after the murderer has repented; *vid Tefillah*, XV, 3, and *Tosafot, Menachot* 109a. Such a disqualification is inapplicable to prayer. The privilege and right of prayer cannot be denied to anyone, not even to the most wicked. The Psalmist already stated that everyone is admitted to the realm of prayer: שומע תפלה עדיך כל בשר יבאו, "O Thou Who hearkenest to prayer; unto Thee doth all flesh come." (Even drunkenness does not disqualify the person, but nullifies the act of prayer because of the lack of *kavvanah*; see Maimonides, *Tefillah* 4, 17.) In fact, the Midrash never stated that a sinner has been stripped of the privilege of prayer. It only emphasized that prayer requires a clean heart and that the prayer of a sinful person is imperfect. The Midrash employs the terms תפלתו זכה and תפלתו עכורה, which denote pure and impure prayer. Maimonides quoted the Midrash not in the section on *Tefillah*, which deals with the Halakhic requirements of prayer, but in that of *Teshuvah*, which deals with the metaphysical as well as the Halakhic aspects of repentance, where he says distinctly that the immoral person's prayer is not fully acceptable to God — צועק ואינו נענה שנאמר גם כי תרבו תפלה אינני שומע, "He petitions and is not answered, as it is written, 'Yea, even ye make many prayers I will not hear.'" As a matter of fact, Maimonides extended the requirement for moral excellence to all *mitzvah* performances — עושה מצוות וטורפין אותן בפניו, "He performs *mitzvot* and they are thrown back in his face." It is of course self-evident that the imperfection inherent in the deed does not completely nullify the objective worth of the deed. Maimonides' statement at the end of *Tefillah* 'that you do not prevent the wicked person from doing a good deed' is not only Halakhically but also psychologically relevant. We let the sinful priest, as long as he has not committed murder or apostasy, impart his blessings to the congregation. Likewise, we encourage the sinner to pray even though he is not ready yet for repentance and moral regeneration, because any *mitzvah* performance, be it prayer, be it another moral act, has a cleansing effect upon the doer and may influence his life and bring about a complete change in his personality. *Vide* also, Introduction to *Beth Halevi* on Genesis and Exodus.

In Saadya's enumeration of the reasons which prevent prayer from being accepted we find a mixture of Halakhic and metaphysical considerations. The first reason for the rejection of prayer is of a purely metaphysical nature: one's prayer is not answered if it is offered "after the decree was issued against" the person. As an illustration, Saadya introduces the case of Moses beseeching the Lord to allow him to cross the Jordan and not being answered. On the other hand, the second reason—the lack of sincere intention—is Halakhic. It is, therefore, hard to determine whether the five reasons which are related to moral impurity are classified as Halakhic or metaphysical deterrents to prayer.

38 It is quite characteristic that Aristotle, the man of science, derived time from motion, while Plotinus, the philosopher-mystic, even though, as a pagan, unaware of the idea of the covenant, reversed the order. Of course, for Aristotle, even though he knows of three kinds of motion, the highest is related mainly to morphological change, the transition from possibility to actuality.

39 In reality there are no pure typological structures and hence the covenantal and majestic communities overlap. Therefore, it is not surprising that we come across the three-dimensional time experience, which we have presented as typically covenantal, in the majestic community as well. The historical community rests, in fact, upon this peculiar time experience. What is historical belonging if not the acceptance of the past as a reality to which one is indebted and the anticipation of a future to which one is responsible? Historical action is never confined to the "now." It crosses the frontiers of perceptible time and relates itself to a unitary experience of time embracing the "before" and the "after." If the stream of time be broken down into micro-units, there would be no place for history. Living in history means experiencing the total drama of history stretching across calendaric time. This peculiarity of the historical experience was known to E. Burke and E. Renan. However, this time awareness was borrowed by majestic history from covenantal history.

40 אמר in Hebrew means both to say and to think.

41 Man's dialectical see-sawing between the cosmic and the covenantal experience of God is reflected in the benediction formula in which we address God in both the second and third person. See Nachmanides, Exodus 15:26, and Shlomo S. Aderet, Responsa, V, 52. To be sure, the mingling of grammatical persons is quite normal in Hebrew syntax. In this case, however, our medieval scholars attributed particular significance to the change.

42 Not only Halakhic teleology but also positive Halakhic thinking is dialectical. The latter follows the rules of an N-valued logic rather than those of a two-valued logic. Positive Halakhah has never honored the sacrosanct classical principle of the excluded middle or that of contradiction. Quite often it has predicated of x that it is neither a nor b or that it is both a and b at the same time.

It is worth mentioning that it took scientific thinking a very long time to make the discovery that the complex cosmic occurrence does not lend itself to a two-valued logical interpretation.

The role of the multi-valued logic in Halakhah will be discussed by me, God willing, in a forthcoming paper.

[43] *Vide Berakhot* 35b; *Shabbat* 33b. Maimonides distinguishes between two kinds of dialectic: (1) the constant oscillating between the majestic and the covenantal community; (2) the simultaneous involvement in both communities, which is the highest form of dialectical existence and which, according to Maimonides, only Moses and the Patriarchs achieved. See *Yesode ha-Torah,* VII, 6: "Hence it may be inferred that all prophets when the prophetic power left them returned to their tents, that they attended to the satisfaction of their physical needs. Moses, our teacher, never went back to his former tent. He, accordingly, permanently separated himself from his wife, and abstained from similar gratifications. His mind was closely attached to the Rock of the universe . . ." This, however, is not to be interpreted as if Moses had abandoned the majestic community. After all, Moses dedicated his life to the fashioning of a majestic-covenantal community bent on conquest and political-economic normalcy on the one hand, and the realization of the covenantal *kerygma* on the other.

Maimonides is more explicit in the *Moreh,* III, 51 where he portrays the routine of the Patriarchs who, like Moses, achieved the highest form of dialectical existence and resided in both communities concurrently. "The Patriarchs likewise attained this degree of perfection. . . . When we therefore find them also engaged in ruling others, in increasing their property and endeavoring to obtain possession of wealth and honor, we see in this fact a proof that when they were occupied in these things their bodily limbs were at work while their heart and mind never moved away from the name of God . . ." In other words, the Patriarchs were builders of society, sociable and gregarious. They made friends with whom they participated in the majestic endeavor. However, axiologically, they valued only one involvement: their covenantal friendship with God. The perfect dialectic expresses itself in a plurality of creative gestures and, at the same time, in axiological monodeism.

The concluding paragraphs of *Hilkhot Shemitah Ve-Yovel* should be interpreted in a similar vein. Cf. *Nefesh ha-Chayyim,* II, 11.

The unqualified acceptance of the world of majesty by the Halakhah expresses itself in its natural and inevitable involvement in every sector of human majestic endeavor. There is not a single theoretical or technological discovery, from new psychological insights into the human personality to man's attempts to reach out among the planets, with which the Halakhah is not concerned. New Halakhic problems arise with every new

scientific discovery. As a matter of fact, at present, in order to render precise Halakhic decisions in many fields of human endeavor, one must possess, besides excellent Halakhic training, a good working knowledge in
those secular fields in which the problem occurs.

This acceptance, easily proven in regard to the total majestic gesture, is
most pronounced in the Halakhah's relationship to scientific medicine and
the art of healing. The latter has always been considered by the Halakhah
as a great and noble occupation. Unlike other faith communities, the
Halakhic community has never been troubled by the problem of human
interference, on the part of the physician and patient, with God's will. On
the contrary, argues the Halakhah, God wants man to fight evil bravely
and to mobilize all his intellectual and technological ingenuity in order to
defeat it. The conquest of disease is the sacred duty of the man of majesty
and he must not shirk it. From the Biblical phrase, "Only he shall pay for
the loss of his time and shall cause him to be thoroughly healed" (Exodus
21:18), through the Talmudic period in which scientific medicine was
considered authoritative in situations in which the saving of a human life,
פיקוח נפש, requires the suspension of the religious law, to the Judaeo-
Spanish tradition of combining Halakhic scholarship with medical skill,
the Halakhah remained steadfast in its loyalty to scientific medicine. It
has never ceased to emphasize the duty of the sick person to consult a
competent physician. The statement quoted in both the *Tur* and Karo's
Shulchan Aruch, ואם מונע עצמו הרי זה שופך דמים, which can be traced
indirectly to a Talmudic passage, is a cornerstone of Halakhic thinking.
Vide Yoma 82a, 82b, 83a. *Kiddushin* 82a, Rashi sub טוב, *Bava Kamma*
85a, *Tosafot* sub שניתנה, *Tur Yoreh Deah* 336, *Bayit-Chadash* sub תניא.
See also *Pesachim* 56a, Rashi and Maimonides' Commentary.

Nachmanides' observation in Leviticus 26:11 refers to an ideal state of
the covenantal community enjoying unlimited divine grace and has no
application, therefore, to the imperfect state of affairs of the ordinary world.

The passage in II Chronicles 16:12: "yet in his disease he sought not
to the Lord, but to physicians" referred to priest-doctors who employed
pagan rites and magic in order to "heal" the sick.

The doctrine of faith in God's charity, בטחון, is not to be equated with
the folly of the mystical doctrine of quietism which in its extreme form
exempts man from his duty of attending to his own needs and lets him
wait in "holy" idleness and indifference for God's intervention. This kind
of repose is wholly contrary to the repose which the Halakhah recom-
mends: the one which follows human effort and remedial action. Man
must first use his own skill and try to help himself as much as possible.
Then, and only then, man may find repose and quietude in God and be
confident that his effort and action will be crowned with success. The
initiative, says the Halakhah, belongs to man; the successful realization, to
God.

Certainly, "except the Lord build the house, they labor in vain that build it," but if those who labor stop building, there will be no house. The Lord wants man to undertake the task which He, in His infinite grace, completes.

[44] I hardly believe that any responsible man of faith, who is verily interested in the destiny of his community and wants to see it thriving and vibrant, would recommend now the philosophy of *contemptus saeculi*. I believe that even within the classical medieval tradition the monastic-ascetic approach was just an undercurrent and that the philosophers and moralists moving with the mainstream of religious thought preached the doctrine of human optimism and activism.

[45] Jewish eschatology beholds the great vision of a united majestic-covenantal community in which all oppositions will be reconciled and absolute harmony will prevail. When Zechariah proclaimed "the Lord shall be King over all the earth; on that day the Lord shall be one and His name one," he referred not to the unity of God which is absolute and perfect even now, but to the future unity of creation which is currently torn asunder by inner contradictions. On that distant day the dialectical process will come to a close and man of faith as well as majestic man will achieve full redemption in a united world.

[46] According to Kant, the need for a rational metaphysics is constantly reasserted by the pure reason even though the latter cannot gratify this need. However, what the pure reason cannot achieve is accomplished by the practical reason or the moral will which is an integral part of the free, creative cultural consciousness. The three postulates of the moral will—freedom, God, and immortality—have very little in common with the covenantal doctrine pertaining to these postulates. They are pure, rational ideas which make the ethical performance meaningful. In other words, the need for religion is part of the all-inclusive human need for cultural self-expression.

[47] The idea that certain aspects of faith are translatable into pragmatic terms is not new. The Bible has already pointed out that the observance of the Divine Law and obedience to God leads man to worldly happiness, to a respectable, pleasant and meaningful life. Religious pragmatism has a place within the perspective of the man of faith.

[48] Our description of the "individuality" and autonomy of the faith gesture should not be associated with Tertullian's apothegm *credo quia absurdum est*. Neither should it be equated with Kierkegaard's "leap into the absurd."

Tertullian tried not only to free the act of faith from its subservience to the intellect but actually to posit them as two inexorable foes. Thus, he considered any attempt to translate aspects of faith into cultural majestic categories as illegitimate and negating the very essence of faith. This kind of antirationalism led to complete rejection of majestic man willed and created by God. Small wonder that Tertullian's contemporary Tatian condemned the majestic gesture as the work of the devil.

Tertullian was wrong also in another respect. The terms "reasonable" and "unreasonable" belong exclusively to the realm of the logos and are, therefore, inapplicable to the act of faith. Neither does one believe because it is reasonable to do so, since the reasonable is affirmed on logical grounds and is in no need of being affirmed by an act of faith, nor is it sensible to say that one has faith because the latter contradicts human reason. The faith gesture is not motivated by intellectual insights or convictions.

The term "absurd" in the Kierkegaardian philosophy is both a logical and psychological category. It refers not only to logically false statements but also to unreasonable psychological motivation. The act of "repetition" precipitated by failure and resignation is absurd and belongs, therefore, into the realm of faith. In a word, for Kierkegaard, faith supersedes the majestic posture of man. The world of faith rises upon the ruins and debris of the world of majesty.

This thesis is unacceptable, as we indicated in the text, to the Halakhah which insists upon the dialectical movement between these two worlds. They do, indeed, exist concurrently according to the Halakhah. Moreover, Kierkegaard lacked the understanding of the centrality of the act of objectification of the inner movement of faith in a normative and doctrinal postulate system which forms the very foundation of the Halakhah. The Halakhic world of faith is "terribly" articulate, "unpardonably" dynamic, and "foolishly" consistent, insisting that feeling become thought, and experience be acted out and transformed into an objective event. Kierkegaard's existentialist world, like Schleiermacher's pietistic world, is a place of silence and passivity, far removed from the complex array of historical events, not hungering for action or movement.

[49] Vide Maimonides, Hilkhot Teshuvah, X, 3, "What is the love of God that is befitting? It is to love the Eternal with a great and exceeding love, so strong that one's soul shall be knit up with the love of God, and one should be continually enraptured by it, like a lovesick individual whose mind is at no time free from its passion . . ."

MAIMONIDES' UNBENDING OPPOSITION TO ASTROLOGY

MAIMONIDES' LETTER TO THE JEWS OF MARSEILLES IN 1194

by LEON D. STITSKIN

INTRODUCTION

The final years of the life of Maimonides were rewarded by the correspondence which he carried on with Provencal Jewry who looked upon him as the divinely appointed instrument for the purification and revival of Judaism. The taste for scientific investigation was nowhere more pronounced than among the Jews of Southern France where Bar Hiyya, Ibn Ezra, the Tibbon and Kimchi families had scattered seeds of Jewish culture. The letters of Maimonides to communities of Marseilles, Lunel, Montpellier—in contrast to his pietistic letters to some Eastern communities such as Baghdad whose severe opposition to his *magnum opus, The Guide to the Perplexed,* prompted him to write the epistle "On the Resurrection of the Dead"—reflect more authentically his uncompromising rationalism, and almost natural hostility to benighted obscurantism, blind dogmatism and vulgar superstition. Without any apologetics, he engaged the weight of his mighty intellect and wide erudition against any insights and practices not grounded in the dictates of the intellect. One should never abandon his own intellectual independence, he argued, even at the risk of disagreeing with a contrary opinion of a learned sage which could be demonstrated by scientific proofs to be false. For the latter may have

Reprinted from *Tradition*, Volume 13, 1972.

expressed his contrary individual view allegorically or for a specific occasion, which in either case was not meant to be taken literally. Alas, the concluding words of Maimonides, in the following letter to the Jews of Marseilles wherein he states: "One should therefore look ahead of him and not behind him. I have thus revealed to you with these words my whole heart," reflect the authentic thought mode of our philosophers.

At a time when belief in astrology was irresistible and widespread, Maimonides sought to eradicate it root, branch and all. He charged against it with all the force of reason at his command. In his *Commentary on the Mishnah,* he devotes the eighth chapter of *Shemonah Perakim* to the subject of Providence and Free Will in order "that thou mayest not believe the absurd ideals of the astrologers." In his *Sefer ha-Mada* he branded this universally-held belief of astra determinism as akin to idolatry ("Idolatry II"). In the *Guide* he condemns astrology[1] as "intimately connected with witchcraft . . . leading to the worship of stars" (Part III:37). In the "Epistle to the Jews of Marseilles," he denounces astrology as an irrational illusion of fools and a baseless deception that was subversive to the faith and teachings of Judaism.

Maimonides reached this conclusion after having studied every extant astrological treatise—as a matter of fact, astrology was the first branch of secular learning he pursued—and convinced himself that none of them had any scientific[2] foundation or could be demonstrated by proofs. While astronomy[3] was a science demonstrating the movement of the spheres, the eclipse of the sun and the moon, the subject of astrology was not science at all but an irrational illusion adhered to by simpletons who believe anything or by people who wish to deceive others.[4] No authentic scientist ever devoted time to this enterprise or wrote on the subject of astrology.

By the same token, on the ethical level, he argued that if the fate of man depended on the constellations and everything was preordained then the formulation of the precepts of the Torah was superfluous and observance of the Commandments unnecessary. Moreover, by what justice could God punish the wicked or reward the righteous? Obviously if religion were to have any meaning in helping to shape one's moral being, one's destiny could not be entrusted to the whims of the comets.

The halakhic element in his denunciation of astrology was the most poignant. A belief in this pseudo-science was tantamount to a belief in idolatry. In the face of several utterances by the rabbis who implied a belief in the potency of the stars at a person's nativity, Maimonides declared that "it is forbidden to be an 'observer of times' . . . and whoever is influenced in his actions by astrology and arranges his work or journey to take place at the time fixed by the astrologers, is punished with stripes, as it is said, 'ye shall not observe times'" (Lev. 19:26), (Hil. Avodat Kochavim, 11:9). He concludes this chapter with an appeal to his fellow Jews, "endowed as they are with superior intelligence, should not be drawn to such follies nor regard them as advantageous. For is it not written, 'For there is no enchantment with Jacob, neither is there any divination with Israel?' (Num. 23:23). Were we not warned, 'For these nations, that thou art to dispossess, hearken unto soothsayers and unto diviners; but as for thee, the Lord thy God hath not suffered thee so to do?'" (Deut. 18:14).

Apparently Maimonides adhered to the declaration of Rab (B. Tal. Shab. 156a), shared by R. Johanan, the Palestinian amora, that "there are no planets for Israel—ein mazal l'yisrael." Rab's contemporary, Samuel of Babylon, also stated, "Torah cannot go together with the art that studies the heavens as we read, 'It (The Torah) is not in heaven.'" (Deut. 30:12; Deut. R. 8:6). On the other hand, statements like that of Raba to the effect that "duration of life, progeny and subsistence are dependent upon the constellations" (B. Tal. M.K. 29a), to which he specifically alludes in his letter as well as others must be taken as allegorical.

Moses Maimonides was thus one of the very few outstanding Jewish scholars[6] who resisted the belief in the hypnotic witchery of astrology which was so generally widespread during the Middle Ages. In communication with authentic intellectuals he dared to articulate an unbending rationalism in Halakhah and philosophy which he applied with equal vigor to this pseudo-science.

What follows is my translation of Maimonides' letter to the Jews of Marseilles written in the year 1194.

A Letter of Maimonides to the Jews of Marseilles

Several intimate wise friends of mine in Marseilles, well-versed in Jewish law and legal matters put to me several pertinent questions. May the Almighty protect them and increase their wisdom, magnify and glorify their erudition and vouchsafe His abundant blessings unto all their endeavors. The prayers and heartwarming solicitude of Moses Maimonides for their well-being bears testimony to the purity of their souls and their sincere pursuit of wisdom and understanding in order to rise to a high level of authentic knowledge "and discover acceptable words written in an agreeable script, even words of truth."[7] May the Lord's grace abide with them and help them to disclose the mysterious and straighten out every convexity! Amen.

Your question, although it has many ramifications and subdivisions, may be reduced to one basic issue, namely the problem of the astrologers[8]— the star gazers. Apparently, my work *Mishneh Torah* on the laws of the Torah has not reached you yet; otherwise you would have known my opinion on the questions you posed as I have expounded upon them in the chapter on Idolatry and pagan statutes. I am certain, however, that my work will reach you before this reply as it has spread already to the Island of Sicily as well as to the East, West and Yemen. Nevertheless, I wish to respond to you directly and elucidate the issues you raised.

Know my masters that no man should believe anything unless attested by one of three principles. First, rational proof as in mathematical sciences; secondly, the perception by one of the five senses; for instance, the judgment or color by one's eyes, taste by the tongue; touch to distinguish between hot and cold; hearing between clear and confused sounds and smell between that which is distasteful or pleasant; and thirdly, tradition derived from the prophets and the righteous. It is accordingly incumbent upon every wise person to investigate his doctrinal beliefs and classify them according to one of the three basic sources which they are drawn from, namely tradition, sensation or rational insights. One, however, who grounds his belief in any other but one of those guiding principles Scriptures refers to him as "the simple believeth every word" (Prov. 14:15).

Moreover, you should know that some misguided people wrote thousands of books on the subject and many ignorant people wasted their precious years pouring over them, mistaking vanity for knowledge and ascribing consummate wisdom to their authors. There seems to be a fatal disease and abysmal mischief among most people, with the exception of a select divinely inspired remnant, to the effect that whatever is found in books is instantly acceptable as truth, especially if the books are ancient. Moreover, if the books are used extensively, the impulsive reader immediately construes them to be works of wisdom for the reason that the pen never belies its author,[9] nor does one engage in the art of writing in vain. However, this kind of involvement in false astrological works whose notions are essentially pagan led to the loss of our kingdom, the destruction of our Holy Temple and extended the duration of the exile to the present day. Our ancestors sinned and disappeared, for as we explained they strayed after false notions, ascribing to them purposeful ends, while neglecting the arts of martial defense and government. No wonder the prophets referred to them as ignorant and foolish. They were surely correct in this, for they pursued "vain things which cannot profit nor deliver because they are vain" (Samuel 12:21).

Know my masters that I investigated these matters extensively. My early training included knowledge derived from the movement of the stars, such as predictions regarding impending international and national events or the well-being of an individual person. I also read extensively about all pagan practices. There was not a single book translated into Arabic on the subject that I have not studied and .investigated in depth. As a matter of fact from these works I derived a rationale for all the *mitzvot,* in contradistinction to those who maintained that *mitzvot* are just dogmatic decrees and have no deeper meaning. I have written a large work on the subject in Arabic expounding upon every *mitzvah* but this is not my intention here. Let me therefore return to the subject you inquired about.

You should realize that all the assumptions of the astrologers with regard to the forecasting of impeding events, or the determination of one's destiny by the constellation at the time of one's birth are irrational superstitions devoid of any scientific basis. I have clear flawless proofs invalidating their essential theories. For one thing we should take note of the fact that none of the Greek thinkers who were surely authentic scientists ever engaged in such notions or wrote any treatises on the subject. They never made the mistake of calling astrology a science as did the Chaldeans, Egyptians and Canaanites who even regarded it as a fundamental doctrine of their religion. The Greek philosophers, who were involved in almost all scholarly disciplines, utterly repudiated these notions, root, branch and all. Also the Persian scholars regarded the astra-deterministic concepts of the Chaldeans, Egyptians and Canaanites as deceptions. It should be pointed out in this connection that the reason we do not believe the proponents of this theory is not simply because their concepts lack sufficient evidence for validation but rather because we possess such clear and flawless proofs to the contrary that their notions are utterly repudiated. It is therefore incumbent upon us not to accept their beliefs which only a simpleton who believes anything or the person who wishes to deceive others adheres to.

You should know, however, my masters, that there is an authentic wisdom concerning the celestial bodies which consists in knowing the form of the spheres, their number, measurement, the course of their movement, the different velocities of their motions, their deflection toward north or south; their revolution eastward and another sphere westward, the orbit of every star and the courses they traverse. These notions and others are contained in large volumes composed by Greek, Persian and Indian scholars and constitute a praiseworthy discipline. By virtue of knowledge derived from this study we can determine the eclipse of the planets, the time of its occurrence in different places, the reason why the moon appears first as a bow gradually increasing until it reaches its full size and then reverts to its original size, as well as the time of its appearance and disappearance. This science further explains to us why one day is longer than another; why two stars appear to rise together but set separately; the reason why the duration of the day time in one place lasts thirteen hours and in another fifteen, sixteen or twenty; or why both day and night are forever equal in one place while in another the day lasts a month, two, three or six months so that the year is equally divided between six daylight months or six sunless months. There are many other related matters we can learn from this wisdom which is without any doubt authentic. This is the science of mathematical astronomy, which our sages confirmed to be the true wisdom in the sight of the people. But the theories of the astrologists are devoid of any value.

Accordingly, I shall presently proceed to expound philosophically upon these secret matters in outline form.[10] You should know that all philosophers who are men of wisdom and science agree that the world has a Ruler Who is the Prime Mover and that the sphere is not self-moving. For this they have conclusive evidence and clear proof which no one refutes. Differences among them arise only with reference to the nature of the existence of the sphere and its properties. Many contend that the universe is not transient but eternal. Just like God Who is its Prime Mover is eternal so the moved object never exists without the other.[11] Others maintain that the universe is transient and the Creator brought it into existence out of a primeval stuff coexistent with the Creator like clay in the hand of a potter. Out of a portion of the primeval matter He fashioned the heaven and out of another part the earth, and at another time as a result of His Will, He may mould out of the stuff He originally fashioned the celestial sphere another phenomenon. But *creatio ex-nihilo* they maintain is impossible.

Other philosophers, however, in consonance with our prophets project the theory of *creatio ex-nihilo* and assert that the Creator had no co-existent matter but created all that exists from nothing. The wide differences among philosophers centered on this question as our patriarch Abraham apprehended. Countless books were written containing convincing arguments in support of each theory. The basic principle of our Torah is that the Creator is the First and Last and that there is no one besides Him and that He created all from nothing. One who does not acknowledge this is a heretic and a destroyer of his faith.

I have compiled a large work in Arabic on these matters and formulated with valid demonstration and clear proof the existence, authentic unity and incorporeality, in the sense of a physical body or a force in a corporeal body, of the Creator. In addition I have repudiated the contrary claims of the philosophers on the eternity of the universe and resolved the various questions pertaining to our theory of *creatio ex-nihilo*.

Now, the aforementioned three sects of philosophers from ancient times to the present day—those who maintain that co-existent with the Creator was a primeval matter of our prophets who denied eternal matter and stressed God's unity Who created the world with His Will out of nothing and finally the eternalists who asserted that the universe was neither created nor transient but existed eternally, moved by the Prime Mover so that the mover and the moved always exist simultaneously—all agree, however, that existence in the sublunar world from living beings, vegetation and minerals, God created through the motion of the spheres and the stars. The spirit of God at first hovered above the spheres and stars and later through them radiated and expanded in this world and brought into being all existence. Just as we maintain that the Almighty performs miracles and wonders through angels, so these philosophers ascribe similar potency to the spheres and stars who are also endowed with life and intellect and are responsible for the existing order of things in nature. The claims of the philosophers are correct and as I have already elucidated with conclusive proof that not only are they not damaging to religious beliefs but as is apparent from the midrashic statements of our sages, there is no dichotomy between them and the philosophers on these matters.

Now, the three sects of philosophers who concurred on the creative faculty of the spheres and the stars, also maintained that casual events befalling individual people are the result of accident and chance and not caused from on High, or from man's nativity or his natural endowment. They see no difference between a human being torn by a lion, and a mouse killed by a cat, or a fly by a spider. Nor do they distinguish between a person fatally struck by a fallen rock and a stone torn off a hill falling upon a tree or another stone and breaking

them. Both are the result of chance. By the same token the philosophers hold that bellicose activities carried on by warring people against
each other for the sake of enhancement of their respective kingdoms
arc the result of the constellations as much as a horde of dogs fighting
over a dried out carcass. On the other hand, the fate of one's personal
fortune reflects in material well being or progeny is left to chance.
The general principle they lay down is that events occurring to individual members of the human, animal, mineral or plant species are the
result of accident, whereas for the species including inanimate genera,
the determination of their fate comes from spheres and stars derived
from the Almighty. This is the point of contention. We who follow
the authentic teachings of the Torah affirm that events befalling men
are the result not of accident, but of God's justice as we read: "He is
the Rock, His work is perfect; for all His ways are just" (Deut. 32:4).
The prophet comments: "Thou whose eyes are open over all the ways
of the sons of men; to give unto everyone according to his ways and
according to the fruits of his deed" (Jer. 32:9). The Torah further
admonishes and bears witness to this fact when it states: "But if you
will not hearken unto me" I will administer punishment unto you.
Should one, however, maintain that these punishments are not inflicted
on account of sins committed, but are simply casual events which
occur accidently, we are admonished that the Almighty will keep on
increasing similar "events" as we read . . . "But if you will walk contrary unto me then I will also walk contrary unto you . . ." (Lev.
26:21). It is a fundamental doctrine of the Law of Moses, that all
events that happen in the world and suffering that befalls collective
man are the result of strict judgment. Our sages indicated this when
they said: "There is no death without sin nor suffering without iniquity" (B. Tal. Shabbot, 55).

You should know further my masters that another fundamental
assumption of our faith, concurred by the philosophers, is that man is
morally responsible for all of his activities and there is no hetero-
nomous force to determine his actions. He is free to worship God
always and pursue his studies to acquire wisdom or to follow the
counsel of the wicked and engage in theft and adultery. And since no

natural endowment or the accident of one's birth is responsible for one's pursuits, we were commanded and admonished to act in a certain prescribed way as I have indicated in my Arabic work (*The Guide*) or the *Commentary* on the Mishnah as well as my other works.

Accordingly, we have rational proofs that the vicissitudes that befall man are different from those that occur to animals, as the philosophers maintain. For as we find there are three divergent groups in this regard. First the opinion of the philosophers who argue that if, for instance, Reuben was an impoverished tanner whose children died during his lifetime while Simeon was an affluent pharmacist with children. And then suddenly the wheels of his fortune turned and he suffered reverses and became like Reuben. All this the philosophers maintain was due to pure chance. For no natural force in the world, not the potency of the stars was responsible for the divergent fates of both men.

A second group consists of the astrologers whom you have heard disseminating their irrational folly among you to the effect that it is impossible for anything to undergo a reversal in this world inasmuch as one's fate is sealed by the stars at the time of birth. Hence Reuben was destined to remain forever in his inferior state while Simeon in a more exalted position.

To be sure both assumptions are false in the light of our true faith. The position of the astrologers has been proved to be groundless by science as well as by theonomy. For if man's life is predestined by an external force that coercively casts him into a frozen mould or impels him to act in a certain way without his own choice, then of what value are the precepts and the teachings of the Torah? It would appear thus that their views are not only invalidated by scientific thought with the same proofs employed by the philosophers against the notions of the Chaldeans and their associates, but in their folly the astrologers tend to reject the Mosaic Law.

By the same token the concepts of the philosophers that everything comes upon us by accident is false in accordance with the dictates of our Torah which we follow scrupulously and rely upon. We affirm that the incidents pertaining to Reuben and Simeon respectively with regard to their financial position and their reverses are not accidental, but a result of the Creator's Will in keeping with strict justice. To be sure we cannot apprehend the ultimate wisdom of the Holy One which would enable us to ascertain by what measure He decrees the fate of each person. For our ways are not His; nor our thoughts His. It behooves us, however, to affirm that if Simeon sins, he will be punished and suffer financial and family deprivation. On the other hand, if Reuben repents and mends his ways he will prosper in all his pursuits, in substance, progeny and duration of life.[12] This is a fundamental principle of the Torah. The fact that many virtuous people do not prosper should not lead one to question our thesis for any misfortune visited upon them may be due either to some iniquities committed by them of which we were not aware or should be construed as a test and a stepping stone to something better in the future. A general principle to hold on to is that our finite mind cannot comprehend the nature of the Creator's judgment of mankind in this world or the hereafter. With abiding conviction we can only affirm the principle validated by men of science that all the assumptions of the astrologers are false.

I am aware that it is possible to find some individual opinions of our sages in the Talmud, the Mishnah and Midrashim supporting astrological assumptions about the potency of the stars at a man's nativity. This should not be disturbing to you inasmuch as we must never abandon practical Halakhah for the sake of upholding dialectical arguments. Moreover, it is not feasible to surrender demonstrative rational knowledge and embrace the opinion of one individual sage who might have missed a crucial point at that time or he may have proffered an allegorical remark not to be taken literally or that his statement was meant as a temporary measure referring to a specific incident. For is it not apparent that many statements of the Torah cannot be taken literally but, as is clear from scientific evidence, require interpretation that will make them acceptable to rational thought? Our eyes are set in the front and not in the back. One should therefore look ahead of him and not behind him. I have thus revealed to you with these words my whole heart.

NOTES

[1] Known as a "chaldean science," astrology was considered of celestial origin as having been revealed to mankind by defiant angels (Enoch VIII:3). In its earlist stages among the nations of antiquity its importance lay in reckoning times and seasons as well as in its supposed power of forecasting the future and controlling the planets. The Assyrio-Babylonian kings received from their astrologers a monthly forecast of coming events and Haman regulated the time for annihilation of the Jews by means of astrological calculations (*Pirke R. El.* 1). In the Roman empire astrology took on an additional aspect. The Roman emperors believed in the allegedly powerful influence of the stars upon the destinies of man and nature. Tiberius was a master in the art of casting a horoscope and regulated all his activities according to his astrological deductions (Josephus, *Antiq.* 18, 6). In all of its aspects astrology was cultivated in Arabic speaking countries, favored by al-kindi and the *Ihwan al-safa.*

Astrology as a cult was introduced into Judea originally through the medium of Hellenism and in the course of centuries it met with an ever widening acceptance. Already Isaiah uses the term *hobre shomayim* (Isaiah 47:13) which the Greek translation renders as astrologers. The Talmud is replete with references to the practice (Comp. *B. T. Shab.* 156a, *Moed Katan* 28a. Of special interest is the comment of Tosafot on *Nid.* 16b and *Meg.* 25a to the effect that astrological predictions are out of the hands ot God).

[2] It is interesting to note that although many medieval illustrious thinkers like Ibn Gabirol, Abraham ibn Ezra, Yehudah ha-Levi, Abraham ibn Daud and Isaac Abravanel accepted the influence of astrology, it was Abraham Bar Hiyya who did not accord it the rank of a science. (See his Introduction to *Zurat ha Arez* and Friemann's Int. to *Heg. ha-Nefesh.*)

[3] Astronomy was called *hokmat ha-hizzayaon* (wisdom of star-seeing) which was practiced as a science in the Middle Ages in distinction to *hokmat ha-nissayon* (wisdom of prognostication).

[4] *Shemonah Perakhim,* ch. 8 where he states "that our Law agrees with Greek philosophy which substantiates with conclusive proofs that man's conduct is entirely in his own hands."

[5] "Every person had a particular star as a guardian spirit with which his fate was closely interwoven" (*Shab.* 146a). Causeless fear in man is a sign that his star sees danger (*Meg.* 3a). God tells Eliezar ben Pedat that

his state of poverty is due to having been born in an unlucky hour (*Taanit* 25a).

[6] On the other hand, the daring Biblical exegete, Abraham ibn Ezra, yielded to this hypnotic lure and became its foremost expounder. He translated astrological works from Arabic and also wrote a treatise on it, *Reshit Hokmah*, edited and translated by Raphael Levy and Francisco Contera, *The Beginning of Wisdom* (John Hopkins Press, 1939). See also his commentaries in Gen. 2:9; 2:12; 4:24; 26:34. Ex. 3:15. Lev. 16:8.

[7] Ecclesiastes 12:10.

[8] *Hobre Shamayim* is found in Isaiah 47:13 and generally translated as astrology.

[9] Cf. a similar statement in his *Igereret Teiman*, "Regard not all that you see in books as convincing proof. The liar lies with his pen as readily as with his tongue." See also his admonition in *Kiddush-ha-Shem*.

[10] Maimonides proceeds to formulate the Aristotelean theory on the basis of its lack of conclusive demonstrative proof which Aristotle himself acknowledged. See *Guide* 11:15.

[11] "The Universe is inseparable from God. He is the cause, the Universe, the effect and this effect is a necessary one" (*ibid.,* 19).

[12] Reference is here to Rabah's statement in *B. Tal. Moed Katan* 28a.

RALBAG'S INTRODUCTION TO THE
BOOK OF JOB

by LEON D. STITSKIN

INTRODUCTION

Levi ben Gerson, *Ralbag* (commonly called Gersonides or Gershuni, in Hebrew) was born at Bagnols, Southern France, in 1288. He was a philosopher, exegete, physician, and mathematician. As a philosopher, his chief philosophical work, *Milchamot Hashem,* occupies a distinguished place alongside of the *Guide* of Maimonides. As a commentator of the Bible, he depicted the philosophical essences of Biblical thought and brought them into harmony with Aristotelianism. This was especially true of the Book of Job which he, like Maimonides, regarded as purely a philosophical work dealing with the problems of good and evil and God's providence.

Though a distinguished Talmudist, Levi ben Gerson never held a rabbinical post. He earned a livelihood most probably by the practice of medicine. He was a descendant of a family of scholars. His father was Gershon b. Solomon, the author of *Shaar ha-Shamayim,* and Nachmanides was his maternal grandfather.[1] He was only in his late twenties when he began writing his magnum opus, *Milchamot Hashem.* In addition to his commentaries on the Bible and Talmud, he wrote treatises on logic,[2] mathematics,[3] physics,[4] medicine,[5] and a résumé on Averroes.

The Book of Job offered for Gersonides, as well as for Maimonides before him, an excellent opportunity to project the representative opinions held by philosophers on the nature of providence and theodicy. There is first of all the Aristotelian view that God's providence

Originally published in "A Treasury of Tradition", 1965.

147

extends only to species and not to individuals. Then there is the notion held by the majority of our people that God provides for every individual of the human race—*hashgachah peratit.* The third view maintains that some individuals are specially provided for but others are under the protection only of "general" providence.

Essentially the problem resolved itself into a consideration as to whether God's omnipotence is so central that we can circumscribe His goodness or vice versa. Now if we assume as some traditionalists do that it is inadmissible that evil proceed from God, we are confronted by the shocking dilemma: why are the righteous oppressed by miseries while the wicked are triumphant? What is even more paradoxical is the question why evil exists altogether in a universe which is apparently orderly and purposefully-directed.

Classical and medieval philosophers (unlike some modern thinkers who, geared as they are to a scientific view of reality, assert that we must learn to live with our dilemmas and not waste our energy attempting to resolve them in a rational manner, inasmuch as paradoxes abound in all fields of natural research) worked over in massive theological schemes the contradictions and aberrations posed by the problem of evil. Their doctrines ranged from the Platonic view (adopted by Philo) that evil, being simply the absence of good, is not anything positive or absolute, to the notion that good and evil are distributed in this world according to the law of justice and that in the sublunar world God's omnipotence limits His goodness.

Abraham bar Chiyya, Maimonides, and Gersonides, in the tradition of a philosophy of personalism, maintain that moral evil befalling man is due to the defect of the recipient rather than the dispenser. When man fails to realize his potentialities and rational faculties, he is subject to the immutable, determining laws of nature. He can only escape the rigor of the iron laws of the physical environment by developing his intellectual excellence. The higher he stands in the scale of creation, the greater solicitude and protection is bestowed upon him. The degree of divine protection is proportional to the degree of development through man's free choice. Thus those who strive to develop the faculties of the soul enjoy the care of a special, individual providence, while those who grope in ignorance are guarded only by "general" providence.

What follows is my translation of a major portion of Ralbag's introduction to Job which contains in essence his notions on theodicy and providence, expanded upon in his *Milchamot Hashem.*

Levi ben Gerson said: it is appropriate to interpret this book, the Book of Job, in a broad perspective, and to delve deeply into its content in accordance with the dictates of our wisdom, considering especially the great value derived from this work for man's political and intellectual well-being. In fact, the Torah generally is conceived on the principle elucidated in this book. For this reason, our sages ascribed the authorship of this work to Moses our teacher and observed: "Moses authored his book as well as the portion of Balaam and Job." To be sure, there were differences of opinion among them whether the episode of Job was an allegory or an actual event.

The central problem we shall investigate in this book is whether God's special providence is extended to each person individually, in keeping with basic Biblical doctrine, and whether the Almighty watches over all human activities or not. Accordingly, if we establish the premise that God's providence is over all His creatures individually in consonance with the doctrines of the Torah, it follows inevitably that we ascribe an injustice to the Almighty on account of the apparent evil order in the world pertaining to good and evil that befalls particular individuals. For, invariably, we can find a righteous person who suffers and a wicked one who is prosperous. This paradox led philosophers to believe that the Almighty does not apprehend particular things in the sublunar world, as we indicated before.

Doubts about the doctrine of divine providence continued to receive renewed impetus among ancient and later thinkers and even among the prophets and revered sages. Our sages maintained that even Moses, our teacher, already made reference to this cosmic paradox when he beseeched the Almighty: ". . . Do make me know Thy way that I may know Thee" (Exodus 33:13). From the very response by the Almighty to this supplication, it is apparent that this was the problem agitating

Moses. For the Almighty proclaimed: "The Lord is the immutable, eternal Being, merciful and gracious" (*ibid.*, 34:6).

The prophet Habakkuk likewise was concerned about this doctrine when he queried: "Wherefore wilt Thou look upon those that deal treacherously, be silent when the wicked swalloweth up him that is more righteous than he?" (Hab. 1:13).

The Psalmist David similarly was troubled when he stated: "For I was envious of the arrogant, when I saw the prosperity of the wicked. For there are no pangs at their death but their strength is firm. . . . Behold, such are the wicked, and they that are always at ease increase riches. Surely in vain have I cleansed my heart and washed my hands in innocence. . . . And when I pondered how I might know this, it was wearisome in mine eyes" (Ps. 73:3, 4, 12, 13, 16).

Before we commence the interpretation of this book we shall preface one postulate that is all-embracing in this work. It is our contention that the evils that befall men are generally due to human potentialities that have not been actualized, or to pure accident. This is because tragic incidents basically originate either with the recipient of the misfortune himself or with an object external to him. As regards the former, the roots of evil occurrences in the recipient are to be found either in human temperament, one's character, or psychological disposition. If it is due to human temperament, then it must surely be ascribed to one's potential faculty. For the cause of the disorder here is the submergence of the passive powers to the active ones as demonstrated in the fourth proof. The same explanation holds true for the other factors of man's character or psychological disposition as the cause of evil. For in those instances as well, danger strikes when man does not channel his potentialities in the proper direction, that is, when they are not guided by his rational mind. For alas, it is only one's rational spirit that leads man in the right direction in everything that has to do with human needs.

By the same token, tragedies originating outside of man, which have their roots in human temperament or man's free choice, as is the case with wars, may be explained in the same manner as previously and ascribed to man's potentialities not developed.

Misfortunes, however, that do not have their genesis in human temperament or in man's free-will, such as earthquakes, violent storms, lightnings, and similar disorders are the result of pure accidents. For what is involved in this instance are destructive forces whose very nature is to destroy by design. It is necessary to assume, therefore, that in some cases there are celestial causes determining and guiding them so that at one time one malevolent force prevails over the other and vice versa. This takes place according to a determined rhythmic design and a permanent plan as has been indicated by our physical sciences. For this reason, too, we find at one time the element of fire predominant; at another time air, or water, on earth in accordance with the relation that exists between the active and the passive forces. In this way it is possible to maintain the sublunar forms of existence whose survival depends upon the uniform elements found in the substances that compose them. The cause for the unity in sublunar nature is the impact upon the substances from heavenly bodies.

From this standpoint, then, we deduce that such calamities strike us as pure chance. Consider, for instance, the case of one individual struck down by a conflagration or a group of people, who by chance dwell in a certain area, suddenly overtaken by a calamitous earthquake. Surely in those instances only a chance element is involved. In general, then, it is inadmissable that evil can proceed directly from God. That is why we often hear the expression that no tragedy ever descends from on High.

NOTES

1 *Yuchasin,* Abraham Zacuto (ed. Fillipowski, p. 224).
2 *Sefer ha-Hekkesh ha-Yashar*—a treatise on syllogism.
3 *Sefer ha-Mispar*—a treatise on algebra and *Melo Chofnayim* on Euclid.
4 *Dillugim*—a treatise on the seven constellations.
5 *Meshichah*—a remedy for gout.

This year marks the one hundredth anniversary of the passing of Samuel David Luzzatto (1800-1865). Permeated with a deep love for Torah Judaism, Luzzatto attempted to meet up with the theological challenges of his day. He was at home in both cultures and in his *taame-ha-mitzvot* made a unique contribution to an ethical interpretation of Judaism grounded in a broad theological scheme. The ethical formulations of Luzzatto are especially compellingly contemporaneous in view of their psychological insights.

We know that there are many ways of refuting wrong notions. In his prolegomena to *Emmunot V'deot,* Saadia posits the soul as the verifier of truth "causing errors to vanish, doubts to be removed, proofs to be clarified and arguments to be well-grounded." Clearly sound reasoning and empirical experimentation are reliable means to disprove erroneous ideas.

But what can one do about irrational instincts that tend to corrode body and mind. How can one resist evil passions, repugnant desires that impair our personal and social well being? To repress and inhibit them is simply to force them into our unconsciousness whence they will reappear to set up their infectious disorders. Psychiatry has made us aware of the processes by which the unconscious hands over to the mind its mental disorders resulting from repressive drives and transmits them in turn to the body. The unconscious is not a dead end but a laboratory where certain derisive mental mechanisms such as repression, fantasy, projection, rationalization and compensation are worked over and eventually reappear as detrimental consequences to plague us.

Over a hundred years ago there lived a Jewish scholar in Italy, Samuel David Luzzatto who set out to grapple with this deep seated psychological problem. He was keenly aware of the seductive power of human passions to rise repeatedly in the human frame — although the terms unconscious and repression were unfamiliar to him — and resolved to meet the challenge on its own ground. Reason alone or a sense of social welfare he argued, were not strong enough deterrents of man's overpowering instincts which persist within us and exert such influence upon our moral behavior. No maxims even that of Kant's "act as if the principle on which your action is based were to become by your will a universal law of nature" can succeed in the face of an irrational drive for egotistical advantage. It is therefore important to delve directly into the emotional springs of human action and behavior when confronted with the overmastering passions governing man. We must turn to the human emotions themselves as a base for a sound ethical system and utilize the power of some of our benign instincts to counteract our irrational passions for evil and immorality. The ethical basis of Torah Judaism, Luzzatto argued, constitutes a total approach to existence taking into account the emotional responses to human situations.

In his *Yesodei Hatorah,* Luzzatto set out to interpret the *Mitzvot ha-Torah* in the light of the principle of employing certain human instincts to counterpoise human passions. The Torah which always takes into account the nature of man has given us precepts designed to offset derisive instincts by the cultivation of desirable impulses such as compassion, self assertiveness and fear of retribution. Once we accept emotional drives not as exceptional conditions or as illnesses but as concomitant of human nature we have begun the race to guard against their ravages which always take us unawares as something from "outside."

This study of a modern traditional thinker and philosopher — for Luzzatto was traditional both in his religious practices and in his beliefs — reflects the general objective of our series. We have set as our purpose in these studies to underscore the conviction that Torah Judaism has a rationale and that our doctrines and beliefs are grounded in ideological constructs and philosophic schemes with which reflective traditional scholars of every generation have come to grips. Luzzatto was an eminent exponent of such a school of thought. He was at home in the intellectual currents of his day and applied them to the organic resources of Torah Judaism to revitalize its creative faculties and render them in modern thought modes.

The translation of *Yesodei ha-Torah*, "Foundations of the Torah" at the end of the monograph is of special significance. This is the first time that this most important study of Luzzatto has been translated into English.

LUZATTO'S
THE FOUNDATIONS OF THE TORAH

Translated by NOAH ROSENBLUM

FIRST PREFACE

Samuel David to his dear father-in-law, the venerable sage, man of integrity, piety, great in Torah and knowledge, linguist and scholar, R. Raphael Baruch son of the venerable R. Yechiel Benjamin Segre of blessed memory. May you have peace and tranquility, joy and happiness, from now on and forever.

My father, My father!

To you, who taught me German and Latin thirty years ago; who loved and befriended me ever since; who raised and reared three daughters and taught them wisdom, piety, love of justice, and humility; who gave me Bilhah Bath-Sheva in marriage, whose re-markable qualities only her sisters can equal; who for many years shared my bitterness and during her dreadful illness drank with me the cup of poison; who helped and consoled me in my adversity and, together with your God blessed family, assisted me, my wife and children in times of need; who had compassion upon me and my children and gave me, after my saintly wife's death, her sister, Leah, to take her place and be a mother to her children, who since became like her own; to you I bring today my best work, my essay, *The Foundations of the Torah*, as a gift. I present it to you because you deserve it. For the cup of Divine wrath which we shared may have been the main factor that opened my eyes and made me realize the truth in these matters. Having endured with me in my troubles, may you, in joy, partake with me in the honey I extracted from my tribulations.

Happy is the man whom Thou dost discipline, Lord,

And Thou teachest him Thine instruction.[1]

With all my heart I praise the Lord Whose hand bore down heavily upon me for many years. With a strong hand, He separated me from the erring, who believe in their own power and devices, and forget the Supreme Power in Whose hand our strength is as clay in the hand of a potter. Loudly and haughtily, they declare: "By the strength of our hands we have done it, and by our wisdom, for we are prudent. We have removed the bounds of the ancients. We shall discover every day the wonders of science and control the powers of nature. The former generations were like asses and only we are human.[2] We were created to perfect our intellect. The greater one's intelligence, the more praiseworthy he is. God's care for man is in proportion to his intellect and it determines the extent of Divine Providence. (*Guide of the Perplexed* III Chapters XVII-XVIII). Success, too, is in proportion to intellect. "And a blessing is conveyed in the Scriptural text: 'And David had success in all his ways and the Lord was with him'"[3] (Deoth V, 11).

We inherited this type of human wisdom from the Greeks, and I term it *Atticism*. Were it not for the vicissitudes that I had experienced, perhaps I, too, might have accepted it. However, my experiences convinced me that man's wisdom is naught, and complete trust in our intelligence for success, unfounded. All that is abiding is the joy of performing acts of goodness, kindness, and love, for no one can deprive us of the pleasure of helping and loving our fellow man.

Then while meditating on the Torah and the books of the Jewish heritage, I realized that their main purpose is to fortify the sense of compassion and love in man's heart, and mitigate his confidence in his own power; to trust in Divine Providence which is related to man's charitableness, kindness and integrity rather than intellect. This is Divine wisdom, the beginning of which is in the words of

Moses and its end in the words of Rashi and his disciples. For this reason, I termed it *Judaism*.

Then my eyes began to discern faults in the thinking of some of the great Spanish scholars, whose wine comes from the vine of Greece.[4] After expressing my views in public I became, against my will, "a man of strife and a man of contention to the whole earth."[5] I lent money but could not borrow.[6] I spent my energy to fulfill the wishes of men I never knew and rendered my services freely, "yet every one of them doth curse me."[7] However, the fire within me[8] enabled me to endure. I hardened my face like a rock and was convinced that I will not be disgraced. For, either during my life or after my death, truth and justice will find their way into men's hearts.

Then I began to probe and analyze the laws of the Torah and reflect upon their foundations. I wrote this essay which, though incomplete, due to the vicissitudes and tribulations that beset me, constitutes merely a part of a larger work encompassing all of Judaism throughout the generations. In each generation the analysis consists of two parts, the normative and the narrative. This essay deals only with the normative part of the Torah, as I already explained the narratives to my students in my commentary on Genesis. As to the rest of the work, I shall continue to labor as much as my strength and time will permit me. Should others, however, complete it before me I will be delighted "like one who attains great wealth."[9]

Now my father, my father, blessed of the Lord, having almost reached your eightieth birthday, may you continue to live many more years and may they be better and happier than those which passed.

Peace to you and peace to your house and may all of you have peace, as you desire, and as the one who writes and signs this, here in Padua, wishes.

Today, "It is good for me that I have been afflicted that I might learn Thy statutes."[10]

Your student, friend, and son-in-law

SHaDaL

SECOND PREFACE

Said SHaDaL: I wrote this letter to my father-in-law, of blessed memory, in (5)602 (1842), and the essay *The Foundations of the Torah* was written a year or two before. I had intended to publish it before my wedding, which took place on Kislev 20, (5)603. However, due to reasons unknown to me, it did not appear in print until now. Since that time I neither added anything to it nor did I begin to work on the other parts which were to follow. Though twenty years have elapsed, I publish it without any changes because my views concerning the principles of wisdom and faith have not changed since.

I know that some views expressed in this letter will not be readily accepted by most readers. For it is difficult for those who know and witness many great and wonderful discoveries attained by man's intellect and reason, to consider the same detrimental to human welfare. But, the wicked employ them for evil purposes because they think that everything is within their power, and with their knowledge they will escape any punishment or trouble.

When has one seen in the world such great discoveries as in our days? And yet, did they decrease war, murder, theft, poverty, destitution, disease, jealousy, hatred, suffering, anguish, and untimely death?

Were one to ask me: "Does that not imply that you despise wisdom (*haskalah*) and detest understanding?" I would reply that since my early youth till the present I have always loved to search and contemplate in order to find truth, comprehend what is unknown, and recognize deception and error. I will never desist from the pursuit of truth. However, I never liked nor will I like wisdom (*haskalah*) for my personal gain nor for the furtherance of my personal good fortune and success. I always believed, and I continue to believe, that neither wisdom, intelligence nor prudence, can save man from all troubles and tribulations, and make his prosperity endure.

Were one to argue that in Hebrew, wisdom, (*haskalah*) and success (*hatzlachah*) are synonymous, I would point out that there are two kinds of wisdom (*haskalah*).

The ancient Jews and non Jews believed strongly in Providence of God (or deities). The wise man (*maskil*) amongst them, was one whose acts were done with great care and thoughtfulness. When he was about to undertake something, he considered, not merely the natural consequences that might result, but also that of Providence, (whether of God or the deities). Whoever disregarded Providence or did not fear God was considered neither prudent nor wise (*maskil*). Therefore, the Psalmist said: "There is no fear of God before his eyes...He hath left off to be wise (*lehaskil*) and to do good."[1] To see if there were any that did understand (*maskil*), that seek after God";[2] And they say, the Lord shall not see, neither shall the God of Jacob consider. Consider ye brutish among the people and ye fools, when will you be wise (*taskilu*)?"[3] Also in the Torah is written: "Oh that they were wise (*yaskilu*), that they understood this, that they would consider their end. How should one chase a thousand and two put ten thousand to flight, except their Rock had sold them?"...[4]

Thus, what was in those days called wisdom and *haskalah* included also the belief in God and His Providence in the world. For this reason success (*hatzlachah*) and wisdom (*haskalah*) are properly considered in Hebrew as synonyms, because the wise man (*maskil*) also believed in Providence, and considered it among the factors that might help or hinder him. He was, therefore, careful not to do anything that might displease God.

But in our generation, and in that of Maimonides, wisdom (*haskalah*) no longer includes religion. Even an atheist or a non-believer in Providence, is called *maskil* and wise man, and according to some, the only wise man and *maskil*. It is this wisdom (*haskalah*) which, in my opinion, is detrimental to man.

However, a discussion about Providence "is longer than the earth and broader than the sea,"[5] and this is not the place for it. Nevertheless, to forestall the philosopher's arguments, I will state that, in my opinion, it is immaterial whether one believes in a continuous Providence in which changes are frequent — although according to Maimonides whoever considers God subject to change is an unbeliever — or, after profound contemplation, professes that all the changes of Providence have been set at the time of Creation and that the Torah employs human terms.

Finally, the most important thing to recognize is that the world was planned and fashioned with great wisdom by a thoughtful designer. Not only was the physical realm created by Divine wisdom but the good and evil that befall us also emanate from Divine wisdom and are neither accidental nor blindly determined. The wicked who considers himself to be his own master, deludes himself. His doom evolves in a natural manner but is concealed from him until it overtakes him. Similarly, the salvation of the righteous is set in a natural way, and is unknown to him until its time comes.

All this I examined, tried, explored, saw, reflected upon. I believed and attained peace. I trusted and became refreshed. I was downhearted, but I was not crushed. I was disliked, but I was not diminished. I trust in God and I did not wander. I was young and I grew old.[6]
Padua Nisan 30, (5)625.

I

The people of Israel did not acquire their religion from Moses, but inherited it from their ancestors, Abraham, Isaac, and Jacob. Therefore, when Moses came to them he merely said: "The Lord, the God of your fathers, the God of Abraham, the God of Isaac, and the God of Jacob hath sent me unto you."[1]

What was the nature of that religion? Moses did not specify for there was no need to expound it to his contemporaries who were already familiar with it. However, for the sake of the future generations, he described its character by portraying the biographies of Abraham, Isaac, Jacob, and his children. Judging from these narratives, we realize that they believed in one God, creator of heaven and earth, judge of the world, Who protects and rewards His faithful, and punishes the wicked in accordance with their deeds. Thence, too, we note that they believed in signs, miracles, angels, and prophecy. Their concern with the location of their interment indicates their belief in immortality and resurrection. They prayed to God in time of distress, whether for themselves or others, as Abraham on behalf of Abimelech.[2] They made vows to God and, upon their salvation, expressed their gratitude to Him and offered sacrifices. The way of God with which Abraham charged his children and household was: "to do righteousness and justice."[3] (A)

A) The way of God which Abraham taught his children is not, as Maimonides maintained in *Hilchoth Deoth* I, 5, the same as the mean taught by Aristotle. The Aristotelian way is that of reason and calculation, and its aim is that we benefit ourselves and that we win praise from men. The Abrahamic way is that of love and kindness, and its aim is that we benefit others and please God. Maimonides himself realized that the mean is neither the way of the Torah, the prophets, nor of the sages of Israel, and he, therefore, stated, in the above chapter, that "the ancient saints trained their dispositions away from the exact mean towards the extremes." Why, therefore, did he state in that chapter that the attributes, merciful, gracious, long-suffering and abounding in kindness, righteous

II

After Abraham had abandoned, by his own reason and integrity, the idols of his ancestors and came to believe in one God, the Lord elected him, revealed Himself to him, and blessed him, so "that he may command his children and household after him, that they may keep the way of the Lord."[4] He was, therefore, not chosen for his own sake but that he may become the progenitor of a holy nation. (B)

holy, and upright, and others — by which the Creator is called — are the mean and comprise the way of God that the patriarch Abraham taught his children? Why did he not say that the way of God and his attributes are the ways of saintliness and supererogation? Is it possible that attributes like long-suffering, abounding-in-kindness, and holy, should indicate the mean? Consider the fact that among the Divine attributes he also listed "mighty and powerful." This he did because the philosophers included "power" in the scale of attributes. However, the attributes "powerful and mighty," concerning the Creator, were not mentioned for the same reason as the attributes "gracious and merciful," namely, that we may imitate Him in these qualities. Instead, they were mentioned that we may fear Him, and that our trust in Him be strong and abiding. Our sages never said, "Even as He is powerful so be thou powerful; Even as He is mighty so be thou mighty." This would have been merely mockery and irony. For were we to explain might and power in their ordinary connotation, then it is common knowledge that it is impossible for man to equal the Creator in strength. On the other hand, were we to interpret them metaphorically, in the sense as "Who is mighty? One who subdues his passions,"* does the Creator have passions or an evil inclination?

B) Divine Providence did not intend to elect this nation merely for its own sake, but for the benefit of all peoples, as it is explicitly stated in the prophets: "For out of Zion shall go forth the law; And they shall beat their swords into plowshares" etc. (Isaiah, II:3, Micah IV:2). For indeed, the God of Israel is not their own particular and private deity but the God of all mankind and all the nations are His children. This was the belief of the Jews throughout all generations.

---

*) Aboth IV 1.

In order that his children do not intermingle with the heathens, he was given the commandment of circumcision,[5] which constituted the only Divine precept (C) in the religion of that time. Subsequently,

This was also the belief of Rashi who interpreted "How would I put thee among the sons,"[*] "amidst the rest of the sons, commingled with the nations." Rabbi Yehudah Halevi (Kuzari IV:23), too, believed that the dispersion of the Jews in the diaspora constitutes one of the mysteries of Providence and is for the benefit of all nations.[**] This Divine intention is gradually being realized. However, if one will argue that the Christians are idolators, (as maintained by Maimonides in the Laws Concerning Forbidden Foods, Chapter eleven, *halachah* seven, in old editions: "Nevertheless, the Christians are considered idolators and no one may derive any benefit from their wine"), we will reply that it is not true. And this was also the view of Rashi that they are not to be considered idolators (Tur Yoreh Deah CXLVIII).[***]

C) We know that the Egyptians were circumcised (Jeremiah IX 25),[****] and it seems far fetched to say that they learned it from Abra-

---

[*]) איך אשיתך בבנים, את עדתי ואומתי בתוך שאר בנים מעורבת בין האומות לפיכך
ביררתי מנה יפה ואתן לך ארץ חמדה (רש״י, ירמיהו ג׳ י״ט).

[**]) Luzzatto refers to the reply of the Rabbi to the king of the Kuzars about the suffering of the Jews.

... Besides this, God has a secret and wise design concerning us, which should be compared to the wisdom hidden in the seed which falls into the ground, where it undergoes an external transformation into earth, water and dirt, without leaving a trace for him who looks down upon it. It is, however, the seed itself which transforms earth and water into its own substance, carries it from one stage to another, until it refines the elements and transfers them into something like itself, casting off husks, leaves, etc., and allowing the pure core to appear, capable of bearing the Divine Influence ... (*The Kuzari*, translated by Hartwig Hirschfeld, (New York, 1964) pp. 226-227).

[***]) והאידנא כתב הרשב״ם בשם רש״י שהכל מותר דלאו עובדי אלילים הם ולא אולי
ומודי. ואע״ג דמתנדבין ונותנין המעות לכהניהם מותר לו להלוותן שאין כהניהם קונין מהם
לא תקרובת אליל ולא גויה אלא אוכלים ושותין אותם. ועוד כיון שעיקר פרנסתינו מהם ואנו
נושאין ונותנין עמהם כל ימות השנה ואם היינו פורשים מהם ביום אידם היה לנו איבה, לכך
שרי... (טור יורה דעה, הלכות עבודה זרה, סימן קמ״ח).

[****]) Luzzatto refers to the verses in Jeremiah: "Behold, the days come, saith the Lord, that I will punish all them which are circumcised in their uncircumcision; Egypt and Judah and Edom and the children of Ammon and Moab and all that have the corners of their hair polled, that dwell in the wilderness: for all the nations are uncircumcized, and all the house of Israel are circumcised in heart" (Jeremiah IX:24-25).

Luzzatto's view that the above verses imply that the Egyptians were circumcised is not shared by the biblical commentators.

the Israelites restricted themselves not to eat the sinew of the thigh-vein, commemorating the event and miracle, which happend to their forefather, Jacob, who then received the honorific name — *Israel.*[6]

III

This religion was adequate for the Israelites as long as they had constituted one family. However, when they became a great people and the time drew near to bring them to the land, promised by God to their forefathers, the Lord realized that they were in need of instruction, laws, education, and proper guidance for the perfection of virtue and social welfare, as well as for the maintenance of religion. Thus, the Torah that God gave Moses was to forestall the possibility of the people abandoning their religion for those of their neighbors or remain without religion at all.

IV

To attain these two objectives the Lord selected three means, one of which was designed for the perfection of virtue and two for both,

---

ham. Apparently, at first it was customary in Egypt only for the priests to circumcize. God commanded Abraham to circumcize all males, implying that all will be a kingdom of priests, as He explains, "and it shall be a token of a covenant betwixt Me and you."[*] Thus, cirucmcision symbolized the bond between the Israelites and their God, and betokened their distinction and separation from the masses, analogous to the idea of circumcision of the Egyptian priests.

Subsequently, however, circumcision might have become prevalent among the Egyptian masses. Sanchuniathon, the Cannanite, writes that when famine and plague occurred, Kronos sacrificed his only son to his father, Ouranos, circumcized himself, and commanded his people to circumcize themselves. It seems that this story was taken from the story of Abraham, who circumcized his household and offered his only son Isaac, but it was distorted by the Canaanites.

---

*) Gen. XVII:11.

the perfection of virtue and the maintenance of religion. These three constitute the foundations of the Torah.

V

The first foundation — which is the special means designed for the perfection of virtue — is compassion. The latter is an innate quality and constitutes the basis of love, kindness, and righteousness. (D) It is the only factor which motivates us to do good without expecting to be rewarded neither naturally nor supernaturally, neither in this world nor in the world-to-come. Compassion is its own reward, for the compassionate man identifies himself with the suffering person and does not rest until he helps him, and alleviates his pain.

VI

The Greek sages and the philosophers who followed in their footsteps, made various endeavors to base the perfection of virtue on principles other than compassion. Their theories, however, proved empty and barren.

D) Compassion which is the root of love and kindness, is also the source of love, justice, and hatred of violence. Just as our heart aches at the sight of a suffering man who is in pain, so does it ache when we see another person inflicting pain, (unless we are prejudiced by love for one and the hatred for the other). Therefore, barring any personal reasons, we naturally abhor violence and desire that everyone be treated properly, for all people are the same to us and our love and compassion for people, heretofore unknown to us, is the same. Also, the famous scholar Heineccius in the introduction to his book *Elementa Juris Naturae et Gentium*, wrote that, in his opinion, all of jurisprudence, and the laws regulating interpersonal and international relationships, emanate from the love for others which is implanted within us, *Ex eo (amore) solo, tamquam limpidissimo Fonte, totum Jus naturae et gentium prono alveo fluere censeo.*

VII

Some of them taught that the pursuit of passion never brought man any lasting happiness. Its benefits were only illusory and fleeting, causing tribulations and suffering. This is indeed so. However, the recognition of this fact does not enable man to master his passions, because his strong desires, particularly when young and passionate, prevent him from considering the consequences. There are also many, though fully aware that their way of life does not lead to tranquility and peace of mind, prefer, nevertheless, a riotous and stormy life, coupled with enjoyment and gratification, to a quiet uneventful life, devoid of storms and excitement. Sagacious preachings will neither help nor be effective, since God did not create all men with the same nature. It was not the Divine will that the same thing or condition should appeal to everybody. Just as it is inconceivable that all people should have the same occupation, so it is impossible that all should behave alike. Just as some prefer to live on land while others spend most of their lives on the high seas, and just as some love peace and security, while others enjoy weapons and war, so it is natural for some men to prefer a peaceful existence, few in pleasures but few in troubles, while others desire a noisy and stormy life in which sadness and passions commingle.

The philosophers who wish to guide men by reason and understanding, actually negate nature or rather the will of the Creator, and, consequently, most people do not heed them.

VIII

Some maintained, that since the welfare of society demands that its constituent members follow the path of righteousness it is important for every individual to be righteous and further the welfare of the group, since his security is contingent upon its security.

This is undoubtedly true. However, will this really enhance the morals of every man? The latter may argue: "You philosophers are telling me that unless all members of society rectify their deeds the social order will collapse and anarchy will ensue. You are correct. It would indeed be wonderful if all members of society would be like brothers pursuing justice and loving truth and peace. However, as long as I see that most of the people of my community are greedy, then woe, woe unto me, for I will perish in my righteousness, since only I will have pursued it."

Far worse is the attitude of the wicked who orally agree with those philosophers, and pay lip service to the idea that society can only exist on the basis of justice and righteousness. Deep in their hearts, however, they devise plans to be exempted and deviate from the path of righteousness, whenever it is to their advantage. Any attempt by the philosophers to convince them of the unfairness of an individual to benefit at the expense of the group is bound to fail, since man is governed by what he sees. Believing that a given disadvantage to society may be in his interest and promote his success, will he heed the advice of his mentors and abandon that, which in his opinion, is beneficial to him? Did not his teachers stress that his concern for the social welfare was only for the sake of his own good?

IX

Some based it on the principle of human equality, maintaining that what is right for A must be right for B. Since both are human, neither may have prerogatives the other does not have. Should theft robbery, and murder be permitted to A, they ought to be permitted also to B. As long as A disallows them for B, he has to admit that he is not allowed either, unless he could prove that B is not human.

This, too, is correct. However, man's evil inclination has many arguments. The villain thinks that equality is merely an illusion. Nature itself made people unequal in their physical ability and intellectual capacity. Since nature saw fit that I be strong and the other weak, I clever and the other foolish, it undoubtedly wanted that my lot should be better than his and it never intended that our fate be the same. By stealing from him, robbing him or showing my superiority over him, at any given opportunity, I do not violate any principle or law. I merely enjoy the boon with which nature had intentionally endowed me. Were it so, as the philosophers maintain, muses the villain, that neither strength nor power nor craftiness give a person right (*jus*) over another, why do the nations consent to settle their disputes by arms, warfare, and might?

X

Some relied on honor. They told the people to avoid anything which may bring about disgrace and humiliation. Man should choose good deeds which will bring honor upon him. The proper course which man ought to pursue is the one which is an honor to him and which gets him honor from men.

This teaching, however, may be very effective with regard to outward behavior but not for inner morality. For not all human deeds, nor even most, are publicly known. A person will frequently commit evil or refrain from doing good and will not, thereby, incur any disgrace. Many people attain fame and glory through slyness and perfidy, though their ways are evil, and their deeds perpetrated in secrecy, are shameful and abominable.

XI

Some stated that man differs from all beings in possessing the Divine gift of reason, which includes the categorical imperative, (*Imperativus categoricus*), to choose good and reject evil. However, what should people do who do not sense this imperative? Were this imperative inherent in all men, what accounts for the numerous evils on earth?

XII

Some maintain that events in human life are neither good nor evil, and only the righteous person is genuinely happy. Though he may be beset with many vicissitudes and troubles, he will remain unaffected and unharmed. However, how many people will agree with this view? Of what value is a theory which fails to gain acceptance?

XIII

Some assert that man must abide by the laws of nature. Since nature made man a social being and in need of other men, it attests that nature intended man to live and act in a manner beneficial to society and for the furtherance of its existence. By his improper deeds, man brings about social disorder and the disintegration of the group defying, thereby, the dictates of nature.

What is the evil-doer's reply? "Why? Why must I heed the laws of nature in general and disregard my own nature? Do I not act in accordance with my nature when I steal, commit adultery or murder? It is by refraining from these acts that I go contrary to my nature, and the weariness I experience by overcoming my inclinations is a punishment for having defied nature."

XIV

Some emphasize the nearness of God. They say that man ought to disregard all mundane things and concentrate on attaining wisdom, and the knowledge of God. However, is it possible that all men, or even most of them, should pursue this course? Should even one in a thousand attain this objective, will he, thereby, benefit anyone else? Will he not be as contemptuous about some one else's problems as he is about his own? Moreover, such a person can neither be pleasant to others nor be liked by them, since the latter seem to him worthless, and only he is superior. All men appear to him as animals, while only he is a person.

XV

These are some of the views of the Greek philosophers and of their followers and these are their main teachings in their attempt to construct a system of ethics. To mention all, is impossible, since they are numerous. They have, however, one thing in common, namely, that they are ineffective in inducing the masses to pursue goodness, since their theories are not based upon a natural principle common to all men.

XVI

The feeling of compassion, however, is inherent, to a larger or lesser degree, in the nature of every man. As clear evidence may serve the fact, that even the most stout-hearted egotists, who spend all their lives in amusement and feasting, cannot bear the poor, the destitute, the sick and the tormented. Why? Because the sight and cries of these unfortunates mar, to a degree, their enjoyment, and sadden their hearts, in spite of themselves. Why? Because the sense of compassion is inherent even in egotists.

It is undeniable that there are many factors which may weaken man's sense of compassion and mercy, and render him cruel and severe. This, however, is merely accidental, not natural. If we ever witnessed or heard of people who treated others cruelly and without mercy, it was caused by hatred, wrath or vengeance, which affect man and make him irrational, or by expediency designed to attain a specific goal. There is, however, no doubt that even people who seem most cruel are at times also compassionate and merciful.

XVII

The sense of compassion, alone, can make man choose good and reject evil. Anyone who is affected by another man's pain or suffering will undoubtedly cause no one any harm. On the contrary, he will endeavor to be kind to people, help them and save them from trouble. This sense of compassion will bring about love of righteousness and justice. For when I see two men for the first time, I like them both equally, and I will not help one to the detriment of the other, but wish them both well. Were I to see one robbing the other I would want to take the goods from the robber and restore it to the rightful owner.

XVIII

Consequently, if we desire to teach a child to pursue the proper course, so that our guidance be truly beneficial for the perfection of virtue, we must endeavor to fortify his inherent sense of compassion by word and deed. Just as conditioning a child to witness cruelty and listen to the praise of selfishness, will undoubtedly weaken his sense of compassion, and will gradually harden him and make him insensitive, so by conditioning him to see acts of compassion and kindness and listen to their praiseworthiness as well as the contemptibility of selfishness and harshness, his sense of compassion and mercy will be strengthened and he will grow up to be compassionate, merciful, righteous, just, and trustworthy.

XIX

The Torah, Moses gave to the people of Israel, guides us in the way of compassion and kindness, having commanded to leave the gleanings,[7] the forgotten sheaf[8] and the corner of the field[9] for the poor, the stranger, the orphan and the widow; by prohibiting to take from the poor any interest[10] or increase[11]; by forbidding to enter his house to fetch his pledge[12]; by commanding that neither the mill nor the upper millstone be taken in pledge,[13] nor the garment of a widow[14]; by ordaining: "If thou, at all, take thy neighbor's garment to pledge, thou shalt restore it unto him before the sun goeth down."[15] Reflect about what is written after that commandment: "For that is his only covering, it is his garment for his skin; wherein shall he sleep?"[16] Here is the case of a creditor who loaned his money and, realizing that it was overdue, rightfully takes a pledge. He is legally entitled to take the debtor's garment unless the latter gives him something else. However, if he will return it to the debtor every evening the debt will, undoubtedly, never be paid. "Had he asked it as a gift — argues the creditor — perhaps I would have given it to him. But since he promised to repay and he does not, he is a swindler and bent upon robbing and harming people. Now having taken his garment in pledge, why should I return it to him? How will I get my loan back? What concerns me in what he will sleep?" However, though philosophers and exponents of the honor theory will agree with the creditor, the Torah teaches compassion and kindness and says to him: "Wherein shall he sleep?"[17] (E)

Similarly, after the Torah ordered the remission of debts on the seventh year, there is no doubt that any man with common sense will be careful not to lend any money at the end of the sixth year,

E) What I wrote, that "he must return it to him every evening," is according to the *halachah*, though this, in my opinion, is not the obvious meaning of the text, since the Bible does not state that he, (the creditor) ought to take it back in the morning. It seems to me, therefore, according to the actual meaning of the text, that since he, (the debtor), is so poor and has nothing to give in pledge except his garment, the Torah allowed to take it from him and humiliate him in public in order that he may repay his debt. However, if in spite of it he will not repay, the Torah believed that he was unable to do so and obliged the creditor to return the pledge and leave him alone. This, however, refers only to a creditor who takes the pledge forcibly, for the expression *Habalah* does not connote a pledge given voluntarily at the time of the loan, but, rather, that which is taken from the debtor who fails to pay when it is due (see Rashi). This law, however, does not apply to a pledge given by the debtor at the time of the loan, since it is evident, as maintained by Gersonides, that he can get along without this garment. The Rabbis say in the *Mechilta*, "During the night one may take as a pledge a garment worn by day, and during the day one may take as a pledge a garment worn by night. And one must return the garment worn by day for the day and the garment worn by night for the night."* They were lenient

---

*) English translation of *Mekilta de Rabbi Ishmael* by Jacob Z. Lauterbach Vol. III (Philadelphia, 1949) p. 150.

knowing that the borrower already thought not to repay it. What philosopher or exponent of the honor theory will dare censure anyone refusing a loan at such a time? However, what did the Torah say? "Beware that there be not a base thought in thy heart, saying: 'The seventh year, the year of release, is at hand'; and thine eye be evil against thy needy brother, and thou give him, nought... Thou shalt surely give him and thy heart shall not be grieved when thou givest unto him."[18]

XX

Compassion was so important to the blessed Lawgiver that immediately after Revelation when He came to teach the people the laws of conduct, He began "If thou buy a Hebrew servant."[19] The status of slaves in antiquity is well known. They and their children, not unlike the ox or ass, were the property of their master. The latter had the right to beat and even kill his slaves with impunity. However, the Torah in its first ordinance did not permit a Hebrew slave to work more than six years,[20] and prohibited the killing or even the severe chastisement of a Canaanite one.[21] It decreed the punishment of a master who caused the death of his slave by smiting,[22] and compelled to set free a slave if the master destroyed his eye or felled his tooth.[23] It ordained the slave to rest on Sabbath and holidays.[24] The Torah even had compassion for female war captives commanding to grant them a month for mourning their parents,[25] and forbade selling them after having had with them conjugal relations.[26]

The Torah insisted upon compassion and kindness, not only towards man but also towards animals and birds for the latter's sake, since

---

with the creditor in order not to discourage others from lending. And Rabban Simon ben Gamliel (Baba Metzia IX, 13) was even more lenient and said that even to the debtor himself the creditor need only restore the pledge during the first thirty days, and after that he may sell with the permission of the court. However, his opinion is not accepted.

God's mercy extends to all creatures, (F) as well as for the sake of man himself that he may learn compassion rather than cruelty. To this category belong the precepts: "Thou shalt not muzzle the ox when he treadeth out the corn,"[27] "Thou shalt not plow with an ox and an ass together,"[28] — as Abraham Ibn Ezra explains — because the strength of an ass does not equal that of an ox. Similarly, "whether it be cow or ewe, ye shall not kill it and its young both in one day,"[29] and the precept about the rest of animals on the Sabbath.[30]

F) In *Midrash Rabbah, parshath Ki Tetze* we read: "And just as God shows mercy to man, so, too, has He shown mercy to cattle. Whence this? For it is said, 'But from the eighth day and thenceforth it (the animal) may be accepted for an offering' (Leviticus XXII:27). And what is more, God commands, "Ye shall not kill it and its young both in one day (*Ibid.*, 28).' And in the same way that God had compassion upon the cattle, so, too, was God filled with mercy for the birds, as it is said, 'If a bird's nest chance before thee (thou shalt not take the dam with the young).'" The statement in the *Mishnah Berachot* Chapter V p. 345; *Megillah*, Chapter IV p. 25a) that if one says may Thy mercies reach the nest of a bird he is silenced, seems to me, with due apologies to the sages of the Talmud for their interpretation, that since it is stated, "*May* Thy mercies reach" and not "*did* Thy mercies reach," we may conclude that it does not refer to the commandment concerning the sparing of the mother bird, but rather to the people of Israel. The latter is like a bird wandering from its nest and any one who asks God to have mercy upon them, the Tanna feels that he ought to be silenced for the language he employs is strange and not understood by everybody. Since communal prayer must be understood by everyone, therefore, when the people will hear the poetic metaphor "May Thy mercies reach the nest of a bird," they will not comprehend it and it will cause laughter and ridicule. I have already pointed out in *Oheb Ger* how skilfully Onkelos avoided figures of speech in his translation because the masses would have misunderstood them. However, not all generations are alike. Thus, in the days of the Tannaim they were compelled to silence anyone who referred to the people of Israel as bird's nest. However, subsequently, Kalir came and he referred to them as "valley of roses," "a nation that is firm as a rampart"; likened to a palm-tree"; "lake-like eyes"; and similar strange metaphors and no one silenced him. Why? Because in his days poetic metaphors were commonplace.

The Torah commanded to respect and be kind to animals or birds, when they show acts of kindness, as is evident in the law concerning sparing the mother bird.[31] For the dam sitting on the young or the eggs could have flown away and saved serself when she heard or saw a man approaching. Why did she not fly away and save herself? Because she had compassion for her children. Had man been permitted to take her, he would get the impression that compassion is bad, foolish and deleterious. On the other hand, the prohibition of taking the dam indelibly impresses upon man the paramount importance of compassion. (G)

XXII

The Torah forbade any cruel practices even in case of sacrifices and stated: "When a bullock or a sheep or a goat is brought forth, then it shall be seven days under the dam; but from the eighth day and henceforth, it may be accepted for an offering made by fire unto the Lord."[32] Similarly, the prohibition to seethe a kid in its mother's milk[33] — in the opinion of Rabbi Samuel ben Meir and Abraham Ibn Ezra — is on account of the cruelty to seethe an offspring in its own mother's milk. Although, after the kid was slaughtered, what does it matter to it or to its mother in what liquid it is boiled? Nevertheless, such an act will adversely affect the mentality of the perpetrator

G)   The seeming wisdom — Greek philosophy — treats such small matters lightly and disregards them. But true wisdom knows that these small matters constitute the source of the important ones. There is no great thing which was not young and insignificant in its beginning. A child who rejoices at the outcry of an animal will, in the future, laugh at the cry of his parents. Whoever delights in the burning of a mouse will eventually delight in setting fire to a city, should the opportunity arise. If you see a person laugh at another man's misfortune without any personal reason — do not trust him for when he will not need you he will laugh at your troubles too. Stay away from a person who enjoys reading in history books how the crafty succeeded by their cunning.

and the onlooker. Suppose one makes spoons out of his father's bones and a dish from his skull and eats from them.[34] Although he does not harm his dead father, it is a cruel deed, nevertheless, and this act destroys in him and in the onlookers the quality of compassion and kindness. (H)

XXIII

In order to emphasize the importance of compassion, the Torah attributes this quality to the Creator, blessed be He, by saying: "For I am gracious"[35]; "The Lord, God merciful and gracious"[36]; "He doth execute justice for the fatherless and widow"[37] etc. (I)

H) I surmise that it was the custom of some people or even of some Israelites to offer the first born sheep in their mother's milk. It is possible that just as they gave the priest the first fleece, so they considered to be good and proper to offer the first milk. They slaughtered, therefore, the first-born and boiled it in its mother's milk and gave it to the priests to eat (or they gave him the first-born and the milk, and he boiled them together and consumed them, or you may say, that they boiled and burned them upon the altar). Thus, they presented the most High with both the first born and the first milk.

Therefore, after the Torah mentioned the first fruit from the earth, it also mentioned the seething of the kid in its mother's milk. It is also clear why it mentioned seething and not eating, because the seething was most important and not the eating, since the latter is impossible without the former.

I) Though the Torah considers compassion to be of great value, it endeavored to eliminate it in certain instances. This was not with regard to individuals but to the community and judges. Because compassion for the wicked constitutes cruelty to the just. Therefore, in civil matters the Torah told the judge: "Thou shalt not respect the person of the poor, nor honor the person of the mighty, but in righteousness shalt thou judge thy neighbor."* For just as it is improper for a judge to pervert justice in favor of the rich so it is equally improper for him to do it out of

---

*) Lev. XIX:15.

XXIV

Owing to the guidance of the Torah, compassion and mercy became an inherent characteristic of the people of Israel in all generations, so that their neighbors commented: "Behold now, we have heard that the kings of the house of Israel are merciful kings."[38] Consequently, too, the Israelites never wrung any confession by torture, on a mere suspicion, without testimony and proof, a practice common among the peoples of antiquity. It existed only in the times of Herod, who was not of Jewish descent, was contemptuous of the Jewish mode of life, and followed that of the Romans.

XXV

Though compassion constitutes a strong and important foundation for the perfection of virtue, it is, nevertheless insufficient to enable

compassion for the poor. Justice ought to be the same for the small and the great alike. In the case of capital punishment and other penalties, the Torah told the community and the judges not to have mercy on the wilful murderer if he managed to escape to one of the cities of refuge, but they should bring him back and kill him. They must not have any sympathy for a false witness but do unto him as he had planned to do to his brother.* They must not have any mercy for a woman who injures a man's genitals, but they should punish her measure for measure (in accordance with the interpretation of Abraham Ibn Ezra since she has no testicles, they should cut off her hand).

This seems to me to be the meaning of the text. Similarly, when the Lord commanded to exterminate the Canaanites and the Amalekites on account of their wickedness He admonished not to have mercy upon them and never to forget (see below XXVIII, XXIX). And only due to the severity of the sin of idolatory, which is injurious and damaging to the entire social structure of the Jewish people and destroys the order Divinely instituted in Israel, the individual and even relatives were commanded not to conceal the enticer and not to pity him.** Similarly, the Torah threatened the members of a family who conceal a relative who sacrificed a child to the Moloch.

---

*) Deut. XIX:16-21.
**) Ibid., XIII:7-12.

man to control himself and to overcome his passions and deficiencies, since man has more pity on himself than on anyone else. Therefore, when in need of something, be it real or imaginary, he feels it more keenly than somebody else's need. Should he be able to satisfy his need at another man's expense, compassion alone will not deter him from perpetrating evil. The blessed Lawgiver, therefore, added another foundation for the perfection of virtue — the hope of reward and the fear of punishment. Since reward and punishment affect one personally, their impression is more profound and, surpassing frequently, that of need and passion. The gratification of the latter will, thus, be inhibited by the fear of punishment and hope of reward.

Reward and punishment, which were made a foundation for the perfection of virtue, are not to be meted out by mortals, who only see the visible things while many others are concealed from them, but by God Who sees the heart, and from Whom nothing is hidden. The belief in Divine Providence and His reward and punishment constitutes the second foundation of the Torah of Moses, and serves as a means to attain both aims — the perfection of virtue, and maintenance of religion.

XXVI

Faith was not commanded by the Torah. The Israelites had already believed since the days of Abraham, and if they had not believed, such a command would have been futile. The blessed Lawgiver, however, strengthened the belief in Providence by showing them in Egypt the severe plagues He inflicted upon their oppressors and by rescuing the groaning and sighing Israelites.

Whenever Moses spoke to the people, he always emphasized God's Providence to pay man according to his conduct and deeds. He ordained to remind our children of all that God wrought to Pharaoh and his people[39]; and instituted the festival of Passover[40] and the consecration of the first born[41] in remembrance of the Exodus from Egypt.

The reward and punishment designated in the Torah refer to precepts regulating relations between man and man as well as between man and God and, therefore, this foundation constitutes a useful means for both the perfection of virtue and maintenance of religion.

XXVII

The spoilage of the Egyptians, taking from them silver and golden valuables and garments, constituted one of the signs of Providence, reward and punishment, demonstrated by God to His people at the time of the Exodus. It was as He had promised them when He had first spoken to Moses: "And I will give this people favor in the sight of the Egyptians. And it shall come to pass, that when ye go, ye shall not go empty; but every woman shall ask of her neighbor and her that sojourneth in her house. . ."[42]

Some argue about this and say, "How could God command such an act, even though the Israelites were entitled to be compensated for their many years of labor, and for the houses and movable goods they had left behind at their departure? Did not the Egyptians believe that the Israelites were merely going to sacrifice to their God and then return, and for this reason they made the loan? The Israelites, on the other hand, at the time when they asked for the valuables were already determined not to return them. Was not, therefore, their request an act of deceit and absolute fraud? Did not this Divine command make a bad impression upon them, learning from it to speak deceitfully and act treacherously? Could God not have prospered His people without ordering them to act dishonestly?

This argument which seems so weighty to our contemporaries would have seemed ridiculous to those who departed from Egypt. For they who endured the oppression of the Egyptians and were aware of the latter's evil deeds did not consider this act, neither at the time of the command nor at its execution, as permission to deceive and defraud. On the contrary, it impressed them that God recompenses man according to his deeds and punishes the wicked who are cruel to their fellow-men, for they did not do it wilfully. Anxious to flee from their oppressors and from the land which destroyed their children, they would not have even entertained such a thought. They did it only because their leader commanded them to in the name of God.

The impression they got was that God detests evil-doers, but helps and rewards the oppressed. Should they, therefore, while successful, oppress others, God will avenge the victims and give them the wealth of their oppressors. Thus, they were, subsequently, so frequently admonished by Moses to remember that they were slaves, and the Lord redeemed them. As proof may serve the fact, that the Torah explains in three places[43] that it was God who caused the Egyptians to like the Israelites and loan them, i. e. the Israelites recognized and were taught by their leader, Moses, that were it not for the will of God, manifested through a miracle, their Egyptian enemies would never have loaned them their valuables. For this reason, it is explicitly stated that the Israelites did as Moses told them,[44] to indicate that they did not do it wilfully but merely carried out their leader's command, in the name of God, Who helped them through signs and miracles. It also contradicts the view of the heretics, who haughtily apologize for our ancestors by saying that it is understandable that slaves who succeed in breaking their shackles should not hesitate to deceive their former oppressors.

"In order to evaluate properly the ethicality of a people it is necessary to know its distinct concepts of right and wrong, and not to judge the former generations by our concepts of today." (Cahen)[45]

O fool! O dullard! Listen to what you say yourself. If indeed we cannot judge the ancients by our present views, why do you rise to judge your ancestors, saying, that it is natural for slaves, who break their shackles, to allow themselves to deceive their oppressors? Why do you not realize that they did not do it wilfully, but merely obeyed God's command. If you do not believe that it was ordered by God, how can you deny that they thought so? If you do not believe in

Providence, reward and punishment, how can you deny that your ancestors did? Why can you not understand that they had no intention of deceiving their oppressors, but presumed that God took from the wicked and gave to the righteous, in order to give one in accordance with his deeds? How can you judge the ancients according to your thoughts and not according to their own? Do you not know that not only the Israelites, but all people of antiquity attributed human events to the will of God? The only difference between the Israelites and the other peoples in this respect, was that the latter attributed these events to the will of many deities, whereas the Hebrews only to one God. If the sophisticated contemporaries fail to realize God's Providence — though the remarkable philosopher Bacon, (J) whose

J) "The third part, the history of Providence, has been dealt with by some pious pens, but not without a mixture of party politics. This history is employed in observing the agreement which there sometimes is betwixt the revealed and secret will of God. For, although the counsels and judgments of God are so secret as to be absolutely unsearchable to man, yet the Divine goodness has sometimes thought fit, for the confirmation of his own people, and the confutation of those who are as without God in the world, to write them in such capital letters, as they who run may read them. Such are the remarkable events and examples of God's judgments through late and unexpected sudden and unhoped for deliverances and blessings, Divine counsels dark and doubtful, at length opening and explaining themselves, etc. All which have not only a power to confirm the minds of the faithful but to awaken and convince the consciences of the wicked."

(Francis Bacon, *The Advancement of Learning, World's Great Classics* Book 2 Chapter XI 3 (New York, 1900) pp. 66-67.*

I know that many contemporary intellectuals accept the belief in Providence. However, in their opinion, it extends to mankind in general,

---

*) This quotation from Bacon must have impressed Luzzatto for after quoting it in Latin he added: "Since these words are very important to us I decided to publish also their French translation of Buchon for those who do not understand Latin." In the edition *Mech-kerei Hayehaduth*, I (Warsaw, 1913) pp. 26-27, there appeared also a German translation.

wisdom enlightened all contemporary scholars, did not — how do you judge the ancients by the ideas of the contemporaries? O fool! O dullard!

XXVIII

The underlying reason for the order to exterminate the inhabitants of Canaan[46] is analogous to the commandment to borrow the valuables from the Egyptians. God could have given His people fields and vineyards without ordering them to commit violence and cruelty by exterminating peoples who never molested them. The Blessed One, however, wanted them to exterminate these peoples so that they learn a lesson and witness how God punishes the evil-doers, as Moses told them: "For all these abominations have the men of the land done, that were before you and the land is defiled, that the land vomit not you out also, when ye defile it, as it vomited out the nation

rising gradually to perfection, but not to the individual in particular, nor to the detailed occurrences that affect him. I, however, consider their words contradictory since it is impossible for Providence to be on the general, unless it is also on the particular. For what is the general if not an aggregate of particulars. Is it possible for a man to read a letter without reading the alphabet written in it? Is it possible that one of the great kings should be commissioned by Providence without Divine Providence extending to all the men that surround him from the day of his birth. For, indeed, everyone of them who surrounds him, as a child and as a young man, leaves an impression upon him. Had any one of them any peculiarity, the king may not necessarily receive it but it may affect him nevertheless, and perhaps even change him altogether. Similarly, is it possible that Divine Providence extends to all men who surround the child destined to become a great king without extending to the men that surround them from the day of their birth? For each of these men, too, was impressed by those who surround him and thus it goes back to Adam. Therefore, if Providence exists for mankind in general it must extend to each individual and to all the detailed occurrences of every one of the human species.

that was before you."[47] The Torah also prefaced God's statement to Abraham: "And the fourth generation they shall come back hither for the iniquity of the Amorite is not yet full,"[48] to inform that the destruction of these people was due to their wickedness and, until their measure was full, the Israelies would not be able to take their land. Also from what Moses told them: "Speak not thou in thy heart, after that the Lord thy God hath thrust them out from before thee saying: 'For my righteousness the Lord hath brought me in to possess this land',"[49] is clearly indicative that every nation's success is contingent on God's decree and His Providence, and is not accidental, as the contemporaries maintain. Consequently, by exterminating the Canaanites they did not get a negative immoral notion, but they were strongly impressed that these people became subject to extinction on account of their abominations and that by exterminating them, the Israelites were merely the messengers of God.

This belief was further strengthened when they witnessed the signs and miracles the Lord wrought for them when they came to conquer the land: He made them cross the Jordan on dry land; He hurled stones from heaven upon the Canaanites who made war on them; He halted the sun in mid sky. Should the sophisticated — who show compassion and pity for the remote and dead — say: "Is it conceivable that God order the slaughter of an entire people, innocent men and women, young and old, infants and sucklings?" Set their teeth on edge and tell them: In time of an earthquake, do not houses collapse on their dwellers? During a plague in a land, do not half of its inhabitants die? Did not God command it?

I am not here to defend God. It suffices that I proved clearly that, God's command to the Israelites, whether concerning the borrowing of the valuables from the Egyptians or with regard to the extermination of the inhabitants of Canaan, did not leave upon them an immoral impression, but, on the contrary, was useful to strengthen their belief in Providence, reward and punishment.

XXIX

The command to exterminate the Amalekites and the admonition "thou shalt not forget"[50] is analogous to this. It was intended to make deceit loathsome to the Israelites as the Amalek affair was. For the latter had no cause to quarrel with the Israelites, nor were they threatened by war. Nevertheless, the Amalekites attacked them from the rear, at a time when the Israelites were faint and weary. They murdered all the feeble Israelites without compassion and fear of God. Therefore, after the admonition against deception in measures and weights and the concluding remark, "for all that do such things, even all that do unrighteously are an abomination unto the Lord thy God,"[51] the Torah mentioned the Amalek affair which was a case of injustice and deception. It revealed its shamefulness by saying: "How he met thee by the way and smote the hindmost of thee, all that were enfeebled in thy rear when thou was faint and weary and he feared not God."[52] It exposed him as an example for deceivers and commanded his extermination which should not be forgotten nor neglected. This was to serve as a lesson that God despises traitors and punishes them severely. This command too, undoubtedly, left no immoral impression upon the Israelites but, on the contrary, realizing how much God detested disgraceful acts and punished their doers, it enabled them to abstain from such deeds.

XXX

Indeed, the extermination of an entire people, men, women, infants, and sucklings is considered nowadays a shockingly cruel deed. Nevertheless, should a prophet presently arise, whom the people would consider a messenger of God, and command a given nation to destroy the men, women, and children of a certain city, notorious for their evil deeds, there is no doubt in my mind that the former would not be adversely impressed by executing the prophet's command. On the contrary, from that day on, they would fear that God and avoid to incur His wrath. In antiquity, when genocide in wartime was a common occurrence, pregnant women were ripped open and infants were disemboweled and dashed against rocks, the command to exterminate the Canaanites and Amalekites was, most certainly, not as strange as now. Behold, whom did Saul and the people pity in the war with the Amalekites? The old, the women, the pregnant, or the infants? No! They merely pitied Agag and the good sheep and cattle. Is this considered compassion? They let the king live for their own glory and kept the good sheep and cattle for consumption. God was, therefore, angry at Saul, for He knew the truth, that his disobedience was not motivated by compassion but by his own and his people's desire for indulgence and self-aggrandizement.[53]

XXXI

Retribution in the Torah is directed to both, the collective, and the individual, to the entire nation as well as to the individual Israelite. To the entire people, for sins committed openly, and to the individual, for those committed in secret. By making all Israelites mutually responsible, the blessed Lawgiver intended it to constitute a strong deterrent, for the prevention of the spread of evil and corruption in the nation. As a result of the fact that Divine retribution affected the entire nation, no one seeing a person committing a sin will be able to say: "What does it concern me?" but will reprove the sinner. Should the latter continue to sin, the witness will testify against him in court, where he will be punished, so that all people may learn a lesson and fear to do likewise. Therefore, all the blessings and maledictions were directed to the entire nation and only on such sins which are naturally committed surreptitiously or involve the abstention from a positive commandment in secret — as Rabbi Samuel ben Meir, Abraham Ibn Ezra, and Rabbi Abraham ben Nathan in *Eben Haezer XLV* pointed out — it said: "Cursed be the man."[54] The reason God desired upon the entrance into the land that the Levites inform the people of the blessings and maledictions, "And it shall come to pass if thou shalt hearken diligently"[55] . . . "But it shall come to pass if thou will not harken"[56] was to impress upon them this idea of mutual responsibility, since reward and punishment apply to the entire nation.

For two reasons, however, God wanted the Levites to preface the blessings and admonitions with "Cursed be the man who will sin in secret."[57] Firstly, that the sinner in secret should not think that his sin does not matter since the rest of the people are good. "Will God be angry with the entire community for the sin of one individual?" Secondly, that the people do not despair saying: "We are all lost for perhaps one man sinned in secret and the entire community will be punished." They will know and remember that "the secret things belong unto the Lord our God and only the things that are revealed belong unto us and our children,"[58] to punish the sinners. Thus, the statement, "Cursed be the man who will sin in secret,"[59] constitutes a blessing to the entire nation, that they will not be punished for sins committed in secret. Therefore, it is stated in Joshua: "As Moses, the servant of the Lord had commanded, that they should bless the people of Israel first of all. And after he read all the words of the law the blessing and the curse."[60] (That is the way the profound meaning of these verses seem to me).

XXXII

Similarly, the rite of the breaking of the neck of a heifer[61] was not to discover the murderer — as Maimonides maintains in the *Guide of the Perplexed,* III, Chapter XI — but had a dual motive: Firstly, to strengthen the idea of the Israelites' mutual responsibility and "No expiation can be made for the land for the blood that is shed therein, but by the blood of him that shed it."[62] Consequently, since the murderer is unknown and cannot be punished, the neck of the heifer had to be broken in his place and the elders had to wash their hands, signifying, that they and the ones they represent are innocent, and their hands were not defiled by the victim's blood. Secondly, that their belief in the punishment of the land in which a murder was committed should not prompt them to kill an innocent man suspected of murder without absolute proof and clear evidence. For, although they knew that the entire people do not bear responsibility for a murderer, who killed a man in secret, they might interpret it to refer only to a case when the victim was unknown. In the given case, however, where the victim was found, the community might be punished unless they endeavor to discover the murderer.

XXXIII

The belief that God elected the people of Israel as His chosen people and concluded with their ancestors an eternal, irrevocable covenant constitutes the third foundation of the Torah of Moses and serves as a means to attain both, the perfection of virtue and the maintenance of religion.

This belief needs to be explained not by sophistic equivocation but in a way that it may be truly comprehended and not confused, by false analogy, with beliefs prevalent among other peoples of antiquity. Actually, the tendency to judge Jewish matters either by contemporary views or by those of the ancient peoples, constitutes the source of all errors encountered by the sophisticated. This is indeed a great error, since the ancient Israelites — those who adhered to the teachings of their God — were very different in their ways and ideas from both, the ancients, and the contemporaries.

XXXIV

Some of the ancient peoples worshipped a distinct deity, not worshipped by their neighbors, and believed, therefore, that it watched over them, loved them, was alien to their neighbors, and hated them for serving another god. Not so the Israelites. Their God was the

creator of everything, the God of all flesh Who had mercy on all
His creatures. Though Israel was His first-born, all peoples were
His children. He was never angry with the nations for worshipping
other deities and the prophets never said that a given nation will
be punished for worshipping wood and stone, but for the sin of
violence, abominable practices, and lack of compassion.

XXXV

Some of the nations of antiquity despised and hated others who
differed from them in knowledge and beliefs, called them "barbarians"
and considered them as animals. However, the Israelites and their
ancestors did not hate nor despise other nations. Abraham was the
confederate of the Amorites: Aner, Eshcol, and Mamre.[63] He and
his son, Isaac, made a covenant with Abimelech, the king of the
Philistines.[64] Jacob cursed the anger and wrath of two of his sons
for having killed the Shechemites, who had dishonored their sister.[65]
Judah entered into partnership with Hirah, the Adulamite.[66] Joseph
said: "How then can I do this great wickedness and sin against God?"[67]
although his master was an Egyptian. Joshua and the elders fulfilled
their oath to the Gibeonites, although they were Canaanites and
although the oath was made in error.[68] Ezekiel said that Zedekiah
will be captured by the Babylonian king because he rebelled against
him, after concluding with him a covenant and swearing allegiance to
him.[69] The prophet does not justify Zedekiah's rebellion, although
Nebuchadnezzar was an idol worshipper and a tyranical king. In
general terms he stated, that it is impossible for anyone violating a
covenant to prosper and escape. "Shall he prosper? Shall he escape
that doeth such things? Shall he break the covenant and yet escape?"[70]

XXXVI

Judaism notes the difference between Jews and other peoples, in
the fact that the Jew considers all men as the children of one Father,
created in the image of God, and that nobody should be judged

by his beliefs, but by his acts. He believes, however, that since all nations remained heathens and only Abraham clung to the one God, creator of heaven and earth, God made a covenant with him to multiply his children and be their God; to demonstrate to him His Divinity through signs and miracles, and give his children the land of Canaan. As a token of this covenant, He commanded him and his children to be circumcized. When God came to give them the Torah through Moses, He confirmed and strengthened in them this belief and said to them: "Now therefore, if ye will hearken unto My voice indeed, and keep My covenant, then ye shall be Mine own treasure from among all peoples; for all the earth is Mine."[71] All mankind is dear to Me, "and ye shall be unto Me a kingdom of priests and a holy nation."[72] And in order to impress them with this belief, He gave them many teachings and precepts that the ordinary Israelites should be on the same level as priests among other nations who, in order to sanctify them to their God, were separated from the rest of the masses by special precepts and laws.

XXXVII

The numerous precepts and laws in the Torah of Moses, are useful for the maintenance of religion, since, thereby, the Israelites are separated from the heathen nations. They are also beneficial for the perfection of virtue, for two reasons: One, by observing the Divine precepts, man is always reminded of God, Who commanded them, and the thought of God, of His Providence, and of reward and punishment, serve as deterrents which prevent man's passions to overwhelm him as well as instil in him the fear of God that he may not sin. The second reason is that the numerous precepts and laws condition man to control himself, to endure and abstain, since man is unable to overcome his passions and control himself, unless he trains himself to abstain from pleasures, and endure pain and hardship as it is written: "It is good for a man that he bear the yoke in his youth."[73] The philosopher Epictetus[74] also said, that if a man will always remember these two words, "Suffer and abstain," (*sustine et abstine*), meaning endure pain and abstain from pleasure, he will never sin and live in peace all his life.

XXXVIII

However, although the Torah strengthened the belief that Israel is the chosen people, and prevented their assimilation with the heathen nations, the Torah never differentiated between a Jew and a non-Jew with regard to the laws of justice and equity that govern interpersonal relations. The Torah did not say: "Do not murder your compatriot," "Do not commit adultery with a Jewess," "Do not steal from a Jew." (*K*). Only in four distinct cases did the Torah distinguish between a Jew and a non-Jew since they are not legally obligatory nor are they accepted even among the most righteous people. The Torah commanded these novel laws to the Israelites so that their interpersonal relations may be not only in accordance with the requirements of the law, but transcend it, as if they were all brothers. These were:

a) To lend money without interest, regardless of the rate.[75] This of course is not required by law, and limited interest is permitted by all peoples.

b) Not to ask for payment after the Sabbatical year.[76] This regulation, too, is beyond the requirement of the law and does not exist among other peoples.

c) To release slaves after six years[77]; to espouse a maid-servant or to espouse her to his son and facilitate her redemption. This, too,

---

K) This is the statement of Rabbi Abraham ben Nathan, who lived in Mayence seven hundred years ago, " 'Thou shalt not steal' is analogous to 'thou shalt not murder and thou shalt not commit adultery' which does not differentiate between a Jew and a non-Jew." (Eben Haezer p. 91.)

is beyond the requirement of the law and does not exist among other peoples.

d) Not to take vengeance nor bear a grudge,[78] is most certainly beyond the requirement of the law and constitutes rather an act of piety. What does the Bible refer to? Since the Torah already forbade to hurt a person's body or property and stated the punishment, it undoubtedly refers to the prohibition to say "I will not lend you, because you did not lend me," which is also beyond the requirement of the law.

XXXIX

In all other laws concerning equitable relations between men, however, the Torah did not differentiate between a Jew and a non-Jew. It either stated the command in general terms like: "Thou shalt not murder. Thou shalt not commit adultery. Thou shalt not steal,"[79] or employed the term neighbor (Re'a), like "thou shalt not bear false witness against thy neighbor (Bere'echa).[80] The term Re'a does not refer to co-nationals, but to everybody, as it is written, "And let them ask every man of his neighbor (Re'ehu) and every woman of her neighbor Re'utah,"[81] which shows that the Egyptians were referred to as Re'im of the Israelites. (L) The term Achicha, however, which refers to co-nationals is never employed in legal commandments. The statement "Ye shall not wrong one another" (Ish Et Achiv),[82] does not imply permissibility to defraud a non-Jew. The Torah merely employed Achicha since it concerns the sale of land, whereas a non-Jew did not possess any land in Israel. Similarly, the

L) The Sages of the Talmud, too, did not consider that the term, "neighbor," (Re'a), refers only to a Jew, for they said: "But I might here assert that you are on the horns of a dilemma. If the implication of 'his neighbor' has to be insisted upon... If (on the other hand) the implication of 'his neighbor' has not to be insisted upon..." (Baba Kamma p. 38a).

term *Achicha,* employed in the chapter dealing with restoration of lost property and assistance to lift fallen beasts,[83] does not imply that lost property of a non-Jew is permitted. For Scripture does not state: "When you see your brother's ox or his sheep driven away, do not take them for yourself" but it states: "Thou shalt not see. . . and hide thyself from them."[84] The commandment, therefore, is not to let lost property go unnoticed but take it home, an act which transcends the requirement of the law. This was also the command to assist on the road in lifting of a fallen beast. Also the prohibition "Thou shalt not hate thy brother (*Achicha*) in thy heart,"[85] goes beyond the requirement of the law, since Scripture does not refer to causless enmity, but to hating a wicked man and sinner, as is borne out by the conclusion of the verse: "Thou shalt surely rebuke thy neighbor."[86]

XL

Hence all the precepts and laws that God gave His people aim, either at the perfection of virtue, national well-being, and welfare of the people, to maintain the religion among the people, or both.

XLI

All commandments of the Torah are divided into two major categories: commandments between man and God, and commandments between man and man. The latter aim at the attainment of well-being for the group and the individual through the perfection of virtue, just, equitable, and merciful interpersonal relations, and punishment for the sinner, so that the people will take heed. However, most of the commandments between man and God are for the maintenance of religion, to remember God, fear Him and not forget Him — which is the aim of all religions in the world. Furthermore, all the Israelites should be separated and sanctified by special laws like priests among other nations. Thus, proud of the idea that they are a chosen people, a kingdom of priests and a holy nation, they will not intermingle with the heathen peoples nor imitate their acts, but always cleave to their God and follow in His righteous and holy ways. Furthermore, these commandments are useful either for the perfection of virtue in a general way, the two reasons of which had already been previously explained, (§37) or in a particular one, as it will be explained.

XLII

All dietary prohibitions are prohibitions of sanctity, designed for the separation of the Israelites and for their sanctification as priests, and not for hygienic purposes. If the Torah wished to teach the people how to guard their health, there are many other things it should have warned them about. Thus, the Torah prohibited the consumption of camel meat, though it is known that the Arabs eat it and consider it a good and wholesome food. Therefore, although some dietary prohibitions may have a special reason, it is unnecessary to look for a rationale for each one. For knowing that the general intention is that some foods should be forbidden, what difference does it make which food is forbidden.

XLIII

The prohibition of unlawful marriages was not designed, as Maimonides maintains, for the limitation of sexual intercourse, for the Torah neither prohibited polygamy — except in the case of a king — nor the frequency of intercourse with one woman. These laws, however, are for the good of society. The reason for the prohibition of sex relations with a married woman is to eliminate violence, quarrels and murders that result from adultery. Even when one willingly permits his wife to have relations with a wealthy man, it is forbidden due to the corruptive influence it is bound to have on the morals of the nation. Sodomy and bestiality are acts contrary to nature, and were such practices permitted marriage would decrease. Consanguinary relations are forbidden[87] for the sake of the preservation of domestic happiness, the perfection of virtue, and the well-being of the state. Thus, the marriage with a mother, father's wife, father's sister, and father's brother's wife, constitutes an insult to one's parents, which in turn would be injurious to morality and domestic relations. Similarly, the marriage with a daughter-in-law, who is considered like a daughter to her father-in-law and mother-in-law, will cause disrespect to the father-in-law, mother-in-law, father and son. The marriage with a woman and her daughter puts them on an equal basis and, thus, brings about the disrespect of the mother. The prohibition of marrying a woman and her sister is explained by the expression "to be a rival."[88] This means, not to cause any jealously between two sisters, turning them into rivals, hating one another instead of loving. It is well known that hatred among lovers is stronger by far than between strangers, for the intensity of the subsequent hostility equals the former love, and this causes damage to morals and to domestic happiness.

The marriage with a brother's wife, too, will cause jealousy and hatred among brothers and even the marriage of a sister-in-law, after his brother who left children died, will bring about animosity between himself and his brother's children, as well as between his children and those of his brother. This too, will damage morality and domestic happiness. This, however, is not the case when the brother died childless. The prohibition to marry a sister of the same father or the same mother, seems to be for the sake of the well-being of the state. For had the marriage of a sister been permitted, most people would have married their sisters and each family would be like a separate nation. Families would neither intermarry nor intermingle with one another and, thus, the nation would not be unified but would consist of many unrelated nationalities disliking one another.

XLIV

The cases of impurity consist of two categories, those which require an offering for their purification and those which do not. We shall begin with leprosy,[89] which constitutes the most severe impurity of the first category. Many thought that the removal of the leper was due to contagion. However, aside from the fact that the contagion of leprosy is not unanimously accepted by physicians, (M) it seems to me that if the Torah were concerned with the communicability of this disease, why are there not any regulations about other communicable diseases? Why did the Torah not command about the plague? It seems to me, therefore, that any discoloration of the skin was considered by the ancients as a sign of Divine condemnation. In their view, the leper was afflicted by God as a punishment for a terrible sin. They, therefore, kept themselves apart from him as from a man censured by God. The discoloration in a garment or house, too, was considered a sign of Divine condemnation, as if the leprous garment or house were detested by God due to a terrible sin committed in them.

Since this belief was conducive to the belief in Divine Providence and reward and punishment, the Torah confirmed it. It ordered the removal of the leper, the burning of the leprous garment, the demolition of a leprous house, as well as its sprinkling and cleasing. It

---

M) The famous physician Joannis Petrus Frank in his book *De currandis hominum morbis Epitome* §460, testified that many lepers cohabited with their healthy wives without any deleterious consequences. He also said that he saw a woman who had been afflicted with leprosy for many years and during her illness cohabited with her husband without any deleterious effects. She also conceived and gave birth to healthy children without the slightest defect.

Innumeri leprosi cum sanis uxoribus, insatiabili quidem cum libidine, sed sine dammo istarum manifesto, concumbunt. Mulierem a lepre squanosa jam multos per annos insigniter affectam, ac non modo prolium, hoc tempore genitarum, sanissimarum matrem, sed cum proprio marito, codem in lecto, sine noxa istius, cubantem, nos ipsi conspeximus.

commanded that upon his cure, the leper bring an offering. Thus, as soon as the Divine condemnation and censure, which barred the leper from God's presence is removed, he had to go to God's house, submit to Him, thank Him for having accepted him again, and implore Him not to condemn him again nor cast him away. This is the meaning of "And the priest shall make atonement for him that is to be cleansed before the Lord."[90] By the offering, God will forgive him and be gracious to him. It seems to me, that the two birds, the cedar-wood, the hyssop, the scarlet, and the sprinklings are a sign of atonement signifying that the leper is no longer condemned by God.[91] Thus the scarlet symbolizes sin, for sin was pictured red, as it is written "Though your sins be as scarlet,"[92] on account of bloodshed which constitutes the gravest sin. The cedar-wood and hyssop symbolize great and small analogous to "from the cedar that is in Lebanon even unto the hyssop that springeth out of the wall."[93] The cedar-wood, hyssop, and scarlet symbolize great and small sins. The blood of the slaughtered bird symbolizes a great cleansing i. e. cleansing of a great sin, for only life can serve as an expiation for blood. The living water symbolizes a small cleansing i. e. cleansing of a small sin. The two birds are an atonement and substitution for the leper. One was slaughtered and its blood atoned for life. The living one was joined with the sins — cedar-wood, hyssop and scarlet — dipped in blood and water and sprinkled with on the leper, as a symbol that the latter's sins were forgiven, and he returned to the state of purity. Subsequently, they sent away the living bird into the open fields signifying that the leper was permitted to leave his quarantine and go wherever he wished.

XLV

The cases of a menstruant,[94] a man or woman who has flux,[95] and a woman after childbirth[96] are similar to that of a leper. They too, appear to be condemned by God, for any discharge of blood, or involuntary emission of semen is the beginning of death and signifies that the given man or woman deserves to die. Hence we were commanded to stay away from them and not come in contact with them and, therefore, upon purification they bring an offering, and the priest has to atone for them as for the leper. The reason that the Torah did not require a menstruant to bring an offering was out of consideration for Jewish women, so as not to trouble them to leave home every month and go to the Temple. It is incorrect to say that no offering was required because it is unlikely that a woman would pray for the discontinuance of her menses, since she could have requested that her menstruation be not unduly prolonged, leading to flux. Similarly, the atonement necessary for a woman after childbirth was not to atone for having wished not to bear any more children, but to pray that she does not die in childbirth, for bleeding betokens death and the life of every woman in childbirth is in danger.

XLVI

The impurities which do not necessitate an offering for their purification are: uncleanliness contracted from a corpse,[97] uncleanliness of carrion,[98] the uncleanliness of semen unattributable to illness.[99] These do not require any atonement since they are not caused by God, but are contingent on man's will, whether to defile himself or not and conseqeuntly these defiled ones cannot be considered condemned by God. (Since we are not concerned with exceptional cases, therefore, there is no special command about the accidental defilement of a Nazirite when a man died suddenly beside him, etc.[100]) A corpse and a carrion convey impurity, for death constitutes a most severe condemnation of God. Since a leper or a Zav contaminate by contact for they are considered condemned by God, how much more so a corpse. Due to the severity of the impurity of a corpse, the person who touched it was condemned for seven days and had to be sprinkled upon with the water of purification. However, a slaughtered animal was not considered impure, since its death was not caused by Divine condemnation, but by man and for his own needs. On the other hand, the body of a slain person, though killed by man, is impure, for man is watched over by God and is subject to reward and punishment more than an animal. Consequently, when a man dies, though his death was caused by man, it is considered nevertheless a result of God's decree and His condemnation. There is, however, no such implication in the case of a slaughtered or slain animal.

The uncleanliness of semen is for the respect of the Temple and the sacrifices, so that no one may enter the Temple or partake of the offerings on the day he indulged in bodily pleasures not as essential as food and drink. It is analogous to the command which preceded the event of Revelation: "Be ready against the third day; come not near a woman."[101] This prohibition will enhance the glory of the Temple, and the offerings in the mind of the people and the importance of its service in the mind of the priests. All this was designed to instil in the priests and people the fear of God.

The sprinkling of the water of purification[102] symbolized the absolution of sin. The redness of the heifer symbolized sin. The cedarwood, the hyssop, and the scarlet symbolized great and small sins, and when burned together seemed to void these sins. The ashes symbolized the remission of the sin. Therefore, the sprinkling decontaminated the severe uncleanliness conveyed by a corpse. Although the sin was burned, it was not completely nullified, for the remaining ashes still contained something thereof which caused a light degree of contamination upon contact and had to be removed by immersion. One need not wonder why the red-heifer purified the contaminated and contaminated the pure, removed a severe form of uncleanliness and caused a lighter form. It is similar to a copper vessel which has to be first scoured with sand to remove what cannot be done by water, and subsequently rinsed with water to remove the pasted sand, as it is written: "It shall be scoured and rinsed in water."[103] The one who scours it must wash his hands of the pasted filth. Similarly, the ashes of the heifer constitute a strong detergent which removes the severe defilement to be followed by the immersion of those who occupied themselves with the water of purification and the water sprinkled upon.

XLVII

The origin of sacrifices was not by Divine command but were freely and voluntarily offered by men to God in gratitude for His goodness, as a gift to appease Him, or to induce Him to fulfill their desires. For men's attitude to God was similar to their attitude to a mortal king. Wishing to offer a gift to God, they considered burning the best mode, since, thereby, the gift was removed from their domain as well as from the domain of men, animals and fowl. Its burning and the ascension of its smoke gave them the impression that it went up to God. They called the object burned in God's honor *Kadosh* from the words *Yekod Esh* and this term *Kedushah* was subsequently applied to other things.

The Divine Torah, the aim of which is not to impart wisdom and knowledge to the people but to guide them in the path of righteousness, did not abolish the institution of sacrifices, not due to its inability but because the practice *per se* was neither bad nor harmful to people or their morals, but was rather useful. Had the Torah told the people that God does not desire burnt offerings and sacrifices they would have subsequently said: "What does it matter to God that we are just, and why mend our ways?"

Since one of the foundations of the Torah is that God observes man's actions, loves the righteous, and detests the wicked, it was imperative not to describe Him in His true ultimate sublimity but in a more comprehensible way, that people think of Him as a great king, Who understands them, hears their cries, and accepts their gifts. This need was not limited to that generation but is equally present in all generations. Had God substituted prayer, songs, scriptural reading, ethical preachings, in lieu of sacrifices, the masses would not have been that much impressed with God's greatness and awe. They would have thought the deities of the other nations, to whom their worshippers offered many sacrifies, to be far greater and more important than our God Who is served with mere words. This is the attitude of the masses in all generations, not only of the masses but of all people. Whom do they respect? They respect the pretentious and imperious person and ignore the affable and modset one. (N)

Although the true God does not need man's honor, it is considered important to instil in us the fear of Him for our sake that we do not sin. Since in those days it was impossible for people to fear God unless they brought sacrifices, He ordered them to do so. The impression that the people got from the sacrifices they offered in the Temple was that a great God and king dwells in their midst Who loves them and commands them these desirable services, and by performing them they please Him daily and cause His love for them to endure forever.

N) This is what Ezekiel said: "Wherefore I gave them also statutes that were not good, and ordinances whereby they should not live; and I polluted them in their own gifts, in that they set apart all that openeth the womb, that I might destroy them, to the end that they might know that I am the Lord. (Ezekiel XX:25-26.) The verbs "I gave" and "I polluted" indicate here, not what had taken place but what should have taken place, like "They were wont to speak in old time, saying: They shall surely ask counsel at Abel"; (II Samuel XX:18); Ye should certainly have eaten it in the sanctuary"; (Lev. X:18); "But thou shouldest not have gazed on the day of thy brother," (Obadiah I:12); and the rest (Ibid., 12; 13; 145); "Neither did thy shepherds search for My sheep" (Ezekiel XXXIV:8); and as I explained, "And Thou canst not bear with them" (Isaiah II:9); "Surely, now I had put forth My hand" (Exodus IX:15). The meaning is, that since they disregard and violate My laws and statutes which, due to their reasonableness and beneficence to the state, are for man's welfare, I should have, therefore, given them irrational laws and statutes which would be useless to the welfare of society. I should have polluted them by commanding them to offer Me gifts their first born, and by sacrificing their children, they would become desolate. Had I done this they would have revered and feared Me. Then they would have known and believed that I am the source of all good and evil, Who ought to be worshipped. For they worship their abominations and sacrifice their children (as explained Ibid., 31), not because they consider them effective nor because their laws are better than Mine but because the idols oppress their worshippers commanding them to burn their children and therefore they honor them more than Me.

XLVIII

The Torah's prohibition of the erection of private altars and its demand that all people offer their sacrifices in a special place designated by God[104] was not, heaven forbid as Maimonides maintains, to curtail the sacrificial cult, but for the good and well-being of the nation, as well as for the perfection of virtue and the maintenance of religion. By having one sanctuary for all the people, they will all meet in one place, thus, a sense of brotherhood will be engendered and they will become united forever. Thus, no tribe nor family will remain isolated. If the erection of private altars were permitted, one would have been satisfied that God was pleased with him and accepted his offerings and would remain unconcerned with the rest of the nation. The Torah, however, wishes that reward be general, for the entire nation, and all should bear mutual responsibility (*ibid.*, §31). Furthermore, the centralization of worship in one place prevented the possibility of any family or tribal deviations, ritual changes, heathen rites, practices abominable to God and sacrifices of children, for to do so the consent of the entire nation was required. (See what I wrote on Numbers XV:15.) (*O*)

O) For this reason, the Torah strictly insisted that the stranger should not deviate from the laws regulating the sacrifices. It dwelled extensively and stated: "And if a stranger sojourn with you, or whosoever be among you throughout your generations, and will offer an offering made by fire, of a sweet savor unto the Lord; as ye do, so he shall do. For the assembly, there shall be one statute for you, and for the stranger that sojourneth with you, a statute for ever throughout your generations: as ye are, so shall the stranger be before the Lord. One law and one ordinance shall be for you and for the stranger that sojourneth with you." (Numbers XV:145-16). All this was that the strangers should not gradually introduce their customs and the rites of worship among the Israelites.

XLIX

In order to impress the Israelites with the idea that God is in their midst, is their king and leader, observes their deeds and rewards them accordingly — an idea inconceivable by the masses unless concretized — communal sacrifices were instituted which necessitated a tabernacle and Temple for Divine worship.[105] The Temple had to be like a royal palace, with a table and candelabrum. On the table had to be a row of bread-loaves, and utensils for the table like dishes and spoons. Since it was customary to offer victuals to God, foods and drinks had to be brought to our King. The sacrifices represented food, and the libations, drink. The priests were like the attendants who surround a king and serve him and the high priest was like the chief minister. The Temple and its vessels, the priests and their garments had to be ostentatious to impress the people with the greatness of the King dwelling there, that they may fear Him and abstain from sin. While formerly, when private altars were permitted, the service could be performed by any man or by the first-born, at the time of centralization of worship, one family acted on behalf of the entire people. As dedicated to God's service, this family had to be free of any other work or occupation, and since it served in the Temple on behalf of the entire people, it had to be supported by them.[106] The Torah, however, left it to the discretion of every Israelite to give the priestly allotment to priest or Levite of his choice. Since the latter were not equally pious, the Torah did not insist that they be maintained uniformally. As a result, the priests and the Levites would endeavor to please the people with their good conduct and righteous deeds.

L

The Torah similarly, endeavored to impress the soldiers who leave their country for war with this belief that God dwells in their midst. by commanding: "When thou goest forth in camp against thine enemies, then thou shalt keep thee from every evil thing. If there be among you any man that is not clean... thou shalt have a place... For the Lord thy God walketh in the midst of thy camp... therefore shall thy camp be holy..."[107] This was — as Maimonides maintains — to strengthen in the soldiers the belief that the Divine presence is in their midst, that they do not become unbridled, casting off the teachings of the Torah and morality, as most soldiers in antiquity.

LI

The sacrifices of the individual were for the sake of the individual to be offered on various occasions.[108] When one prospered he offered a sacrifice of thanksgiving to God. This was designed to impress him that his prosperity came from God and consequently this man will trust in God, mend his ways that God may continue to love him and be kind to him. When in trouble, man would pray to God and pledge a sacrifice to be offered when the Lord will save him. Then upon his deliverance he will fulfill his pledge, impressed thereby, that it was God who had saved him. When a man committed a sin inadvertently, he brought a sacrifice which impressed him that God pardoned him and again accepted him. Had there not been any atonement for an unintentional sin, the sinner would have thought: "Who shall save me from this stern God? If on account of an unintentional sin He cast me away in His anger without any hope to appease Him, I may as well continue to sin." For this reason the deliberate sinner was not supposed to bring any sacrifice that he should not get the impression, entertained by the people of antiquity, that God receives bribes from sinners and forgives their iniquities. (P)

P) The idolatrous people of antiquity believed that their deities could be bribed by sacrifices, do what their devotees desire, and fulfill their requests regardless whether their deeds were satisfactory or not. This was also the error of Korach and his company who, unlike the heretics, did not deny Moses' mission, for otherwise, they would not have said: "All the congregation are holy, every one of them and the Lord

There are only three sins which require a sacrifice since it is possible for a man to commit them without realizing that they constitute a sinful act.

a) He who "hears a voice of adjuration, he being a witness, whether he has seen or known"[109] and fails to testify. Anyone adjured to offer the testimony may abstain rationalizing "no one can compel me to involve myself to testify in a dispute not of my concern? Why should I harm the other party?"

b) He who "deals falsely with his neighbor in matter of deposit, or of pledge, or of robbery or have oppressed his neighbors or have found that which was lost and deal falsely therein and swear to a lie."[110] The sacrifice[111] is not an atonement for the robbed goods which he must restore but for perjury. The sinner reasons "I swore falsely to obtain the money, but now having restored it, I am no longer sinful."

c) "Whosoever lies carnally with a woman that is a bondmaid, designated for a man, and not all redeemed nor was freedom given to her"[112] and the master uses her as a slave as well as a sexual partner. This is against the will of the blessed Lawgiver who wants the master to set her free and marry her "after the manner of the daughters" otherwise she is *Bikoreth,* ownerless — as Nachmanides interprets it — free for everybody. No one having relations with her may be prosecuted on the charge of adultery, since she was not released. Such a charge applies only to a free woman whose marital status is legally recognized. This it is stated concerning a war-captive: "Thou shalt not deal with her as a slave because thou hast humbled her."[113] On one hand this bondmaid belongs to the master who

is among them" (Numbers XVI:3). They believed, however, that after Moses had been initiated by God and learned from Him the rites of worship acceptable to Him, he did whatever he pleased, and God consented just like a person who readily agrees when persuaded. (See my comments on Isaiah I:11.)

bought her and supports her. She must, therefore, not be promiscuous, and anyone having relations with her commits a sin. On the other hand she is ownerless, for the Torah penalized her master that until he sets her free she should not be considered his wife. There is, therefore, a mitigating aspect for the man who has relations with her, which could be atoned by a sacrifice.

We are not concerned here with the guilt offerings in the cases of Temple misappropriation, Nazirite, leper and suspensive guilt offering, for these are brought either for unintentional sins or for sins of which the sinner is unaware.

In the case of misappropriation, it is explicitly stated: "If anyone commit a trespass, and sin through error, in the holy things of the Lord."[114] The Nazirite brings a sacrifice to atone for a previous sin of which he was not aware and for which he was condemned by God who rejected the Nazirite causing his defilement by the sudden death of a man. The leper, too, as it was already stated, is condemned by God though he is unaware of the reason. In a suspensive guilt offering it is explicitly stated "concerning the error which he committed."[115]

LII

The individual sacrifices served yet another purpose, in that the sacrificial meat given to the owner, after the priests got their share, could not be left until the following day or the day thereafter,[116] nor could it be preserved to be consumed with the family outside of Jerusalem but had to be shared in company with other people. Thus, when a man fulfilled his vow to God for a kindness received, he had to make others rejoice with him.[117]

Thereby he entered into fellowship with people he never knew or had at least to share his meal with the poor and destitute. Therefore, in the portion of Kedoshim after mentioning "And when ye offer a sacrifice of peace-offerings unto the Lord... it shall be eaten the same day ye offer it, and on the morrow... and if it be eaten at all on the third day... But every one that eateth it shall bear his iniquity,"[118] it is immediately followed by another precept, seemingly unrelated, "And when ye reap the harvest of your land, thou shalt not wholly reap the corner of thy field," [119] to indicate that the precept of consuming the sacrifice within a day or two days is comparable to the precept of leaving the corner of the field because both aim at the furtherance of generosity and kindness.

LIII

The aim of the Sabbath for the Israelite differs from its aim for slaves and animals. For the latter, it is a matter of compassion and kindness, whereas for the former, who as a free man may rest at any time, it has another meaning. To begin with the precept of the Sabbath, as all prohibitions of sanctity, was designed to give the Israelites a feeling of importance. Resting on the day that the Lord rested after having created heaven and earth, [120] they would consider themselves a kingdom of priests and a holy nation. Consequently, the Sabbath constitutes a sign between God and Israel marking their covenantal relationship. In addition, the Sabbath is important for the perfection of virtue, national well-being, and the maintenance of religion. Indeed, everyone rests occasionally and enjoys some serenity. However, by everyone choosing his own day of rest, aside from personal satisfaction, no benefit will result. But when the entire nation will rest on the same day, good fellowship will be promoted by eating and drinking together, having talks with one another, as well as listening to scholars and sages lecture on Torah and ethics. Sabbath is the day on which the rich and the poor, the master and the slave, the small and the great, are equal, and the slave is free from his master. It, therefore, makes the wealthy modest, and reminds them that we are all the children of one Father.

LIV

The aim of the three major festivals is the same as that of the Sabbath, though their beneficial aspects are even more universal. Thus, on the Sabbath, only the people of the same town can get together, whereas on the festivals the entire nation is able to congregate, which promotes national cohesion, good fellowship, as well as religious observance, as was explained (§XLVIII) as the reason for centralization of worship.

The times designated for these festivals are: the time of harvest, *Shavuoth*,[121] the time of ingathering, *Succoth*,[122] when the landowners are happy, and thus celebrate the festival of God with joy and delight, grateful for His bounty. Passover[123] commemorates the deliverance from Egypt. On *Rosh Hashanah*[124] the shofar is blown to herald the beginning of the New Year, just as we blow shofar in the Jubilee year to herald freedom.[125] In the Jubilee year the shofar was blown on the tenth day of the month to differentiate between the Jubilee year and the ordinary years. The tenth day, thus, was singled out as the first festival after *Rosh-Hashanah*. The precept of the Day of Atonement[126] aimed at strengthening the belief in God's goodness and kindness, and at instilling in us our love for Him and trust in Him.

The precept of *matzah* was added on Passover to commemorate the haste with which the Egyptian king dispatched the Israelites, though previously he kept them by force.[127] This attests that it was God who compelled Pharaoh to surrender. The precept of *Succah* was added on the festival of ingathering that the people remember that the good land they enjoy was given to them by Divine grace, for their ancestors dwelt in tents possessing neither houses nor fields.[128] The four species[129] symbolized the quality of the land which produces big and beautiful, fragrant and delectable trees, and plentitude of water (symbolized by the willows). By taking these species, the people rejoiced in the quality of their land, and expressed their gratitude to God Who gave it to them.

LV

The commandment of the Sabbatical year[130] is similar to that of the Sabbath. Just as the aim of the latter was to strengthen in the people the belief that they are a holy nation, the commandment of the Sabbatical year aimed at instilling in them that their land, too, is holy since it has to rest in the seventh year, as God rested on the seventh day. (See the words of Don Isaac Abravanel in *Nachlath Aboth,* Chapter III *Mishnah, Galuth Baah L'olam Ki Naemu*). Furthermore, just as God had given them food in the wilderness on the sixth day to last for two days, so, when dwelling in their land, God will bless their produce on the sixth year to suffice for the Sabbatical year.

The belief in the holiness of the land constituted a strong deterrent for the people not to contaminate it nor desecrate it by abominable deeds. Furthermore, as a result of the rest of the land, the slaves and animals, too, will get some rest similar to the kind they enjoy on the Sabbath.

The fact that the produce of the Sabbatical year was ownerless, constituted an act of compassion to the poor. It also equalized the rich with the poor, diminished the vanity of the wealthy and reminded them that all men were alike. The remission of the debts,[131] too, constituted an act of compassion and kindness to the poor.

LVI

Just as the people were given, in addition to the rest of the seventh day, other holidays on which to rest and rejoice before God, the Holy Land, too, received the Jubilee year[132] in addition to the

Sabbatical year. (Q) The latter, like the Sabbath, also equalized the rich and the poor by cessation of work in the field and by declaring all produce ownerless. Moreover, the restoration of the land to the original owners and the liberation of the slaves constituted great acts of compassion for the poor and a strong factor for the equality of all the people of the state.

LVII

The object of the commandment of the firstling,[133] the heave-offering,[134] the first-fruit,[135] and the first shearing,[136] are for the maintenance of religion, that man be mindful that everything is from God, thank Him on the day of his joy and give Him the first things of which God had endowed him. Giving it to God's servants, the priests, is as if he had given it to God.

Since these gifts are not burned but given to the priests, it helps to support them. For the maintenance of the Levites, we were ordered to give tithe. In order for the latter, too, to be mindful of God, they were told to give the priests tithe out of the tithe they received. The priests themselves, however, were not required to set aside anything for God from their heave-offering, on account of their great holiness, but were merely commanded to eat it in purity which will suffice to remind them of their sanctity.

LVIII

There is another type of heave-offering, fruit of the fourth year[187] and the second tithe[138] which had to be consumed by the owner only

---

Q) There is one Jubilee for every seven Sabbatical years, and one festival for seven Sabbaths of the year. For the annual Sabbaths are more than forty-nine but less than fifty-six and the festivals are seven; the first and the seventh day of Passover, one day of Shavuoth, one day of Rosh Hashanah, one day of Yom Kippur, first day of Succoth, the Day of Shemini Atzereth together constitute seven. However, all this may or may not be merely coincidental.

in Jerusalem. The reasons for eating in the place singled out by the Lord were manifold. The stay in the holy city in which the Temple is situated will bring about the fear of God and the recognition of His greatness, as it is stated "That thou mayest learn to fear the Lord thy God always."[139] Furthermore, the gathering of all people to eat and rejoice in one city will strengthen national unity and cause people to meet and become friendly as well as love their nation.

The fruit of the fourth year was "holy for giving praise unto the Lord,"[140] as an expression of gratitude to God for the fruit of the new tree. Since the Torah wanted that its first fruit be "holy for giving praise unto the Lord" it, therefore, ordered — as maintained by Gersonides — to wait until the fourth year, that it may be praisworthy and wholesome. Until then it was considered defective and forbidden as the bread, parched corn, and fresh grain prior to the offering the *Omer*.

LIX

To strengthen in the people the idea of their sanctity and chosenness the Torah stated: "Ye are the children of the Lord your God, ye shall not cut yourself nor make any baldness between your eyes for the dead. For thou art a holy people unto the Lord thy God."[141] "Ye shall not round the corners of your heads, neither shalt thou mar the corners of thy beard. Ye shall not make any cuttings in your flesh for the dead"[142] — is to be included according to the opinion of some scholars, as quoted by Abraham Ibn Ezra.[143] The practices of disfiguration, baldness and marring of one's beard, aside from inflicting harm and pain to the body, cause man to act foolishly, impetuously, instead of learning patience which gives life, peace and saves us from sin (§XXXVII).

In order to impress the priests and the people with the sanctity of the priesthood, these prohibitions were reiterated with special emphasis for the priests: "They shall not make baldness upon their head, neither shall they shave off the corners of their beard, nor make any cuttings in their flesh. They shall be holy unto their God."[144] In addition they were not permitted to defile themselves other than to close relatives, and the High Priest was not permitted to contaminate himself even to his parents.[145]

It is important to note that the Torah appreciates constructive compassion and kindness which influence man to be useful and of assistance to his fellow man, but frowns upon empty sentimentality which causes one to mourn excessively, disfigure himself, and make himself bald over the dead. For this is not a good trait, but shows irrationality and lack of faith in God. The Torah, however, wants all the people to believe strongly in God, even more so the priests and the High Priest most of all.

LX

To maintain religion and prevent the Israelites from defecting from the true God, the Torah forbade not only idol-worship, but commanded that there not be in our midst "one that uses divination, a soothsayer, or an enchanter, or a sorcerer, or a charmer, or one that consulteth a ghost, a familiar spirit or a necromancer,"[146] since all these cause man to place his trust in someone other than God. Therefore, anyone dealing with them or trusting in them is like an idol-worshipper. For this very reason all kinds of mixtures were prohibited — "Thou shalt not let thy cattle gender with a diverse kind; thou shalt not sow thy field with two kinds of seed; neither shall there come upon thee a garment of two kinds of stuff mingled together."[147]

It was due to the special significance and importance the heathens attached to the combination of diverse kinds believing, thereby, to unite the various deities, of which each governs a different kind. Since this constitutes a denial of monotheism, the Torah objected to it.

LXI

Finally the precepts of *Mezuzah*,[148] *Zizith*[149] *Tephillin*[150], are for the maintenance of religion, that we always remember God and His Torah, as it is explicitly stated in the Torah: "That ye may look upon it, and remember all the commandments of the Lord,"[151] . . . "And it shall be for a sign unto thee upon thy hand, and for a memorial between thine eyes that the law of the Lord may be in thy mouth."[152]

Notes

FIRST PREFACE

1. Psalms XCIV:12.
2. Shabbath 112b.
3. I Samuel XVIII:14.
4. Paraphrase of Deut. XXXII:32.
5. Jeremiah XV:10.
6. *Ibid.*
7. *Ibid.*
8. *Ibid.*, XX:9.
9. Psalms CXIX:162.
10. *Ibid.*, 71. In the Hebrew text some of the letters of this verse are printed in bold type טוב לי כי עניתי למען אלמד חקיך their numerical equivalent is 602 representing the Hebrew year 5602 or 1842 C.E.

SECOND PREFACE

1. Psalms XXXVI:2, 4.
2. *Ibid.*, XIV:2.
3. *Ibid.*, XCIV:7-8.
4. Deut XXXII:29-30.
5. Iob XI:9.
6. Psalms XXXVII:25.

FOUNDATIONS OF THE TORAH

1. Ex. III:15.
2. Gen. XX:17-18.
3. *Ibid.*, XVIII:19.
4. *Ibid.*
5. *Ibid.*, XVII:7-14.
6. *Ibid.*, XXXII:25-33.
7. Lev. XIX:9.

8. Deut. XXIV:19.

9. Lev. XIX:9.

10. Ex. XXII:24; Lev. XXV:36-37; Deut. XXIII:20.

11. Lev. XXV:36-37.

12. Deut. XXIV:10-13.

13. *Ibid.*, 6.

14. *Ibid.*, 17.

15. Ex. XXII:25.

16. *Ibid.*, 26.

17. *Ibid.*,

18. Deut. XV:9-10.

19. Ex. XXI:2.

20. *Ibid.*

21. *Ibid.*, 20.

22. *Ibid.*

23. *Ibid.*, 26-27.

24. *Ibid.*, 10; XXIII:12; Deut. V:14.

25. Deut. XXI:10-13.

26. *Ibid.*, 14.

27. Deut. XXV:4.

28. *Ibid.*, XXII:10.

29. Lev. XXII:28.

30. Ex. XX:10; Deut. V:14.

31. Deut. XXII 6-7.

32. Lev. XXII:27; Ex. XXII:29.

33. Ex. XXIII:19; XXXIV:26; Deut. XIV:21.

34. Mishnah, Yadaim, IV:6.

35. Ex. XXII:26.

36. Ex. XXXIV:6.

37. Deut. X:18.

38. I Kings XX:31.

39. Ex. XII:27; XIII:14-16.

40. *Ibid.*, XIII:6-8.

41. *Ibid.*, XIII:1-2, 15; Num. III:13; XVIII:17-18.

42. Ex. III:21-22.

43. Ex. III:21; XI:3; XII:36.

44. *Ibid.*, XII:35.

45. Samuel Cahen (1796-1862), founder of the *Archives Israelites* and translator of the Bible into French.

46. Deut. XX:16-18.

47. Lev. XVIII:26-28.

48. Gen. XV:16.
49. Deut. IX:4.
50. *Ibid.*, XXV:19.
51. *Ibid.*, 16.
52. *Ibid.*, 18.
53. I Samuel XV.
54. Deut. XXVII:15-26.
55. *Ibid.*, XXVIII:1.
56. *Ibid.*, 15.
57. *Ibid.*, XXVII:15.
58. *Ibid.*, XXIX:28.
59. *Ibid.*, XXVII:15.
60. Joshua VIII:33.
61. Deut. XXI:1-9.
62. Num. XXXV:33.
63. Gen. XIV:13.
64. *Ibid.*, XXI:22-34; XXVI:26-33.
65. *Ibid.*, XLIX:5-7.
66. *Ibid.*, XXXVIII.
67. *Ibid.*, XXXIX:9.
68. Joshua IX:18-19.
69. Ezekiel XVII:15.
70. *Ibid.*
71. Ex. XIX:5.
72. *Ibid.*, 6.
73. Lamentations III:27.
74. Greek philosopher and moralist of the first century C.E.
75. Ex. XXII:24; Deut. XXIII:20-21.
76. Deut. XV:1-3.
77. *Ibid.*, 12-18.
78. Lev. XIX:18.
79. Ex. XX:13.
80. *Ibid.*
81. *Ibid.*, XI:2.
82. Lev. XXV:14.
83. Deut. XXII:1-4.
84. *Ibid.*, 1.
85. Lev. XIX:17.
86. *Ibid.*
87. Lev. XVIII.
88. *Ibid.*, XVIII:18.

89. *Ibid.*, XIII-XIV.
90. Luzzatto's quotation is incorrect. He paraphrased two verses in Leviticus XIV:18-19.
91. *Ibid.*, 4-7.
92. Isaiah I:18.
93. I Kings V:13.
94. Lev. XV:19-24.
95. *Ibid.*, 1-18; 25-30.
96. *Ibid.*, XII:1-8.
97. Num. XIX:11-22.
98. Lev. XI:31-44.
99. *Ibid.*, XV:16-18.
100. Num. VI:9.
101. Ex. XIX:15.
102. Num XIX:1-22.
103. Lev. VI:21.
104. Deut. XII:1-28.
105. Ex. XXV-XL.
106. Deut. XVIII:1-8.
107. *Ibid.*, XXIII:10-15.
108. Lev. I-VII.
109. *Ibid.*, V:1.
110. *Ibid.*, 21-22.
111. *Ibid.*, 25.
112. *Ibid.*, 20-21.
113. Deut. XXI:14.
114. Lev. V:15.
115. *Ibid.*, 18.
116. *Ibid.*, VII:15-18.
117. *Ibid.*, XIX:9.
118. *Ibid.*, XIX:5-8.
119. *Ibid.*, XIX:9.
120. Ex. XX:8-11.
121. Lev. XXIII:15-21
122. *Ibid.*, 33-43.
123. *Ibid.*, 5-8.
124. *Ibid.*, 24-25.
125. *Ibid.*, XXV:9.
126. *Ibid.*, XXIII:26-32.
127. Ex. XII:39.
128. Lev. XXIII:42-43.

129. *Ibid.*, 40-41.
130. *Ibid.*, 1-7.
131. Deut. XV:1-11.
132. Lev. XXV:8-55.
133. Deut. XV:19-23.
134. Lev. XVIII:8-20.
135. Deut. XXVI:1-11.
136. *Ibid.*, XVIII:5.
137. Lev. XIX:23-25.
138. Deut. XIV:22-27.
139. *Ibid.*, 23.
140. Lev. XIX:24.
141. Deut. XIV:1-2.
142. Lev. XIX:27-28.
143. See Ibn Ezra Commentary on Lev. XXI:5.
144. Lev. XXI:5-6.
145. *Ibid.*, 1-12.
146. Deut. XVIII:10-11.
147. Lev. XIX:19.
148. Deut. VI:9.
149. Num. XV:37-41.
150. Ex. XIII:9; Deut. VI:8.
151. Num. XV:39.
152. Ex. XIII:9.

SALANTER'S MUSAR MOVEMENT

A Quest for Excellence
in Character Education

by

ZALMAN F. URY

EDITOR'S INTRODUCTION

A contemporary theologian and philosopher, Paul Tillich, maintains that in the course of history the human predicament expressed itself in three different forms. Ancient man was obssessed with the fear of death; medieval man was overwhelmed by a sense of guilt and modern man has an apprehension of the meaninglessness of life.

In Judaism, throughout its long history, man's existential situation was dominated by an overwhelming passion for life's meaningfulness. The crucial issue in Judaism was not between life and death, innocence and guilt, but between a life that is meaningful and a life that is stagnant.

There were several roads leading to a meaningful and self-fulfilling life. The cognitive, the pragmatic, the pietistic, the meditative. The Musar movement attempted to combine the cognitive with the pragmatic. It aimed at behavior modification through a coalescence of the theoretical with the applicational. The often quoted Talmudic dictum seems to express this notion: פלוני שלמד תורה, ראו כמה נאים דרכיו, וכמה מתוקנים מעשיו (יומא פ"ו) "Observe how beautiful are the ways and how perfect the deeds of one who has studied the Torah" (Tal. B. Yoma 86).

The unique contribution of Salanter's Musar is in its attempt to bridge the behavior gap between one's knowledge of the ideal good and failure to live by this knowledge. While the road to moral excellence is arduous involving self-understanding, self-evaluation, self-discipline, Salanter believes that human nature is perfectible.

The author of this significant study has concentrated on the educational implications of the Musar Movement. The copious works by Rabbi Dov Katz in Hebrew and Rabbi Kopul Rosen and Menahem Glen in English have covered the general background, history and contribution of the movement. The major thrust of this monograph, based on Dr. Ury's doctoral dissertation, is psycho-educational utilizing Salanter's methods for transforming cognitive knowledge into attitudinal knowledge. Draw-

Originally published by Yeshiva University Press, 1967.

223

ing upon Salanter's writings,[1] and the works of his disciples[2] as well as modern psychological research, the author affirms Musar's relevance for modern man and proposes the appointment of *mashgiah*-type ethics counselors in elementary and secondary schools.

Dr. Ury is a lecturer in education and ethics at the West Coast Division of Yeshiva University. He serves also as Head Consultant of the Bureau of Jewish Education of the Jewish Federation — Council of Greater Los Angeles in charge of all traditional schools in the area, as well as spiritual leader of Young Israel of Beverly Hills. Ordained at Beth Medrash Govoha, Dr. Ury earned a Doctor of Education degree at the University of California majoring in educational philosophy, psychology and ethics.

This study is the first to emanate from a member of the faculty of our West Coast Division. It was my privilege to have been appointed by our learned President Dr. Samuel Belkin seven years ago to help in the establishment of the school. Dr. Ury was the first lecturer to be appointed as a member of our faculty in our Teachers Institute, in which capacity he has served ever since with distinction and dedication.

As always, I am deeply indebted to our dynamic President Dr. Belkin for encouraging the publication of the creative works of our people. I am also appreciative to my distinguished colleague and co-worker Dr. Sidney B. Hoenig for assisting in the editing of this study.

---

1. *T'vunah, Or Yisrael, Even Yisrael.*

2. *Or Yisrael* by Blazer (Reb Itzele Peterburger) ; *Hokmah Umusar* by Braude ("Der Alter of Kelm") and *Madregat ha Adam* by Hurwitz ("Der Alter" of Navarodock) *Daat Hokmah Umusar,* by Yeruhum Levovitz of Mirer Yeshivah and *Miktav ma-Eliyohu* by Eliezer E. Dessler of Ponovetz Yeshiva.

PREFACE

The course of human history is marked by a reciprocal relationship between man's theoretical faculties and his practical skills. Without ideas civilization would not have been possible. Without technical know-how, ideas could not have been implemented. Faced with the ever present struggle for survival, and driven by needs and incentives, men have come to know that their very existence is predicated on a harmonious *combination* of intellectual power with technical competence. To be sure, intelligence, being more distinctly human than mere activity, gives direction and lends meaning to man's work. Yet, the value of ideas can only be tested and realized in real life situations. Society can function only when ideas are put to work.

In such instances where theory was not properly applied to life's realities men made little advance. The field of ethics, in which humanity has made insufficient progress, serves as a somber illustration that without *interaction* between thought and deed there can be no meaningful achievement.

Moral philosophers have been concerned with the discovery of what is good and right. Some philosophers have developed *Normative Ethics,* a system of general ethical principles that are valid and defensible. Other moral philosophers have refuted the claim that there are universally valid ethical norms. Basing themselves on anthropological and psychological facts and theories, they argue that there are few, if any, universally valid ethical principles. What is right in one society, may be considered wrong in another. Accordingly, they have formulated relative or critical ethics, known as *Metaethics.*

Moral philosophers are commonly concerned with such questions as "What kind of acts ought men to perform?" and "What sort of acts ought men to avoid?" Utilitarians answer, that men ought to do such acts that lead to good *consequences,* and avoid those acts which produce bad consequences. Intuitionists reply, that men must guide themselves by the approval or disapproval of their moral sense, or *conscience.*

225

There are some moral questions which philosophers do not consider at all, at least as professional philosophers, although they must answer such questions in daily life, like everybody else. Such questions are *specific* questions about *specific* situations. For example, should I make a substantial contribution to charity or spend most of the money on a new car? My friend is seeking my advice regarding a business venture. Am I obligated to give him sound counsel though he may become my competitor? Answering such questions is not the philosopher's task, as a philosopher. What he is usually concerned with is the formulation of general principles which may have some clues for answering particular questions. Thus many moral philosophers had separated thought from deed and removed themselves from the daily affairs of men.

As a result, the *practice* of morality was not considered the professional duty of the moral philosopher; it became the task of the moralist. This is unfortunate for the development of ethical theory and practice. Whereas ideally ethics should have been every person's pursuit, philosophers have shown, by example, that this need not be so. Ethics, instead of becoming a universal endeavor, became the almost exclusive concern of the moralist. The philosopher became the ethical theoretician and the moralist the practitioner, with the average man receiving little guidance from either. This dichotomy between ethical theory and practice may be considered as one of the causes for the failure of humanistic ethics to regulate human conduct.

There are a few more apparent weaknesses in humanistic ethics. Secular moral philosophers have seldom been albe to awaken in man a *love* for the good or to stimulate them to *do* right. Even if we grant there is within man a desire to do what is right, that desire, by itself is generally not strong enough to overcome passion and those social forces which are opposed to the right and good. These philosophers, by creating a division between thought and deed and by injecting too much scientific objectivity in their ethical systems, have not generated the necessary moral *incentive* or *motive*. Without such motivation one does not usually behave ethicaliy if temptation or selfish interests stand in his way.

A secular moral philosophy may present men with an *ideal*, to be followed, but seldom offers the example of one who follows it. And this is regrettable, for some of the finest moral qualities are attained through the *influence* of ethical persons and *participation* in the life of a moral community.

The history of Jewish ethics is *not* marked by a dichotomy between cognition and action. Jewish ethical thinkers have generally been moralists who lived what they preached. Having set a good personal example, some Jewish moralists have usually been able to elicit people's love for morality and the needed motivation to live morally.

Rabbi Israel Salanter, an ethical thinker and a practicing moralist of the highest order, is a classic example of what Jewish ethics, or Musar, can do for men. Salanter's life and thought are a reaffirmation of the optimistic traditional belief that man can be his own moral master. As a moral philosopher, Salanter dealt with *ends,* and as a moralist he was concerned with *means.* He concentrated unswervingly on the *combined* task of formulating the "why" and the "how" of ethics. By being a living example of the good man, Salanter inspired others to do good and thus the Musar Movement came into being.

Salanter's Musar, and the teachings of the later masters of Musar, is a normative ethics because it is based on the revealed universal truths of Torah. Though a religious ethics, it is *not* authoritarian for it allows and encourages individual differences and expressions. It is a *balanced* ethics because it combines man's cognitive faculties with his emotive powers. Musar does not entirely depend on man's conscience, for it takes into consideration man's vulnerability to the intricate influence of his subconscious drives. It does agree that the moral act is a *means* to good consequences, but also sees *intrinsic good* in the performance of a Mitzvah. *Musar* may be described as an eclectic ethical theory, placing special emphasis on the importance of the *interplay* of thought and deed. In Musar, the idea and the act are inextricably intermingled.

Chapter I

HISTORICAL BACKGROUND

Introduction

Because ethics is so important to Judaism it is no wonder that over the centuries there developed a considerable musar literature. Suffice it to mention here two of the major moralists. The first one to formulate a system of Jewish ethics was probably Bahya ben Joseph Ibn Pakudah (circa 1050-1120). In his classical work *Hovot Ha-l'vavot* (Duties of the Heart), Bahya placed the duties of the heart above other commandments.[3] Moshe Hayim Luzzatto (1707-1747), the versatile mystic, poet and Talmudist expressed his abiding concern for man's search for meaning when he coined the immortal phrase "Mah hovato b'olamo?" (What is man's duty in this world?). Luzzatto evolved his ethical theory into a total *weltanschauung* based on reverence for G-d and man.

> Said he: The foundation for saintliness and the root of perfection in the service of G-d lies in a man's coming to see clearly and to recognize as a truth the nature of his duty in the world and the end towards which he should direct his vision and his aspiration in all of his labors all the days of his life.[4]

Bahya and Luzzatto, and other major moralists, have given Musar scope and depth and transformed it into a systematic Jewish worldview. Yet, their ethical theories remained sealed in their books, sharing the fate of many other great ideas which lie dormant within scholarly folios.

It was the destiny of Rabbi Israel Lipkin (1810-1883), known as Reb Yisroel Salanter, to redeem the great Musar teachings of the past from obscurity. Salanter, one of the most prominent nineteenth-century Lithuanian Talmudists, went beyond the preservation of the

229

works of the past masters; he became one of the greatest moralists of all time.

In his youth Salanter had been exposed to two distinct modes of thought and conduct. His father, a well known Lithuanian Talmid Hakham, represented the world of scholarship. His learned mother embodied the nobility of man's spirit and kindness of heart. The young boy must have learned from his parents that there are many dimensions to human existence and many levels of greatness — a lesson which was to remain with him through life.

When Salanter matured and became known as a *Gaon* (genius), he must have come to know more nuances and additional qualities in men and their ideas. Indeed, it seems that a historical dialectic was at work in his background. Rabbi Elijah Gaon of Vilna (1720-1797), the acknowledged master of Lithuanian scholars, was an individualist on a grand scale. His chief follower, Rabbi Haim ben Isaac of Volozhin (1749-1821), took a different road; he engaged actively in communal affairs and built the famous Volozhin Yeshivah. His student, Rabbi Zundel of Salanty (1785-1865), returned to the extreme individualism of the Goan, only to see his disciple, Rabbi Israel Salanter follow a different path altogether. Salanter was both, an individualist and a social reformer. The dialectical ebb and flow of ideas of three generations of masters had culminated in Salanter's *Musar synthesis,* expressed in the individualist's concern for the social order while retaining his individual spiritual privacy.

As Salanter studied the community, its mores, standards and problems, he became concerned and anxious. Men, he observed, conceive of religion primarily in terms of ritual, failing to give sufficient attention to moral precepts. *Musar, decided Salanter, must be applied towards social reform.* Men must be taught that to be truly religious means to serve man while serving G-d.[5]

When Salanter reached this decision he left the little Lithuanian town of Salanty and began traveling extensively from community to community and from country to country — something unusual for a nineteenth-century rabbi. Salanter's life-long efforts were directed towards men, not just books. He published very little, but succeeded to create the Musar Movement which lives on to this day.

Salanter's Definition of Musar

Musar, the Hebrew term for ethics, has a complex etymological structure. It is a comprehensive concept containing several meanings and connotations. Musar refers to chastisement, reproof, admonition, exhortation, instruction, prohibition, transmission, discipline, politeness, proper conduct and imprisonment.[6]

Musar posits ultimate authority in G-d and His Law. The religious ethic espoused by Musar is an all-embracing morality which recognizes no distinction between moral law and statutory law. In Judaism *morality and law are one.*

Salanter's unique contribution to Mussar consists in his formulation of Musar as a dynamic process and adding to it a psychological dimension. Salanter's theory of Musar includes such elements as introspection, self-criticism, self-discipline and continuous emotional involvement and stimulation. Salanter's definition of Musar is *a life-long process of self-improvement,* service to man and reverence for G-d.

Differences Between Musar and Hasidism

The eighteenth-century Hasidic Movement, founded by Rabbi Israel Baal Shem Tov (circa 1689-1759) developed into a vibrant mass movement, gaining momentum even in twentieth-century America. Salanter's nineteenth-century Musar Movement never became a mass movement. Why did not Musar appeal to the masses? A brief analysis of the nature of these movements should help us understand their historical differences, and, in turn, bring out some of the salient points of Salanter's Musar.

Let us first begin by dispelling some popular misconceptions about both, Hasidism and Musar. Musar, we are told, represents somber Lithuanian scholasticism, devoid of enthusiasm and emotion, whereas non-scholastic Hasidism offers a dynamic, emotional and happy way of life. It is therefore claimed that Hasidism appeals to the masses and Musar to scholars only. It is the opinion of this writer that these allegations are based on a narrow and oversimplified interpretation of both movements.

It is true that there have been some excesses among certain Hasidim
to the point of anti-intellectualism. Likewise *some* Musarites have
gone to the other extreme of negating the satisfactions and joys of
living — something that Luzzatto, for example, had strongly opposed.[7]
But one ought not judge a movement by its splinter-groups. There is
sufficient scholarship in the mainstream of Hasidism, and Salanter's
Musar, as we shall demonstrate later in this study, is based on
psychological and emotional foundations, not only intellectual ones.
Musar and Hasidism, then, are not mutually exclusive.

A most interesting assertion was made by the late Rabbi Abraham
E. Kaplan that Salanter intended to synthesize Lithuanian scholarship
with Hasidism through Musar, rather than to oppose Hasidism.[8] This
writer is not convinced that this was Salanter's original intent.
However, that later Musar masters such as the late Rabbi Elijah E
Dessler, for example, would seek such synthesis, remains within the
range of probability.

Having asserted that Hasidism and Musar share some common
elements, we now turn to evaluate the causes responsible for the
popularity of the former and the exclusiveness of the latter. We will
first take up that which may be considered an open question namely,
did Salanter ever intend to organize a mass movement?

There seem to be some contradictions in Salanter's teachings and
practices regarding this issue.[9] It is true that Salanter taught that
every person, man or woman, scholar or non-scholar must study
Musar,[10] and in his early years Salanter did address himself to the
masses trying to imbue them with his Musar ideals. But when only
the intellectual elite, which fully grasped and appreciated his Musar
theory, responded to his teachings, Salanter increasingly associated with
intellectuals.[11] This would seem to indicate that Salanter having
decided to pay less attention to the general public, gave up the idea
of organizing a mass movement.

It is the opinion of this writer that theoretically Salanter remained
committed to teaching Musar to all people. However, he must have
gradually realized that his exacting requirements for self-discipline
have placed his moral standards beyond the reach of most people who
spend the better part of their lives in the struggle for exsitence,
having little time left for contemplation.

Salanter must therefore have decided to reach the masses through their spiritual leaders, who do understand his Musar teachings.[12] This notion that the scholarly elite bears greater moral burdens is substantiated in Talmudic sources.[13] Thus Salanter must have evolved the idea that scholars are required to maintain much higher Musar standards than non-scholars.

If this supposition is accepted, we can readily understand that even if Salanter ever meant to organize a mass movement he had to abandon this plan. But there are other significant reasons for the proliferation of Hasidism and the containment of the Musar Movement.

When Hasidism arose in the eightenth-century in the wake of the upheavals caused by such false Messiahs as Shabbtai Zevi and Jacob Frank, Jewish misery was at its worst, marked by despair and frustration.[14] Scholars, who drew strength and inspiration from their Talmudic studies, were not overly affected by the general spiritual crisis. The masses, however, lacking this source of inspiration, found it very difficult to hold the line of faith in face of extraordinary suffering. A general lowering of morale resulted and the people were ready for new leaders. Hasidism could not have come at a more opportune moment in history. Basing itself on a spirit of optimism and cheerfulness, Hasidism held out to the forlorn common man the hope and the promise that he, too, could find G-d, not only the Talmid Hakham. Dispelling frustration and despondency, Hasidism brought to the masses the beauty of joyous emotional experiences and a new consciousness of their inherent spiritual strength.[15]

In Lithuania, where the standards of Talmudic scholarship were the highest, Hasidism exerted little influence. The only significant proliferation of Hasidism in Lithuania and its surrounding provinces was carried out by *Habad,* the Lubavitch movement in Hasidism.[16] This Hasidic school espouses substantial rational teachings and therefore appealed to some Lithuanian Jews.

Inasmuch as the influence of Habad was not too great, and in view of the fact that the emerging secularist forces of science and Haskalah were posing serious threats to tradition, Lithuanian Jewry too was ready for something new, particularly such ideas which would appeal to man's heart rather than his mind alone. Salanter's Musar came to fill this need. Yet, though Musar possessed in some degree the emotional dimension lacking in Lithunian life, it did not succeed to emulate Hasidism for the following reasons.

Generally speaking there are seven sets of conditions favorable to the development of a mass movement: (1) leadership, (2) followership, (3) major ideas and ideals which fire the imagination of people, (4) social, economic and spiritual bonds between leaders and followers, (5) historical events which set the stage for change, (6) the emergence of a powerful leader at the right time and the right place, (7) that this leader be both, an efficient administrator and a man of vision capable of inspiring people to transcend the vicissitudes of the present and strive ceaselessly towards an ultimate goal.

Hasidism met these conditions remarkably well, so it flourished. Rabbi Israel Baal Shem Tov was an extraordinary leader of men, with alleged transcendental powers, buttressed by mysticism and the practice of wondermaking.[17] His appearance at a time of crisis; his finding a receptive audience; his "applied mysticism" that elicited the awe and admiration of many had created a permanent bond between Rebbi and Hasid; and his joyous and simplified way of worship all converged to create a mass movement. This movement was cemented through economic and social ties between leader and follower. The Hasid was eager to offer material assistance to his Rebbi, who, in turn, served as the Hasid's mentor, guide, and therapist. Although Hasidism urged man to strive for spiritual improvement, it reassured him that there is much good in him as he *is*.

But Musar came to teach man how he *ought* to be, telling him that he is not sufficiently good as he *is*. Musar did not encounter such conducive circumstances as Hasidism did. Musarites shunned the Hasidic "personality cult" and, being basically individualistic, never developed common social and economic bonds between leader and follower. Whereas the Hasidic Rebbi accepted "quitlakh" and gifts from his Hasidim, the Musar master would have none of it.[18] The Baal Shem Tov seemed to be a more practical leader than Salanter. Whereas the Baal Shem Tov was a wanderer in his early years, he later settled down and led his people from a home-base. Salanter, however, after having left Salanty, travelled almost continously dissipating his energies and failing to establish a center of Musar.

Hasidism came to sooth the masses, so the people embraced it. Musar came to disturb the people's smug complacency by insisting on higher moral standards so the masses remained aloof. Unfortunately lofty ideas alone do not attract large numbers of people.

Salanter the Man of Musar

Salanter not only taught Musar — he lived it. Already during his life he became a living legend. There have been many stories abroad about Salanter, not as a miracle maker, but as a man with an impeccable record of kindness and consideration beyond the call of duty even for a Tzadik. He would never tire in his incessant efforts to help those in need.[25]

People were attracted to him because of his personality as much as his teachings. He was an impressive figure, with an appearance of distinction which conveyed his inner greatness.[26] Though exceedingly humble and wearing the simple garb of the common man, he had courage and strength. Thus he defied the Czarist authorities by refusing to lecture at a government-sponsored Rabbinical seminary, an institution, which as Salanter predicted, was not in the best interests of the Jewish community.[27] Salanter rose to his height of courageous independence when he ordered the Jews of Vilna to eat on Yom Kippur of 1848 during an outbreak of cholera, an act that was not condoned by the local Rabbinate.[28]

Salanter was a man of rare purity of soul and dignity. When some rabbis initially opposed his Musar teachings he did not engage in any personal polemics and controversy, relating himself with respect and humility towards his opponents.[29]

He was a saintly man, living in self-imposed poverty and refusing to hold public office. For Himself Salanter needed precious little, but he would lavish his attention on others, never giving preference to his children over his students.[30]

Salanter was a serious man, and he would move his audiences to tears when he discussed man's moral duties and the grave consequences of immorality. But, Salanter also possessed a keen sense of humor which he would put to good use, either to entertain lonely and forlorn persons or to ridicule man's weaknesses and unethical behavior.[31]

In his final days, Salanter came to Koenigsberg, a city he frequently visited. He returned, at the age of 73, ailing and exhausted from a life of continuous wandering. On the last night of his life his disciples and friends left him under the care of an old man. When Salanter's followers returned in the morning they found their master dead. The disciples were anxious to know what their master did in his last moments. The old man told them that Salanter repeatedly assured him that there is really no reason to be afraid of a corpse. The body of a man is harmless and there is nothing which should make one afraid at the sight of dead body, said Salanter. Rather than to concentrate on *vidui* (confession) and his own salvation, Salanter, knowing he was dying, was concerned lest the old man, remaining alone at night, would be perturbed at the sight of a dead body.[32] To Salanter, there was no better way to earn salvation than bestowing kindness on a human being.

Chapter II

THEORETICAL FOUNDATIONS

Introduction

Salanter's ethical theory is based on theological and psychological foundations. His ethics, though flexible and humanistic in approach, is a *religious* ethics. He shed some new light on certain aspects of Jewish morality[33] and added a new psychological dimension to Musar, making it attractive to modern man.[34] Although Salanter had advanced some psychoanalytical concepts, he would not have subscribed to such Freudian teachings that sex and pleasure are the major drives motivating man.

Salanter's Musar, as well as that of Luzzatto, comes much closer to Frankl's Logotherapy, which sees in man's *search for meaning and purpose* the primary force in life.[35] Frankl's Logotherapy, coming much closer to spirituality, or even religion, views the meaning of human existence as something detected by man, rather than invented.[36] Man's search for an ultimate purpose in life, says Frankl, drives him on to meet challenges and to find meaning even in suffering. Frankl disagrees with other psychologists who believe that what man needs most in an inner equilibrium. In his theory, there is no place for a tensionless state in man. Quite to the contrary, it is the power of *spiritual dynamics,* which is the *tension in man towards a meaningful purpose to be fulfilled,* which according to Frankl, directs man to make life more than just biological existence.[37]

Salanter's Musar, too, finds meaning in suffering, not suffering for its own sake but as a prerequisite to spiritual satisfaction, joy and serenity — the ultimate goals of Musar. As we shall see in the following chapter, Salanter conceived self-discipline in two stages, the first being "bitter" and the second "sweet" and there is as much meaning in the "bitterness' as there is in the "sweetness." This is why, we reiterate, Musar and Hasidism have common interests, for

237

both seek to enable man to serve G-d in serenity and joy. However, there can be no doubt about the *difference*: whereas Hasadism offers almost instant ecstasy and happiness, Musar *predicates* this state on the arduous road of introspection and self-criticism.

Besides illuminating old moral concepts, and in addition to adding psychological components to Musar, Salanter made an important contribution to Jewish ethical theory by *synthesizing reason with emotion*.[38] This synthesis had historic value, for Lithuanian Jews were strict rationalists and infusion of Musar ecstasy and emotion was a welcome addition to their way of life.[39] This synthesis is as important today as it was then, for human existence is generally marked by the old-new struggle between mind and heart and whoever offers a working synthesis of these two opposing forces is a benefactor of humanity. We now proceed to describe some of the theological and psychological foundations of Salanter's ethic.

The Centrality of Ethics

The Torah commands man to imitate G-d.[40] This concept of *Imitatio Dei* is a central principle of Judaism.[41] This commandment to emulate G-d is open to misinterpretation, for *some* of the Biblical attributes of G-d are stern and one might think that he ought to imitate G-d through fanatic vengeance and the like. But revenge is forbidden, except in the case of war, and even then it is subject to regulatory laws. This is why the Talmud formulated this principle of *Imitatio Dei* in terms of G-d's beneficent modes of expression.[42] Furthermore, this emulation of G-d is generally not expressed in terms of worship and ritual, but, rather through ethical relationships between men.[43] Judaism, then, does not view morality as an area that is outside the sphere of Law. In Jewish thought, *morality is law*,[44] and its centrality is established by the cardinal injunction to imitate G-d ethically.[45]

Man as a Free Moral Agent

Judaism views each individual as a free moral agent whether he is capable of maintaining only the minimum standards of morality or reaching its maximum standards. Man has both, the capacity

and the obligation to improve his character. The principles of freedom
of choice and man's responsibility for his actions are clearly stated
in Biblical,[56] Talmudic[57] and later sources.[58]

In Salanter's ethic we find an underlying optimistic assertion that
human nature can be improved, and that his character is *not determined* by environmental conditions.[58*] Reports from German concentration camps seem to substantiate Salanter's views. There were
some individuals, though admittedly few in number, who managed
to maintain their *Tzelem Elokim* (the image of G-d). Though
living under subhuman conditions, facing death every moment, they
extended aid and comfort to as many inmates as possible.[59]

Salanter, in keeping with the mainstream of classical Jewish
thought, rejected any form of determinism. But, due to the complexity
of human nature and the various environmental temptations, man
must make Musar a lifelong pursuit.[59*]

The Psychology of Man

Salanter espoused the traditional dualistic view that man, composed
of body and soul, possesses innate forces of good and evil. Salanter,
steering clear of strange forms of asceticism and the condemnation of
the flesh, retained the traditional doctrine that man has a *Yetzer Tov,*
a disposition towards good, and a *Yetzer Ra,* an inclination towards
evil. Salanter added depth to this doctrine by evolving a psychological
theory that man's inner self is much more complex, than was
formerly assumed.[59**] He reportedly based his view on general
philosophical and psychological works, which he studied.[60]

According to Salanter, man's inner self consists of two parts. There
is the *vivid,* or conscious part, and a pale, or *dull,* non-conscious part.
The latter, harboring primary instincts and acquired characteristics,
is much stronger, than the former, which possesses reason, common
sense, and purity of spirit.[61]

Salanter maintained that these two realms of the self correspond
to the traditional conception of man. The *Yetzer Tov,* consisting of
reason and the human soul, operates mainly through the *conscious*

self, and the *Yetzer Ra* combining passions and evil spiritual inclinations, functions primarily within the non-conscious self.[62]

Salanter's formulation of the concepts of the nature and psychology
of man were in the main uniquely his own and is considered as an
original contribution to Jewish religious thought.[63]

The psychology of Salanter, particularly his views on the subconscious part of the human personality, played an important role
in the formulation of his Musar study methods, as shall be discussed
later. Though the Socratic dictum, "Know Thyself," was a favorite of
Salanter, he believed that knowing right from wrong does not always
precipitate proper conduct. Observing that reason and knowledge do
not, in fact, withstand the pressure of passion, Salanter was deeply
concerned with his gap between knowing and doing.[64] One of the
probable causes for the failure of reason to regulate conduct, he
asserted, is the strong influence that the subconscious drives have on
man's behavior. This prompted Salanter to develop his unique
methods of Musar study.[64*]

The Vagueness of the Moral Law

According to Salanter, there is an additional reason why action lags
behind moral knowledge. It is the vagueness which characterizes
moral laws and moral situations, leaving many people confused as
to what constitutes proper conduct.[64**]

The vagueness of moral laws is strikingly evident when compared
to other religious laws, whether in matters pertaining to ritual or
civil and criminal justice.

> One is not permitted to depend on his own judgment in
> such matters as dietary laws, for example, and consequently
> he submits to the rabbi's ruling. But in matters pertaining to
> relations between men ... very few turn to the rabbi for counsel,
> though objective knowledge and guidance are most needed in
> making moral decisions.[65]

For example, when does a father, dealing with a rebellious teenage
son, show patience and when anger? Or, when should one react

strongly to an insult, and when overlook it? The Law is vague in such matters and people tend to rely on their own subjective judgment, which in many cases is incorrect.

Solomon tells us that "there is a time to break down, and a time to build up; a time to weep, and a time to laugh; a time to keep silence, and a time to speak; a time to love, and a time to hate; a time of war, and a time of peace..."[66] But what the wisest of men did not tell us is *when* to keep silent, and *when* to speak; *when* to wage war and *when* to sue for peace, etc. Each man, it seems, must be his own judge. But, is every person qualified to judge in such matters? Salanter thought that without Musar one is a poor judge indeed. This problem is further complicated by the fact that in everyday life men must make decisions in a hurry, having neither time nor patience to do otherwise.

Salanter believed that people should be given independence in making moral decisions. He never demanded from his students to follow a single theory or method in Musar, for he believed in a plurality in Musar.[67] Accordingly, the vagueness of the moral law may have appeared to Salanter as a blessing in disguise, for it allows individual choice of expression. However, this freedom of expression is not to be exercised indiscriminately; it must be regulated by Musar.

Salanter was convinced that without full knowledge of Musar, one is incapable of rendering fair ethical decisions.[68] Man, said Salanter, will solve his moral problems when he will learn how to continually make conscious efforts to regulate his conduct according to the teachings of Musar.[69]

The Musar Equilibrium

Salanter's Musar avoids extremism and seeks to develop a balanced Musar method. In trying to counteract the vagueness of moral law, and to reduce the subjectivity of the doer, Salanter did not resort to extremism in either direction. He recommended neither fanatic asceticism nor light-headed self-assurance. Instead, Salanter sought the element of balance in concrete moral situations, or the *mean* between excess and deficiency, not merely ethical generalizations.

The major thrust of Salanter's theory was directed towards the uncovering of the *moral underpinnings* of Judaism. The Burden of his argument was that without Musar the entire structure of Judaism cannot endure. What he wanted was to make sure that man should not be carried away by any delusions of grandeur. Whatever one's achievements, no matter. how lofty his thoughts and how noble his deeds, he must submit himself to self-analysis and self-evaluation. For no man can ever hope to exercise self-control if he does not know the extent of the influence of the subconscious forces operating within his self. When the student of Musar learns to view himself critically, said Salanter, he is approaching the enviable state of moral equilibrium.[73*] The term "approaching" was used advisedly, for there is no final and permanent state of moral equilibrium. Man leads a dynamic life and he cannot really attain a static equlibrium. All that man can do is to continously travel on the road of perfection, coming ever closer to his ultimate goal. Having thus defined the place and role of morality in Judaism, Salanter had indeed become one of the guardians and interpreters of the *ethos* of the Jewish people.

Chapter III

MUSAR AS A PROCESS

Introduction

The study of Musar until Salanter, was a cognitive experience. Numerous Musar books were published and some students *read* those books at random, for the study of Musar was not mandatory even in Yeshivot. This sort of study of Musar texts generally made little impact on the reader's behavior. This, then, was the gap between learning and doing, discussed above. What makes Salanter's Musar more than an intellectual exercise? How did Salanter intend to close this behavior gap?

Salanter's Musar is not mere study; it is a *process,* involving the student's emotive and cognitive faculties. His Musar provides emotional stimuli sufficiently strong to overcome man's bad inclinations.[74] Whereas ordinary study of a Musar text reaches only the conscious realm of the self, Salanter's Musar affects the subconscious realm as well as the learner's reason and common sense. While reason alone may not be able to conquer emotions and passions, especially those residing at the subconsious level, reason, reinforced by emotion and ecstasy, may regulate and subdue passion and emotion.[75]

Therefore, assumed Salanter, frequent emotionally-charged periods of Musar study will keep one alert and aware of his weaknesses, resulting in consistent and lasting ethical behavior.[76] He repeatedly stressed the need for *constancy* in Musar study, cautioning against naive expectations of quick changes in character.[77]

Salanter's Musar, then, is the *ongoing process of man's search for meaning and relevance,* with the concomitant concern for *discharging ones responsibilities.* For man wants to know, more than anything else, what is the meaning of life and what is his function in this world.

Musar as an Emotional Experience

According to Salanter's interpretation of the nature and psychology of man, cognitive Musar is ineffective in regulating behavior because it affects only man's conscious region, leaving the subconscious forces to their own devices. But Salanter wanted to verify his theory, at least by observation, and so he began studying human behavior.

As he observed the people about him — people who were deeply religious, carefully following the prescribed religious duties and even studying Musar — he noticed some inconsistencies in their conduct. Thus, he saw individuals who would meticulously fulfill their duties to G-d, yet neglect their obligations to men.[80] And these were not mere isolated incidents, for case after case, in community after community, verified Salanter's general conclusion that reason nay, even, knowledge of Musar does not produce ethical behavior.

If Musar is to help man control his desires and passions, it must possess emotional stimulus strong enough to combat man's intricate subconscious forces.[81] Said Salanter in his *Iggeret Ha-Musar* (epistle of Mussar):

> Our impulses are swiftly running currents which drown our intellect if the latter is not carried over them on the boat of emotion and enthusiasm.[82]

What did Salanter mean by "the boat of emotion and enthusiasm?" It seems that he had in mind the transformation of Musar study into an emotional experience using the following methods.

Musar must be studied with ecstasy, "which shall stir the soul to seek self-improvement."[83] Ecstasy cannot be aroused by the mere reading of a text or silent study; it will be engendered by reading aloud, with a dirge-like chant.[84] Fervor, or ecstasy, will be evoked if the learner will make use of "vivd mental imagery."[85] The student is requested to project in his mind the halakhic extent of the moral obligation he is studying, and the dire consequences of unethical behavior.[86]

Such an emotional study of Musar must be sustained and constant.

This will cause the emotions aroused by it, to eventually become an acquired part of the self, thus enabling these emotions to combine with reason in subduing the subconscious forces in the self.[87] Salanter was optimistic about the improvability of human nature and he asserted that the *constancy* of an emotionally-charged study of Musar will result in *consistency* of ethical conduct.[88] Accordingly he proposed that a regular period for learning Musar be set aside daily, and he designated a *Beth-Ha-Musar,* (Musar Conventicle) for this purpose. The conventicle, a simply furnished room containing various Musar books, was to be open at all times. Such a place, where one could come to study Musar either individually or with a group, is conducive to meaningful Musar study, thought Salanter.[89]

Self-discipline

Studying Musar with ecstasy is the first stage of the Musar process, and in and of itself it cannot produce ethical conduct. Following it are two more stages of self-discipline.[90] Being therefore concerned with the application of ethics to every-day-living, Salanter considered self-discipline as *the* regulator of such living.

According to Salanter, there are two stages of self-discipline. The first stage is *K'vishat Ha-Midot* (subjugation of bad inclinations), and the second is *Tikkun Ha-Midot* (correction of bad inclinations). The first stage is "bitter", for it constitutes an unrelenting struggle with one's evil inclination. The second stage is "sweet", because it culminates in permanence and happiness.[91]

Salanter thought that the subjugation of bad tendencies, including some mild forms of self-denial, though difficult, is not impossible. But, since these tendencies remain potentially active, subjugation may not be a permanent solution, for passion may be stimulated anew by temptation. The correction of evil tendencies, however, which follows the first stage requires sustained effort. But, since this form of self-discipline yields prudent regulation and canalization of needs and desires, it may, in time, become as permanent a part of the self as acquired characteristics. The final outcome of the second stage of self-discipline results in contentment, joy and serenity.[92]

Self-analysis

Self-discipline is predicated on self-analysis. If one wants to exercise self-control he must first understand his problems so that he may properly apply this control. A person who does not fully grasp his own problems, may practice self-restarint in easy or "soft" areas, while overlooking more urgent and difficult ones. For instance, an alcoholic controlling his food intake may be adhering rigorously to a prescribed diet, but he is not solving his obesity problem unless he is also willing to foreswear the caloric content in alcoholic beverages. This individual is solving relatively minor difficulties while overlooking his major problem namely, insufficient self-control. Or, let us take the example of the polite executive who, though considered by his business associates to be a paragon of virtue, at home is angry and crude as a husband and father. Whatever the psychological reasons for this behavior, his exemplary conduct in the office does not compensate for his unworthy behavior at home. Such men are in need of a balanced over-all self-discipline, not partial self-control.

Salanter, therefore, taught his students to be more critical of themselves than others. Toward this end, he republished the book *Heshbon Ha-Nefesh* by Lefin, which contains many practical suggestions for self-evaluation plus a check list for this purpose. Salanter also directed his students to keep a diary in which they would enter a daily record of their achievements and failures. The check list included the following virtues: (1) Peace of mind, (2) Forbearance, (3) Ordeliness, (4) Spiritedness, (5) Cleanliness, (6) Humility, (7) Righteousness, (8) Thrift, (9) Zeal, (10) Silence, (11) Gentleness, (12) Truth, (13) Abstinence.[94]

Group Therapy

Recognizing that one's subjective judgment may weaken or impair self-analysis, Salanter devised new methods of group analysis, or group therapy. Small groups of like-minded Yeshivah students would meet and evaluate the conduct of each individual member. Each member of the group was obligated to accept the group's recommendations for his improvement.[95] It is interesting to note that a Harvard University experiment with juvenile deliquents, using self-evaluation and group-evaluation methods resulted in success in some cases.[96]

Salanter believed that a group will be more objective than an individual can ever be regarding himself.[97] He, therefore, advised his students to exercise patience and to disregard pride when their behavior was discussed by the group. But, knowing that groups may at times be influenced by prejudice, Salanter urged all members to take sufficient time for deliberation; not to mock anyone; and to consider the *whole individual*, his failures as well as his achievements.[98]

This group, known as the *Vaad*, respected the dignity and rights of each individual. There were no secret sessions and the individual whose conduct was under discussion was usually on hand to clarify his actions. In order to assure freedom of expression, neither Salanter nor the later Musar masters attended the Vaad's sessions. The Vaad was conducted exclusively by the students.

The Musar Yeshivah

Reference was made earlier to Salanter's preoccupation, in his later years, with the scholarly elite. It is within these scholarly circles, in the Lithuanian Yeshivot, that Salanter's Musar process was tested and refined.

Historically, the Yeshivah G'dolah has been a school of higher learning. Its curriculum comprises Talmud, Responsa, and the Codes. Primary attention is given to the Talmud, its commentaries, and to Maimonides' Mishneh Torah. In Salanter's time, Lithuanian Yeshivot gained prominence by their high scholastic standards and the pursuit of intellectual excellence.

Religiosity and ritual were a matter of course. Each Yeshivah student was, by definition, a religious person. The students were not overly concerned with religious and ethical problems, an dthey studied little Musar, if any. The Yeshivah students generally yearned for intellectual — not moral — excellence.

The rationale for pursuing intellectual excellence rather than moral excellence was as follows. Scholastic proficiency can be attained only after years of itensive Talmudic studies. But one need not aim directly at morality; it will come of itself as a result of Torah study and everyday observance of Mitzvot.[99] This belief was so widespread that some rabbis were opposed to Salanter's Musar theories, fearing lest students may begin to view Musar as more important than Talmud. There is no doubt that Salanter himself would not place Musar above the study of Talmud.[100]

What Salanter did challenge was the assumption that morality is a by-product of religiosity, or *frumkeit*. He pointed out that various immoral acts are perpetrated by religious individuals — even by scholars.[101] If morality is attained so easily, why do not most people act morally? Salanter, therefore, concluded that the attainment of morality requires special efforts, and is a life-long process.[101*] For this he decided to convert the Lithuanian Yeshivot into *Musar Yeshivot*. This transformation, which took many years, required the following changes.

1. The Beth-Hamusar

In the Yeshivah, Talmud is usually studied in a large study hall, the *Beth Hamidrash*. But, Salanter did not think that Musar, which requires reflection, should be studied in a large study hall. For this purpose he provided a *Beth-Hamusar,* the Musar Conventicle. In the quiet atmosphere of this relatively small room the Musar learner would find peace of mind, a sort of spiritual retreat.[101**]

2. The Mashgiah

Before Salanter, most Yeshivot either had no Mashgiah at all or, if there was one, he was regarded as an overseer with some administrative duties. The real leadership of the school was vested in the

Rosh Yeshivah.

The office of the Rosh Yeshivah has been an exalted one. He is usually the one who sets the srhool's scholastic standards and patterns of learning. In his regular Talmudic lectures, he presents his own *hiddushei Torah* (creative new interpretations and solutions of difficult Talmudic problems). Though the Rosh Yeshivah is generally a most pious man, a *Tzadik,* he is primarily regarded as a scholarly authority, a *Gaon* (a genius). In the person of the Rosh Yeshivah are blended piety and scholarship, and he represents the intellectual aristocracy.

> An integral part of the curriculum of the Yeshiva is the character improvement program. This goes under the general term of "Musar".... The underlying theme is the cultivation and the awareness of the inner "self"... The "self" must be scrutinized, evaluated and spurred on to ever higher levels of fulfillment and realization.... One of the central figures of the Yeshiva is the "Mashgiah" or Supervisor....

> ...The Mashgiah... continously prods, stimulates and elates the inner "self".... One of the illustrious Mashgihim of recent years was Rabbi Eliyahu E. Dessler of the Poniewez Yeshiva, Bnei Brak. One of his talks is centered on the theme, "The meaning of life." Rabbi Dessler expounds that in life we should be aware of two principles: (a) awareness of our existence, (b) awareness of our deficiencies.... We should be able to distinguish between what is lacked "by" us and what is lacked "in" us. Rabbi Dessler draws a distinction between "achievements" which are possessions "by" us, and "values" which are attainments "in" us.[105]

Not all Yeshivot consented to become Musar Yeshivot, but over the years the number of Musar Yeshivot increased. Salanter succeeded in developing a number of prominent Mashgihim in his lifetime. They, in turn, trained subsequent generations of Mashgihim who exerted considerable influence on their students.[106] Salanter had transformed the Mashgiah from monitor or disciplinarian into a mentor and spiritual guide.

3. *Individualized Guidance*

As a rule the student body of the Yeshivah is relatively small.[107]

The Mashgiah has, therefore, a chance to know each student and to provide individualized Musar guidance. In guiding the individual student, the Mashgiah refrains from infringing upon his privacy and dignity, leading him instead towards self-understanding and spiritual self-sufficiency.

To attain these ends, the Mashgiah conducts informal and friendly discussions with individual students. He encourages the student to express himself freely, prods him to remember his ultimate responsibility in life, and makes some pungent comments and suggestions relative to the student's conduct.[108] The student, who was treated with dignity and respect, was thus led to the realization that there is a place for him in this world, and that he is ultimately his own master.

4. Group Guidance

Knowing that social experiences play an important role in the student's moral development, the Mashgiah provides group guidance, too, and this takes two forms.

The Mashgiah gathers small groups of like-minded students for informal Musar discussions. These groups do not have a regular schedule, and the sessions are not lengthy. The informality of the meetings is reinforced by a friendly atmosphere and the opportunity to ask questions and exchange views with the Mashgiah.[109] The second form of group guidance is provided by the student-run *Vaad*, which was discussed above. These group guidance sessions provide an objective medium for guidance that eventually leads students towards self-guidance.[110]

5. The Musar Schmuess

One of the Mashgiah's important media for teaching Musar has been the Musar lecture, or *schmuess*. This lecture deals with human problems, conflicts, values, and incisive analyses of Biblical or Talmudic personalities. Each Mashgiah makes his own original contribution of Musar ideas and psychological insights. Rabbi S. Z. Braude's *Schmue-*

ssen, which became an integral part of his Yeshivah's curriculum, have reportedly made a profound impact on his students.[111]

Not all *schmuessen* were alike, nor were all Mashgihim equal in stature. But the ecstasy, the total concentration, and the listeners' attention and attachment to the master are general features of all Musar lectures.

One of the great Musar masters of the preceding generation was the late Rabbi Yeruham Halevi Levovitz, Mashgiah of the Yeshivah in Mir, Poland. His schmuessen were very popular in the Yeshivah world. His students state: "... he revealed deep and hidden meanings in Musar... his lectures had shed new light on fundamental human problems."[114]

Today, the Musar schmuess is still prevalent in various Yeshivot here and in other countries. It is assumed that the Musar lecture "helps students form their own *weltanschauung* and develop a spiritual value system."[115]

6. Quest For Moral Excellence

The hallmark of a Musar Yeshivah is the quest for moral excellence on the part of the *individual student.* If Salanter would not have achieved this end result, his entire Musar effort would have been of little consequence. The following discussion points out the significance of the quest for moral excellence, as conceived and attained by Salanter.

The process of education operates along two basic lines of human development. The first is chronological or quantitative, ranging from nursery through graduate school. As the educand progresses from grade to grade and from school to school, he gathers more information and acquires more knowledge. The second line of development is a qualitative form of growth. It is generally assumed that, as the learner ascends the educational ladder, he gains not only more knowledge but also better knowledge.

"Better" knowledge means fuller comprehension, more meaningful conceptualization, consistent association and organization of facts, ideas and theories. Generally speaking, these two lines of development ultimately converge to form a harmonious union as a result of the student's physical and mental maturation and learning. This is probably the case in cognitive learning and intellectual development.

However, when it comes to moral and religious education, the qualitative development seems to lag behind its quantitative counterpart. In other words, the progressing student may acquire more religious and moral knowledge, but he does not necessarily show a concomitant deepening and keener comprehension of this knowledge. As such knowledge accumulates, it does not generally become better knowledge. It is not "better" knowledge for it is not paralleled by growth in commitment, and improvement of conduct — the touchstone of the effectiveness of moral education.

Salanter was puzzled and baffled by this seemingly inherent weakness in moral development, and this prompted him to launch his Musar programs. In the words of a noted student of Salanter's disciples:

> It is a strange historical phenomenon.... Musar, one of the important areas of Jewish thought was neglected and ineffective in the pre-Salanter days.[116]

What, indeed, accounts for this "strange historical phenomenon?" And what is essentially the distinction between Salanter's Musar and that of his illustrious predecessors?

Rabbi S. Z. Braude, exponent of Salanterian Musar education, pointed out the educational implications of this "strange historical phenomenon." He suggested that, in most instances, "childish understanding of religious beliefs persists throughout life, resisting change.[117] Childish beliefs, asserted Braude, are only *professed beliefs,* and they remain superficial cognitive concepts which cannot lead men to commitment and ethical conduct. Such beliefs are not internalized by the individual, and they do not become *actual beliefs.* Only *actual beliefs* guide human conduct.

Current psychological thought bears a striking resemblance to

Salanter's and Braude's views. For example:

> The actual moral beliefs of an individual are the truest measures of his character. If they could be validly ascertained it would certainly be found that they are significantly related to conduct. The widesperad opinion that belief and conduct are unrelated, springs from (a) the confusion between moral belief and moral knowledge; (b) the confusion between *expressed* and *true* beliefs.[119]

Even intelligent persons, possessing outstanding mental abilities, do not necessarily do as they know they should do. This is because their knowledge of the good is only a cognitive knowledge, never becoming emotionally internalized i. e. that this knowledge had no effect on their subconscious forces. *Such knowledge is lacking the essential binding quality of obligatoriness.* According to psychological research, there are no significant correlations between intelligence and helpfulness, for example.[120] Other psychologists also report that they found no relationship between honesty or "service" behavior tests and moral training in schools.[121]

This is why Salanter stressed that one's quest for moral excellence, which will result in ethical behavior, must be constant and intensive. Moral development must be a life-long pursuit, not merely a reliance on childhood learning.

7. *Practical Wisdom*

In order that one may transform childish religious notions into mature ideas, Braude suggested the adoption of the Salanterian reflective study of Musar *plus* a sound understanding of life.[122] This sound understanding of life was termed by Salanter "practical wisdom."[123] This wordly or practical wisdom, is the ability to detect one's own hidden inner motives, as well as those of others, which are inconsistent with overt action. A person who is practically wise, can foresee future complications arising from present conduct. Salanter considered this wordly wisdom as "the key to Wisdom and Musar."[124]

To predict future developments, and to conduct exacting self scrutiny is admittedly no mean accomplishment. Salanter, therefore, warned that *"practical wisdom is not to be found in Musar books ... each man is left to his own devices in acquiring such wisdom."*[125] This, of course, reminds us of the vagueness of the moral law, discussed in the previous chapter.

In fine, worldly wisdom is the practical side of Musar. It makes the quest for moral excellence easier by helping the Musar student relate life's realities to Musar theories. It is through practical wisdom that the student becomes fully aware of his *actual* and *potential* failings and limitations as well as those of others. Musar teaches how man *ought* to be; practical wisdom shows *how* man is, and the two check and balance each other.

8. Safeguarding Individual Dignity

Salanter's own practical wisdom, which has been demonstrated in many ways, was primarily directed at safeguarding the dignity of the individual Talmid Hakham and Yeshivah student. A few illustrations will suffice.

As far as religious doctrine and practice is concerned, Salanter stood out as both, a *Gaon* and *Tzadik.* He opposed any group that challanged the validity of faith and attacked the rabbinate. This is why he fought the Haskalah movement, and organized his Musar Movement as a counter-force against Haskalah. However, Salanter was flexible enough that he did not hesitate to adopt some of the modern methods used by his opponents. Any method, having some practical value, that was in consonance with religious thought was acceptable to him.[126] For example, he went against the custom of his Russian Talmudic colleagues by studying science. What was his reason for doing this? He certainly did not consider science for its own intrinsic value. He was probably the only Russian Rabbi to wrestle with the conflicts between religion and science, especially after the appearance of Darwin's work on evolution.[127]

Being convinced that one must possess scientific knowledge if he is to attempt to bridge the gap between religion and secular knowledge, Salanter thought it necessary to be familiar with the latter.

By acquiring this knowledge Salanter also hoped to maintain the dignity of the Talmid Hakham in general, for one of the favorite charges of the Maskilim was that the rabbis do not understand the dynamics of a changing world.

Salanter guarded the dignity of the Yeshivah students in many ways. He instructed his students to emulate him by "modernizing" their attire and modes of behavior. Since he was generally opposed to ascetism, he cautioned his disciples against fasting and other excessive forms of self-denial.[128]

Salanter also changed another established procedure in the pre-Musar Yeshivah. Because most of the out-of-town Yeshivah students were poor fellows, unable to support themselves, they would dine each day with a local family. This was known as "essen teg" ("eating days"). But, as the Maskilim gained some influence in the small towns of Lithuania, this practice was frowned upon and they began to ridicule these poor scholars, calling them beggars and parasites. The young students, who therefore had been held in esteem by the tradition-abiding populace, were unaccustomed to the new criticisms. Because of this there was a resultant lowering of student morale. Salanter was the first to do away with this practice of "eating days." He determined that the students would no longer receive hand-outs, and instituted a system of scholarships. In this way Salanter protected the students' integrity and dignity.[128*]

The strengthening of student morale and dignity was also due to their relationship with the Mashgiah. This relationship was *not* *master-directed;* it was rather *student-directed.*

The similarities and distinctions between the Musar Movement and the Hasidic Movement were discussed above. One obvious distinction between these two movements is to be found in the relation between the disciple and his master. The Hasid stands in awe before his Rebbi because he ascribes to him some mystic powers. The more difficult it is for the Hasid to comprehend his master, the more he venerates him. The Musar student, in true Lithuanian rationalistic fashion, respects his master the more he understands him. The Musar student ascribes no transcendental powers to his mentor; his purpose is to learn from him and to emulate him. The Hasid, too, attempts to emulate his master but he intends to remain his satellite. The disciple of the Mashgiah, although he will always honor him as his Rebbi, seeks to gain spiritual independence.[129] The Musar master, to be sure, is the leader but, he is a leader of spiritual equals, *primus inter pares* — at least potential equals.[130]

We reiterate: the relationship between the Hasid and his Rebbi is master-directed and that of the *Baal-Musar* (Musarite) is student-directed. Both the Hasid and the Baal Musar derive great benefits from their masters. But, the difference is striking: The Rebbi is the protector of his Hasid whereas the Mashgiah safeguards his disciple's dignity and spiritual independence.

It is quite possible that Hasidism trains the individual Hasid, particularly the non-scholar, to live a content life filled with ecstasy and joy. Musar, on the other hand, may not immediately offer these experiences to its adherents. Yet, there is one important redeeming factor in the Baal Musar's quest for excellence which more than compensates for the initial absence of contentment, ecstasy and joyous living.

The constancy of Musar study, the unrelenting drive for subjugation and control of all unworthy inclinations, create within the Baal Musar a permanent *inner state of deep concern and tension*. This inner tension drives on the Musar student towards the ultimate goal of individual excellence.[131]

Psychiatrists, treating neurotic patients, try to help the latter develop "waiting power," i. e. continuous and persistent occupation with life's ongoing experiences.[132] Dr. Henry Raphael Gold, pointed out that the religious Jew rarely suffers from "spiritual unemployment." To him it is always Shabbat or Erev Shabbat, Yom Tov or Erev Yom Tov. This continuous state of readiness and preparedness generates waiting power. Religious ritual, then, is a great source of occupational therapy.[133]

If this be true in the routine process of Shmirat Mitzvot it is even more so in the case of the Baal Musar. The latter is virtually never free from his abiding and all-embracing drive for self-improvement.

The waiting power that the Baal Musar thus gains has substantial therapeutic value. Having achieved this, the Musarite has gone far beyond immediate contentment or joy — he found the road to life's ultimate meaning. And when the Baal Musar has traveled extensively on this road he will ultimately attain joy and serenity.

Salanter's educational programs within the Musar Yeshivah, such as the Beth-HaMusar, the Mashgiah's activities and the various guidance programs have culminated in a genuine pursuit of moral excellence. Many students of Salanterian Musar are agreed that Salanter succeeded in generating a quest for moral excellence almost equal to the quest for intellectual excellence.[134]

Chapter IV

THE KELM SCHOOL OF MUSAR

Introduction

Among Salanter's followers there were six autstanding disciples who have been credited with the dissemination of Musar. The six chief disciples were: Rabbi Simhah Zissel Ziv Braude (1829-1898) known as "Der Alter" of Kelm, Rabbi Naftali Amsterdam (1832-1916), Rabbi Isaac Blazer (1837-1907) Rabbi of St. Petersburg and known as Reb Itzele Peterburger, Rabbi Jacob Joseph (1848-1902) who served as chief Rabbi of New York and was called Reb Yankele Harif, Rabbi Yosef Yoizel Hurwitz (1848-1919) called "Der Alter" of Navaradock, and Rabbi Nathan (Note) Zevi Hirsh Finkel (1849-1928) known as "Der Alter" of Slobodka.[135] We shall now discuss the theories and activities of the three disciples, who founded distinct schools of Musar and earned the affectionate title *"Der Alter"* — The Elder.

Rabbi Braude the Elder of Kelm

Reb Simhah Zissel, born to a distinguished scholarly and wealthy family in Kelm, received an intensive religious training plus a modern education. Even as a young boy he displayed unusual scholastic ability, always seeking to grasp the essence of things.[136]

As an adult, Braude followed a rigorous schedule, studying and contemplating about twenty hours a day. He was an orderly and well-organized person. Braude wore modern European clothes; he was a meticulous and well-mannered person and his speech was deliberate and well controlled. He was a kind and considerate man with a warm and friendly smile.[137]

Among Salanter's chief disciples Reb Simhah Zissel was the *educator par excellence*. When Salanter left Russia for his extensive travels, Reb Simhah Zissel became the central figure in the Musar Movement. He opened *Batei-Musar* in Vilna and Kovno for the layity, a Musar Yeshivah in Kelm, and unique preparatory schools for boys, which were the forerunners of our modern Day Schools.[139]

Educational Philosophy

Salanter laid the general foundations of Musar but did not insist on a single theory. He believed that Musar may be varied to suit changing conditions and different environments, and this is precisely what his major disciples have done. Braude was the first one to evolve a Musar theory of his own and to implement it.

Braude, though he was given to philosophizing, believed that the essential part of Musar is its practical application. The application of Musar must be *gradual*, for there are no shortcuts to perfection. The attainment of Musar's goals is a difficult and complex process.[140] The progression of Musar must be *deliberate, consistent, constant* and *systematic*. The Musar student must realize that perfectibility is an individual pursuit, for no one can do this for him. The Musar student must be a serious self-analyzer, but not without feeling and emotion. He must be humble and faithful.

Self-Improvement is a life-long process. Jewish scholars, said Braude, are called *Talmidei* Hakhamim, to indicate that they are perpetual students. He was fond of Socrates' statement that "to know that I do not know" is a sign of wisdom.

Man's powers of reflection and observation are the mind's weapons in its struggle against animalistic tendencies. Said Braude: "The person who neglects his reflective faculties commits spiritual suicide."[141]

Braude attached much importance to Salanter's "practical wisdom" which was discussed earlier. He believed that self-analysis must be accompanied by a study of the world of things and people.[141]* Said he: "The entire world is a Beth-Hamusar and each person is a Musar book."[141]**

As was previously stated, Reb Simhah Zissel thought that most people retain their childhood concepts of good and evil, of religion and the world around them. Attitudes and opinions formed in childhood change little in later life in spite of the acquisition of new moral knowledge, hence the gap between knowing and doing.

Braude sees the solution to this problem in man's reflection on Torah, life and man. Only *systematic reflection,* with the attendant Musar methods of Salanter, has the power of breaking childhood habit-formations and thought-patterns.[141]***

Braude's notion that attitudes and personality traits are developed in early life, is substantiated by recent psychological research.[142] Said one prominent educator: "teachers are asked to mold what has already been largely molded."[143]

In order to enable the student to foster his moral development that has been arrested since childhood, Braude suggested the following three methods of Musar study: (1) Whatever one studies must be internalized through emotion; a pleasant subject or event must arouse *happiness,* an unpleasant event — *sadness,* (2) after concluding the lesson, the learner should ask himself: have I learned this lesson thoroughly enough? And, what new ideas have I acquired?" (3) to form associations between various facts and ideas.[144]

In summarizing Braude's educational philosophy, we may say that it is based on a *synthesis* of three basic objectives: (1) *Torah* — to be studied *lishmah* with total concentration and dedication; (2) *Musar* — for the development of an ethical "self"; (3) and the study of *general subjects* — to acquaint the student with, and help him adjust to, his physical, economic, and social environments, as well as to prepare him to earn a livelihood.[145] Braude's educational philosophy is both idealistic in outlook and practical in application.

Braude based his educational synthesis on the theory of Maimonides that Torah must be correlated with reason and science. Braude, like Salanter, showed historical perspicacity by stating that young boys, unlike their predecessors, can no longer be trained to be religious on the basis of faith alone. Their faith, said Braude, will be strengthened if supported by reason.[146]

Braude's Preparatory Schools

Braude was a Talmid Hakham of note, an educational theorist, and an experimenter in education. His experimental schools for boys in the Lithuanian towns of Kelm and Grubin were unique — even revolutionary in some respects.

Reb Simhah Zissel's schools were distinctive in several ways. The students studied such general subjects as geography, mathematics, and language for three hours a day. One who knows the social and educational climate in nineteenth-century Russia, can fully appreciate the significance of this innovation in the curriculum of the Jewish school. This was truly a revolutionary practice in Lithuania, for no religious Jewish school offered such a program in Lithunia, or Russia.

To be sure, Braude alloted more time to the religious subjects than to general studies, but the signifiicant fact is that he did *not* consider the latter as "a necessary evil." Indeed, Braude believed that a knowledge of science and general environment is necessary, not only for better living, but for a *better understanding of religious teachings* as well.[147]

In Braude's preparatory schools there was a strict adherence to order, discipline, cleanliness, and decorum, much more than was customary in those days. Rules were strictly enforced without distinction between poor and rich students. In those schools, children from wealthy families studied together with the children of the poor, and mingled with each other freely.[148]

The *Vaad* preceedings, originally developed by Salanter, were refined by Braude. The *Vaad* conducted group-analysis sessions in a spirit of comradeship and equality. Each member of this group was genuinely concerned with the development of proper conduct-patterns. The *Vaad* was run democratically with one of the older students serving as chairman.

The *Vaad* issued many regulations governing decorum, proper dress and speech. The following are a few typical regulations: "Do not interrupt any speaker"; "Do not seek self-justification"; "Rebuking a member should be done with dignity and respect"; "One ought to be as careful and prudent with his words as with his money."[150]

The Beth Hatalmud in Kelm

In the Beth Hatalmud Yeshivah of Kelm, also known as *The*

Talmud Torah, Braude's Musar program reached its highest level. All the teachings of Salanter, which were intended to produce a quest for moral excellence, were implemented here in a well-organized and systematic fashion.

The improvement of the self was the major objective of the *Beth Hatalmud.* It is reported that one of the regents of a German University informed his colleagues that there is one subject that is taught only in the Yeshivah of Kelm namely, the improvement of human nature.[151]

Reb Simhah Zissel's schmuessen, though they would, at times, last several hours, were extremely liked by his students. Unlike the other contemporary Mashgihim whose schmuessen would reach a high emotional pitch, Braude delivered his lectures in a quiet and dignified manner. His lectures were very well organized and well thought out.

Braude's concern for each individual student was phenomenal. It is reported that he knew every students' strengths and weakness. He would, however, begin his individual guidance work by first elaborating on one of the good qualities of the student. This would strengthen the students' self-confidence and prepare him to accept criticism.

In other Yeshivot students were ranked according to their scholastic achievements, but in Kelm they were evaluated on the basis of their moral attainments. Admission to the Beth Hatalmud was also stipulated on the applicant's personality traits, not so much on his mental abilities.

Braude, did not distinguish between "Jew" and "human being"; to him they were synonymous. The slogan of the secular Haskalah Movement was: "Be a Jew at home and a human being on the outside." Braude's credo was: "Be a Jew *and* a human being everywhere."[152]

Chapter V

THE NAVARADOCK SCHOOL OF MUSAR

Introduction

Kelm and Navaradock are at the opposite poles of the Musar Movement. Whereas the former sought to accommodate religion *and* general knowledge, the latter aimed at separating the two. In Kelm they stressed order, meticulous cleanliness and appearance, in Navaradock they negated all of this. The Kelmites approached the formidable task of self-improvement in a step-by-step organized fashion. In Navaradock they stormed the inner powers of evil, stressing self-denial and deprivation. Kelm and Navaradock share a common goal namely, the improvement of man through Musar, but their methods are totally different.

Rabbi Hurwitz the Elder of Navaradock

Rabbi Joseph Hurwitz, also known as Reb Yoizel, was a man with strong convictions, a highly efficient organizer and administrator, and a man with an iron will. This man, who built Yeshivot and worked with people, was also given to extremism and mysticism and for some time lived a hermit's life. It was Braude who influenced him to give up his isolationism and to take his place in the community.[153]

Reb Yoizel founded his first Yeshivah in Navaradock, White Russia. The school enrollment grew rapidly and many branches of this Yeshivah were opened in other communities. During World War One, Reb Yoizel and his students spent the difficult years of war, pogroms, and revolution in various Russian cities. Reb Yoizel, disregarding danger and adverse conditions, kept on building Yeshivot. When bread was rationed in Kiev, he would distribute the daily half pound ration of bread among his students before giving it to his hungry grandchildren.

Reb Yoizel was a man of determination and action and he would usually take extreme positions, rejecting neutrality. Said he: "In spiritual matters one can either be warm or cold, not lukewarm."[154]

The Elder of Navaradock spent most of his life as a leader of men and a master of Musar. How do we account for his initial tendencies towards separatism and a hermit's life? It seems that he was really seeking this retreat not for its intrinsic value but so that he might learn to exercise self-control before attempting to guide and control others. Said the Elder: "Only a man who is capable of complete self-discipline is qualified to become a leader of the community."[155]

Life in the Navaradock Yeshivah

Life in the Navaradock Yeshivah, named later "Beth Yoseph" after their master, has been dominated by the ascetic spirit of Reb Yoizel. The students lived a life of self-imposed poverty, disregarding external appearance and mannerisms. Their sole purpose was to study Torah and to obtain true religiosity, Yir'at Shamayim.[156]

The students tended to be as aggressive and dynamic as their master. They would help him in organizing new branches of their school in every possible way, sometimes by infiltrating other Yeshivot and "converting" them to Navaradock's Musar.[157]

The teachings of The Elder favoring extremism and rejecting compromise were fully implemented in these schools. Reb Yoizel's students negated this-worldly matters, dedicating themselves to the life of Musar. The students' disregard for their safety and very lives was demonstrated during the Bolshevik revolution, when they heroically continued to study in spite of starvation and persecution.[159]

It seems that Reb Yoizel did not embrace fanatic extremism for its own inherent worth; he rather considered it as a *means* to an end.[159*] He indicated that after considerable exercise in self-denial one may return to the golden mean approach.[160] But, he did not indicate clearly when the Navaradock Musar student is to abandon his negative attitude to life and follow a more moderate course. As it turned out, his students never quite managed to return to the stage of moderation.

The extreme self-denial and self-struggle of the Navaradock students took many forms. They would eat little and sleep on the school's hard benches. In order to crush the passion for money and property they would *share* their belongings. A student who received a package from home would distribute its contents among his schoolmates. For the sake of breaking one's vanity they would purposely neglect their clothing and appearance, and grow their hair long.[161]

One of the characteristic methods of Navaradock was its extreme ecstasy. The Elder, as well as his students, tried to take the body's evil inclination by storm. During holidays their ecstasy would take a happy form, but on other occasions like before the High Holidays, they would appear anxious and troubled.[162]

The *Vaad* of the other Musar Yeshivot was transformed by the Navaradock Baalei Musar into a *Boerse* ("stock exchange"). During such sessions, small groups of students, sometimes consisting of pairs, would discuss their personal problems and jointly seek methods of self-improvement. These "exchange" discussions exerted a deep influence on students and helped them develop life-along friendships.[163]

Reb Yoizel, in keeping with Salanter's teachings, would not let his students rely completely on such group sessions. He believed that the Musarite must strike a balance between individualism and group life. For this end he and his students were accustomed to make solitary retreats, known as *hit'bod'dut*, for reflection and Musar study.[164]

Chapter VI

THE SLOBODKA SCHOOL OF MUSAR

Introduction

This school of Musar is more akin to the Kelm than to Navaradock. The basic difference between Kelm and Slobodka was in their approach to man. In their efforts to subdue man's evil inclinations, all Musarites — not only those of Navaradock — stressed the limitations and shortcomings of man. They taught their students to abstain from vanity, for man's life is brief and full of suffering. Man comes from the dust and to dust he shall return. Why, then, should man entertain notions of grandeur? Let him better remember his inevitable end and prepare for the hereafter.

The Slobodka approach was altogether different. according to Rabbi Nathan Z. Finkel, the old Musar method was no longer suitable. There is more than enough suffering these days, argued Rabbi Finkel, and if you constantly stress man's finiteness and helplessness you may completely crush his spirit. Instead, his argument went, let us teach man that he is a great being with unlimited potential for spiritual development.

Slobodka rejected the ascetic tendencies of Navaradock. But even the more moderate system of Kelm was not acceptable to Slobodka Musarites, who argued, that the Kelmite step-by-step approach is not too conducive to the attainment of greatness in Musar. The Musar student may never get out of the tedious and lengthy stages of preparation. This is why Slobodka decided to hold out to the student the *promise* of Musar, not so much the *burden* of Musar.

Rabbi Finkel the Elder of Slobodka

Rabbi Nathan (Note) Zevi Hirsch Finkel, a native of the town of Rossein in Lithuania, was orphaned at an early age and little is known of his childhood. At the age of fifteen he was already known

266

as a Talmudic scholar. After his marriage he became a student of
Reb Simhah Zissel in Kelm. The latter was deeply impressed by
the former's personality and scholarship. At the age of twenty Reb
Note became Reb Simhah Zissel's assistant.[165]

Though the master and his young associate admired each other,
they did not always agree on educational and Musar matters. Reb
Note therefore decided to open his own Musar Yeshivah. His first
Yeshivah was a *Kollel* for young married scholars. Later he opened
a Yeshivah in Slobodka which developed into a great Torah center,
taking the place of the famous Volozhin Yeshivah that closed down
in 1892. The Slobodka Yeshivah attracted some of the most illustrious
Roshei Yeshivah and brilliant students. Reb Note, now called Der
Alter of Slobodka, and his students opened many Yeshivot in other
communities as well as in Hebron. Though he encountered resistance
to Musar on several occasions, Rabbi Finkel weathered all the storms
of opposition and continued his Musar work. In his declining years
he settled in Hebron where he dedicated all of his energies to his
Yeshivah.[166]

The Elder's schmuessen were distinguished in their profound and
masterful array of ideas. Though given to ecstasy, he would always
attempt to keep reason in firm control. He objected to emotional and
tearful outbursts during Musar study, claiming that even Salanter
would not have condoned that. He praised however, the student whose
deliberate and rational Musar reflections moved him to tears and
ecstasy.[167]

The Elder's life-long self-analysis was phenomenal. He would
scrutinize his own motives, always searching for the undesirable
n'giah — ulterior motive. Posterity would have probably never known
of this if not for the accidental discovery of his diary which is filled
with incisive self-analysis and criticism. His diary deals primarily
with human relations. The Elder's concern for others knew no limits.[168]

Pedagogical Principles and Methods

The Elder of Slobodka possessed unusual abilities in guiding the
individual student. He had the combined qualities of the expert
psychologist and the master pedagogue. He *knew* each student intimately and remembered all details of a student's life. He would

diagnose a student's behavior and personality, always seeking to get to the core of the student's character.

He would not entertain any preconceived opinions about a student. Instead, he preferred to judge for himself on the basis of observations and numerous conversations with the student. When talking to a student he would discuss with him his home background and other non-school matters. The Elder believed that such conversations reveal a student's attitudes and character traits more than scholarly discussions.

The Elder would chastise students even for seemingly small offenses in derekh eretz and external appearance. He maintained that major offenses are the result of a series of smaller ones, and it is therefore necessary to combat insignificant failings before they develop into behavior-patterns. In insisting on proper care of one's clothes, the Elder used to say: "A wrinkled or deformed hat is indicative of a disorganized mind."[169]

Reb Note Hirsch created a relaxed and happy atmosphere in the Yeshivah. Not only during holiday seasons, but even on ordinary school days Slobodka was a happy place. The master considered a happy and joyous mood as a prerequisite to study, reflection and creativity. Although Der Alter cared for all students his concern for the gifted ones was without precedence. He would spend much time with brilliant students, guiding them on to greatness. Even during strikes he would not agree to expel the leaders of the student revolts because they were among the scholarly elite. Ultimately his efforts bore fruit and many of the restless students became noted scholars.

As a result of The Elder's pedagogical efforts the students of Slobodka developed into wholesome and dignified individuals. Those students were well-mannered, well-dressed, alert, happy and friendly persons.[170]

Major Premises and Concepts

The Elder of Slobodka taught Musar for more than half a century. He was a most creative and productive thinker and practitioner of Musar. The following brief discussion contains a few of the major premises and concepts of his Musar theory.

1. *Spirituality of Man.* The human being is endowed with great spiritual powers. Instead of burdening the Musar student with ascetic requirements or tedious preparations for greatness we must begin by inspiring him to *recognize* and *utilize* his own potential.[171]

2. *Man's Transcendental Quality.* To say that man's spirit is transcendental is to tell only part of the story of man. Even the physical part of the human being is endowed with a transcendental quality.[172]

3. *The Origin of Man's Drives and Emotions.* Musarites have generally assumed that there is a dichotomy between man's intellect and emotions and drives. Whereas the former is the manifestation of man's spirit, the latter are the functions of his body. Slobodka rejects this dichotomy.

Even man's so-called physical drives and emotions flow from his spirit. When the Torah said that man was created in the "image of G-d" it referred to the *whole* man, not only part of him. This is why the requirement of *Imitatio Dei* is both logical and feasible, for finite man has a transcendental link with the infinite Creator.[173]

4. *To "Know" G-d is to Imitate Him.* The more man imitates G-d, the more he comes to "know" Him. To know G-d's essence is impossible, but to "know" His ethical manifestations *is* possible. It is possible because man was given a measure of these manifestations, even though they are admittedly finite. Man, therefore, has the opportunity to relate to G-d and to "know" Him by emulating Him. Because the imitation of G-d is expressed in ethical terms, and since man is social being, there is almost no limit to the opportunities for moral living.[174]

5. *To Serve Man Means To Serve G-d.* Inasmuch as man's transcendentality is so complete one must relate to every human being as to a *Tzelem Elokim* — the image of G-d. Moreover, whosoever deals kindly with man is in fact, dealing kindly with G-d.[175]

6. *The Purpose of Kindness.* We are obligated to bestow kindnesses on our fellowmen for the purpose of alleviating their suffering and serving their needs. There is an additional purpose in dealing kindly with others, namely, the elevation and edification of the *doer*. Thus,

when the Baal Musar meets a person who is either unaware of his physical or spiritual needs or fails to express them, it is the duty of the Baal Musar to make this individual aware of his deprivation. In other words, kindness is not a passive response to an external stimulus; it is rather an *active* process of seeking to *do* good for the sake of both the giver and the recipient.[176]

7. *Humanistic Ethics and Torah Ethics.* Much of what has been said thus far may be assumed by humanists, without Torah. The distinct contribution of Torah to ethics lies in the delicate and intricate area of motive and intent. For example, "Thou shalt not murder" prohibits more than actual murder. The Torah's Musar demands the *total absence of tendencies and inclinations* towards murder. Furthermore, this concept of "murder" includes, in a broad sense, such acts as putting one to shame or depriving him of a livelihood. The Torah is very much concerned with the roots of action which lie deep in man's psyche. The uprooting of such tendencies, not stressed by humanistic ethics, is the primary purpose of Torah ethics.[177]

8. *Man's Happiness.* It was the intention of the Creator to make man happy, not only in *Olam Habba* but *also* in *Olam Hazeh.* If man lives an unhappy life he must blame himself, not G-d. The purpose of the Mitzvot is to afford man bliss and happiness in this world *and* in the hereafter. Those who observe the Mitzvot for their intrinsic value — not for the sake of happiness or any other reward — will obtain satisfaction, fulfillment and happiness. Even as man's body has a transcendental quality, so does the entire creation. One should not, therefore, reject the wholesome and proper pleasures of life.[178]

Chapter VII

MUSAR'S RELEVANCE TO CONTEMPORARY PROBLEMS

Introduction

The preceding discussion of the Musar Movement which was primarily pedagogical in scope, dealt with the early history of the movement. We have not discussed the present day state of this movement, for this would require a separate study. Suffice it to say that the Mussar Movement continues to exist. After the Holocaust it was transferred from the destroyed Yeshivot of Europe to a number of Yeshivot in Israel and in the United States. Apparently the Musar Movement has the flexibility to adapt to new environments.

Assuming, therefore, that the Musar Movement will continue to play an important role in the Yeshivot, we now turn to a brief discussion about its relevance to some contemporary problems. We shall try to suggest possible future directions for Musar so that it may make its rightful contribution to the Jewish community. While we agree that Musar's role in the Yeshivah should be maintained, we would like to see, some accomplished Baalei Musar *reach out to the community at large* even as Salanter did. If present trends are any indication of the mood of humanity today — and we think they are — then we assume that people are now ready for some sound ethical teachings.

Freedom and Free Will

Philosophers have pondered the problem of man's free will vs. determinism for millenia. Moralists, particularly religious moralists, are agreed that man's will is not completely determined by outside forces, and that there is a measure of freedom in our lives. Freudian psychoanalysts claim that man's will is determined not so much by external stimuli as by his hidden subconscious drives. As we have noted earlier, Salanter, though he was aware of the dark region in the human psyche, maintained that man *is* free *if* he so chooses.

This Musar concept is of crucial importance today. In our society we tend to sacrifice the needs of *men* to the needs for *things*. Our economic development retards social development because it is based on efficiency and capacity rather than prudence and justice. Our youth, sensing the degradation of man, are protesting against what seems to be the perpetuation of an aimless machinery. And Jewish youth is no exception. Indeed, we hear that Jewish youth is in the forefront of student groups challenging our social institutions.

Should we not bring to our youth the meaningful message of Musar which places the *needs of men above the needs for things?* Should not our schools, on all levels, develop curricula and methods for teaching Jewish morality?

The Dignity of man

Much has been said in recent times regarding the degradation of the individual in our technological age. Many concerned persons feel that our technological age has transformed man into a consumeer, leading a stereotype machine-like existence. Among the many modern maladies troubling our society, there is one that stands out as a distinct threat to the dignity of man namely, "computerities." This malady may cause man to develop such self-affacing symptoms as the phobic fear that the computer will soon supplant man's mind.

Some recent research findings in neuro-anatomy sound somewhat reassuring:

> It is still commonplace to hear the brain compared with a computer. For parts of the brain the analogy is accurate enough, but as a whole organ, the human brain is so complex that a billion computers of the most advanced design could not equal its capacities.[181]

Yet, one's anxiety concerning the computer's threat to man is not completely dispelled. As technology advances it may very well create such complex computers which may be superior to the brain, or at least rival it. But even if this could never happen we should not console ourselves with the fact that the brain *is* more complex than the computer, for the real question is what does man *accomplish* with his brain? How much of the human quality is left in a brain that does not elevate man above the machine?

Would not a Slobodka-type Musar theory, which vests even man's body with the dignity of spirituality, constitute a good antidote to "computeritis?"

Towards a Synthesis of Musar and Hasidism

It seems that a process of synthesis has been under way for some time in the American Yeshivot. This refers to the fusion of Lithuanian *lomdut* with Hasidic *fervor*. This is due to the fact that many of the Roshei Yeshivot are either Lithuanian-born, or Lithuanian trained, and many of the students come from Hasidic homes. On the basis of observations it seems that this is a wholesome development. What is needed, however, is to combine Lithuanian scholarship *and* Musar with the qualities of Hasidism.

As we pointed out earlier, Musar and Hasidut share some common interests. The Hafetz Hayim praised Hasidim.[184] The Baal Shem Tov urged his followers to study Musar each day.[185] Musarites admire the Hasidic zeal, frankness, youthfulness and resistance of environmental pressures.[186] Hasidic leaders have expressed ideas that are remarkably similar to those promulgated by the Musar masters. The following is a characteristic example. Salanter once stated: "Kaas ha-panim v'lo kaas ha-lev." i. e., anger, even when justified, must be an external expression only, not an internal state.[187] The Baal Shem Tov is credited with a comparable statement: "Even if one has to display righteous indignation he must take pains to confine it to an outward manifestation only. Within his heart he ought to remain calm and friendly."[188] In fact, such Musar masters as Levovitz and Dessler have incorporated Hasidic and Kabbalistic concepts in their works.[188*]

Having spiritual affinity, and co-existing in today's Yeshivot, both Hasidim and Baalei Musar would greatly benefit from an exploration of mutuality. That the historic controversy between Hasidim and Mitnagdim had some positive effects is acknowledged by Hasidic leaders.[189] But the old disputes and debates seem to be no longer relevant. What is needed now is understanding and cooperation.

To continue maintaining the separation between Hasid and non-Hasid is detrimental to both. Salanter once said: "The Hasid feels that he *has* a Rebbi, and the Mitnaged thinks that he *does not need* a Rebbi. The truth is that both live in error."[190] Rabbi Menashe Illier put it this way: "Both the Hasid and the Mitnaged will be reprimanded. The former, for claiming, I do not need the book, for I have a rebbi, and the latter for saying, having the book, I need no Rebbi."[191]

There is really no justification for perpetuating the error of separatism. The historic split between Hasid and Mitnaged can be eliminated in today's Yeshivot where the aforementioned good qualities of Hasidism would be fused with the *combined* virtues of the Musar Schools of Kelm and Slobodka. Such a synthesis may lead to a renaissance of Jewish ethics.

Ethics Counselors for our Schools

School curricula generally prescribe programs for the teaching of moral and spiritual values. It is taken for granted that the responsibility for teaching these values rests with the classroom teacher. The teacher's work in this area can not be, and should not be, taken over by anyone else.

Yet, the appointment of a mashgiah-type ethics counselor has now become necessary more than ever. The gap between cognitive knowledge and affective knowledge has widened considerably. *The* need for *behavior modification* which Salanter has sought, is now more urgent in view of the current erosion of morality in our society.

This counselor, who, having studied Musar and psychology, would be a moral philosopher, should conduct the school's *moral guidance program.* His functions would consist of conducting discussions and debates on ethical issues, arranging essay contests, serving as a moral guide and mentor to individual students, and conducting group-analysis sessions.

The ethics counselor should be appointed in high schools as well as in elementary schools. Guidance programs must not be restricted to high schools. Current psychological thought tends to stress the cognitive and emotional potential of the young child as being far superior to that previously ascribed to him. It seems that educators have been underestimating the importance of the young child's moral consciousness.[192]

A recent experiment with elementary school children caused some educators to observe that "the children's discussions were in many ways on a level with first-year law students."[193] According to the findings of Piaget, children of eleven years, for example are capable of mastering formal operations in the mind.[193*]

Traditionally the mashgiah's guidance program has been *preventive* and *developmental* rather than remedial. This Salanterian approach has recently been accepted by guidance experts for use with elementary school children, in preference to remedial guidance, characterized as "waiting for the casualties to fall."[194]

Accordingly, the objective of the ethics counselor would be to provide guidance to *all* students and to prevent maladjustments as much as possible.

Israeli high school students have been studying a special course called Mahshevet Yisrael (a Jewish world-view). This program, reportedly a result of the influence of Salanterian Musar, may be termed a *problems course*. During such sessions, the students and the teachers analyze ethical problems, ranging from personal dilemmas to international conflicts.[195] In the opinion of this writer, upper and middle grades of the elementary school are also ready for such a program.

It may be expected that where such a program is instituted, school people, along with the ethics counselor, will be concerned with *character development* — not only intellectual growth. Hopefully, students, too, will grapple with ethical issues so that they may develop an *ethical* and *social conscience* which will guide their behavior. This kind of guidance may also have therapeutic value and reduce students tensions and pressures. The desirability of achieving this end can scarely be denied.

SUMMARY

The Musar Movement has made a lasting contribution to Yeshivah education. The current Musar programs in the Yeshivot ought to be fostered and intensified. There is presently a shortage of Musar masters, or Mashgihim. Therefore, special efforts should be made by Yeshivah leaders to train high caliber Musar teachers.

It seems desirable to carry Musar's teachings outside of the four ells of the Beth Hamidrash, even as Salanter himself presented his ethic to college students and wider audiences.

Presenting Musar to larger audiences would involve the following new approaches: A rapprochement between Hasidim and Musarites, which would be beneficial to both groups. Jewish institutions of higher learning ought to give Musar a more prominent place in their curricula. Endowments for chairs of Jewish ethics in American universities should be encouraged. Musar publications for the English-reading public would help popularize Salanter's legacy. Many writers have popularized Hasidism, but few have attempted to present and interpret the mystique and relevance of Musar.

Jewish schools, elementary and secondary, must begin attaching more importance to character education. To this end mashgiah-type ethics counselors should be appointed. These counselors, who would conduct formal and informal programs of ethics with particular emphasis on self-analysis, self-understanding, and self-discipline, would have a salutory effect on children.

Educators ought to pay more attention to behavior modification through developmental and preventive guidance programs. Much research and experimentation will be needed to find better methods for transforming cognitive knowledge into attitudinal knowledge, and to motivate children to translate their attitudinal, or emotive, knowledge into positive behavioral patterns. This sort of research, being admittedly complex, calls for team-work involving psychologists, guidance experts, educators, Musar scholars and other social scientists.

The current crisis in morality in our society and the complex international situation seem to warrant special efforts in the area of character education. We and our children are in need of the spiritual strength and the integrity which are inherent in a genuine Musar program.

NOTES

1. *Vayikra Rabbah,* IX, 3.
2. He expanded the term "Kadmah" by adding to it the connotation of "hakdamah", an introduction.
3. Bahya ben Joseph Ibn Pakudah, *HOVOT HA-L'VAVOT* (Warsaw: Goldman Publishers, 1856), pp. 13-25.
4. Moshe Chayim Luzzatto, *MESILAT YESHARIM — THE PATH OF THE JUST,* Shraga Silverstein (tr.), (Jerusalem: Boys Town Press, 1967), p. 17.
5. Dov Katz, *T'NUAT HA-MUSAR* (Tel-Aviv: Beitan Ha-Sefer, 1952) I, 145-46.
6. Eliezer Ben-Yehuda, *MILON HA-LASHON HA-IVRIT* (Tel-Aviv: La-Am Publishing House, 1948) VI, 2849-2853, 3137.
7. Luzzatto, *op. cit.,* introduction.
8. Abraham E. Kaplan, *B'IKVOT HA-YIR'AH* (Jerusalem: Mossad Harav Kook, 1960) pp. 26-27.
9. Kopul Rosen, *RABBI ISRAEL SALANTER AND THE MUSAR MOVEMENT* (London: The Narod Press, 1945), pp. 101, 113-14.
10. Israel Lipkin Salanter, *OR YISRAEL,* Isaac Blazer (ed.) (Tel-Aviv: Israel-American Offset, 1959), p. 44.
11. Kaplan, *op. cit.,* p. 18.
12. Rosen, *op. cit.,* pp. 113-114.
13. Babylonian Talmud, Tractate *Yoma,* p. 86a.
14. Max L. Margolis and Alexander Mark, *A HISTORY OF THE JEWISH PEOPLE* (Philadelphia: The Jewish Publication Society of America, 1947), pp. 581-583.
15. Heinrich Greaetz, *HISTORY OF THE JEWS* (Philadelphia: The Jewish Publication Society of America, 1939), pp. 378-386, Vol. V.
16. Kaplan, *op. cit.,* p. 26.
17. S. A. Horodetzki, *HA-HASIDUT V'HA-HASIDIM* (Tel-Aviv: D'vir Publishers, 1928), pp. 1-73.
18. Salanter onre told a visiting Hasid who offered him a gift: "You consider as a Tzadik the one who accepts offerings, but we designate the title of Tzadik to the one who gives..."
19. Z'ev Yawetz, *TOLDOT YISRAEL* (Tel-Aviv: Achiever Publishers, 1937), XII, 229-50.
20. Rosen, *op. cit.,* pp. 88-92.
21. Katz, *op. cit.,* pp. 178-182.
22. Yehiel Y. Weinberg "The Musar Movement and Lithuanian Jewry" in Leo Jung, (ed.), *MEN OF THE SPIRIT,* (New York: Kymson Publishing Company, 1964), p. 217.
23. Katz, *op. cit.,* pp. 178-186, 225.
24. *Ibid.,* pp. 183-220.
25. Louis Ginzberg, *STUDENTS, SAINTS AND SCHOLARS* (New York:
26. Rosen, *op. cit.,* p. 23.

27. Menahem G. Glenn, *ISRAEL SALANTER, RELIGIOUS-ETHICAL THINKER* (New York: Bloch Publishing Co., 1958), p. 42.

28. *Ibid.*, p. 41.

29. Meir Berlin, *FUN VOLOZHIN BIZ YERUSHALAYIM* (New York: Orion Press, Inc., 1933), p. 273.

30. Hayim I. Lipkin, *RABBI ISRAEL MI-SALANT SHITATO V'TORATO* (Tel-Aviv: Nezah Publishing Co., 1953), I, p. 98.

31. Glenn, *op. cit.*, p. 181.

32. Rosen, *op. cit.*, p. 28.

33. Ginzberg, *op. cit.*, p. 178.

34. Katz, *op. cit.*, p. 92.

35. Viktor E. Frankl, *MAN'S SEARCH FOR MEANING: AN INTRO-DUCTION TO LOGOTHERAPY*, (Boston: Beacon Press, 1959), p. 99.

36. *Ibid.*, p. 101.

37. *Ibid.*, pp. 106-107.

38. Z. E. Kurzweil, *MODERN TRENDS IN JEWISH EDUCATION* (New York: Thomas Yoseloff, 1964), pp. 74-93; Ginzberg, *op. cit.*, pp. 158, 178; Glen *op. cit.*, p. 5.

39. Rosen, *op. cit.*, p. 105.

40. *Deuteronomy*, X:12; XI:22; XXVII:9.

41. Joseph H. Hertz, "Fundamental Ideas and Proclamations of Judaism", in Leo Jung, (ed.), *THE JEWISH LIBRARY*, Second Series (New York: Bloch Publishing Co., 1930), p. 71.

42. Babylonian Talmud, Tractate *Sotah*, p. 14A.

43. Katz, *op. cit.*, p. 381.

44. Hertz, *op. cit.*, p. 59.

45. Babylonian Talmud, Tractate *Shabbat*, p. 31 A; *Sifra* K'doshim, IV; *Tanna D'vay Eliyahu*, XV.

46. *Deuteronomy*, VI:8; Proverbs, II:20.

47. Babylonian Talmud, Tractate *Bava M'tzia*, p. 30 B; *Bava Batra*, pp. 12 B, 88 A, B.

48. *Leviticus*, XIX:1.

Nahmanides, *Commentary on Leviticus*, XIX:1.

50. Blazer, *op. cit.*, pp. 23, 26.

51. Babylonian Talmud, Tractate *Yoma*, p. 86a.

52. This sheds some further light on the previously discussed question of why did not Salanter concentrate on establishing a mass Musar Movement. As we pointed out earlier, Salanter, in his later years, preferred to work primarily with the scholarly and ethical elite. We now see that he did so because he wanted to foster the development of those maximum moral standards. He believed that only such leaders who adhere to high moral standards are capable of inspiring the community to maintain its minimal standards.

53. This list is exclusive of the "baal metzra" — a neighbor who has property adjoining the field offered for sale. A "baal matzrah's" claim to the field is much stronger than that of the others and, if sold to another, the sale is voided.

54. Maimonides, *MISHNEH TORAH*, Hilkhot Sh'khenim, XIV, 5.

55. *Ibid. Commentary of Harav Hamagid.*

56. *Deuteronomy,* XI:13-21, 26-28; XXX:15.

57. Babylonian Talmud, *Tractate Avot,* III, 19.

58. Salanter, *op. cit.,* pp. 80-81. This is, of course, the central theme in the entire Musar literature.

58*. *Ibid.*

59. Frankl, *op. cit.,* pp. 35, 46, 58, 65, 67, 72.

59*. Salanter, "Iggeret Ha-Musar" *in OR YISRAEL, op. cit., pp.* 103-108.

59**. B. Blazer, *op. cit.,* p. 49.

60. Katz, *op. cit.,* pp. 186, 254, 330.

61. Salanter, *op. cit.,* p. 49.

62. *Ibid.,* pp. 49, 105.

63. Kurzweil, *op. cit.,* p. 76; Katz, *op. cit.,* p. 65; Rosen, *op. cit.,* pp. 34-44.

64. Israel Lipkin, Salanter *T'VUNAH in SHLOSHA S'FARIM.* (New York: Grossman Publishing House, 1965), pp. 14, 15, 64, 84, 94.

64*. Salanter, *OR YISRAEL, op. cit.,* pp. 49-54; 100-102.

64**. Israel Lipkin Salanter *in* Schneur Z. Hirshowitz *EVEN YISRAEL* (Vilna: Funk Publisher, 1912) pp. 16, 17, 33-34, 67, 72, 92.

65. Abraham E. Kaplan, *DIVRAY TALMUD* (Jerusalem: Mosad Harav Kook, 1958), p. 48.

66. Ecclesiastes, III:3-9.

67. Lipkin, *op. cit.,* pp. 107-108.

68. Katz, *op. cit.,* p. 278.

69. Rosen, *op. cit.,* pp. 80-81.

70. Salanter, *EVEN YISRAEL,* p. 34.

70*. Salanter, *OR YISRAEL, op. cit.,* pp. 84-86.

71. *Ibid.,* p. 103.

71*. *Ibid.,* p. 100.

72. Rosen, *op. cit.,* pp. 104-105.

73. Babylonian Talmud, Tractate *B'rahot,* pp. 5 B, 63 A; Tractate *AVOT,* I; 17; II, 2.

73*. Salanter, *OR YISRAEL,* op. cit., pp. 48-55, 72-75.

74. Rosen, *op. cit.,* p. 65.

75. Katz, *op. cit.,* p. 251.

76. Salanter, *OR YISRAEL, op. cit.,* p. 50.

77. Salanter, *EVEN YISRAEL, op. cit.,* p. 48.

78. Gordon W. Allport, "Preface," *in* Viktor E. Frankl, *op. cit.,* pp. XI, XII.

79. Mario D. Fantini and Gerald Weinstein, "Reducing the Behavior Gap." *THE PEDAGOGIC REPORTER,* XIX (June 1968), 4.

80. Salanter, "Iggeret Ha-Musar", *in OR YISRAEL,* op. cit., p. 106.

81. Rosen, *op. cit.,* p. 65.

82. Salanter, *OR YISRAEL, op. cit.,* p. 103.

83. Blazer, *op. cit.,* p. 32.

84. *Ibid.,* pp. 26, 33.

85. Katz, *op. cit.,* 259.

86. Rosen, *op. cit.,* p. 77.

87. *Ibid.*, p. 65.

88. Israel Lipkin Salanter, *T'VUNAH in SHLOSHAH SEFARIM, op. cit.*, pp. 15, 32, 100.

89. Blazer; *op. cit.*, pp. 36, 50.

90. Salanter, *op. cit.*, p. 103.

91. Salanter, *OR YISRAEL, op. cit.*, pp. 80-85.

92. *Ibid.*, p. 83.

93. Rosen, *op. cit.*, p. 80.

94. *Ibid.*, pp. 83-84.

95. Lipkin, *op. cit.*, p. 20.

96. William L. Griffen, "A Needed Dialogue: Schools and Values." *THE PEDAGOGIC REPORTER*, XVI. (Dec. 1964), 6.

97. Hayim I. Lipkin, *TORAT RABBI ISRAEL MI-SALANT* (Tel-Aviv· Nezah Publishing Company, 1954), II. 12.

98. Salanter, *OR YISRAEL*, op. cit., p. 42.

99. Katz, *op. cit.*, p. 262.

100. Berlin, *op. cit.*, p. 268.

101. Katz, *op. cit.*, p. 64, 302.

101*. Salanter, *OR YISRAEL, op. cit.*, pp. 64-65.

101**. Blazer, *op. cit.*, pp. 36-38.

102. This has been the situation in Lithuania and Israeli Yeshivot. In America this trend continues with a few exceptions where there is a president and several Roshei Yeshivah in a single institution, such as Yeshiva University of New York and the Hebrew Theological College of Chicago.

103. Aaron Greenbaum, "Official and Unofficial," *THE JEWISH HORIZON* XXVI (June 1963), 9.

104. Avraham Ronn, "Darkei Ha-Hinukh Ba-Y'shivot," *Bisdeh Hemed*, VI (February 1963), 251.

105. Greenbaum, *op. cit.*, pp. 7, 8.

106. See Katz, *T'NUAT HAMUSAR*, op. cit., Vol. II, III, IV, V. Unlike modern colleges, Yeshivot have not developed large student bodies. Except for a few larger American Yeshivot, a Yeshivah generally has no more than a few hundred students. The students come to know each other, and the individual student is not subjected to the problem of anonymity within a multitude.

108. A personal note is pertinent. The writer was a student at the Yeshivah "Etz Hayim" in Kletzk, Poland, and in Lithuania where the Yeshivah moved after the outbreak of World War II. The Mashgiah, Rabbi Joseph Leib Nenedick of blessed memory was a student of Rabbi Simhah Z. Braude, Salanter's chief educational disciple. Though the writer was then only a lad of fifteen, the Mashgiah had several discussions with him. Those discussions, centered around the importance of learning and self-improvement even under adverse wartime conditions, made a salutory impact on him. He remembers how he stood in reverence before this sage, absorbing each of his words with total attention and deep concern. The Mashgiah spoke slowly, carefully considering each word he uttered, telling the young student of the higher purposes of life. In those moments, the writer felt deep gratitude towards the Mashgiah for taking a

personal interest in his spiritual welfare and for teaching him tow to search for life's meaning.

109. Reported from personal experience.

110. Katz, *op. cit.*, II. 203, 205.

111. *Ibid.*, 205.

112. Rabbi Joseph was one of the first of Salenter's dsciples to fouŋd a Musar Yeshivah. He later became the Chief Rabbi of New York, and thus the first to bring Musar to America.

113. A. A. Friedman, quoted *in* Katz, *op. cit.*, II. 367-68.

114. Student Committee of Mirer Yeshivah, *HATVUNO* (New York: Mirer Yeshivah Publication), I. (1947), 10.

115. Ronn, *op. cit.*, pp. 249-50.

116. Yehiel Y. Weinberg, "T'nuat Ha-Musar V'shitatah," *PANIM EL PANIM C L I* (March, 16, 1962). 14.

117. Katz, *op. cit.*, II. 127.

118. *Ibid.*, pp. 128-30.

119. David P. Ansubel, *THEORY AND PROBLEMS OF ADOLESCENT DEVELOPMENT* (New York: Grune & Stratton, 1954), p. 265.

120. David P. Ansubel, *THEORY AND PRACTICE IN CHILD DEVELOPMENT* (New York: Grune & Stratton, 1958), p. 397.

121. Harold W. Stevenson, (ed.), *CHILD PSYCHOLOGY,* National Society for the Study of Education, Sixty-second yearbook (Chicago: NSSE, 1963), pp. 279-80.

122. Katz, *op. cit.*, II. 128-130.

123. Salanter, *op. cit.*, *OR YISRAEL, op. cit.*, p. 43.

124. Katz, *op. cit.*, I. 297.

125. Salanter, *OR YISRAEL, op. cit.*, p. 43.

126. Katz, *op. cit.*, I. 172, 186, 343.

127. *Ibid.*, pp. 186, 225.

128. *Ibid.*, pp. 172, 323, 343.

128*. Rosen, *of cit.*, pp. 91-93; Katz, *op. cit.*, pp. 171-173.

129. Kaplan, *B'IKVOT HA-YIR'AH op. cit.*, p. 23.

130. Y'shayahu Wolfsberg, *IYUNIM BA-YAHADUT* (Jerusalem: Mossad Harav Kook, 1955), p. 53.

131. Wolfsberg, *op. cit.*, pp. 25-53.

132. Henry Raphael Gold, "Can We Speak of Jewish Neuroses?" *in* Normal Kiel (ed.), *THE PSYCHODYNAMICS OF AMERICAN JEWISH LIFE,* (New York: Twayne Publishers, Inc., 1967), p. 136.

133. *Loc. cit.*

134. Blazer, *op. cit.*, p. 5; Hirshowitz, *op. cit.*, p. 2; Katz, *op. cit.*, I, 174; Rosen, *op. cit.*, p. 113; Ginzberg, *op. cit.*, p. 163; Glenn, *op. cit.*, p. 55; Kurzweil, *op. cit.*, p. 92.

135. Glenn, *op. cit.*, p. 69; Katz, *op. cit.*, Vols. II, III, IV.

136. Katz, *op. cit.*, II, pp. 27-28.

137. *Ibid.*, II, 30-39, 42-43.

138. *Loc. cit.*

139. Glenn, *op. cit.*, p. 70.

284

140. Simhah Zissel Ziv Braude, *HOKHMAH UMUSAR,* Vol. II (Jerusalem: Hat'hiyah Publishers, 1964), pp. 10, 24.

141. Simhah Zissel Ziv Braude, *HOKHMAH UMUSAR* Vol. I (New York: Aber Press, Inc., 1957) p. 137.

141*. *Ibid.,* p. 386.

141***. Braude, *op. cit.,* pp. 380-383.

142**. Katz, *op. cit.,* II p. 120-130.

142. Percival M. Symonds, *WHAT EDUCATION HAS TO LEARN FROM PSYCHOLOGY* (Bureau of Publications, Teachers College, Columbia University, 1960), p. III.

143. John I. Goodlad, "Understanding the Self in the School Setting," *CHILDHOOD EDUCATION,* XLI, (September 1964), 10.

144. Katz, *op. cit.,* II pp. 125-129.

145. *Ibid.,* pp. 193-194.

146. *Ibid.,* p. 218.

147. Braude, *op. cit.,* I pp. 423-424.

148. Katz, *op. cit.,* II p. 184.

149. *Ibid.,* p. 202.

150. *Ibid.,* pp. 203-205.

151. *Ibid.,* p. 172.

152. *Ibid.,* pp. 176-192.

153. Hayim E. Zaichyk, *HA-M'OROT HAG'DOLIM* (New York: Balshon Printing & Offset Co., 1962) p. 153.

154. Glenn, *op. cit.,* pp. 82-87.

155. Joseph Hurwitz, *MADREGAT HA-ADAM* (Jerusalem: Israeli Publication Committee, 1964), pp. 58-29.

156. Zaichyk, *op. cit.,* p. 159.

157. *Ibid.,* p. 164.

158. *Ibid.,* pp. 168, 171.

159. *Ibid.,* pp. 232-251.

159*. Hurwitz, *op. cit., pp.* 271-274.

160. Katz, *op. cit.,* II p. 256.

161. *Ibid.,* pp. 257-272, 291.

162. Zaichyk, *op. cit.,* pp. 156-158.

163. *Ibid.,* p. 157.

164. *Ibid.,* p. 160.

165. Katz, *op. iit.,* III. 17-19.

166. *Ibid.,* pp. 20-115.

167. *Ibid.,,* pp. 208-214.

168. *Ibid.,* pp. 220-261.

169. *Ibid.,* pp. 276-289.

170. *Ibid.,* pp. 276-297.

171. *Ibid.,* pp. 119-124.

172. Abraham S. Finkel, *N'TIVOT HA-MUSAR* (Tel-Aviv: A. Tziyoni Publishers, 1961) pp. 26, 48, 165.

173. *Ibid.,* pp. 126-133.

174. *Ibid.,* pp. 55-58.

175. Katz, *op. cit.*, III, pp. 161-162.
176. *Ibid.*, p. 163.
177. *Ibid.*, pp. 180-189.
178. *Ibid.*, pp. 199-207.
179. Wolfsberg, *op. cit.*, p. 53.
180. Kurzweil, *op. cit.*, p. 92.
181. Harry Nelson, "Mysteries of Brain Being Unlocked." *L. A. TIMES*, July 15, 1968, part II, p. 1.
182. Moses D. Tendler, "Medical Ethics and Torah Morality" *TRADITION*, IX (Spring 1968), 12-13.
183. See Elihu D. Schimmel, "A Rejoinder," and Nachum L. Rabinovitch, "What Is The Halakhah For Organ Transplants?" *TRADITION op. cit.*, pp. 14-27.
184. Moshe M. Yoshor, *HE-HAFETZ HAYIM* (Tel-Aviv: Nezah Publishers, 1959), pp. 582-83.
185. Horodetzki, *op. cit.*, p. 47.
186. Kaplan, *B'IKVOT HA-YIR'AH*, *op. cit.*, p. 22.
187. Student Committee, *HAYEI HA-MUSAR* (Bnei Brak: Hokhma Umusar Publishers, 1963), p. 20.
188. Horodetzki, *op. cit.*, p. 42.
188*. See Yeruham Levovitz, *DAAT HOKHMAH UMUSAR* Vol. I. (New York: Balshon Printing & Offset Co., 1967) & Vol. II. (New York: Deutsch Printing & Publishing Co., 1969) and Eliyahu E. Dessler, *MIKHTAV MA-ELIYAHU* Carmel and Friedlander, (eds.) Vol. I. (Jerusalem: Hathiyah Press, 1955) Vols. II, III. (Tel-Aviv Shem Publishers, 1964, 1965).
189. Yoshor, *op. cit.*, p. 583.
190. Kaplan, *B'IKVOT HA-YIR'AH*, op. cit., p. 20.
191. *Loc. cit.*,
192. Lee J. Cronbach, *EDUCATIONAL PSYCHOLOGY*, (New York: Harcourt, Brace & World, Inc. 1963), pp. 329, 598.
193. "Elementary School Children Learn Bill of Rights by Socratic Method," *UCLA Educator*, 9:2 (May, 1967).
193*. Cronbach, *op. cit.*, p. 329.
194. Moshe Kranzler, "Elementary Guidance — A New Horizon In Yeshiva Education," *The Jewish Parent*. 17:8 (June, 1966).
195. Kurzweil, *op. cit.*, p. 191.

BIBLIOGRAPHY

Ausubel, David P. *Theory and Problems of Adolescent Development.* New York: Grue & Stratton, 1954.

——————— *Theory and Practice in Child Development.* New York: Grune & Stratton, 1958.

Babylonian Talmud. Tractates *B'rahot, Yoma, Sotah, Shabbat, Bava M'tzia, Bava Batra, Avot.*

Bahya, ben Joseph Ibn Pakuda. *Hovot Ha-l'vavot.* Warsaw: Goldman Publishers, 1856.

Ben-Yehuda, Eliezer. *Milon Ha-Lashon Ha-Ivrit.* Tel-Aviv: La-Am Publishing House, 1948.

Berlin, Meir. *Fun Volozhin Biz Yerushalayim.* New York: Orion Press, Inc., 1933.

Blazer, Isaac. *Or Yisarel.* Tel-Aviv: Israel-American Offset, 1959.

Braude, Simhah Zissel Ziv. *Hokhma Umusar.* Vol. I. New York: Aber Press, Inc. 1957.

——————— *Hokhma Umusar.* Vol. II. Jerusalem: Hat'hiyah Publishers, 1964.

Cronbach, Lee J. *Educational Psychology.* New York: Harcourt, Brace & World, Inc., 1963.

Dessler, Eliyahu E. *Mikhtav Ma-Eliyahu.* Carmel & Friedlander (eds.) Vol. I., Jerusalem: Hathiya Press, 1955, Vols. II, III, Tel-Aviv: Shem Publishers, 1964, 1965.

Deuteronomy.

Ecclesiastes.

"Elementary School Children Learn Bill of Rights by Socratic Method," *UCLA Educator,* IX:2 (May, 1967).

Fantini, Mario and Gerald Weinstein. "Reducing The Behavior Gap" *The Pedagogic Reporter,* XIX (June 1968), p. 4.

Finkel, Abraham S. *N'tivot Ha-Musar.* Tel-Aviv: Tziyoni Publishers, 1961.

Frankl, Viktor E. *Man's Search for Meaning: An Introduction to Logotherapy.* Boston: Beacon Press, 1959.

Ginzberg, Louis. *Students, Saints and Scholars.* New York: Meridian Books, Inc. 1958.

Glenn, Menahem, G. *Israel Salanter, Religious-Ethical Thinker.* New York: Bloch Publishing Company, 1958.

Gold, Henry Raphael. "Can We Speak of Jewish Neuroses?" in Norman Kiel, (ed.) *The Psychodynamics of American Jewish Life.* New York: Twayne Publishers, Inc. 1967.

Goodlad, John I. "Understanding the Self in the School Setting." *Childhood Education* XLI (September 1964)., p. 10.

Greaetz, Henrich. *History of the Jews.* Philadelphia: The Jewish Publications Society of America, 1939.

Greenbaum, Aaron. "Official and Unofficial", *The Jewish Horizon.* XXVI (June 1963), p. 9.

Griffen, William L. "A Needed Dialogue: Schools and Values", *The Pedagogic Reporter,* XVI (Dec. 1964), p. 6.

Hertz, Joseph H. "Fundamental Ideas and Proclamations of Judaism". *in* Leo Jung (*ed.*) *The Jewish Library.* Second Series. New York: Bloch Publishing Company, 1930, p. 71.

Hirshowitz, Schneur Z. *Even Yisrael.* Vilna: Funk Publishers, 1912.

Horodetski, S. A. *Ha-Hasidut V'Ha-Hasidim* Tel-Aviv: D'vir Publishers, 1928.

Hurwitz, Joseph. *Madregat Ha-Adam.* Jerusalem: Israel Publication Committee, 1964.

Kaplan, Abraham E. *B'ikvot Ha-Yir'ah.* Jerusalem: Mossad Harav Kook, 1960.

——————— *Divrai Talmud,* Jerusalem: Mossad Harav Kook, 1958.

Katz, Dov. *T'nuat Ha-Musar.* Tel-Aviv: Beitan Ha-Sefer, 1952, Vol. I; 1954, Vol. II; 1956, Vol. III; 1957, Vol. IV.

Kranzler, Moshe. "Elementary Guidance — A new Horizon in Yeshiva Education", *The Jewish Parent* XVII:8 (June, 1966).

Kurzweil, Z. *Modern Trends in Jewish Education.* New York: Thomas Yoseloff, 1964.

Leviticus.

Levovitz, Yeruham. *Daat Hokhmah Umusar.* Vol. I. New York: Balshon Printing & Offset Co., 1967. Vol. II. New York: Deutsch Printing & Publishing Co., 1969.

Lipkin, Israel Salanter. *T'vunah in Shloshah Sefarim.* New York: Grossman Publishing House, 1965.

——————— *in Or Yisrael.* Isaac Blazer (ed.) Tel-Aviv: Israel-American Offset, 1959.

Lipkin, Israel Salanter. *in Even Yisrael.* Schneur Z. Hirshowitz (ed.) Vilna: Funk Publishers, 1912.

Lipkin, Hayim I. *Rabbi Israel Mi-Salant Shitato V'Torato.* Tel-Aviv: Nezah Publishing Company, 1953.

———— *Torat Rabbi Israel Mi-Salant.* Tel-Aviv: Nezah Publishing Company, 1954.

Luzzatto, Moshe Chayim. *Mesilat Yesharim.* Shraga Silverstein (tr.) Jerusalem: Boys Town Press, 1967.

Maimonides. *Mishneh Torah.*

Margolis, Max L. and Alexander Mark. *A History of the Jewish People.* Philadelphia: The Jewish Publication Society of America, 1947.

Nelson, Harry: "Mysteries of Brain Being Unlocked", *Los Angeles Times,* July 15, 1968, part II, p. 1.

Ronn, Avraham. "Darkei Ha-Hinukh Ba-Y'shivot" *Bisdeh Hemed* VI (February 1963.) p. 251.

Rosen, Kopul. *Rabbi Israel Salanter and the Musar Movement.* London: The Narod Press, 1945.

Sifra.

Stevenson, Harold W. (ed.) *Child Psychology.* Chicago: National Society for the Study of Education. 1963.

Student Committee, *Hayei Ha-Musar.* Bnei Brak: Hokhmah Umusar Publishers, 1963.

Student Committee of Mirer Yeshivah. *Hatvuno.* New York: Mirer Yeshivah Publication, I. 1947.

Symonds, Percival M. *What Education Has To Learn from Psychology.* Bureau of Publications, Teachers College, Columbia University, 1960.

Tanna D'vay Eliyahu.

Tendler, Moses D. "Medical Ethics and Torah Morality", *Tradition* IX (Spring 1968). pp. 12-13.

Vayikra Rabba.

Weinberg, Yehiel Y. "The Musar Movement and Lithuanian Jewry", *in* Leo Jung (ed.) *Men of The Spirit.* New York: Kymson Publishing Company, 1964, p. 217.

———— "T'nuat Ha-Musar V'shitatah", *Panim El Panim* CLI (March 16, 1962) p. 14.

Yawetz, Z'ev. *Toldot Yisrael.* Tel-Aviv: Achiever Publishers, 1937.

Yoshor, Moshe M. *He-Hafetz Hayim.* Tel-Aviv: Nezah Publishers, 1959.

Zaichyk, Hayim E. *Ha'M'orot Hag'dolim.* New York: Balshon Printing and Offset Company; 1962.

RABBI KOOK'S PHILOSOPHY
OF REPENTANCE

A Translation of
"Orot Ha-Teshuvah"

By ALTER B. Z. METZGER

A firm conviction in the inevitable progress of humanity constituted for Rabbi Kook the moral implication of the Hebraic heritage. The human species was constantly moving forward and approaching the ideal good which is elemental in the universe. Steeped in the teachings of mystical concept of world unity, Rabbi Kook maintained, that in all people there glowed a divine light. The full splendor of the light was frequently dimmed by an imperfect vessel in which it was cast, but some light was present everywhere as the footprints of God's presence. The light manifested itself in man's unlimited goals, in his unquenchable aspirations and relentless search for human progress and messianic idealism.

The Divine covenant with man after the deluge that "all flesh shall never again be cut off by the waters of the flood," was in effect a reassurance of the upward sweep of human history. By the same token, the very notion of God's omnipresence was an indication that the primary force in the world is *ratzon ha-tov,* the Good Will ultimately affecting the ascendant course of all existence. The good was everywhere in all things. The physical was linked with the spiritual as the foundation on which the spiritual rests. Despite the regressive manifestations of evil, the good was destined to assert itself and to triumph as the sparks of the divine light immanent in the universe continue to dispel the surrounding darkness in increasing measure.

Rabbi Kook's confidence in the ultimate triumph of goodness based on Divine Omnipresence was reflected especially in man's endless yearning for *teshuvah* — penitence — a return to the source of its being. Penitence was a perpetual process, an expression of the restless yearning of our creaturely nature. The essence of the soul by virtue of its developmental nature was repentance. Through penitence the soul sheds the fetters of its static self, renouncing its errors and transcending its inadequate virtues and rising to levels of perfection. "The will to repentance," wrote Rabbi Kook in *Orot Ha-Teshuvah* is always present within the heart. "At the very moment of backsliding the impulse to repent lies dormant within the soul and it radiates its influence which becomes manifest when remorse sets in calling for a return."

Originally published by Yeshiva University Press, 1968.

The growth in virtue and goodness is properly called a return. For as the soul which emanated from the Divine draws close to God it is only retracing its steps to the source whence it came. God is the Soul of all souls. The vast drama of life is one endless yearning to return to God.

The *Orot ha-Teshuvah* (Tel Aviv, Israel: Tarbut 1955) was commenced by Rabbi Kook prior to World War I and concluded in 1924. It was structured and edited by his son, Rabbi Zvi Yehuda Kook. It is one of the most significant books on religious thought as its doctrine of penitence underscores the underlying motif of Kook's ethical system. It also has its pragmatic ramifications. For as his ideas of *teshuvah* crystallized, the term "return" 'took on a practical meaning of the return to the land as a prerequisite for the people of Israel's return to a spiritual wholeness shattered by the *galut*.

The publication of the translation of *Orot Ha-Teshuvah* by Yeshiva University Press is a genuine contribution to Jewish scholarship as the work constitutes an authentic contemporary Jewish classic. The introductory chapter by Dr. Metzger focuses on the psychological dimensions of Rabbi Kook's thoughts and the Appendix is an attempt by the author to convey in simply language the mystical, poetic and often elusive concepts of Rabbi Kook's mystical but radiant insights. It should be remembered that a translation of any of Rabbi Kook's works is a staggering task. This is the first attempt at such an effort. It is our hope therefore, that the Appendix as well as the introduction will serve to clarify the often involved and poetic language of Rabbi Kook.

Dr. Metzger is Assistant Professor of Religious Studies at Stern College. He holds an Ed. D. degree from Teachers College, Columbia, and was ordained by the Rabbi Isaac Elchanan Theological Seminary of Yeshiva University. He has written frequently on chassidic literature and Jewish mysticsm in Tradition and other scholarly magazines.

OROT HA-TESHUVAH
LIGHTS OF REPENTANCE

Chapter I

For a long period of time I have been involved in an intense inner struggle and a strong spirit impels me to speak on the subject of repentance, and all my thoughts are centered on this theme. Repentance encompasses the major part of Torah and life; upon it are based all the hopes of individual man as well as the community. It is the commandment of God that, on the one hand, is the simplest to perform, for the slightest thought of repentance is in itself repentance. Yet in another sense, repentance is the most difficult of all commandments to fulfill, for indeed it has not been fully actualized in the world and in human life.

I find myself tending to think and to speak constantly only of repentance. Much is written in the Torah, the Prophets and the teachings of our Sages regarding repentance; however, to our generation these matters are obscure and require clarification. Literature, which explores all areas wherein are to be found poetry and life, has not at all penetrated within this wondrous treasure of life, the treasure of repentance. Actually, it has not yet shown the slightest interest in repentance, to know its character and value, nor even its poetic aspect, which inspires beyond comprehension, and most assuredly has not exerted any effort to bring about its practical realization, particularly as pertains to the conditions of modern life.

NOTE: See Appendix for explanation of difficult passages, either partial or complete.

293

I am compelled, from my innermost self, to speak of repentance. I draw back from this very thought, "Am I then worthy to speak on the subject of repentance?" The great of all past generations, the Prophets and the most saintly Sages, the greatest men of piety, wrote of repentance and how can I stand in their assemblage? But no inadequacy in the world can free me from this inner demand. I am compelled to speak about repentance, particularly its literary and practical aspects, to clarify its inner content for our generation, and to speak of the means of implementing it in the life of the individual and in the life of the community.

REPENTANCE: NATURAL, FAITHFUL, AND INTELLECTUAL

Repentance may be divided into three categories: one based on nature, one on faith and one on intellect.

Natural repentance possesses physical and spiritual aspects.

Physical repentance encompasses all transgressions against the laws of nature, as well as against the moral conscience and Torah, which are bound up with the laws of nature. The result of all evil conduct is sickness and pain, and the individual as well as society suffer intensely on account of it. Once a person clearly realizes that he is himself responsible for the deterioration of his life-strength, he will undertake to rectify the situation and he will turn back to the laws of life and abide by the laws of nature, ethic and Torah, so that he may return and live, and then life will be restored to him in all its vigor. The science of medicine occupies itself extensively with this matter, but apparently this great labor has not been brought to completion. As yet there has not been found the proper solution to all the problems of physical repentance; medical science has not yet learned to what extent there is within the limitations of life the possibility of restoring all that has been lost as result of the sins which have weakened the body and its powers. Apparently, this area of repentance is dependent upon and inextricably bound up with the other parts of spiritual repentance — natural, faithful and intellectual.

The innermost repentance is the natural repentance that pertains to the soul and spirit. It is that which is called "the ethic of the inner organs." It is the nature of the human soul to proceed upon an upright way. When a person strays from this way, and has fallen because of sin, if his soul is not as of yet completely corrupted, then this sense of uprightness pains his heart and causes him to waste away from great anguish, and he hastens to return so as to adjust that which is perverted until he senses that his sin is erased. This aspect of repentance is extremely complicated and dependent upon many conditions, both internal and external, and there are therein many paths of error of which he is obligated to take heed. Nevertheless, this type of repentance is one of the foundations upon which the content of repentance is based.

Consequent upon natural repentance there occurs repentance based on faith, with its source in tradition and doctrine, which concern themselves greatly with repentance. The Torah assures forgiveness to those that return from transgression. The prophetic writings are replete with exacted matters regarding repentance. The sins of the individual and of the community are erased by means of repentance. In general, the whole significance of the remonstration of the Torah is based upon faithful repentance. In its depths there are details beyond inquiry, and even their basic principles require extensive clarification and much exploration.

Intellectual repentance can be achieved after natural and faithful repentance have been undergone. It is ascent to the highest level. Not only bodily pain or spiritual anguish, the influence of heritage and tradition, whether through fear of punishment or from the effect of law and statute — none of these in themselves causes intellectual repentance. It is caused by a clear awareness that emerges from a total perception of life and the world, an awareness which has ascended to its level after the natural and faithful tasks have effectively exerted their impressions.

Encompassing the preceding stages, intellectual repentance is pervaded with infinite happiness. It transforms all sinful acts into acts of merit. From all errors it derives lofty teachings and from all degradations glorious exaltation. This is the repentance toward which the eyes of all are uplited and which inevitably must occur and ultimately shall occur.

Chapter II

SUDDEN AND GRADUAL REPENTANCE

As for the extent of the time entailed, repentance may be divided into two categories — the sudden and the gradual.

Sudden repentance derives from a spiritual flash entering the soul. All at once the individual recognizes the evil and ugliness of sin and is transformed into another person. Immediately he experiences inwardly a complete change for the good. This comes about by means of a manifestation derived from an inner spiritual quality, by means of a great soulful influence whose paths merit scrutinizing to the very depths of their concealment.

As for the gradual repentant, no flash has gleamed within him to transform him from the abyss of evil to virtue. Rather, he feels that he must go forward and improve the paths and ways of his life, his will and manner of thought. In this way, he advances and gradually acquires for himself paths of uprightness. He rectifies his qualities, improves his deeds, disciplines himself as to the manner in which he may constantly improve, till he finally comes to the exalted level of purification and rectification.

An upper level of repentance occurs from a flash of the general virtue, of the Godly virtue which exists in all the worlds, the Light of Him Who is eternal. The soul of Allness, so emanant, takes form before us, to the extent that the heart can assimilate; and, indeed, in truth, are not all things, in their essence, highly upright and virtuous? And the uprightness and virtue within us, do these not come from our harmony with all things? How is it possible, then, to be torn from everything with incredible severance — a separation comparable to fine grains of sand devoid of worth? And from this awareness, which in truth is Godly awareness, there shall come repentance motivated by love unto the life of the individual and the life of humanity.

Chapter III

PARTICULAR AND GENERAL REPENTANCE

There is repentance corresponding to a specific sin as well as to many sins. Man places his sin "before his face" and is remorseful for it. He is pained because of his having been caught in the snare of sin. His soul climbs and ascends till he is completely freed of bondage to sin; he senses within himself the sacred freedom, so pleasant to his weary soul, and is progressively cured. And the radiant lights of the sun of mercy, transcendental mercy, cast their rays upon him and he becomes joyful, he becomes filled with inner pleasure and delight, though simultaneously enduring a broken heart as well as a humbled and contrite soul — for he senses within himself that this very feeling, appropriate to him according to his present state, increases his inner spiritual pleasure and aids him toward true perfection. He constantly senses that he is coming ever closer to the source of life, to the Living God from Whom he was but a short while ago so remote. His yearning soul remembers with joyful heart its inner affliction and anguish and it is overwhelmed with feelings of thankfulness; with praise and song it lifts its voice:

> Bless the Lord, O my soul,
> And forget not all his benefits;
> Who forgiveth all thine iniquity;
> Who healeth all thy diseases;
> Who redeemeth thy life from the pit;
> Who encompasseth thee with loving kindness and tender
>   mercies;
> Who satisfieth thine old age with good things;
> So that thy youth is renewed like the eagle.
> The Lord executeth righteousness and acts of justice for all
>   that are oppressed. (Psalms 103:1-6)

Oh! how oppressed was the spirit while it yet bore the burden of sin,

298

when the dark, coarse, frightful endurance lay yet upon the spirit! How degraded and bludgeoned it was even if wealth and external pride were its lot! Of what worth is all wealth if the inner content of life is impoverished and decayed? How joyous and happy is the spirit now when it senses within itself that its iniquity is already forgiven and that the nearness of God animates and illumines within; that its inner burden is lightened, for it has already fulfilled its obligation and it is no longer suffering from inner oppression and turmoil. It abounds in virtuous repose and tranquility.

> Return O my soul unto thy rest;
> For the Lord hath dealt bountifully with thee. (Psalms 116:7)

Of another kind, again, is the elemental, general repentance. This comes to one who, though no specific sin or sins of the past come to his mind, in general senses within himself that he is greatly pained, that he is filled with iniquity, and that the light of God does not shine upon him. There is no "willing spirit" within him: his heart is calloused; his soul's qualities and characteristic do not proceed along the straight and desired way conducive to fulfillment of life appropriate unto a pure soul; his conceptions are coarse and his emotions are a confusion of darkness and lust which causes him spiritual revulsion. He is ashamed of himself and he is aware that God is not within him, and this is his greatest anguish, his most frightful sin. He is embittered at himself and finds no escape from the snare of his pursuers, which has no specific nature, but he is as one taken completely captive. From amidst this spiritual bitterness repentance emerges as healing by means of a skillful physician. The sensing of repentance and a profound knowledge thereof — of its great affinity to the depth of the soul, to the mysteries of nature and all inner recesses of Torah, faith and tradition — repentance with its full strength comes and streams into the soul. Intensive faith in the healing and in the all-embracing renascence which repentance extends to all that cleave to it shall cause a spirit of "favor and grace" to pass over him:

> As one whom his mother comforteth,
> So will I comfort you. (Isaiah 66:13)

He feels with the advance of each day to be in greater harmony with the general upper level of repentance. This feeling becomes more assured, clarified to a greater extent, increasingly illumined by the light of intellect and increasingly elucidated in accordance with the laws of the Torah. His face then beams, the visage of wrath passes, the light of acceptance casts its brightness, he abounds with strength, his eyes are filled with sacred light, his heart is immersed in "streams of pleasure," sanctity and purity hover over him. His spirit is filled with infinite love, his soul thirsts for God and his soul is satiated "as with marrow and fatness" from this very longing.

The spirit of holiness reverberates about him like a bell and he is informed that all of his transgressions are effaced, those known to him as well as those of which he is unaware, for he is created anew as a new creature, for the entire world and all worlds are renewed with him; all things sing praise to God; a divine gladness pervades all creation. "Great is the power of repentance for it brings healing to the world, and even if one individual repents, both he and the entire world are forgiven" (B. T. Yoma 86a).

Chapter IV

PARTICULAR INDIVIDUAL REPENTANCE AND GENERAL COLLECTIVE UNIVERSAL REPENTANCE—IN THE WORLD AND IN THE CONGREGATION OF ISRAEL

I.   The currents of individual and general repentance are sweeping forward. They are comparable to the waves of flames upon the surface of the sun, which in infinite battle leap forth and ascend. They give life to a multitude of world's and to creations beyond number. No power can encompass the great multitude of varying colors which emanate from this great sun, the sun of repentance that illumines all worlds. This cannot be done because of their rapid flowing and great profusion; because of their wondrous speed; because they themselves come from the source of life wherein even time is only one of many concentrated forms. The individual and collective soul of the universe and the infinite cries out as an awesome lioness in its pangs of suffering for complete rectification, for the ideal existence, and we sense the pains and they cleanse us; as the salt which sweetens meat, they sweeten all our embitterment. It is impossible to express in words this thought which is as the vastness of the heavens. We unite unities, we meditate upon the names of God: a dot — new heaven and earth in their entirety are concealed therein; a letter — and worlds are revealed; words — and tens of thousands of infinite worlds and multitudes of creations, tranquil and rejoicing, abounding with the gladness of the Almighty, abounding with peace and truth. And the soul proceeds toward its rectification.

II.   By means of repentance all things return to Godliness; by means of the existence of the power of repentance, which prevails in all the worlds, all things return and are united with the perfect Godly existence. By means of the conceptions of repentance, its

301

attitudes and emotions, all thoughts, conceptions and attitudes, wills and emotions are transformed and return to be established in the essence of their character, in a content of Godly sanctity.

III.   General repentance, which is the ascent of the world and its rectification, and particular repentance, related to the specific personality of each individual even to the extent of the most delicate details of specific means for rectification so as to achieve repentance, means which the sacred spirit can particularize to their most isolated details — they together form one content. Similarly, all those rectifications of culture, by means of which the world emerges from its state of ruin, as well as social and economic life-orders which advance toward perfection with the rectification of all sin and iniquity, from those most severe to minor prohibitions of the scribes and the most minute ethically pious observances — all of these constitute one distinct form and cannot be torn asunder from each other. "All of them ascend to one realm." (Zohar, II 162b)

IV.   The nature of the world and every particular creation, human history and each particular person and his deeds, must be viewed in one perception, as one content composed of various aspects. Then shall the light of knowledge hasten — the light which brings unto repentance shall hasten to appear.

V.   In actuality the ascent to spiritual yearning for general salvation is impossible without deep inner repentance from all sin and iniquity. In truth an individual who repents in this manner brings about forgiveness both for himself and the entire world. Similarly many can ascend to the ideal character concealed in the soul of the nation by means of individual repentance, this person returning with the purpose of enabling the pure emanation of the yearning toward the nation's grandeur.

VI.   The "summit's peak" of the nation's soul is the general purpose toward which the nation strives with the essence of its being, and this striving affects general existence. The idea of repentance is set fast in this exalted concealment.

VII. The soul of the congregation of Israel is absolute righteousness, which in its realization encompasses all actualized ethical virtue. Therefore, every ethical defect which the individual Jew commits weakens his bond with the soul of the nation. The primary basic repentance is to unite himself with the soul of the nation. At the same time it is necessary to rectify all his ways and actions in accordance with that qualitative content which is within the soul of the nation.

VIII. Prior to all categories of repentance, which occur subsequently, is the repentance to the glory of God; notwithstanding that with the diffusion of the light there is ascent of the conceptions till the content of glory, with all its breadth, is too narrow to contain the great flow of the lights of repentance, whose quintessence is more precious than wisdom and glory. This is the basis of the repentance whose light shall be revealed in the era prior to the advent of the Messiah. That repentance shall include within itself all the lesser paths of repentance, for they all are contained therein. With its great light at the onset of its breaking, it would appear as though the lesser lights are dispelled. And the "children of the violent" arise and uplift themselves to "establish a vision and stumble," but their stumbling comes only by means of the lesser lights which appeared to have been dispelled. The great light continues to exert its influence, and its "hand shall not rest" till it shall return to be revealed in all its major and minor qualities. "Repair my breach with the son of Peretz and from the thorn pluck the rose." (See Appendix, Item 1, for explanation of this paragraph.)

IX. From various aspects shall repentance come and be revealed. One of its most unique aspects shall be the pain over the humiliation endured by the great spirit concealed in all that has been transmitted to us by our ancestors, incalculable in its power and glory.

The source of this great spirit is a source of life, the Godly exalted source, which advances and extends from generation to generation. When we concern ourselves with it then all is to be found therein, all preciousness and all beauty. The darkness of denial caused the uprooting from this "very fruitful hill," as well as the erring in strange fields wherein there is for us neither vigor nor life.

This great pain shall break out with force, and it shall be accomplished by the strength of calmness and deliberation, so as to obtain knowledge of what may be derived from all the paths of error wherein stumbling has occurred; the freedom of the inner sanctity that is within the soul shall emerge from its imprisonment, and with mighty thirst every awakened spirit shall commence to draw and drink in abundance from that very source of exalted life.

Knowledge and feeling, the sense of life, the world view and the desire for national renascence, rectification of the soul's defects and enhancement of bodily strength, societal order and communal desire for honorable conduct, appropriate forbearance coupled with intense anger against everything that is abominable and evil against everything that is ugly and blemished, an inner dedication of soul for all the means whereby the general exalted virtue manifests itself and shall be enabled to manifest itself — all of these shall occur and be revealed then in one form. We must sustain all these matters by means of purification of the heart to the true inner light of Torah, the esoteric teachings of Torah, (See Appendix, Item 2.) in accordance with whose effects, exerted on those who cleaved to them without appropriate preparation, there have increased in similar manner those who would reject and cast shame upon these teachings. Specifically from this light of life from which the improper influences cause the growth of peril and world catastrophe — specifically from it shall Israel's salvation flourish, its eternal salvation, the manifestation of the exalted light of virtue by means of which life shall be imparted to mankind as well as to each individual, in order to uplift David's fallen tabernacle and to remove the shame of God's nation from upon the face of the earth.

X.   The insolence of the era prior to the advent of the Messiah (See Appendix, Item 1) occurs because the world has already developed to the extent of demanding understanding as to how all particularities are united with the general, and any particularity unrelated to the greatness of the general causes unrest to the mind. If the world would preoccupy itself with Torah light to such a degree that the spiritual soul would grow to the extent of perceiving the appropriate relationship between the spiritual particulars and their general categories, then repentance, and world rectification which accompanies and occurs by means of repentance, would manifest themselves and emerge to actuality. Since apathy has caused that the inner light of Torah requiring exaltedness and essential sanctity has not manifested itself in the world in an appropriate manner, there occurs the obligation of a life-order in such a manner that the particulars will be understood in terms of the general — at a time such as this, when the culmination of the light's manifestation and the "casting up" of the way to this understanding has as 'of yet not occurred; it is from this itself that the awesome devastation occurs.

Then we are compelled to utilize the most exalted remedy, which is the addition of strength to the spiritual faculty, until the way in which to understand and estimate the relationship of all matters of Torah thought and deed with the more lofty generality shall be something understood and explicated in a clear way by means of the soul's normal sensing; then shall the faculty of spiritual life in deed and thought return to illumine in the world, and general repentance shall commence to give its fruit.

XI. In truth, within the depths of life there gleams every moment a new light of the upper level of repentance, just as a new light surges within all the worlds in their fullness to renew them, and in accordance with the degree of this light of repentance and the abundance of wisdom and sanctity therein — so shall the souls be filled with treasures of new life. The fruit of the most exalted culture in ethic and deed develops and progresses from amidst the surging of this light. Consequently, the light of the entire world and its renewal in all its forms at all times and instances are contingent upon repentance, and how much more so does this apply to the light of Messiah and the salvation of Israel, the renascence of the nation and the land, the language and the literature, which all emerge from the source of repentance — and from the depths they shall be uplifted to the heavens of exalted repentance. (See Appendix, Item 3, for explanation of this paragraph.)

Chapter V

THE NECESSITY OF THE EXISTENCE OF REPENTANCE; ITS EFFECTS ON MAN, THE WORLD, AND THE CONGREGATION OF ISRAEL

I.   Repentance is the healthiest experience of the soul. A healthy soul in a healthy body must inevitably attain the great happiness of repentance, and in this state the soul will feel the greatest natural pleasure. The casting out of the harmful substances exerts its virtuous and healthful effect upon the body when the body is perfect in its character; and the spiritual voiding of every evil deed and all the evil and corrupt impressions caused thereby, of every evil thought, of every withdrawal from the the Godly emanant content in general which is the basis of all evil, the casting out of all coarseness and ugliness must inevitably come — when the organism is healthy both in terms of its spiritual and material aspects.

II.   Corresponding to every segment of abomination which departs from the soul of man by means of his inner assent to the light of repentance, there are reveled complete worlds in their exalted clarity within his soul. Every passing of sin is comparable to the removal of an obstructing object from the perceiving eye, and a complete horizon of vision is revealed, a light of the vast expanses of heavens and earth and all that is therein.

III.   The world must inevitably come unto perfect repentance. The world is not a stationary entity; rather, it is continuously developing and the truly perfect development will inevitably bring unto the world perfect well-being both material and spiritual. And this development shall also bring with it the light of repentant life.

IV.   The spirit of repentance pervades the world, endows the world with its basic character and also impels the world toward its development; with the scent of its fragrances, it refines and gives unto the world all of the world's distinctive beauty and splendor.

V. The obstinacy to remain constantly with one opinion and to be sustained thereby in the bonds of sin that have become habituated, either in actions or in thoughts, is an illness that derives from descent into oppressive enslavement, which does not permit the light of the freedom of repentance to illumine with the power of its strength; for repentance strives toward original, true freedom, which is the Godly freedom completely devoid of enslavement.

VI. Without the thought of repentance, its tranquility and assurance, man would be unable to find rest, and spiritual life would be unable to develop in the world. The ethical sense demands of man righteousness and virtue — perfection. How remote from man is the realization of ethical perfection in terms of actuality! How feeble is his ability to make his deeds correspond to the purity of the ideal of absolute righteousness! How then shall he strive for that which is not at all within the realm of his ability? Therefore repentance is natural to man and perfects him. If man is constantly prone to stumble, to impugn righteousness and morality, since the primary basis of his perfection is the yearning and firm desire toward perfection, this desire itself is the basis of repentance, which constantly triumphs over his way of life and truly perfects him.

VII. The future shall reveal the wonders of the power of repentance. This revelation shall be of interest to the entire world, beyond estimation, to a greater extent than all the wondrous visions which are normally perceived in all the expanses of life and existence. This new revelation shall attract the heart of all in its wondrousness, to such an extent as to exert an influence upon all with its spirit. Then shall the world arise to its true renascence. Sin shall cease, the spirit of impurity shall be consumed, and all evil shall as smoke pass away.

VIII. The congregation of Israel, with its great spiritual sensitivity, is the first in the world with regard to repentance. Israel is the unique universal entity wherein there shall first be revealed the quality of repentance. It is impelled to be in harmony with the Divine light that is in the world, wherein there is no sin or iniquity.

Every withdrawal from this characteristic causes defect in the perfection of this nation's nature; ultimately its mighty power in life shall triumph over the disorder, and perfect well-being shall come unto Israel and with great power shall cause it to reverberate. The light of repentance shall first manifest itself in Israel. Afterwards, Israel shall be the unique channel bestowing the life vigor of desire for refined repentance upon the entire world, to illumine unto the world and to exalt its state.

Chapter VI

THE EXISTENCE AND INNER EFFECT OF REPENTANCE WITHIN THE DEPTHS OF CONCEALMENT—OF MAN, THE WORLD, AND THE CONGREGATION OF ISRAEL

I. From the depths comes repentance, from so great a depth that the individual human spirit is not a unique form in relation to it, but a continuum of the grandeur of universal existence. The will of repentance extends to the will of the world in its most exalted source, and since the mighty current of the life-will's surge turns toward betterment, immediately many streams flow unto the fullness of existence to reveal virtue and to do good unto all. "Great is repentance for it brings healing unto the world, and when an individual repents both he and the entire world are forgiven" (B. T. Yoma 86a). In the great channel, in which there flows the vigor of essential life, there is revealed the unity of all existence in its source, and by means of the hovering life-spirit of repentance, all things are renewed to supreme virtue, illumining and radiant.

Repentance derives from the striving of all existence to be more virtuous and pure, stronger and more exalted than its present state. Within this desire there is concealed the life-force of prevalence over the finite dimensions of existence and its imperfections. The particular repentance of individual man, and most assuredly the repentance of the community, draws its strength from this source of life, which effects ever constantly with its power an unceasing labor. (See Appendix, Item 4, for explanation of these paragraphs.)

II. Repentance is always present within the heart. (See Appendix, Item 5.) Even at the time of sin itself, repentance is concealed within the soul, and it sends forth its rays, which are revealed afterwards at the time when there comes the cry calling for repentance. In the depths of being of existential life does repentance rest, because it preceded the world, and even prior to the occurrence of sin there is in the process of preparation repentance from the sin (B. T. Pesachim 54a). Therefore is there nothing so certain in the world as repentance; ultimately all things shall return to rectification, and most certainly Israel is assured and is in readiness to repent, to come closer to the will of its origin, to actualize in life the nature of its soul, despite all the restraining iron barriers obstructing the revelation of this enduring nature.

III. The natural fear of sin is the healthy nature of humanity in relation to universal ethic, and it is the nature distinctive unto Israel in relation to all sin and iniquity — a nature due to Torah and commandment, "the heritage of Jacob's congregation." This nature can be restored to Israel only by means of Torah study in great assemblage — the study of Torah to engender the growth of sages and also Torah study at established periods of time for the broad masses.

It is impossible for Israel to return to its enduring state and live a natural life unless there is also restoration of Israel's spiritual nature with all its many aspects. One of them, and the most powerful among them being the nature of fear of sin, the recoil from it and the established self-demand of repentance, if heaven forbid there should occur unto man a matter of transgression or iniquity.

When the life faculty of the nation shall prevail, encompassing all its aspects, then shall cease the agitation which confuses the intellect, and the facilitators of nationhood will once again concern themselves regarding the matter of establishing return to natural ethic, profound and distinctive unto Israel, an ethic which is scrupulous to the measurement of a hairbreadth's differentiation between the forbidden and the permissible; and all the minor prohibitions of Torah and all the minor prohibitions of the scribes shall be recognized as the essential ways of life, flourishing national life being utterly impossible without them.

IV. The ethical defects, whose source is the deviation from natural ethic, complete their effect by means of deviation from the Divine ethic, through withdrawal from religion. The departure and rebellion against the commandments of God is an awesome ethical decline which cannot come to man except as a result of excessive pre-occupation with the coarse aspects of material life. It is possible that for a certain extent of time a generation shall be confused, the entire generation or many persons of the generation, in countries and lands, with such confused blindness of ethic to the extent that man will not at all sense the ethical decline entailed in the leaving of God's statute. But the matter shall not lose its value because of this. Repentance must inevitably come and manifest itself, for the malady of forgetting the Divine world cannot assume for itself an enduring place in the nature of man. The matter is comparable to a murky spring which reverts to its former clarity.

V. Existence, man's act of choice, and his established will, are all one great chain, and they can never be torn asunder from each other. The desire of man is bound up with his actions. Even the deeds of the past are not severed from the nature of life and desire in its source. Since there is no matter that can be completely severed, it is within the power of desire to impress a distinctive character even upon actions of the past. This is the secret of repentance which the Holy One, blessed be He, created prior to the creation of the world. That is to say: He extended the soulful spiritual faculty of creativity in its relation to actions and existence to the extent that the past is also included in its domain. The evil deed proceeds cumu-latively, causing abomination and sin, loss and destruction, as long as the will has not impressed a new character upon it. When the will has imposed upon it a character of virtue, the deed itself causes virtue and pleasantness, the gladness of God and his light.

VI. The deeds are speaking within the soul. Every virtuous action develops after many sequences of development from virtue and sanctity. This action flows forth from a sacred source, for the exist-ence of sanctity caused it to come into being and caused its manifes-tation in actuality. Infinite are the causes which developed from exalted concealment till this virtuous action emerged to revealed actuality. Similarly, when it has already emerged to actuality it restores the light to its source and drives back the waves, extends the effect of sanctity and enlarges it from below to above. The reverse is also true. Every action whose source is corrupt, just as the impure source caused this action to come into being, so is the decay revealed within the spirit that created it till the action shall be uprooted from its source by the person who prevails over his deeds and his will with the great power of repentance. For then, particularly by means of repentance's ascent to the degree of love, it shall establish its abode in the depth of virtue and drive the waves from below above in the manner of the virtuous deeds unto virtue. (See Appendix, Item 6, for explanation of this paragraph.)

VII. At the beginning of creation, the taste of the tree was worthy of possessing the taste of its fruit. (Gen. Rabbah 5:9) All the means which strengthened any exalted general spiritual goal were worthy of being apprehended by a soulful sense with that very exaltedness and pleasantness that is to be felt in the essence of the goal when we conceive of it. But the nature of the earth, the instability of life, spiritual weariness, when it is enclosed in bodily enclosure, caused that the taste of the fruit of the ultimate goal, the primary ideal, should be sensed in its pleasantness and splendor. However, the trees bearing the fruit, despite their necessity for the growth of the fruit, had become more gross and corporeal and lost their taste. This is the sin of the earth, for which it was cursed when man was also cursed for his sin.

Every defect will ultimately be recitfied. Therefore we are most certainly assured that there shall come days when creation shall return to its antiquity, and the taste of the tree shall be as the taste of the fruit when the earth shall return from its sin, and the paths of active life shall not cause obstruction to the pleasantness of the ideal light, sustained in its path by appropriate means, which strengthen the light and bring it forth from potentiality to actuality.

Repentance itself, which causes the inner spirit to flow, the spirit sunken in the abysmal depths of the void and the very opposite of the ideal goal, repentance by providing expanse for the spirit of righteousness, which was originally in a state of oppression, shall also give power unto the ideal spirit to penetrate with its might into the parts of the many facilitators, and from them all shall there be apprehended the sense of the ultimate light. And man shall no longer bear the shame of sloth upon the way of true life.

Chapter VII

THE VALUE OF THOUGHTS OF REPENTANCE—ITS CONCEPTIONS AND MEDITATIONS

I. It is the nature of repentance to give unto man peace and oppressiveness of mind simultaneously. Man is consoled with even the slightest thought of repentance, within one small point of its great light there rests already the lofty and exalted happiness of an entire universe. At the same time, it constantly places before the eyes of his spirit the obligations of fulfillment, which save him from arrogance and cast upon him a sweet light, giving great and constant value to his life.

The conception of repentance transforms all iniquities and their confusion, their spiritual suffering and their ugliness, into conceptions of happiness and contentment because, by means of the iniquities, there emanates unto man the profound knowledge of hatred for evil, and love of virtue grows stronger within him with noble strength. Beyond all reckoning and knowledge, he derives from the joy of solace the Divine pleasure which is solely for those who have repented. Most pleasurable of all is this feeling when joined with the refining sense of a broken heart and contrite soul, a soul united with deep faith in redemption and eternal salvation.

II. Every thought of repentance unites the entire past with the future; thereby is the future exalted in the ascent of the will of repentance motivated by love.

III. By means of thoughts of repentance, man hears the voice of God which calls to him from amidst the Torah and from amidst all the heart's emotions, from amidst the world and its fullness and all that is therein. And the desire for virtue progressively grows stronger within him. The very flesh which caused sin is constantly refined, until the light of repentance penetrates within it.

313

IV. The thought of repentance is that which reveals the depth of will, and the strength of the soul is revealed by means of these thoughts in the fullness of its splendor; in accordance with the extent of repentance, so is the degree of the soul's freedom.

V. I hereby perceive the iniquities standing as a barrier before the clear Godly light which radiates with great radiance upon every soul, and the iniquities cast darkness and gloom upon the soul. Actually, even the slightest thought of repentance effects great salvation. However, the soul can achieve full redemption only by means of bringing to actuality the repentance which is potential within it. Nevertheless, since the thought is bound with sanctity and with the desire for repentance, there is nothing to fear. Most assuredly, God, blessed be He, will provide all the ways whereby perfect repentance, which illumines all the dark realms with the light of its life, can be achieved. In accordance with the greatness of the value of repentance, so is Torah blessed and more greatly clarified. Torah study becomes more lucid and clear:

A broken and a contrite heart,
O God, Thou wilt not despise. (Psalms 51:19)

VI. There must be pondering with great depth upon faith in repentance, and there must be assurance that even with the slightest thought of repentance there is great rectification of self and the world. It is inevitable that after every slight thought of repentance man shall be more happy and content with his soul than he was at the onset. How much more true is this when the mere thought has already come unto man's acceptance of repentance, and the thought is joined with Torah, wisdom and fear of Heaven. Most assuredly is it thus when the quality of love for Godliness reverberates within his heart. He should console himself and comfort his weary soul, strengthening it with every manner of strength to be found in the world, for it is the word of God:

As one whom his mother comforteth,
So will I comfort you. (Isaiah 66:13)

And if he should find within himself sins in matters "between man and his fellow man," and his power is weak as regards their rectification, nevertheless, let him not despair at all from the great rectification of repentance, for the iniquities "between man and his maker" are forgiven once he has repented for them. Therefore, we may surmise that the remaining segments hitherto unrectified will be nullified by the majority, since the greater part of his iniquities have already achieved forgiveness as a result of his repentance. Nevertheless, let him not rest his hand from great caution so as not to fall victim to any sin "between man and his fellow man" and to rectify all that he can from the past in a manner of wisdom and great spiritual courage:

> Deliver thyself as a gazelle from the hand of the hunter,
> And as a bird from the hand of the fowler. (Proverbs 6:5)

Yet let not his "heart fall within him" as regards that which he has been unable to rectify. Rather should he strengthen himself in the fortress of the Torah and God's service with a whole heart — in joy, in fear, and in love.

Chapter VIII

THE PAINS OF SIN, THE SUFFERINGS OF REPENTANCE AND HEALING BY MEANS OF THE EMANATION OF REPENTANCE

I. The pain, sensed with the thought of repentance, at the onset of its shining occurs due to the severances; for the evil parts of the soul, which can have no rectification as long as they are united in one form with the spiritual organism, corrupt the entire soul and cause defect unto it. By means of repentance they become severed and uprooted from the essence of the soul which is basic in its origin. Every severance brings pain, as the pain of uprooting decayed limbs and the pain of their amputation due to reason of therapy. These are the innermost sufferings by means of which, and through which, man emerges to freedom from the dark enslavement of his sins and his base inclinations with their bitter consequences. "By means of the 'major-minor' method this may be derived from the law that a slave is freed upon an inflicted loss of an eye or tooth." "Happy is the man whom Thou instructeth O Lord, and teachest out of Thy law." "Read not 'teachest'; rather, shall Thou teach us; this matter hast Thou taught us from Thy Torah. (B. T. Berachot 5a)

II. The great pains which grip the soul by means of the thought of repentance, although they appear at times to originate in fear of punishment, their inner content is naught but essential sufferings, for the soul is seared by them because of the sin paining it, sin which is contrary to the soul's conditions of life, and these sufferings in themselves cleanse the soul. The man who is aware with an inner awareness of the treasure of virtue, which rests within these sufferings, accepts them with absolute love and his mind achieves tranquility in them. Thereby does he ascend to many levels; his learning remains with him; his inner character is perfected, and the impressions made upon him by his iniquities are erased. They are transformed into virtuous indications, from which there emerges a soulful splendor.

III. Every sin pains the heart because it destroys the unity between the particular personality and the totality of existence. Man is cured only by means of repentance which shines upon him and in which there is the exalted flow of the "ideal" possessed by the causation of existence. Thereby do general accord and correspondence to existence return to become manifest within him. "He returns and is healed." However, the basis of pain is not solely from the essence of sin, but also from the basis of sin and from the content of the way of the soul, which has become contrary to the order of being, shining with the straight Godly light in all existence, existence united in exalted unity and correspondence. Because of this, those whose souls have their basis in evil and the roots of all their sins rest in their thought, in their striving and in the quality of their hearts — their perception is evil and the entire world appears to them in a color infinitely black. It is they who thunder upon the world and life, "masters of the melancholy spleen," whose derision of all existence is the laughter of a fool, who cannot understand that "the Lord is good to all."

IV. What is the source of the rage of the evil? Why is their anger against the entire world? What is the basis of the bitter melancholy which consumes spirit and flesh, which fills life with venom, that is to be found among them? From whence does this corrupt source derive? With clear inner assurance we reply: all this wells forth from the source of evil. "Out of the evil cometh forth wickedness." (Sam. I 24:14) The will is free. Life has been brought forth so that man can be strong and truly free, and the evil which reposes in the depth of the soul, when the will does not desire to depart from it, destroys the equal balance of life — the upright relationship that man's soul possesses with all being, with the totality of existence both in general and in particular. The disruption of the harmony causes intense pains. And when it penetrates to the spirit, great are the sufferings which manifest themselves in the form of trembling, anger, insolence, of levity and despair. Therefore the righteous call out — the men of virtue and kindness, the men of happiness and life — to the suffering wicked: "Come and live. Return from your evil ways. Why should you perish? Take pleasure in the goodness of God and see a life of pleasure and of light, of tranquility and peace, of trust and dignity."

"As dew from the Lord, as showers upon the grass." (Micah 5:6)

V. The great pain, which each righteous person feels within himself on the lessening of Godly cleavage — for he senses within himself that he does not quench his great thirst — from this pain all his limbs are constantly racked due to the great "yearning of the soul." He finds no peace from all the pleasure and satisfaction that exist in the world. This is in actuality the pain of the divine Presence, for the content of life of all the worlds in their entirety strive toward exalted Godly perfection — that it may be revealed within them. This revelation, in its breadth and pleasures, is conditional in that it requires the perfection of mankind's free will with all the talent and action, virtuous and splendrous, entailed therein. Therefore do the righteous constantly yearn for the repentance of mankind, and in the depths of their hearts they pursue the exoneration of the guilty as one pursues after life, for in truth it is our life and the life of all the worlds.

VI. When the righteous repent, they illumine with the light of sanctity all the darkened ways and defects that they find within their souls, and the counsel that they create for themselves, to ascend from amidst the fall and despair within their hearts unto the clear light of sanctity and exalted uprightness, these counsels in themselves become great light to illumine unto the world. Every person who feels within himself the deep remorse of repentance and the embitterment of thought for the rectification of his defects, whether those whose rectification he is capable or those of whose rectification he is as of yet not capable but hopes regarding them for compassion, should include himself thereby in the category of the righteous, for by means of the thoughts of repentance of righteous men the entire world is renewed in new light.

VII. The entire world is filled with harmony, the harmony which unites and penetrates into all recesses and crevices of existence. The inner ethos and its strong demands derive from the united clamor of all parts of existence. These parts all penetrate into each other and the entire soul is filled with them all and united with them all. Every ethical sundering in thought and deed, in character and temperament causes many severances which bring much inner suffering to all the orders of the soul. The basis of these spiritual pains is the terrifying power of the withdrawal of the light of life which is possessed by the general order of all existence, withdrawal from the life channels of the sinning soul. The greater the purity of the soul, the more it feels the tremors of its pains, till the soul stills its pain in the stream of the life of repentance, which wells forth from the upper source, the stream of repentance which unites all the severances and causes to flow forth a dew of life that proceeds unswervingly from all orders of existence, "One is so near to the other," till the parts of the soul which returns to exalted renascence with great mercy and with everylasting gladness.

VIII. When the spiritual anguish, caused by the spiritual life position of one's self, which is the pain of repentance, and of the entire world, become so severe as to obstruct the sources from whence come the thoughts, speech, prayer, outcry, feeling and poetry, then do these all ascend in a leap to reveal lights abounding with life from the source of silence.

And the parched land shall become a pool,
And the thirsty ground springs of water. (Isaiah 35:7)

IX. When the thinker takes to solitude and there is revealed within his soul his inner spiritual faculty, he senses all the defects whereby his soul has become imperfect because of inappropriate deeds and character traits. He is pained then with a deep inner pain, and he probes within his spirit for the means to rectify that which has been perverted. If the inner pain is experienced in its full intensity, when the external state has become weakened, as, for example, at a time of disturbance and distress, then the inner feeling is not very strong. Nevertheless, even then it can achieve its "loftiest height," for even repentance caused by means of suffering is also deemed repentance.

X. The inner pain of repentance is a great theme for the poets of sorrow to strike up upon their harps and for artists of tragedy — to reveal thereby their talent.

XI. Iniquities are the essence of sorrow, and when the soul is purified, it senses the essence of the iniquities; then the sorrow of repentance prevails upon the soul, and there burns within its heart the flame of remorse, shame and awesome fear. This in itself causes the cleansing of the soul, and it shall be able, after the passing of wrath, to return to its strength, to stand in its honor and essential dignity.

XII. There must be great heed from melancholy, but not to so great a degree as to prevent the light of repentance from penetrating into the depth of the soul. At that time, melancholy spreads as a malignant illness to the very extremities of body and soul, for sin saddens the heart and causes melancholy to be intrinsic to the searing bitterness of flaming repentance; for though repentance is possessed of melancholy aspects, they are as a purifying flame, purging the soul, strengthening it upon the basis of constant natural joyousness appropriate to the soul.

XIII. Every sin imposes separate anxiety upon the soul, which can depart only by means of repentance. Commensurate with the intensity of repentance, the anxiety itself is transformed into faith and courageousness. The impressions of anxiety occurring due to sin can be discerned in the lines of the face, in movements, voice, conduct, script, style of language, speech and most particularly in the writings, in the expression of thoughts and their order. In the place where sin obstructs the light, there is the defect discerned; in the manner the writer relates to the theme, thereby the impression is discerned by those who perceive with clear eyes.

XIV. It is impossible to estimate the pain caused by absence of will for virtue and sanctity; wisdom can only ascend in accordance with the blessing of will within it. Iniquities hinder the will preventing its ascent, and man must return in repentance for the clarification of will, so that wisdom may ascend in an appropriate manner. He must particularly return from transgressions toward his fellow man, prior to all — of oppression which hinders ascent of will; he must greatly strengthen himself in this matter and hope for "God's salvation" to achieve the perfection "of ceasing our hand from oppression."

XV. The despair that occurs within the heart, in itself, is indicative of an inner sensitive self-reproach, which flows forth from an exalted awareness of ethic and sanctity. It is therefore appropriate that despair itself should strengthen the heart of man not to fear and to return from all sin with repentance abounding in tranquillity and spiritual courage.

XVI. When there arises within the heart of man to return in perfect repentance, and to rectify all his actions and emotions — even in thought alone, let not his heart fall within him because of his anxiety due to his many iniquities, which he senses now to a greater extent. For this is the nature of the matter: as long as man is pursued by the wrath of coarse habit and the darkness of evil traits which surround him, he does not fully sense his sins — at times he does not sense them at all; thus is he righteous in his own eyes.

However, as soon as his moral faculty is awakened, immediately is there revealed the light of the soul; by means of this light he searches out his entire soul and perceives all its blemishes. His heart becomes concerned with a sense of deep anxiety over his lack of perfection and the depth of his fall. Specifically then should he take to heart that this perception and the anxiety accompanying it are the best indications, for they bring him tidings of eternal salvation as regards the soul's rectification, and he should strengthen himself with this knowledge in the Lord his God.

Chapter IX

THE VALUE OF THE WILL AS REVEALED BY MEANS OF REPENTANCE

I. The fixed constance of the thought of repentance is that which establishes the character of man upon an emanent basis, and he then constantly absorbs within himself a refined spirit; thereby does this thought establish him upon the spiritual basis of life and existence.

The repentance which constantly is to be found within the heart ascertains unto man the great value of spiritual life; the important principle that the virtuous will is allness and all the talents in the world are naught but its fulfillment becomes a content natural to his soul by means of the light of repentance constant within him. Consequently, there rests upon him a great emanation of sacred spirit ever constantly, and a will exalted in sanctity, greater than the fixed measure of normal persons, becomes progressively strengthened within him; and he comes to realize the true virtue of perfect achievement which is dependent only upon man himself, and not upon any external condition — reliant only upon the virtuous will. This achievement is a happiness greater than all treasures and wealth; only it can bring happiness to the world and all existence. For the virtuous will which constantly abides within the soul transforms all of life and existence unto virtuousness, and by means of virtuous perception, whereby he perceives the reality of existence, man effects upon existence and on the paths of confusion in life that they may emerge from their state of corruption; and all things blossom forth and live in happiness as a result of the soulful wealth and contentment within the virtuous will.

This teaching that all world problems are reliant solely upon the virtuous will is promulgated in the world by means of the "Masters of Repentance," for the content of repentance is the constant aspira-

322

tion of their souls; thereby does the will truly proceed to become refined and virtuous, and the world proceeds toward greater perfection.

The will that comes from the faculty of repentance is the profound will of the depth of life. It is not a superficial will which takes hold only of the weak and external aspects of life. Rather, it is that will which is the most inner seed for the basis of life. It is the absolute essence of the soul. Since the will is steadfast in its virtue due to the profundity of repentance, virtue is thereby made constant in the reality and nature of the soul; as a result, all derived consequences, and all the seeds the true penitents bring unto the world, draw their light of life from the basis of virtue. Verily, these persons are possessed of illumining souls, these souls being permeated with the ideal light of exalted sanctity. (See Appendix, Item 7, for explanation of these paragraphs.)

II. The horizon of perception is broadened by means of repentance. The basis of ideal will is lengthened and extends from the very beginning of the world, proceeding and encompassing to the end, to the conclusion of all generations. Due to the great magnitude, length, width, loftiness and depth of this penetrating perception, Godly virtue and kindness are revealed in their true form; particular and general life proceed and are established on the basis of absolute uprightness. The defects which can be seen in the life order are discerned as folds which are straightened and leveled (see Appendix, Item 8) in the grandeur of the life of the virtuous will, which sweeps forward like an enormous river extending across generations and eras, for only fragmentary aspects of life are revealed in each individual generation, and their fulfillment comes with the passage of all generations; piercing, encompassing will of repentance brings unto all generations life, peace and blessing abounding with pleasure. In its revelation there is revealed that happiness and righteous joyous-ness have established their place from the beginning and onset of repentance's will, and all that appeared trivial and all that was regarded as ugly in the past are revealed to abound only in splendor and greatness, having been aspects of the exalted grandeur of the advance of repentance.

III. The basis of repentance brings actual healing to the entire world; the swift flow of will completes its effect forcefully, specifically through its release from constraint. The "Masters of Repentance" draw with exceeding power the strength of life from the source of virtue. All actions and creations are existentially united with the might of will which assumes form in man in the brightness of its glory.

The bases, faculties and consequences are dispersed in all directions. What instills within them the light of life, system and order for the flourishing of virtue and the avoidance of the snare of evil? — the exalted will, the might of ethic which illumines from the speculum above. With the revealed intent of a holy nation are all deeds joined in one unity to fulfill the will of the Holy King Who is exalted in justice and sanctified in righteousness.

IV. The weakening of will which occurs due to constant absorption with repentance, despite this being a physical and spiritual weakness, which requires remedy, nevertheless, there exists therein much of refinement and emanance, which purifies the spirit, and "all of its transgressions shall be concealed by love." (Proverbs 10:12)

V. When preoccupied with repentance, it is particularly necessary to define clearly between the nature of good and evil, so that the remorse and agitation of will from affirmation to negation will take effect only upon evil and not upon virtue; even more, there must be a clarification and strengthening of the virtue to be found in the depth of evil — with that very power by means of which man flees from evil, so that repentance can be a force effecting for virtue, actually transforming all intentionally evil acts into meritorious acts.

VI. Sin obstructs the illumination of exalted wisdom, whose manner of manifestation derives from the relationship of perfecting harmony which the discerning soul bears toward all general existence and .its supreme source. This relationship manifests itself in that . very channel of the soul wherein knowledge and will constitute a unified entity. Every sin in deed severs this ideal unity of knowledge and will, placing the circle of life beyond it. And the manifestation of the illumining of exalted wisdom (see Appendix, Item 9) which flows like a clear spring does not return to flow towards the desecrated will until man repents and is remorseful; and the light of repentance, in accordance with the degree of its clarity of awareness and profundity of assent, shall then restore the harmony to its strength:

> Restore unto me the joy of Thy salvation
> And let a willing spirit uphold me. (Psalms 51:14)

VII. There is a fault in the character of the lower level of repentance, in that it weakens the will of man and thereby causes defect in his personality. This fault is corrected when the thought of repentance comes to its fullest development. For it then is united with exalted repentance, whose primary intent is not the weakening of will and the breaking of the personal character of man, but rather the strengthening of his will and the enhancement of the worth of his personality. Thereby are intentionally evil acts transformed into acts of merit:

> If he turns from his sin and does that which is lawful and right, upon them shall he live. (Ezekiel 33:19)

VIII. Repentance removes that will which has become actualized in deed and has acquired for itself the existential faculty of power to such an extent that it has broken with its force the very force of ethic and faith; when the Godly light is adequately aroused, the will is uprooted from its source and it does not revert to chaos. Rather, the will acts with its power on the foundation of the world to instill within all of existence a mighty will for light and virtue, and intentionally evil deeds are transformed into deeds of actual merit.

IX. Every sin flows from a defect in the capability of man's soul. If the soul is weakened and cannot stand against the inclination toward evil that is within it, then this inadequacy when actualized weakens the power of the will to virtue, and weakness of the will causes weakness of knowledge and the awareness of virtue becomes obscured. Repentance occurs after understanding, when the awareness of virtue is strengthened. This awareness occurs in its perfect form, together with an awareness of evil, "evil tests virtue"; when the depth of evil is made known in its evil, then does virtue shine even more in its virtuousness. To the extent that the awareness of virtue is clarified, and the defect, which caused the sin to darken knowledge is removed through the restoration of the will and the inclination of the soul toward virtue — to that extent is there also aroused by means of this awareness the inclination to establish the will of virtue and to also save it from the defect of sin; and the soul that was weakened acquires its strength thereby to set aright that which was fallen and to rectify its own capability, that it may be in its fullness, capability for virtue; thereby choice is truly made free, and the weighing of virtue is done without disturbance. Consequently, the spiritual drawing force, which exists in each soul to be drawn toward virtue, is effective with respect to the strengthening of the balance in favor of virtue and toward establishing the life order of the individual as well as all humanity upon the goal of absolute virtue, whose last word is — the light of God.

X. Repentance, and all its practical applications together with the general spirit which prevails primarily during the days designated for repentance, repentance with its great benefit to cleanse the soul, refine the spirit and purify deeds from their ugliness — must inevitably conceal within itself some manner of weakness, from which even the most powerful cannot escape.

When there is constriction of will, when the power of life is inhibited due to the inner recoiling and the inclination to return from all sin — the will for virtue is also constricted, and the power of pure life is also weakened; thus it occurs that man endures from his purification weakness comparable to that endured by a sick person who is cured by means of a strong electric charge. For though it has eliminated the virus of his illness, but it has also weakened the vital and healthy power within him. Therefore there return days of sacred joyousness, of spiritual gladness to uplift the will of virtue and the power of pure life — then shall there be perfect repentance. (See Appendix, Item 10, for explanation of these paragraphs.)

Chapter X

THE RECIPROCAL NECESSITY OF TORAH AND REPENTANCE IN TERMS OF THEIR GENERAL NATURE AND IN TERMS OF THEIR EXALTED QUALITIES

I. Truly perfect repentance requires exalted contemplation, ascent to the splendor of the world wherein abound truth and sanctity. This is only possible by means of preoccupation with the profound aspects of Torah as well as the Godly wisdom concerning the esoteric matters of the universe. This, however, requires physical cleanliness and ethical purity to aid that the clouds of desire should not obstruct the radiance of intellect. But prior to all manifestions must come Torah, and specifically exalted Torah, for only it can destroy all the iron barriers that stand between individual man as well as the community and their father in heaven. (See Appendix, Item 11, for explanation of this paragraph.)

Repentance occurs as a result of a lucid reckoning of a clarified world, and repentance itself clarifies and elucidates the world with its power.

II. A good indication of exalted repentance is an inner pleasure and an illumining of the mind with exalted thoughts, clarity of conception and the sacred power of the pure faculty of imagination which garbs exalted understanding — understanding which encompasses all paths of life.

III. Every sin prevents the tranquillity necessary for the emanation of the world's esoteric matters. Repentance opens the gates of understanding just as it occurs only by means of understanding. (See Appendix, Item 12, for explanation of this paragraph.)

IV. Repentance is necessary for comprehension of the divine. Strengthening and illumining of will and strengthening of intellect are united with each other. The deeds increase light upon the exalted sources from whence they issued forth, and the emotions of the soul, which have their basis in the sources of exalted sanctity, reveal by their very existence these sources. Therefore, he who is prepared for constant cleavage to God cannot proceed upon a lesser path; there repose already within his heart compelling circumstances, physical and spiritual, which strengthen him to return to perfect Godly cleavage. However, it is impossible to attain it except through absolute humility, which comes from the exaltation of the soul caused by rejoicing in the light of God. This joy is created within the heart after the acquisition of conceptual knowledge, that the thought of cleaving unto God in all its forms is the greatest happiness of life. To the extent that it shall grow in splendor, to the extent that it will be adorned with the beauty of knowledge and grandeur of spirit, of established life paths and deeds, of expanding social light, and of the soul's grandeur and purity — to that extent life's happiness will increase; consequently, soulful joy shall then penetrate; cleavage itself shall ascend to its exalted level, till the majesty of God will be revealed in the soul. As a result, the humility of righteousness which manifests itself with the majesty of God shall be infinite, for how can man be vain when standing before the source of all perfection — exalted infinite light which transcends all blessing and praise.

V. How coarsening are transgressions to the intellect, both to the intellect of the individual as well as of humanity, of the generation and of the era! When decline causes that condition of life wherein man is caught contrary to the exalted spirit of life shining upon him, contrary to the word of God which comes to him from all the word's manifestations, from Torah, from faith and also from the custom of fathers, from the assent of humanity, and from his inner uprightness, — of which the extension of exaltedness also within all of these develops and is drawn, from the vital, abounding content within the spirituality of the world and the fullness thereof, within the laws of heaven and earth and their most basic reality. When decline causes man to be an object of oppression to the "blind side" within him, to that weak side, and he is unable to summon up enough strength for a mastery of life in an orderly manner as it fully demands of him, namely the demand which separates man from sin, establishing him upright as God had made him — then has not only one aspect of his many aspects descended and declined, nor is there only weakening of temporary will, with his spirit in its essence and degree, his intellect and all the light of life within him remaining intact. The matter is not so. His countenance has changed completely. The light of established intellect, which is united in the depth of soulful existence with all the faculties of life, interwoven in the total fabric of the actual ethical and spiritual order of all that encompasses him, from below and above, this very light is weakened. And this light is the secret of life itself, the power of the grasp of life, wherein the soul finds its spiritual plasma. Only in purity and repentance will light and life itself be restored and revealed. Therefore, repentance is the basis of human culture, the culture so avid sought.

VI.   Transgressions and unrefined qualities coarsen the heart, and as long as the heart is darkened by them it is utterly impossible for clear self-introspection to unfold and extend properly. The seeker, who desires to ascend to the heights of exalted understanding will sense this within his soul, and he shall sense within himself the absolute necessity to return in perfect repentance, so that the exalted understanding itself should not be possessed of defect. However, for all sins of man, between man and God, spiritual repentance immediately restores the joyous salvation of spiritual light, but as regards transgressions toward his fellow man it is impossible for the soul to achieve perfection till the transgressions shall be rectified in actuality. At times he shall encounter obstacles and hindrances over which he cannot prevail; as long as they remain unrectified, they restrain the light of intellect, and consequently they hinder awareness of general righteousness and the desire for its emergence from its concealment. Nevertheless, by means of firm affirmation to be scrupulously heedful henceforth so as not to sin against man, and intensive endeavor to rectify the past — to that degree of the fulfillment of repentance in deed shall there be commensurate increase of the radiance of spiritual light upon the soul, till the power of the spirit by itself shall provide many ways whereby he can perfect his repentance in deed to enable the spiritual light to rest upon the soul, which thirsts for this light in all its fullness and goodness.

VII. When man ascends to the heights of thought, then there immediately come his iniquities and obstruct from him the exalted light. The great thoughts are abased by means of the darkness of iniquities which have made their impressions upon the recesses of the heart. Nevertheless, he should return at that time immediately with clear repentance, which shall restore to him the life of happiness instantly as in the instance of an eye movement. In accordance with the degree that repentance has been actualized in deed in all the orders of life, so shall the fruits of thought be ennobled and the flow of his thoughts blessed.

VIII. It is an apparent matter that it is impossible to succeed in the study of esoteric teachings without repentance. For in those great matters will and knowledge are one unity. And when there is understanding of the innermost content of these subjects — in accordance with the degree of the strength of will for virtue — there is longing and much conception regarding the many particular and general means whereby greater understanding can be achieved of the innermost content. But when the iniquities separate, then there is defect in will, and since man does not rise to the exalted will within him, and his heart does not accord profound significance to the desire for general and particular virtue because he is sunken under the yoke and virulence of sin, then it is impossible for knowledge to shine upon him, and the channels whereby he can comprehend the esoteric matters of Torah are obstructed. Therefore there must be great strengthening with repentance and clarification of will so as to be worthy of exalted knowledge, lucid and clear, regarding exalted matters.

IX. It is impossible to enter the esoteric world of the spiritual and to gaze upon exalted light without the precedence of perfect repentance, for as soon as man perceives exalted light, there is immediately revealed the radiance of absolute righteousness and the beauty of exalted sanctity. An awesome demand takes hold of him that he too should be united with that radiance and beauty, and that his life and all its paths should be rooted in them. Immediately, he reflects upon his deeds and qualities and perceives their defects. Then remorse grows strong within him and he returns with perfect love. In accordance with the intensity of his affirmation to proceed upon the way of virtue, which corresponds to the light of pure intellect — this light ascending to its highest level by means of the illumining of Torah, and the Jewish personality finding only therein the depth of its obligation — to that degree does he ascend to be rooted in the upper world. His thoughts achieve greater radiance without inner inconsistency, and the spiritual visions of exalted intellectuality concerning the esoteric matters of the world stand before him in the essence of their brilliance, in accordance with the level of his soul and its preceding preparation and in accordance with the might of his soul's power and its true spiritual freedom.

X.   When man proceeds upon the way of pure contemplativeness regarding Godliness, he senses within himself that there is a barrier separating him from his clear conceptions; the soul itself discerns that this barrier is the deeds and qualities of character which are not virtuous. Immediately there awakens within his heart the longing for perfect repentance, to the highest form of repentance, which in many instances cannot be appropriately actualized without their being proximate unto it intensive prayer. Then shall the fountain of strength revert and flow forward, flowing and proceeding upon the soul.

XI.   Prayer, outcry and repentance from the depth of the heart, and their revelation in actuality by means of rectified deeds must inevitably precede the manifestation of the light of exalted understanding. And it is impossible for a truly significant literature to be born and manifest itself within the light of life in the world except by means of the revelation of the light of repentance, which renews the appearance of the entire world; verily, the aura of this future literature manifests itself in the gleaming of intellect which precedes the light of repentance. Knowledge infuses the spiritual faculty with perfect freedom and the lofty exalted liberty which leads to perfect repentance, repentance which brings redemption in its wake. This shall occur after inner and outer forgiveness, after healing and economic sustenance, after the ingathering of the exiles and the restoration of power to judges and counselors who are the pillars of literature and its founders. Freedom strives to come, evil is humbled, righteousness ascends, the heart of the nation commences to beat with the very strength of its life toward Jerusalem, and the growth of the crown of a perfect kingdom manifests itself. Every heart's desire is fulfilled by means of the prayer of the upright which abounds with the will of Him Who sustains the world, of "Him Who spoke and caused all things to come into being."

Chapter XI

THE SOURCES OF REPENTANCE IN GENERAL EXISTENCE AND IN THE EXALTED SPIRITUALITY OF EXISTENCE

I.   Repentance occurs due to "understanding." In its sublime loftiness, deeds of evil intent are transformed into meritorious deeds,
and upon these deeds man "shall live." However, in whatever manner
or form that repentance occurs, it endures initially from weakened
will due to the preceding remorse, but subsequent to this, it is
transformed into joy and expansiveness of mind caused by the exalted
awareness of the transformation of intentionally evil deeds into deeds
of merit. The light of wisdom then appears, the light which never
had to undergo diminution because of the pain of remorse. This
light finds the meritorious deeds illumining as "manifest day,"
"Godly joyousness" manifests itself within the light in its radiant
exultation devoid of the constriction of shame and darkness, for all
things have been cleansed by the manifestation of soulful understanding.

Even loftier than this is the manifestation of the "universal crown's"
radiance, the mystical perception from whence wells forth all
pleasure and delight, all that is sacred and virtuous, that encompasses
everything in the treasure of its sanctity. This light does not utilize
at all the preparation of remorse which occurs at the onset of the
radiance of understanding. There is revealed to its light that there is
neither defect nor darkness. There is naught but sacred light and
exalted splendor, the brilliance of life and lofty radiance. Above
"understanding," which voids,

> For the Lord of hosts hath proposed
> And who shall disannul it? (Isaiah 14:27)

above wisdom, which releases, only goodness flowing without hindrance, and all evil and abomination are completely negated from

the very onset of time, for in actuality they have no existence, not in the past, present or future. All that was, is, and will be is nothing other than the light and goodness of God. (See Appendix, Item 13, for explanation of these paragraphs.)

II. The collective sacred spirit which encompasses in one exalted form the union of all the separate streams as one; the sacred spirit of will, intellect, beauty, strength and ethic, when it reverberates in its fullness and exaltedness, gives speech unto the prophets — speech in their full detailedness and thunderous power, as the "voice of a vast expanse of mighty waters," the voice of tumultuousness, comparable to the clamor of a military encampment, as the voice of God in its manifestation. This spirit, which encompasses the five aforementioned kinds of "sacred spirit," gleams and is revealed by the spirit of repentance which constantly abides in every heart desirous of rising from the decline resulting from man's sin and his failure — to the heavens of sanctity "to contemplate the sanctuary of God."

III. As there is a deepening of repentance, so does fear of death decrease, till it ceases completely. Its place is taken by the condition of "and she laugheth of the last day." (Proverbs 31:25) The spiritual state within the true reality of man, as well as the spiritual state of the entire world, assumes its manifest form imposed upon it; the certainty of the spiritual state within man gleams more and more, death loses its name and with it its fear and terror. The individual personality develops and grows, actually achieving full entrance into the encompassing essence of the nation and is assimilated from there into the general existence of the entire world, and with supreme allness finds its true happiness in the Godly radiance and the grandeur of the power of radiance, its light and its pleasure, abounding with life from whence flows forth eternal existence.

IV. The development of all that exists is based on the foundation of repentance. Aspects of existence become manifest by means of their descent from divine reality to worldly reality. This is comparable to awesome abasement and death — all worldly descent from level to level from great talent and mastery to lesser talent and mastery are not comparable thereto. All this is accomplished by the exalted weighing of righteous justice, which reckons the justice of all aspects of existence prior to all creation. The exalted mercy of "a world built in mercy" is possessed also of the quality of strength and law, of "the spirit of God hovering over the face of the waters." However, this descent has concealed within it the basis for exalted ascent, even before the order of time, ascent is already contained therein; "the great depth of judgment" and "the mighty mountains of righteousness" shall kiss each other. The matters become more and more clarified, returning to their power with greater intensity within the spirit of man, for repentance is his portion and inheritance, and it is a paradigm of all that exists in the exalted heights and nethermost depths.

Lord, thou hast been our dwelling place in all generations.
Before the mountains were brought forth,
Or ever Thou hadst formed the earth and the world,
Even from everlasting to everlasting
Thou are God.
Thou turnest man to contrition;
And sayest: "Return, ye children of men." (Psalms 90:1-3)

The more we contemplate as to what extent the most particular matters in existence, spiritual and material, have within them aspects of microcosm and condensation of all generalities, and that every smallness has shades of greatness in the depths of its being, then we are no longer amazed by the mystery of repentance which penetrates to so great an extent in the depths of man's soul; it penetrates and proceeds from the very beginning of man's flight of thought and his world-view till the particularities of his specific acts and the nuances of his qualities of character; the matters continue to revert to their affecting in the historical development of collective man. When we shall have greater knowledge of the qualitative value of man and his spirit and the form he gives to existence by means of his impress, immediately shall we perceive with clarity the illuminating relationship of great cosmic repentance in its broadest, deepest and most exalted sense, with the repentance of man, individual and collective man; upon the orbits of individual and collective man's repentance there circles and revolves the entire order of life, practical and spiritual. "Out of the depths have I called Thee, O Lord." (Psalms 130:1) (See Appendix, Item 14, for explanation of these paragraphs.)

V.   Repentance teaches that the basis of all actions is the spiritual essence within them — that impression which the action impresses upon the very basis of the soul. And since truly the contents of the actions are not merely symbolic concepts but are interwoven in the foundation of the actual world, then we are compelled to declare that the actual world as it is is nevertheless a divided world, with all its orders in harmony with each other, but whose root is the element of thought, which includes and encompasses the world and is above and beyond the world. Repentance uplifts man and his world to the world of repentance, wherein all existence stands in the clarity of its spiritual content, and that world with the intensity of its spirituality prevails over our finite world of action, and according to that impression hewn in the world of upper repentance by means of thought is there established the order of the world of action. (See Appendix, Item 15, for explanation of this paragraph.)

VI.   In accordance with the principle of the mystical doctrines, every virtuous deed of an evil person enters into the realm of evil and impurity; although, the Holy One, blessed be He, does not withhold his reward and repays in this world for even the lightest commandment performed. Nevertheless, this is the portion of evil. (See Appendix, Item 16.) How much more so is it true that every sin and transgression committed by a righteous person, even though "the righteous shall be requited in the earth" and "round about him it stormeth mightily," nevertheless, it all proceeds from the principle of "a good measure surpassing," (See Appendix, Item 17) to strengthen and extend the light of sanctity and virtue. From this we understand as regards the nations in general that every virtuous act of an evil nation strengthens universal evil and the "kindness of nations — is evil," (see Appendix, Item 18), and as regards Israel, "a righteous nation that keepeth faithfulness," (Isaiah 26:2) for the Holy One, blessed be He, is exacting with "those about him" to the extent of a "hair's breadth;" and of the nations in general

You only have I known of all the families of the earth;
Therefore I will visit upon you all your iniquities. (Amos 3:2)

Consequently, all sins that come from a source such as this, a source primarily virtuous, this primacy in itself being a sign that in actuality within the source there is complete virtue — there is truly within the inner concealment of the source of great light and much salvation; and the transgression of the tribes sustained the world in its entirety (see Appendix, Item 19), and "at all times of wrath let their needs be before you." (See Appendix, Item 20.) However, such is the manner that the good and the constructive emerging from sin must be greatly purified till it can be applied towards the perfection of the totality of creation. The purification consists of the measure of suffering which purifies the sin, i.e., that purifies the sin that derives from the depth of virtue of all its outer ugliness and establishes it on its inner basis, whose existence is in truth and sanctity. Since nothing is lost from the deeds of the righteous,

And whose leaf doth not wither;
And in whatsoever he doeth he shall prosper. (Psalms 1:3)

therefore of necessity, every sin, even a light one and the most minute, must be purified so that it may be enabled to serve that general cause so exalted and bright, towards which every movement of a holy soul is destined, "for the Lord knows the way of the righteous." (Psalms 1:6) Only God knows thereof — in a realm unto which the thoughts of no creature can reach. Every act of repentance motivated by love comes unto that inner source, from whence all that is done is virtuous and an edifice of perfection and righteousness retroactively. Intentionally evil deeds are transformed into deeds of merit and do not require creation anew; all that is required is the revelation of their essential source; for even the new heaven and earth that God will create in the Messianic Era do not require renewal, for they are established and are standing as it is said: "For as the new heavens and the new earth which I will make are standing"; "will stand" was not said, rather "are standing." (Gen. Rabbah Ch. 1)

Chapter XII

THE INFLUENCE OF REPENTANCE ON THE PATHS OF THE SPIRIT OF LIFE AS WELL AS ON ACTION IN GENERAL

I.   Repentance exalts man above all the degradations to be found in the world. Nevertheless, man does not become alien to the world; rather, he uplifts with himself the world and life. Those very inclinations of evil become purified within him; the powerful will that shatters all barriers, the will that caused sin, becomes a vital force effecting great and exalted achievements for virtue and blessing. The grandeur of life from the source of supreme holiness hovers constantly over repentance and all its standard bearers who are the select of all life. They call for rectification of life, for the removal of all obstacles and for return to virtuous nature and true happiness, to lofty exaltedness which is truly free, proper to the person who ascends upward in accordance with his spiritual source and his basis in the "image of God."

II.   The more a person contemplates as to the nature of repentance, to that extent he finds therein the source of strength and the most elemental content of active and ideal life.

III.   Repentance! how indispensable and significant it is to illumine the horizon of all life. The spiritual channels are obstructed because of man's sin. The "thirst for Godliness," together with all its means which are the rays within the very essence of the soul, of pragmatic and inward morality, quivers, commences to tremble and move with vitality but draw back and falls, because the "thick mire" of the coarse substance caused by the sin is heavy upon it — not only individual sin but, even more so, collective sin. Singular individuals yearning for the light of God, endure the sin of the community as a whole. Their love for collective humanity is powerful beyond comprehension. The essence of virtue within their souls yearns only for universal virtue. When the singular souls are drawn to collective humanity, collective humanity is prone to defile them with its touch because of the sins that cling to it. However, the truly righteous willingly endure all impediments and all manner of bodily and spiritual suffering, so that they may attain their goal, to achieve comprehension and to do good unto others, to increase virtue and sacred light, to level a cleared path for the light of God and its pleasantness, so that the light may enter directly into every heart and spirit, that all may find delight in the goodness of God, and that "the Lord may rejoice with his works."

IV.   Every sin, even the slightest of sins, impresses within man hatred for some creature; by means of repentance love once more begins to radiate its light.

V.   At the time that a man sins he is in "the world of separation," and then every detail stands by itself, and evil is evil by itself, and it possesses evil and harmful value. When he repents out of love, there immediately shines upon him the existential light of the "world of unity," where all is interwoven into one form. In the general relationship there is no evil at all, for evil combines with virtue to facilitate and exalt even further the significants worth of goodness. Thereby are intentionally evil deeds transformed into veritable deeds of merit.

VI.   It is impossible to estimate the necessity of repentance in terms of actual deeds, as regards the rectification of deeds in accordance with Torah and absolute righteousness, so that the exalted degree of individual and communal spiritual ascent can be achieved. The quintessence of human action encompasses within its smallest point great numbers of ideals and broad concepts that enable this quintessence to serve its purpose and in life. When the quintessential act is defective, then is voided the great value of all the broad ideals in the fullness of the world which are related to the act in a relationship similar to the ethereal expanse of a million cubic feet compressed in one physical atom to create it in its perfect form.

VII.   Repentance preceded the world; ethic encompasses all things. Absolute exalted value penetrates into all the minor extensions. The diverging deed which is not directed to its source reverts to its source in an ascent of will.

VIII.   Exalted repentance comes as a result of an inner impulsion, which results from exalted external impulsion. The entire world, both material and spiritual, is comprehended in its unified form. Ethic, upright and virtuous, is the goal of the will of existence. This goal in the particular details of life must correspond with all that surrounds it, with all existence, both in its inner nature and its external revelation. By means of inner awareness in the depths of the heart regarding uprightness and virtue is specific knowledge gained of ethic, ethic manifest in all existence; with ideal, actual, vital form in existence. By means of Torah, ethic is revealed in the light of holiness, to every human community according to their degree, and to Israel in its most perfect form, ethical harmony in all its revelations. The personality, which finds in its life-paths and in the nature of its spirit defects and disharmony in relationship to the absolute all, both inward and the manifest, experiences infinite pain and strives to return to the source of life and being; the personality is remorseful of its strayings and returns with a yearning heart and with the joy of deliverance:

I have gone astray like a lost sheep;
Seek Thy servant;
For I have not forgotten Thy commandments.   (Psalms 119:176)

IX.   Ethic with its Godly voice enters within the soul from the very life of all the worlds. Existence in its totality is without sin. Sin is to be found when regarding the value of particular details; in relationship to generality all things correspond in eternal harmony; the deeds by means of which eternal harmony is revealed are indeed virtuous deeds, devoid of all sin, transgression and iniquity. Life such as this from whence there emerge such deeds — this is the aspiration of the soul. The soul apprehends the deeds in the light which is the source of the life of all worlds, the light which is the source for the shining forth of infinite light, the source toward which the soul yearns so strongly. The soul is bound to this light and its longing for it transcends finitude or purpose; with upper repentance, with exalted freedom, the exultation of liberty and with the trembling of "holy of holies," abounding with eternal wisdom, is the soul bound to this light.

X.   Repentance is renewal of life. It is impossible that repentance not change the value of all life, as life continues; consequently, it changes life's value for good even when repentance takes place on the last day of life.

> Remember then thy creator in the days of thy youth,
> Before the evil days come and the years draw nigh,
> When thou shalt say,
> "I have no pleasure in them,"
> Before the sun, and the light, and the moon
> And the stars are darkened. (Ecclesiastes 12:1, 2)

All other consolations are means for the strengthening of repentance and clarification of its value, but he who is preoccupied with consolation to such a great extent as to be lax in establishing the values of a sanctified life, to such a great extent that he becomes immersed in the "deep mire of sin" "exclaiming I am saved," this is the deadly manner of "beneficent idolatry," (see Appendix, Item 21) which declares:

> And bring your sacrifices in the morning
> And your tithes after three days;
> And offer a sacrifice of that which is leavened. (Amos 4:4, 5)

The method which departs from truth and justice and follows the promptings of its own heart — this is heresy, which brings in its wake all manner of slaughter and lewdness, despite the fact that "beneficent idolatry" extends her hooves (see Appendix, Item 22) and declares, "See that I am pure" and abounds with empty solace. It is even impossible for this solace to stand in a world of "falsity which has no legs."

> For the lips of a strange woman drop honey,
> And her mouth is smoother than oil;
> But her end is as bitter as wormwood,
> Sharp as a two edged sword. (Proverbs 5:3, 4)

XI.   There must be also an awakening to repentance for the continued existence of the nation. In what manner? We must be united together forever. Our spiritual bond needs sustenance; its sustainers are the paths of life and trends of thought. When we adhere to those paths and thoughts then the harmonious unity is maintained. This adds strength to the unity of the people and to various other signs of unity, even though these signs in terms of themselves are matters subject to transition and change. However, in the instance of spiritual weakness spiritual separation gains in strength. The temporary unity of the people as well as the external matters do not possess enough strength to unite the many separations that life's many conditions, both internal and external, have caused to occur.

XII.   It may occur that a thought declines (see Appendix, Item 23) from its exalted greatness and from the source of its purity, because after it has become actualized in deed and in life unworthy persons have preoccupied themselves with it and have darkened its brightness. This descent is not eternal descent, for it is impossible that spiritual, intellectual virtuousness should be transformed into evil; it is a temporary descent that in itself is necessary for ascent. Those persons who are small qualitatively are possessed of quantitative magnitude, and even this trait, despite its insignificance in relation to quality, nevertheless, when it is united with quality the former adorns the latter:

> In the multitude of people is the king's glory. (Proverbs 14:28)

This quantity is not just quantity in number but also the massiveness of power, the diligence and desire to pursue and achieve, to establish that which is sought by means of paths of action and the manifestation of strength. This character is manifested to a greater extent by persons physically strong, coarse and lacking in nobility of spirit, which usually weakens power in its relationship with the physical. When thought must acquire for itself a material basis, it usually descends from its loftiness. At this time it is cast down to the earth and "violent men come and desecrate its sanctity." But at the same time the thought's adherents grow in number, and the manifestation of its material power develops and increases till that time when the refined in heart are aroused; armed with the power of God's righteousness, they ascend to the peak of the source of purified thought; they delve into its depths, instill in it the purity of their own souls, their refined devotions and pure thoughts; thereby, this general thought by itself, which because of its spiritual pains, from the piercing of the thorns surrounding it, was in a state of weariness and weakness, in a slumber of death, almost without spirit of life, is aroused and begins to bestow upon all approaching it a dew of life with the splendor of might from its innermost depths. (See Appendix, Item 24.) Then there rise with it all who cleaved to it. Also those who cleaved to it in its period of spiritual poverty, who by means of deliberate defiance and evil and barbarous way-wardness have deviated from the main path which leads to the goal of the thought; these persons shall also ascend with it, achieving thereby a clear exalted repentance, like the "flight of an eagle" with wondrous ease, to which no parallel can be found in any manifesta-tion of the phenomenon of repentance occurring due to the awakened faculty of virtue of a particular soul. This revelation shall come hastily and will not be delayed in its occurrence. The light of God which is hidden by dark clouds, concealed in the basic point of Zion, shall emerge, shall lift up from the valley of tears the sanctuary of the king and all its environs. With it shall ascend all that cling to the fringe of its vestment, the near and the far, for true renascence and everlasting salvation.

Chapter XIII

THE PATH OF REPENTANCE IN SPIRIT
AND IN ACTION

I.   It is impossible truly to cleave to the national essence of Israel except in the instance when one's soul has already been purified by means of repentance from the shameful sins of man and his base qualities, or when one's soul is from the very onset a pure soul. For the true basis of Israel's national character is the striving for righteousness on its highest level, the Lord's righteousness in the world, and he who has been coarsened by sin, to that degree of coarseness will the desire for righteousness and virtue fails to shine within him in the appropriate manner, and therefore he will not truly be united with the national character till he is purified.

II.   In order to remove every barrier that stands between general Godly virtue and the particular soul which thirsts for it, there must be separation from all ethical defect in its broadest sense in terms of its general significance. This encompasses the refinement of all human qualities and the intellectual purification of deeds, all of these being the extension of Godly light in the world, in a general manner encompassing humanity and all existence, in every realm where it is appropriate for the ethical quality to take effect.

In order also to remove the hindrance which restrains from the perfection of the vestment of Israel, (see Appendix, Item 25) which garbs the abstract Godly virtue in its own unique manner, there must be removal of every hindrance in deed from all that affects the soul of the Jew. This is the characteristic that necessitates complete repentance from the most minute details of sin and iniquity according to the written and oral Torah, which in its entirety is the soul of God related to Israel.

III.   Man must constantly be united with the essence of Divine goodness, which is joined with the source of Israel's soul in its

344

entirety: thereby does he achieve repentance. For there constantly is revealed before his eyes the inadequacies and sins which flow from the source of alienation, his alienation from the Godly nation, which is "the rock from which he is hewn" and the source of all virtue within him. He should not be dismayed about being united with the source of the nation's soul, even though in the "dividing of the particular branches" evil and coarse persons are to be encountered. This fact does not detract in the least from the virtuous Godly light of the nation in as a whole, and a spark of the Godly soul is to be found even in the most fallen particular souls. And since the congregation of Israel embraces within itself Godly virtue not only for itself but for the entire world, for all living things, man achieves by means of intensive cleavage with the innerness of the nation's soul cleavage with the living God in accordance with the Godly blessing, abounding in all things, and the light of the divine presence rests upon him in all its splendor and might.

IV. It is impossible for a person to be truly pained by the distress of the community without sanctification of his ways and rectification of his character traits, returning with perfect repentance. Participation in communal distress in the depths of one's heart is in itself reward for a meritorious act, this being achieved only by the pure in soul.

Upright in the way
Who walk in the way of the Lord. (Psalms 119:1)

V. The most basic and most effective way to achieve repentance, that which derives from the light of Torah in the world, is intensive study in that part of the law dealing with commerce and all the statutes regarding matters "between man and his fellow man," emcompassed in the study of the "Breastplate of Judgment," with the clearest span of textual knowledge and with all the logical and comprehensive analysis maximally possible.

This study rectifies all "offenses of heart" to be found in life, establishes Divine righteousness on its enduring foundation and removes the wound of doubt and confusion from within the soul by means of its clear light illumining the path of action in life. However, there must be constant betterment of heart and mind by means of the other parts of Torah, especially through a powerful and broad influence, both moral and speculative caused by the "dew of light" of inner meditations of noble, Godly conceptions, so that the soul may be fit to cleave in a proper manner with the Godly righteousness that is to be found in the judicial part of the "Torah of life." Then shall this preoccupation be unto the soul as "oil in his bones" for the uplifting and exaltation of the soul.

VI. When man desires that all his senses and inner faculties should be sanctified in one instance in accordance with the spiritual ascent of his awareness when it ascends, and also that all his defects in deeds should be set aright immediately and become perfect in absolute rectification, he will be unable to again find a station for his soul nor will he be able to strengthen his will to walk on the path of true perfection. However, the principle matter upon which all is dependent is the ascent of awareness, the strengthening of Torah's light; and repentance in deed shall be nearby, at first regarding future matters and subsequently matters of the past which are easily rectifiable; afterwards the periphery shall be extended to include matters whose rectification is difficult. Thus he shall proceed, progressing and ascending till he shall be worthy of complete rectification. But let him not be deflected from his spiritual advance-which is in accordance with that inner degree that his soul within him demands of him.

VII. The primary reason for difficulty of comprehension occurs as a result of the will for virtue and perfection being weakened by defect in human qualities and iniquity. Actually, it would also be proper to fast so as to weaken the power of evil in the material which prevents the will from ascending in its highest degrees, but we must also estimate strength of spirit and body whether they are in accord with this purpose. Under all circumstances one should not despair from "ascent of will," even if there remain some defects that have not been rectified, whether in terms of human qualities or in terms of deeds, one must long for "God's kindness" and deliverance from on high.

Good and upright is the Lord
Therefore doth he instruct sinners in the way. (Psalms 25:8)

VIII. The moral sense cries out within man: "Son of man return from thy iniquities." At times the outcry is so tumultuous that it confuses the entire harmony of life, and man is compelled to rise in spiritual degrees that are beyond his scope in order to establish the order of his inner world. At this instance "strength" must come to his aid; the inner strength of man must aid him at the time of the bitterest weakening of spirit. Due to the powerful might of the ethical imperatives, man is at times confused and cannot be freed from his imprisonment — evil qualities and characteristics, evil deeds, departure from the path of Torah and ethic; all these oppress him. He perceives his path "hedged with thorns," with no means of finding rectification; he is bound in the hand of others and has "no standing," but from all this the "sun of righteousness" shall shine.

IX. Man should not be frightened because of the hindrances to repentance, even if repentance is difficult for him because of matters "between man and his fellow man," even if he is aware that he has not fulfilled his obligation and because of some weaknesses is unable to rectify those matters between himself and his fellow man — he should not permit within his heart any discouragement which causes diminution of the precious value of repentance. Without doubt, by perfecting all those matters wherein there are no hindrances God shall make him worthy to rectify in a proper manner all those matters that confront him with great hindrances and over which he cannot prevail.

X. There is a man in whose soul the ethical demand illumines with great radiance, and upon every conception of ethical exaltation that he conceives immediately his soul makes demands upon him that his life's path be in harmony with this conception. Since the spring of conception flows with a swiftness greater than the movement of action and normal qualities, which are natural to body and soul, therefore he is constantly filled with pain and bitterness regarding his soul because of its inability to perform its obligation to fulfill with depth of will and a feeling of essentiality that which is revealed by the good and delightful light of morality.

Thus it is possible that from this sacred quality there should grow fear of creativity, that he may not want to contemplate upon the clarity of the concepts, wherein are merged forms of ethic, of knowledge, and of the refined perceptions of exalted sanctity, lest his pain be increased to "extreme degree."

In such a situation we must bring spiritual power to bear and to seize at the same time the quality of "repentance of will" which accompanies at all times those who proceed on the path of upper life, as well as the talent of the pleasurable, "upper spirit," to increase sacred bounty to "magnify and glorify Torah."

There should be no submission to decay because of the ethical demands which overwhelm him; rather should he intensively endeavor with the assurance that the light of Torah will constantly restore him to virtuousness in its most exalted form. He should strive to increase his intellectual and conceptual achievements with freedom of spirit most particularly appropriate to him. His heart should not fear.

Let the righteous smite me in kindness and correct me; Oil so choice let not my head refuse. (Psalms 141:5)

XI. Great and sublime is the happiness of repentance. The consuming fire of sin's pain in itself refines will, resulting in a superior and radiant purification of character, till the great wealth of repentance to be found in the treasure of life develops and unfolds before him. Man continues to ascend through repentance, through its bitterness and its pleasantness, through its sorrow and its joy; nothing refines and purifies man, truly uplifting him to the level of man, as does profound contemplation of repentance, "In the place where the penitents stand even the wholly righteous cannot stand." (B. T. Berachot, 34a)

XII. The great flame of remorse, which derives from the "willing spirit" by means of the torch of illumining repentance, is a sacred flame, a flame abounding in light and warmth, abounding in life. When it comes to rest on a pure spirit, a vital soul illumined with the light of "grace and good favor" in the "knowledge of the All-holy," then the great flame of remorse is transformed into a vigorous and mighty force, to an effecting power, refining and purifying, increasing strength and power, clearing paths and endowing new spirits into all facets of life.

A new bestirring and an awakening abounding with youthful vigor accompanies it. This person is made into a new creation, refined and purged. He gazes above to the heavens of knowledge and understanding that lead to repentance; and from the light of the Messiah, from the source of Torah and all the commandments, from the source of all actions and all characteristics in their broadest scope, rays shall shine forth to illuminate his dark ways and desolate paths, and together with his edifices there shall be built an eternal edifice, and many shall go by his light which at first was kindled but for him, "a candle for one and candle for a great multitude of nations."

And thou shalt be called the repairer of the breach;
The restorer of the paths to dwell in. (Isaiah 58:12)

Chapter XIV

PARTICULAR PATHS OF REPENTANCE

I. Just as there must be uplifting of evil qualities and thoughts to their source in order to rectify them and to transform them, similarly one ought to uplift to their source of origin the lesser qualities and thoughts, and to allow the light of "grandeur" to shine upon them for although they are good they are not on a great and radiant level. Just as there is benefit to the entire world through the uplifting of fallen thoughts and qualities, similarly and even more so is there benefit and betterment to the world by means of the uplifting of minor qualities and thoughts when they ascend to great light. This quality of uplifting minor matters to "grandeur" ceases at no time; this is absolute repentance by means of which those absolute in their righteousness ascend to the degree of the "penitent." (See Appendix, Item 26.)

II. At times due to intensive endeavor to cleave to exalted spirituality all the faculties of spiritual life are lifted to the heights of the world of uppermost thought and the body is forsaken by the soul; consequently evil qualities prevail within the body. Afterwards, when the loftiest spiritual contemplation is concluded and the power of life is restored to its normal course, the soul discovers the body racked by its corrupted qualities and there commences an intense perilous inner struggle. Therefore it is necessary that repentance, with the desire for refinement of qualities of character, precede contemplative ascent. Then a relational medium between the body and soul is created even in the instance of the soul's exalted ascent. (See Appendix, Item 27, for explanation of this paragraph.)

III. When one is prepared to repent he must know that there can be no obstacle preventing it. Even those twenty-four matters which hinder repentance, (M. T. Hilchot Teshuvah 4, 1) immediately when one desires to repent they no longer stand in the way. We must not dismiss any inclination of repentance, even the most trivial, because of its inconsequentiality by declaring that this trivial thought is inappropriate to the level where one believes himself to be, nor the noblest, saying that it transcends one's worth. For all matters ascent and unite together for "full stature" and a world abounding with repentance, which is more precious, great and ancient than all other worlds.

IV. Though at times overwhelmed by great obstacles either matters "between man and his maker" or as regards matters "between man and his fellow man," this condition should not at all serve as a deterrent to spiritual repentance, and whenever there is a desire to repent and one repents, this individual is renewed as a new creation. Regarding the "fragments" (see Appendix, Item 28) of action that require great application for their rectification, man should strive constantly to rectify them. He should seek to acquire for himself the quality of great humility as long as the matter has not been actually rectified of those aspects which require practical rectification. He should long for the perfect rectification. And so the matter shall reach a state where the Holy One, blessed be He, shall aid him to rectify all things in actuality.

But even when rectification has not as yet been achieved either because of inner or outer hindrances, in the instance that his will is not yet powerful enough and the ascent to the ways of the practical rectification has not been wholly achieved, he should nevertheless take hold of spiritual repentance with all power and strength, being firmly mindful that despite everything he is united with repentance, which is a matter more precious than anything else to be found in the world. He should increase his preoccupation with Torah, doing so with virtuous qualities, with wisdom and upright conduct as much as possible, "pouring out his prayer before his maker," to actualize those aspects of repentance which have as yet not been actualized — for himself, for all of Israel, for the whole world, for the general rectification of the divine presence, the light of God in the world — that it may exist in perfect completeness; he should yearn for the rectification of all souls and their deriving pleasure from the light of the divine presence so that all may be content with goodness and the flowing of life.

V.   When an act is committed due to mundane inclination, either corporeal or animalistic, if it be but a permissible act, immediately upon the inner prompting to repent for the deed all faculties are uplifted and transformed into emanation and sanctity; "If one transgressed a positive commandment and repented, then he is forgiven before he has moved from his place." (B. T. Yoma 86a.) Regarding permissible acts, (see Appendix, Item 29) as soon as the thought of repentance comes to mind, one is sanctified, and the act and its power are sanctified with him. The melancholy that follows in the wake of mundane pleasures is immediately transformed into the joy of fulfilling God's commandment, "and gladness for the upright in heart." (Psalms 97:11)

VI.   When it is asked, "From whence does melancholy derive?" we must reply, "From the effect of evil deeds, thoughts and characteristics on the soul; the soul senses their bitterness with its penetrating instinct and draws back frightened and melancholy." When the light of repentance appears and when the desire for virtue prevails in its original character, a channel of delight and joy is opened, the soul draws from the "river of pleasures," and when the talent of action absorbs within itself the essence of these pleasant experiences, then pure and exalted ethic emerges, causing life to flourish in its splendor.

VII.   All melancholy comes as a result of sin; repentance illumines the soul and transforms the melancholy into joy. The general melancholy in the world has its source in the "collective coarse substance" to be found in the universe, from the sins of society and individuals and from the concealed sin of the earth which emerged to actuality with the sin of man; the righteous who sustain the world, and the Messiah particularly, return in repentance for the nature of this sin and transform it to joy.

VIII. If it should occur that a person consumes food with an improper or base thought and repents immediately after eating, exalting his thoughts and faculties with repentance based upon love, he thereby rectifies the past; thus it is as if he had commenced eating with pure intent, and the time of nourishment, (see Appendix, Item 30) within which it is still permissible to recite grace, is most appropriate for this exalted uplifting, worthy of the priests of God, who eat the bread of God. "The priests eat and the owners obtain atonement." (See Appendix, Item 31.)

IX. Gluttonous eating, though it occurs due to sickness and necessity, possesses defect; nevertheless, it would appear that it is easily uplifted to sanctity, but repentance must surely be joined with this uplifting and sanctification. The increasing strength when it is utilized for sanctity ascends to its source even though it first comes into being due to gluttonous eating, since there is the impelling of necessity due to illness, weakness or causes similar to these, and it is not comparable to a prohibited matter, whose ascent is greatly hindered.

X. Subsequently, after having eaten without virtuous intent or having succumbed to gluttonous eating, for which one is called "a transgressor" — when there is intent to repent fully after having eaten, and to uplift and separate the sparks of sanctity which were contained in this repast, then there is benefit and hope. Nor should one divided in heart weaken in rectifying all that his "hand can achieve," after every repast, with repentance based upon love, "with joyfulness and gladness of heart," without melancholy, rather, with the "joy of the Lord" and with "a broken and contrite heart" abounding in grandeur and sacred strength — then shall he effect salvations for himself and the world. Even if he experienced during his eating many falls and retrogressions, he ultimately shall repent and ascend, being worthy to consume sacred bread with exalted sanctity, and transgressions shall be transformed into flowing abundance, a flowing of virtue and blessing, mercy and favor;

But he that is of a virtuous heart hath a continual feast.

(Proverbs 15:15)

XI. From such thoughts of sanctity and repentance which lead to melancholy one must at times withdraw, for the basis of joy bound with the depths of sanctity is greater than any content of sanctity or any other kind of repentance. Therefore, when there occur to him thoughts of fear and repentance that are a melancholy character, he should divert his thoughts from them until his thought is firmly established, and he should accept upon himself the entire content of sanctity and fear of God in a glad and joyful manner appropriate to the upright in heart serving God in truth.

XII. There is an inner melancholy that derives from an awareness of the sensing of the soul's defect, particularly when there is defect in the nature of action, and the awareness of one's active responsibility is not very particularized; the soul feels its inadequacy to a greater extent because the faculty of action is proximal to the realm of the soul. This is not so in the case of persons who are close to the realm of action, whose defects extend to a greater degree in the distant world of the spirit; they cannot sense their inadequacies to the extent of suffering from melancholy, and are more liable to be joyful by nature. However, he whose defects in action affect him and who has aspirations that are spiritual and mighty, will concern himself with strengthening the spiritual flow and subjecting it to the world of action in such a manner so as to illumine the vista of action and by preoccupation with the active aspects of Torah this flow shall develop and become a luminary of the upper level of repentance, rectifying all things, practical and contemplative life together. (See Appendix, Item 32, for explanation of this paragraph.)

XIII. Even for defects which have their basis in bodily weakness there is need to repent, both for them and all their consequences. Nevertheless, great efforts should be exerted not to be overly fearful, particularly because of those defects are caused by the sickly disposition of the body. For there is already a "great opening" for "mercy of the most high" "that the Lord will not count unto him iniquity" this is so both in reference to sins of commission or omission. And just as "self reproach is good in the heart of man," so is heartfelt endeavor necessary, in order to achieve steadfastness in the service of the Lord with Torah and sincere worship, with clear thought as far as he is capable of achieving.

XIV. Even regarding those matters which are impossible to rectify by thought alone, but that require action, as in the case of "matters between man and his fellow man," nevertheless, it is impossible to estimate the grandeur present in the slightest thought of repentance, even if it is the result of simple fear — fear of punishment — because even the most minor thought awakens in the soul and in the world the holy and great qualities, and a sacred light, from the "light of the countenance most high," appears in all its radiance with the splendor of love and the "graciousness of the Lord" by means of any thought that tends toward goodness. Even if this thought is possessed of much dross, its inner favor, the basic sanctity within it — this is equal to all wealth, "and all things desirable are not to be compared unto her." (Proverbs 8:11)

XV. Even though melancholy and fear result from negligence of Torah and from all sins, nevertheless, upon the slightest thought of repentance everything is transformed into virtue, and there is an immediate need to seek strength with the power of trust, in the kindness of the Most High, blessed be He, a need to take hold of Torah and service, each person according to his level. If at times it would appear to an individual that the effects evoked by reading writings upon the subjects of ethics and fear of God are not in accordance with his level, he should then reflect deeply on his status seeking to discover its true nature, and strive for strength and steadfastness, particularly regarding his essential level; notwithstanding these circumstances he should not abandon those stirring awakened within him by means of the writings. Although his understanding of those matters not immediately relevant to him is very limited, nevertheless, all levels of virtue and sanctity must be bound together and make up one entity to enable the light to cast its rays upon him — the light of God and His exalted Torah, with the graciousness and goodness of the Lord. (See Appendix, Item 33, for explanation of this paragraph.)

XVI. It may occur that a person reads about levels of holiness and his soul is pained and distressed. It is necessary for him to differentiate the pain into its component parts, and he will discover in certain instances that one aspect is his pain over the fact that this particular virtuous level of which he has read is so remote from him as a result of his iniquities. He must marshal all efforts to repent in order to achieve this high level. Notwithstanding this, it is quite possible that there is within that level an aspect beneath his capacity and he is pained by the limitation that he tends to accept within the moderate narrowness of this virtuous degree. He must clarify for himself to what extent he shall truly be happy when he partakes of this degree, and to what extent his happiness is dependent upon his caution not to remain within its limitations but to ascend beyond its degree. "We strive for higher gradations in sanctity." (B. T. Berachot 28a)

XVII. There are two manners of "grandeur of degree." (See Appendix, Item 34.) One manner is based upon deeds and knowledge, and the second is due to ability and heritage within the source of creation. He whose "grandeur of degree" is based upon knowledge and deeds — when he descends from his degree and must ascend, must take hold of the lesser qualities and return gradually. However, he whose "granduer" is based upon ability rooted in birth due to the greatness of his soul, even when he descends from his level due to internal or external hindrances, he must return with greatness and haste, with a leap as on the "wings of eagles," without concerning himself as to the gradations. Nevertheless, there is also joined to this the repentance of minor degrees and the specific minutiae related to them, except that they are not the major endeavor of repentance for him whose source is great and lofty, but they are rather as the value of joined branches, as spice which sweetens, aids and sustains the primary foundation — which is the great and exalted repentance.

XVIII. Within every degree and every conception of the universe there is a treasure of sanctity, and when man leaps and ascends with great rapidity that transcends his level, then he is deprived of the sacred content possessed by the lesser degrees, which are appropriate to him, nor can he attach himself to the upper degrees because their spirituality is beyond him. Therefore must he return in repentance with broken heart and joyousness to the degree from which he has departed; nevertheless, he shall not forget the impression of the upper degrees, for since he has ascended he shall not descend, — and then everything is transformed into virituousness.

XIX.   Even if a person perceives that notwithstanding the awakening within his heart to persevere in the righteous path and to gain in strength in the service of God, blessed be He, that the evil inclination gains even more in strength within him and casts him down to desire and lowliness, nevertheless, he should not regret at all the fact that he had attained this level of strength, "and he should add strength to his strength," and for the obstacles which he encountered upon his path of ascent he should repent, being aware that all this is encompassed within the principle pertaining to "one who has erred in the commission of a commandment and is not obligated to bring a sin offering" (B. T. Sabbath 137a), he should not fear at all; rather he should derive fear, sanctity and repentance from all things.

XX.   The lack of physical strength is responsible to a great extent for the weakening of will, which causes many obstacles. Even though this weakening is related to many ethical causes, nevertheless, in the rectification of repentance we must be concerned with all the causes of weakened will, and we must strive for general rectification, both as regards ethic and spiritual purity and as regards the body and the strengthening of its faculties, so that spiritual strength be more prevalent with great rectification and sustaining perfection.

XXI.   When we conceive of exalted matters from whose acquisition and possession we are actually remote, it is incumbent upon us to realize that this remoteness is physical and does not pertain to the soul. Therefore, we have great need of repentance, so that we shall be closer to the ideal light which gleams in our thoughts; but we must not allow ourselves to be overcome by melancholy and self-deprecation, which weaken the force of life, rather we must achieve an inner refined self-deprecation which casts down the coarser aspects within us and exalts the entire essence of that which is virtuous and refined.

> The right hand of the Lord is exalted.
> The right hand of the Lord doeth valiantly.
> (Psalms 118:16)

XXII. The lessening of faith in his prayer does not come to man because of lack of faith in divine providence, heaven forbid, but because of the contriteness of heart that emanates from his many sins as well as the intense shattering of spirit wrought by repentance; ultimately, this lessening will be transformed into an exalted and mighty faith, with "the right hand of the Lord exalted," which shall do great wonders with the aid of God, blessed be He, "Who guideth the humble in justice, and teacheth the humble his way." (Psalms 25:9)

XXIII. If a person is so humbled in his own estimation over his intense moral decline caused by his many sins that he cannot uplift his head to concern himself with Torah and commandments, with civilization and human society, in tranquillity and with the joy of a healthy spirit — he must take this to heart: that from contrition of heart such as this for all his sins he is most assuredly at this time perfect in his penitence; thus his level is already exalted, and he can set his mind at rest, being restored to his joy and exultant spirit, concerning himself with all that is virtuous, with tranquil and joyful heart, for "Good and upright is the Lord."

XXIV. The shame that one endures within the heart because of sin, even though this is a normal phenomenon, it nevertheless, possesses a slight measure of atonement. When we become concerned with the extending of this shame, the more it extends the greater the compass of forgiveness for all sins. For they are related one to the other in the context of "one transgression brings another in its wake." (Ethics of the Fathers 4:2) Therefore he who is ashamed because of one sin, is in actuality shamed because of all his sins; consequently, repentance based upon fear of God, which is shame, extends to the full measure of his stature; he is thereby forgiven even for the sins that require "great repentance that is capable of achieving forgiveness of all his deeds."

XXV. Evil qualities result at times as a means of punishment for preceding sins, and it is not enough that one should strive to cleanse himself from the qualities as such, because he will not return to his state of purity till he has closely scrutinized all his actions and has repented from the iniquities which caused that very punishment of corrupted qualities.

XXVI. A lessening of the sweetness derived from the Torah's pleasantness occurs due to deficiency in the Jewish nature of the soul, which must be rectified by repentance consonant with this defect; and as soon as one concerns himself with the rectification the deficiency, immediately the exalted light of the soul's sacred nature shines once again, and the Torah's sweetness once more manifests itself.

XXVII. In accordance to the value of the clarity of repentance which precedes study, so the clarity of the comprehension of one's studies increases; the mind is exalted in accordance with the basis of the exaltation of will and is clarified to the extent of the clarity of will.

XXVIII. The upper level of repentance, achieved by means of great love and clear comprehension uplifts the entire content of study to such a degree of fruitfulness and creativity that it is incomparable to any content of study in terms of mere study.

XXIX. All things aid the ascent of spirit to the upper level of repentance, all Torah, all knowledge, all faculties, all knowledge of the world and life, all human relationship, the entire character of uprightness and righteousness. When a person senses the fear of inner shame, the defilement of body and soul, he must closely scrutinize to the best of his ability all aspects of his defect and rectify them. He should not concern himself with this matter in a superficial manner, for then he shall bring about decline after decline; rather should he do so with penetrating scrutiny and with the strength of a pure spirit.

XXX. Only through true, pure repentance must one return to the world and life; thereby is sanctity restored to its original station, and the reign of the divine presence is established in the world.

XXXI. "He who is lax in the study of Torah will not have strength to endure at a time of adversity." (B. T. Berachot 63a) This is so true even in reference to one commandment, and the Holy One, blessed be He, in his great kindness evokes his mercies to recall at a time of adversity all the aspects of virtue and evocations of sanctity by means of Torah and commandment, and from the midst of this very adversity shall be sensed every particular detail of the many particular matters involved in laxity in regard to Torah and commandment, and there is return in repentance — the Holy One, blessed be He, accepts this repentance and from the midst of adversity brings forth redemption and deliverance.

XXXII. There must be haste in repentance for every sin, even if it is regarding the lightest matters, for delay in repentance is comparable to delay in the retention of impurity in the Temple, delay in the forbidden wearing of flax and wool, or delay in the retention of leaven during Passover, for each moment by itself is a separate sin, and repetition of a light sin many times is comparable to the "cords of a wagon." (See Appendix, Item 35.) Similarly, he who is upon the level of exalted conceptions must repent for each superfluous utterance of his tongue, and even for each necessary and sacred utterance devoid of inner sanctity — intellectual or emotional — appropriate to him in accordance with his degree.

XXXIII. On the eve of the sacred Sabbath one should engage in repentance over all that has happened during the weekdays, so as to receive the sanctity of the Sabbath without the hindrance resulting from any sin or iniquity. (See Likutei Amarim (Tanya) 99b). On the night subsequent to the Sabbath one must return over the content of the Sabbath's radiance, that it may be pure without any impurity, in order that those matters which have lost their strength because of the Sabbath and cannot affect or injure should not disturb the normal course of the weekdays, in which there is not the same safeguard. This is the explanation of the high priest's santification of hands and feet after divesting himself of the sacred garments on the day of atonement; this is necessary because those fragments of impurity which break into the midst of the sanctuary and which because of the grandeur of sacred light strive with all their strength to cling to it but are unable to accomplish anything at the time when sanctity dominates — yet after the passing of the light's radiance one must take heed against them by means of great repentance abounding with exultation, might and humility. (See Appendix, Item 36, for explanation of this paragraph.)

XXXIV. Fear of G-d should never be severed from wisdom; rather, it should constantly be united with it and derive from it and so fear of G-d will exert influence on wisdom. This occurs both within the general radiance of the flashing light of fear and wisdom within the soul and in the instance of their derivative particularities, for on every one of fear's particularities wisdom should shed it's light, and out of every one of wisdom's particularities, the fear of G-d in respect to action, character, emotion and imagination, needs wisdom from which to derive its sustenance; and from the harmonious union of these two great lights the soul of man is illuminated and the manifestation of repentance — abounding with delight, with joy and life — comes unto the world.

XXXV. The clear intellectual endeavors exalt man above the containment of limited action. Whenever they are properly established they impel him to rectification of future action and straighten before him the path of life. However they also bring about a clearing of the path of repentance for the past, so that corrupt actions do not obstruct him in his path of life; this is so because he clearly perceives to what extent the light of knowledge, which readies and establishes repentance, uproots all evil at the principal source and restores them to' virtue; and intentionally evil acts are thus transformed into acts of merit.

XXXVI. When a person desires to be solely in the category of the perfectly righteous, then it is difficult for him to become a "penitent." Therefore it is appropriate for man constantly to take to heart the striving to become a "penitent" deeply preoccupied with the thought of repentance and its practical actualization; then can repentance exalt him above, to the degree of those perfect in their righteousness — and even beyond. (See Appendix, Item 37, for explanation of this paragraph.)

XXXVII.   A penitent person must walk in exalted paths, in the ways of piety and sacred thought. There are indeed such persons that are born with the natural gift of being righteous ones from the very beginning, and even if it should happen that they sin and repent, they are capable after repentance of conducting their lives in the manner of the "righteous from the very beginning," without the strengthening of sacred flame, manifest and yearning constantly; but those who by nature are possessed of such souls, that are in constant need of repentance, it is specifically these who are called upon to be "the pious" and "men of sanctity." (See Appendix, Item 38, for explanation of this paragraph.)

XXXVIII.   It may happen that the spirit falls into "smallness" and a person cannot find pleasure within himself as a result of the paucity of his virtuous deeds and the evaluation of his iniquities, as well as his decreased diligence in the study of Torah; man must strengthen himself with the "mystery of thought" and be aware that "he who understands one matter from another — his thoughts are considered more significant before the Holy One, blessed be He, than all sacrifices and burnt offerings"; thus sacred thoughts and exalted intellectual conceptions possess all the unique qualities of the sacrifice and all the unique qualities of the ritual service entailed in sacrifice, as well as the unique qualities of Torah in deed by means of oral discussion and speech of matters of Torah corresponding to the sacrifices and derived from them. He should derive courage from the fact that at times the paucity of deeds and study derives only from the intensive orientation towards the "mystery of thought," and it is possible that many aspects of his falls have occurred because he did not adequately value the basis of his thought. Therefore he should strive ever more with inner understanding to realize that the rectification of the entire world as well as healing for all souls are all contingent on the basis of thought, and he should exalt his thought to the extent of which he is capable; consequently, he shall ascend to repentance from inner love. (See Appendix, Item 39, for explanation of this paragraph.)

Happy is the people that know the joyful sound;
They walk, O Lord, in the light of thy countenance.
(Psalms 89:16)

XXXIX. There are such among the righteous that when for a second they lack from the full vital measure of exalted Godly union in accordance with their level, they sense their soul in the depths of sin's affliction and rectify their breach by means of the upper level of repentance, by means of full repentance, mighty and great. Even if their union is only perfect in terms of one aspect, either fear by itself, or love by itself, they sense in this already a great defect and disruption in the unity of the world's Godly order. And their soul yearns to take hold of the degree of the upper level of repentance, to rectify that which is damaged. The exaltedly righteous, abounding with kindness and Godly mercy for all creation, for all worlds and all that is therein, from beginning to end, those girded with strength and crowned with glory, with the true glory — they sense the imbalance in their pure category of union. And even if the fusion of fear and love will not sustain the equal balance appropriate to it, one aspect weighing down excessively upon its neighbor, they engage in repentance and ascend to that upper realm, from whence flows forth the treasures of sacred bounty, and they find the exalted sacred balance in its place; they rectify the defect of the "limp of Jacob's side" and proceed upon upright paths.

My foot standeth in an even place;
In the congregations will I bless the Lord. (Psalms 26:12)

These are the upright to whom the Lord's hidden teachings are constantly revealed, "and unto the upright his hidden teachings," and from the radiant conception of their striving for precious worth every searching soul is filled with splendor and life, "and the contemplation of their honor is honorable." (Proverbs 25:26) (See Appendix, Item 40, for explanation of these paragraphs.)

Chapter XV

THE BASIS OF INDIVIDUAL AND COLLECTIVE REPENTANCE

I.   The sensing of truth is the basis of repentance, the awareness that the entire world and all its manifestations are but an emanation of "the enveloping garment of the radiance of the absolute divine truth." This awareness imbues within the heart a clear love of truth, and every expression opposing the basis of truth, whether in speech, movement or action is removed from the world, has bypassed existence and is voided from life. Self-criticism, when it penetrates properly within the soul and clarifies in a proper manner all that was done and contemplated, deepens the remorse for all that is voided of the light of truth in the manifestation of human life. Man senses his debasement, his ugliness and worthlessness. Then man returns motivated by love to the light of truth. "A sage must also recite one verse of prayer for mercy upon retiring, entrusting his spirit to the source of truth, for renewal of strength in the labor of truth — in Torah, of which it is written, "truth" — as for example, the prayer for mercy "In Thy hand do I entrust my spirit; Thou hast redeemed me, O God, Lord of Truth." (See Appendix, Item 41, for explanation of this paragraph.)

II.   Pure logic declares that the entire endeavor of knowledge must be directed towards the ideal foundation imparting to human will the purest countenance appropriate to it, refining the will, strengthening, sanctifying and purifying it, regulating it with various disciplines that its striving should constantly be lofty and exalted. Let the areas of knowledge occupy themselves with how there can be brought forth from the potential to the actual all the particulars toward which the upright and virtuous wills prevailing in the world strive; these particulars are the necessities of dignified life, material and spiritual; however, the loftiest peak of their general objective must be refinement of the will itself, clear intellectuality of will and the ideal realization of its essence. Woe to all mankind when it departs from the upright way, and instead of establishing the goal of all perfections on the basis of ascent of will permits the will itself to remain in its coarseness, without betterment or ascent, and every endeavor is but to fulfill the desires of will, which flow like a "stream of brimstone" and over which all kinds of Gehenom prevail. Then collective mankind falls in the awesome and ugly snare of the coarse substance of idolatry, "which bloodshed shall pursue," and from the depths calls out to God, Lord of Truth, for return to the sacred character based upon general endeavor for ascent of will.

> Then shall thou call, and the Lord will answer;
> Thou shalt cry and He will say, "Here I am." (Isaiah 58:9)

For:

> The Lord is nigh unto all them that call upon Him,
> To all that call upon Him in truth. (Psalms 145:18)

This is the entire basis of repentance: ascent of will and its transformation to virtuousness, emergence from darkness to light, from the "valley of disturbance" to the "gateway of hope."

> And my people are in suspense about returning to me.
> (Hosea 11:7)
> Return, O backsliding Israel. (Jeremiah 3:14)
> Return, O Israel, unto the Lord thy God. (Hosea 14:2)

III. Natural remorse, which burns within the heart as a characteristic of repentance, is the result of the pain the soul endures because it remains on one level (see Appendix, Item 42) instead of constantly ascending from one level to another, and most assuredly is there pain if the soul senses decline within itself; actually, however, if the soul has truly declined completely from its level, then is also lost the sense of spiritual pain — or at least the sense of spiritual pain is impaired, and the bitter piercing is thereby lessened. But the pain of the static condition penetrates to the depths of the soul, and the sensing of pain is very great, because the soul

which has not declined has functioning and active spiritual instincts —
and the consuming pain of remaining in one place, which is
contrary to the nature of the soul and the entire goal of its existence,
"burns as the burning of fire" and is transformed into a flame
of great love abounding in exalted pleasure when the soul intensively
strives to return to its position of ascent, firmly grasping the character
of its ascent at all times.

So that my glory may sing praise to thee and not be silent.
(Psalms 30:13)

IV. It may occur that the heart is constantly oppressed because
of anguish without reason or cause. This comes from the source of
repentance, for the exalted light of the divine radiance is revealed
within the depth of the soul in a highly condensed form. There
must flow upon this seed-like point (see Appendix, Item 43) great
streams from the upper fountain of knowledge. Then it will emerge
into the light of the world with kaleidoscope brilliance in grandeur
and splendor; it shall encompass the entire mystery of life, and the
tree of life shall be revealed in the splendor of its branches upon
the soul. Man shall then be exalted and sanctified, "his mourning
will be transformed into gladness," he shall be consoled and rejoice
out of mist of his sorrow,

And the eyes of the blind shall see
out of obscurity and out of darkness. (Isaiah 29:18)

V. The great significance of human sanctity in the eyes of
humanity need not cause weakness of mind because of the demands
man imposses upon himself, for these demands are in actuality the
basis of that repentance, which leads to that complete elevation that
brings deliverance to the individual as well as to the world in its
entirety. However, this evaluation must awaken the quality of
humility in its fullness, the profound delving into the roots of humility bring forth the crown of the totality of wisdom. For the
heeding of humility and for its penetration within the most hidden
recesses of the soul the quality of strength is required. The outer
splendor accorded by society strengthens the basis of strength enabling

it to shine forth in its gleaming purity after being purged of the coarse substance of pride. (See Appendix, Item 44, for explanation of this paragraph.)

VI. The upper level of repentance, whose basis is sacred contemplation and the ennoblement of the perception of the Lord's graciousness, is the source and basis of the rectification of deed and ascent of refined character, of repentance on a lesser level; the basis of the upper level of repentance is the basis of Torah in the full extension of Torah's roots and branches. If man surmises that apprehending the lower level of repentance in its fullness is temporarily denied him, let him hasten to the upper level of repentance; he shall most assuredly achieve his goal since his inner longing is oriented towards the fulfillment of both levels of repentance. As time goes on the upper level of repentance leads him to repentance of the lesser level, which consists of the sanctification of specific deeds and of physical nature, purity of character and uplifting of natural qualities; "His heart and flesh will sing for joy unto the living God." (Psalms 84:3) (See Appendix, Item 45, for explanation of this paragraph.)

VII. To the extent that a person is aware of his sins, to that extent the brightness of the light of repentance shines upon his soul. Even though seemingly he has not achieved the fixed constancy of repentance within his heart and will, nevertheless, its light protect him and hovers over him and is already engaged in the process of recreating him anew. Even those conditions which prevent repentance, to the extent that a person is aware of them, and does not refuse to accept their existence, to that degree the hindrances decrease in strength and their venom is diminished. Thereby the light of repentance commence to shine upon him, and sanctity of upper joy vests itself in the essence of his soul. Gates that were closed open up before him; ultimately he will attain that exalted state where "all crooked places shall be leveled."

Every valley shall be lifted up.
And every mountain and hill shall be made low;
And the rugged shall be made level,
And the rough places a plain. (Isaiah 40:4)

VIII. When a person repents and does not depart from his repentance, even though he is suffering from conditions that prevent repentance, and he imagines that he cannot repent over them, this notwithstanding he keeps firm hold on the thought of repentance, he will ultimately achieve the strength to repent even over those conditions that prevent repentance. The light of retroactive repentance becomes very intense, and because of its emergence from "the straits" and great hindrances, it acts with overpowering strength achieving thereby inclusion among the most distinguished categories of repentance, that create a passageway for acceptance of repentance from those penitents unworthy of acceptance, as for example Manasseh and his acquaintances. (See Appendix, Item 46, for explanation of this paragraph.) Just "as in the realm where penitent sinners stand the perfectly righteous are unable to stand," similarly, in the realm where the penitent sinners who have returned despite being subject to conditions which hinder repentance stand, ordinary penitents are unable to stand, for they are considered in relation with those penitents, who have come to return possessed of matters hindering repentance, as comparable to the perfectly righteous when compared with the penitent.

This principle applies to prayer as well as to repentance. There are conditions which hinder prayer; he who imagines that he is subject to these conditions and nevertheless takes strong hold of the basis of prayer, and calls out to God at all times, ultimately all these hindering matters shall pass from him. Then the light of prayer which arises out of the midst of the very matters which hinder proceeds upon upright paths with great power, with strength from on high, and breaks through pathways for multitudes of prayers hitherto cast aside, his own and of the entire world, and through him is fulfilled this very passage;

Out of the straits I called upon the Lord;
He answered me with great enlargement.
The Lord is for me, I will not fear;
What can man do unto me?
The Lord is for me as my helper;
And I shall gaze upon them that hate me. (Psalms 118:5-7)

IX. The thought of repentance, always present in man, is the foundation of all virtuous qualities. The melancholy thought that derives from a bond with the depth of repentance is itself the source of joy. The fundament characteristic of repentance is the awareness of the grandeur of exalted Godly perfection. Thereby do our iniquities become highly manifest.

> Thou hast set our iniquities before Thee,
> Our secret sins in the light of Thy countenance. (Psalms 90:8)

As soon as one realizes that the awareness of sin, under all conditions, is a consequence of the divine radiation on the soul, he becomes filled by this very thought with joy and infinte grandeur, and the exultation of a noble happiness becomes intensified concommitantly with the contrition of the heart in "the vestment of the soul," (see Appendix, Item 49) which stands on the level of repentance. Repentance accordingly leads to individual redemption. Through this divine lucidity which becomes more and more intensified, man is redeemed from all enslavement to the alien faculties which prevail over him. The entire world, because it is prepared to experience the concept of repentance, is immediately redeemed by means of the divine radiance which is shed upon it together with the thought of repentance.

X. When one forgets the essential nature of the soul, when one ignores the quality of intospection, everything becomes confused and in doubt. The principal repentance, which immediately illumines the dark places, is the return of man to his self, to the source of his soul, and immediately he will return to God, the Soul of all souls and he will progress higher and higher in holiness and purity.

The principle of chaos occurring at all times because existence is forgetful of itself, applies to individuals, to an entire nation, to all mankind, as well as to the betterment of all existence. And if it will occur to you that existence desires to return to God, but is not establishing itself "to gather in its dispersed" — this then is a repentance of deception wherewith the name of the Lord is borne in vain. Therefore, through the great truth of return to the self shall there be return of man, the nation, the world and all worlds, existence in it's entirety, to its maker, to be illumined by the light of life. And this is the secret of Messiah's light — the manifestation of the world's soul; at whose radiance the world shall return to the root of existence, and the light of God shall be revealed upon the world and from this source of great repentance man shall draw the sacred life of repentance in its true sense.

XI. Our nation shall be built and established, be restored to its pristine state, to all foundations of its life, when its capacity for faith, its capacity for reverence, which constitute its emanant divinely sanctified essence shall extend, become intensified, will become perfected and fortified. All the builders of the nation will arrive at the profound truth of this point, and then with a voice abounding in power and strength they will resoundingly proclaim concerning themselves and their nation with great voice, "Come and let us return unto the Lord." This repentance will be true repentance, and the repentance shall be a foundation of strength. Repentance will give strength and power to all the ramifications of action and spirit, for all the media necessary for the upbuilding of the nation and its perfection, for its renascence and the strengthening of its position. "The eyes shall be opened," the soul shall be purified, its light shall gleam, its scope shall increase, a newly born people shall arise; "a nation great, mighty and populous," upon whom divine light will dwell, and that possesses the magnificence of nationhood, "shall rise as a lioness and as a lion uplift itself." (Num. 23:24)

XII. The feeling that decline in the state of morality hinders literary development is an awareness which Israel is unique in sensing; only we truly perceive that in order to improve literature the authors must first purify their souls, and we sense within ourselves great need for repentance, so that there may be uplifting to the pure heavens of the pure literature so distinctively ours, which flows forth from the source of Israel's wisdom, whose sources are sanctity and purity, faith and spiritual strength.

Chapter XVI

THE SOURCES OF REPENTANCE AND ITS INNER NATURE

I. The foundation of repentance is the "reckoning of the world."
The roots of this reckoning, transcend reckoning itself, just as the
theory of the value of numbers transcends numbers and their par-
ticulars. Therefore, the basic aspect of uppermost repentance trans-
cends particular reckoning, and reckoning occurs as its consequence.
That is why the "Chest of Accounts" had to be specifically below
Jerusalem, because Jerusalem itself is the "joy of the whole earth."
(Exodus Rabbah 52:4) The place in which abides the joy of the
light of uppermost repentance. Therefore did Adam sing:
A Psalm, a Song. For the Sabbath day.
It is a good thing to give thanks unto the Lord,
And to sing praises unto thy name, O Most High.
(Psalms 92:1-2)
For Thou Lord hast made me glad through Thy work;
I will exult in the works of Thy hands. (Psalms 92:5)

In conjunction with:
How great are Thy works, O Lord!
Thy thoughts are very deep.

Transcending all reckoning, for
His understanding is infinite, (Psalms 147:5)

beyond the degree that declares:
How manifold are Thy works, O Lord. (Psalms 103:24)

which are subject to reckoning, which is the degree of the earth:
The earth is full of Thy creatures. (Psalms 104:24)

But of the basis of repentance in its source is said:
For as the heaven is high above the earth,

371

So great is His mercy toward them that fear Him;
As far as the east is from the west,
So far hath He removed our transgressions from us.
(Psalms 103:11-12)

The flow of repentance proceeds constantly from above to below
— from transcendence of reckoning to the basis of revealed reckoning, and from below to above — from the quality of reckoning till

Unto the utmost bound of the everlasting hills, (Genesis 49:26)
Before the mountains were brought forth, (Psalms 90:2)

of which it is said:

And weighed the mountains in scales and the hills in a balance.
(Psalms 40:12)
Even from everlasting to everlasting Thou art God.
Thou turnest man to contrition
And sayest: "Return Ye children of men." (Psalms 90:2-3)

(See Appendix, Item 48, for explanation of these paragraphs.)

II. The dark realms of existence are enveloped by false fears
whose darkness extends into the soul of the individual and society
within the soul of a world bound with conditions of oppression and
laws constraining its true freedom. The penitent fears that his iniquities have already destroyed him and that his hope is already voided.
He does not know that already within his fear all the lights of his
deliverance abide in their concealment. The earth also feared and
did not bring forth the tree in its perfection, so that its taste would
be as the taste of its fruit. The moon was afraid of the contention
of two kings for one crown. Mankind is afraid of the clear and
exalted values of freedom. This world in its entirety is afraid of the
manifestation of the world to come, "glorious in holiness." However,
from the treasure of faith there comes tranquility, and fear is removed
from its basis,

The name of the Lord is a strong tower;
The righteous runneth into it, and is set up on high.
(Proverbs 18:10)

With the sanctity of trust, the defects of the worlds and all within them shall be set aright. (See Appendix, Item 49, for explanation of this paragraph.)

> Trust ye in the Lord for ever,
> For the Lord is God, an everlasting rock. (Isaiah 26:4)

III. It is impossible to estimate or evaluate the intensity of happiness, which man must sense within himself with great contentment, out of the midst of that refined pain he experiences when the spirit of sanctity and purity descends upon him:

> *at the time* that he is absorbed with the consuming thought of happiness due to the complete remorse for all his sins, iniquities and transgressions:

> *at the time* that his soul longs with love for the splendor of sanctity and perfection, longs for her beloved, her Creator Who brought her forth, Who brought all things forth, blessed be He;

> *at the time* when, in fullness of heart and soul, man desires with the depth of mighty will to walk in integrity and uprightness, to be righteous 'effecting righteousness," to be upright proceeding in uprightness,

> *even though* he intensively endeavors for the means whereby he can extricate himself from the mire of sins;

> *though* it is not at all clear to him how rectification can be achieved for the entire past;

> *though* the paths of action are as yet not at all leveled and abound with stumbling blocks;

> *but the will to be virtuous* — (see Appendix, Item 50) this is the spirit of Godly paradise, which sweeps within the soul filling it with infinite happiness to such an extent that even the fire of Gehinom of deepest pain is also transformed into "a stream of pleasure."

IV. Repentance is united with human strength. "Happy is the man that feareth the Lord," (Psalms 112:1) and "happy is he who repents while still a man"; (B. T. Avodah Zarah 19a) and the matter is derived from its context: happy is he who remains a man while repenting. (See Appendix, Item 51, for explanation of this paragraph.)

V. The pain sensed at the time of undertaking any sacred activity is a result of the fact that the soul illumines to a greater extent, and the content of absolute perfection is revealed within the soul. The soul perceives thereby the void of its bounded containment and is embittered over all that causes restraint of spirit and weakness. This, in truth, is the basis of "repentance based upon love," which is appropriate for every sensitive soul: to accept this experienced bitterness in joy and "gladness of heart"; then this depth of pain is transformed into a content of uppermost delight, wherein are revealed abounding pleasures of sanctity.

VI. Repentance is not meant to embitter life but rather to make it pleasant. Pleasantness of life which occurs as a result of repentance manifests itself from the midst of all those waves of bitterness which overwhelm the soul at the onset of its walking in the pathways of the life of repentance. But this is the supreme creative strength — that there should be knowledge and understanding that the pleasantness divests the souls of all bitterness; life — from all pangs of death; eternal delight — from all sickness and pain. This eternal knowledge becomes clearer and clearer, in the emotions, in the nature of the body and in the nature of the soul. Man is refashioned anew, casting with forceful power a new spirit of life over all his environs and bearing tidings to his generation and all "future generations": the gladness of the upright, "joy and singing," faith in redemption, "shouting and singing with gladness,"

> The humble also shall increase their joy in the Lord,
> And the neediest among men shall exult in the Holy One of Israel. (Isaiah 29:19)

VII. Every perfect repentance must inevitably achieve two contradictory effects upon the soul: on the one hand, trembling and sorrow for the sin and evil within him; and on the other hand, trust and joy for the virtue, since it is impossible that man should not discover within himself some share of virtue. Even if at times his reckoning is so beclouded that he can find no vestige of virtue, the very fact that trembling and sorrow encompass him as a result of his awareness of the sin and evil within him — this fact in itself possesses great virtue. And immediately he must rejoice, trustful and filled with strength and might, even for this virtue, till he shall find himself constantly, even amidst the greatest oppression involved in the emotions of repentance, abounding with spirit of life, fortified with the very basis of achievement and action with joy of life and preparation for their blessings.

VIII. Repentance in thought precedes repentance of action, and the repentance of "the hidden longing" precedes repentance in thought; repentance of "the hidden longing" is truly always repentance based on love, even in the case of those whose repentance is based on fear. (See Appendix, Item 52, for explanation of this paragraph.)

IX. Uppermost repentance, intellectual and emotional, contains within itself all lower levels of repentance of diverse categories with all the details of their laborious calculations, in an emanant, pleasant and gentle form.

X. A "Master of Torah" cannot achieve the rectification of repentance other than with Torah and by means of Torah; a "Master of Inner Thought" (see Appendix, Item 53) has no penance other than with this thought and by means of this thought. And if a Master of Torah shall declare: "I shall fast and thereby shall repent," there is no significance to his words, and "let the dog consume his repast." (See Apepndix, Item 54.) And the "Master of Inner Thought" who declares: "I hereby repent with outer physical diligence" does not achieve repentance. His repentance must be exalted, spiritual and refined, free and filled with the light of the "Holy of Holies," adorned with the most excellent beauty of uppermost life; then he will achieve healing for himself and the entire world.

XI. Repentance has two points which we categorize by the names "the upper level of repentance" and "the lower level of repentance." The upper level of repentance is repentance for himself, and the lower level of repentance is for the world. (See Appendix, Item 55.) At all times the essentially unique point within man is far higher, far more sublime and exalted than anything that flows outwardly from within. There are individuals who, once having achieved their own personal repentance, would find it necessary to intensify their preoccupation with thought, and would thereby occupy themselves less with study. Such individuals would need to engage more intensively in conceptualization, and thereby minimize action — mainly to purify their inner self so that they may stand purged and truly free. All this is true in the case of the uppermost level of repentance — essential repentance. It is not so, however, in the case of the lower levels of repentance — repentance in relation to the world. Here things are reversed, and it is necessary to intensify one's preoccupation with study and action, even though a diminution in contemplation and thought occurs. At times the lessening of the clarity of contemplation and thought in itself is rectification in relation to the world, because the outer world does not grasp the content of emanant thought and clarity of contemplation. Therefore it is approached specifically by means of restraint of thought in a known manner. But what we must know is that we are constantly called upon to take hold of these two repentances together, and the lower level of repentance is as a body and vessel to the upper repentance. Positions must be established in such a way that every movement of the upper level of repentance will also transpose the lower level of repentance, impelling it toward upwardness, and every transposition of the lower level of repentance will also strengthen and give power to the upper level of repentance; even though in their external form they appear contradictory to each other — in their inwardness they are "as two friends that are inseparable."

XII. The resplendently righteous, who perceive the entire world as judged "in virtue," they refine all things — due to the brightness of their thoughts and the radiance of the upright virtue within their pure will; they remove all the world's corruption and all wickedness from their basis; they place the total activity of the world's folly and wickedness in their proper perspective as veils, which only set aright the shining forth of the light, preparing place for it so that it may illumine in the world, neither corrupting nor destroying it. This condition is dependent upon the degree of the light itself, for condensed sacred light does not require obstruction so as to make possible the pleasure from its light. Therefore in relation to its level all coarseness, all materialistic inclinations and most assuredly all wickedness and folly are in themselves corrupting matters, causing crookedness and sickness; the soul is weakened by them; the soul is filled with wrath, sickness and anger because of their existence.

This is not the lot of the supreme saints, possessors of clear Godly intellect, bearers of pure will, in whom the exalted, gleaming light abides. They realize that the pure light is greater than the world's power to endure it. Nevertheless, it is necessary that it illumine in the world; it is also necessary, due to the nature of the world, that there be many veils to conceal the light. These veils are wickedness and its bearers; consequently, all of these also participate in the betterment of the world order. Therefore, the intensity of their grief is mainly derived from the suffering of those whose light is of a limited character who are unable to perceive how all wickedness in its entirety is naught but a veil setting aright the radiance of light. Therefore "Messiah shall come to bring the righteous back in repentance." (Zohar IV 153b) With the ascent of the righteous to the degree of upper repentance they shall discern that the great light is "vast beyond understanding" and manifests itself in the world with the strength of His "mighty mercies." Were it not for the many veils which occur due to all the categories of wickedness, material and spiritual, the world would dissolve as a result of the great light.

Thus everything returns to world rectification, and all the wicked are rectified and return to virtue when they discern their purpose;

the punishment of the wicked is mainly for the pain they caused the righteous in the world of condensation; and the righteous who stand in the "Godly expanse" come and liberate the wicked from all the straits of the "nether-world," and all things come thereby to abound in "strength and gladness." (See Appendix, Item 56, for explanation of these paragraphs.)

> Passing through the valley of tears they make it a place of springs;
> Yea, the early rain clotheth it with blessings,
> They go from strength to strength,
> Every one of them appeareth before God in Zion.
> (Psalms 84:7-8)

Chapter XVII

THE GREAT REVELATION OF REPENTANCE IN THE LIFE OF ISRAEL AND ITS REVELATION IN ISRAEL'S RENASCENCE IN OUR LAND

I. The renascence of the nation is the basis of the structure of great repentance, which is the exalted repentance of Israel and repentance of the entire world, which shall occur subsequently.

II. When there is true desire to return, even though obstructed by many hindrances, as for example, because of confused thought, or because of physical debility, or because of inability to rectify matters that concern man's relationship with his fellow man, even though the hindrance is very great and the heart will surely be broken because of the knowledge of the great obligation imposed upon him to correct his defects in the best and most complete manner — nevertheless, since the will to return in repentance is firm, even though he does not possess enough strength to overcome all obstacles, one should accept the enlightment of repentance as a purifying and sanctifying content, so that he will not waver, because of the restraints due to his not having achieved perfect repentance; from striving toward every form of exaltation and every degree of spiritual elevations, appropriate to him according to the sanctity of the soul and its sacred character.

And just as this is a fundamental principle insofar as the individual is concerned, so it is in regard to the community as a totality; the illumining of repentance is within Israel. The awakening of the desire of the nation in general to return to its land, to its nature, to its spirit, to its character — truly, this striving contains within itself the light of repentance.

Actually, the truth is expressed with absolute clarity in the expression of the Torah: "Thou wilt return to the Lord, thy God," (Deut. 30:2) "When thou shalt turn unto the Lord, thy God." (Deut. 30:10) This repentance is an inner repentance, but it is concealed with many obstructing veils, and no form of obstacle or hindrance to perfection possesses the power to hinder the supreme light from shedding its splendor upon us.

III. Even, from the mundane shall the sacred be revealed, and also from amidst undisciplined freedom shall come the beloved yoke. Chains of gold shall be woven and ascend from amidst untrammeled poetry. And radiant repentance shall emerge also from amidst secular literature. This fulfillment shall be the supreme wonder of the vision of redemption. This ripening shall come unto fruition, the bud shall flourish, the fruit shall ripen, and the entire world will know that the spirit of holiness speaks in the Congregation of Israel in all movements of its spirit, and ultimately all shall come unto repentance, which brings healing and redemption to the world.

IV. The uprooting of the sacred character of Judaism is responsible for all confusion of thought. They endeavor to be "overly wise" and to discover with logic and speculation what ought to be found in the very depths of the soul's being and in the spiritual and physical nature of the Jewish nation as a whole, and of each son of Israel in particular. This constitutes an abrogation of the covenant, a rejection of the Judaic character in action, in conception, in feeling and thought, in will and existence. There is no remedy for him who breaks the covenant except by return to the covenant, which is firmly bound to the sacred character of Israel with firm .bond, "Return unto me, and I will return unto you." (Malachi 3:7)

V. The emotions of repentance in the full splendor of their brightness, with their most profound anguish of soul, will inevitably be revealed in literature so that the generation of renascence will acquire within the innermost depths of its soul an understanding of repentance in a vital and vigorous manner; "And it shall return and it shall be healed." And there shall arise unto us a poet of repentance, who shall be a poet of life, a poet of renascence, the poet of the national soul which proceeds toward redemption.

VI. We are hindered on the path of perfection and are faint in it because of the great trembling which we sense in the soul at the time that the thought of repentance passes before us; we remain filled with great pain, devoid of strength from the effect of the oppression of repentance. For this very reason we thrust aside this thought, the source of all good fortune, from influence upon our souls and we remain as wanderers in the desert of life. But this situation cannot endure. We must gird ourselves with the strength of the soul, with the power of the poetry of repentance. All its sorrow will inevitably be transformed into vigorous song, which enlivens and sustains, consoles and heals. Then shall repentance with all its meditations be unto us as objects of love, pleasant and sweet, upon which we shall constantly meditate, and in accordance with it shall we order all our paths of life, for our individual and collective good, in this world and in the world to come, for the redemption of the individual and the redemption of the world in its entirety, for the renascence of the nation, for return from its captivity

As in the days of old,
And as in ancient years. (Malachi 3:4)

APPENDIX

EXPLANATORY NOTES

ITEM 1.

Rabbi Kook introduces the basic concept of means and end in an apocalyptic context. The theme of means and end recurs frequently in his writings. In Jewish mysticism the realm of "glory" is below various other spheres. Thus "prior to all categories of repentance" there must be repentance to the "glory of God." In this passage "glory" would seem to refer to ethical means entailed in the achievement of an ultimate ideal; "glory" seems also to refer to minor religious obligations. Though subsequently there will be "diffusion of light" or more exalted spiritual revelations causing the "content of glory" to be "too narrow to contain the great flow of the lights of repentance," nevertheless, glory "is the basis of the repentance, whose light shall be revealed in the era prior to the advent of the Messiah." This era, frequently referred to in the Talmud, will be marked by great social upheaval and strife.

In that period various persons will strive for ends and ideals without concern as to the means entailed. The "children of the violent" will "arise and uplift themselves to establish a vision and stumble." This is because they have disregarded the means or the "lesser lights which appear to have been dispelled." "The great light continues to exert its influence"; the ultimate ideal shall exert its influence until insight is achieved as to the significance of means and ideals — or of "major and minor qualities." Consequently, the Messiah, who is the "son of Peretz," or the descendant of Peretz, in Jewish tradition, will "repair" the "breach" and "from the thorn pluck the rose." This probably refers to the achievement of the ultimate ideal in an appropriate manner. See paragraph ten in this chapter for a similar concept more explicitly expressed. The phrase commencing "repair my breach" is from the liturgy of the seventeenth day of Tamuz, a fast day in remembrance of the breaching of Jerusalem's walls by the Roman army. "Children of the violent" (Daniel 14:11) is a phrase from an apocalyptic prophecy. See special edition of Maimonides, *Rambam Loam* (Jerusalem, Mosad Horav Kook, 5722) Hilchos Melochim 11:4, for a censored segment which cites this verse.

ITEM 2

"The hidden teachings of Torah" is a reference to Jewish mysticism. We may interpret this passage both in a narrow and a more general manner. Since mysticism is the study of God in relation to the world, a concept inexpressible as well as incomprehensible in its fullest sense due to the finitude of the human mind, therefore the various false Messiahs of Jewish history such as Reuveni,

382

Zvi and Frank, "who cleaved" to the hidden teachings of Torah "without appropriate preparation," have caused "the growth of peril and world catastrophe," or have effected much chaos and disaster as the result of their actions.

In a more general sense this may be a re-expression of the means-end concern. Thus those who have striven for human ideals intuitively discerned from an "upper source" without due study of the means entailed in achieving them have caused great destruction and chaos. The various political upheavals of human history commencing with aspiration toward noble ideals and ultimately deteriorating into exploitative self interest such as the phenomenon of Marxism in our own age are manifestations of this concept. (See Item I of Appendix.) See also Dr. Samuel Belkin's *In His Image* (New York, Abelard Schuman, 1960), for an excellent work explicating the unifying underlying principles of Jewish law.

ITEM 3

In Chabad Chasidus, a discipline concerned with the clarification of mystical concepts and their implications for human ethical behavior, there is to be found the distinction between "encompassing light" and "permeating light." "Encompassing light" is equated with God's transcendence, which nevertheless exerts an effect upon the world, and "permeating light" is equated with God's immanence in the world.

Thus "In truth within the depths of life there gleams every moment a new light of the upper level of repentance" may refer to the effecting of God's transcendence within the world. The phrase "just as a new light surges within all the worlds in their fullness to renew them" in all probability refers to the immanence of God as "the permeating light" within the world which animates and ever constantly sustains all existence. Since "within the depths of life there gleams every moment a new light of the upper level of repentance," this being a reference to the primary and transcendent aspect of Godliness, therefore all other "lights," a term describing the inherent spiritual qualities of all existing phenomena, which are the various gradations of "permeating lights," are "contingent upon" and strive toward the transcendence of upper repentance or the source from whence all things came into being. "Consequently, the light of the entire world and its renewal in all its forms at all times and instances," or the renewal of all levels of "permeating light" "in all its forms at all times and instances are contingent upon repentance" or God's transcendence, "how much more so does this apply to the light of Messiah and the salvation of Israel, the renascence of the nation and the land, the language and the literature, which all emerge from the source of repentance,and from the depths they shall be uplifted to the heavens of exalted repentance." All of the aforementioned shall return to their source by means of man's spiritual endeavors.

ITEM 4

The second paragraph of this segment defines the term repentance in the thought of Rabbi Kook and aids us in gaining insight into the complexity of the first paragraph. "Repentance derives from the striving of all existence to be more virtuous and pure, stronger and more exalted than its present state. Within this desire there is concealed the life force of prevalence over the finite dimensions of existence and its imperfections." Teshuva, the Hebrew word for repentance, is literally interpreted as "return." In the thought of Rabbi Kook, just as God initiates action from transcendence to immanence so must man strive for "prevalence over the finite dimensions of existence" and strive for "return" from immanence to transcendence, or from the finitude of physical existence to the realm of the spiritual. This is accomplished by sincere religious and ethical endeavor.

Individual man, humanity and all existence strive for this "return." This thought is expressed in the first sentence of this segment: "From the depths comes repentance, from a so great a depth that the individual human spirit is not a unique form in relation to it but a continuum of the grandeur of universal existence."

In this striving for "return" man evokes the "will of the world" or the "life-will," a quality synonymous with transcendence. "The will of repentance extends to the will of the world in its most exalted source, and since the mighty current of the life-will's surge turns toward betterment, immediately many streams flow unto the fullness of existence to reveal virtue and to do good unto all." The evoking of the "life-will" thus has many beneficial consequences within the world itself.

Even the repentance of individual man can bring blessing to the world. Rabbi Kook cites a passage from Yoma 86a in the Babylonian Talmud to this effect: "Great is repentance for it brings healing unto the world and when an individual repents both he and the world are forgiven."

In the re-establishment of the flow of the life-will from transcendence to immanence by means of humanity's will for repentance there is revealed the "unity of all existence in its source." "In the great channel in which there flows the vigor of essential life, there is revealed the unity of all existence in its source, and by means of the hovering life-spirit of repentance, all things are renewed to supreme virtue, illumining and radiant."

ITEM 5

The striving for repentance or return is inherent within all existence. When God in his transcendence caused the immanent and finite world to come into being it was with the desire that all existence aspire for ascent to Godliness. This quality of return is inherent within the entirety of existence and inevitably all existence will actualize this striving. See *Likutei Amarim, (Tanya)* Chapter 49 where this theme is expressed in more explicit Kabbalistic terms.

ITEM 6

"The deeds are speaking within the sou.. Every act performed causes a subsequent effect within the soul itself. The emergence of a virtuous deed to actuality is the conclusion of a complex process "after many sequences of development from virtue and sanctity." This may be another allusion to the descent from transcendence to immanence. "Infinite are the causes which developed from exalted concealment till this virtuous action emerged to revealed actuality."

This deed "restores the light" of Godliness immanent within the world to its source in transcendence. "It drives back the waves," "waves" probably referring to spiritual phenomena not unlike waves of sound and light. By driving back the waves the deed "extends" the effect of sanctity and enlarges it from "below" within the world to "above" beyond the world. See *Likutei Amarim (Tanya)* 152 a-b.

Rabbi Kook asserts that just as each virtuous deed emerges from a virtuous source, similarly, "the reverse is also true," and the corrupt deed indicates and reveals the decay "within the spirit that created it."

This action is rectified "by the person who prevails over his deed and his will with the great power of repentance." At that time, "particularly by means of repentance's ascent to the degree of love," when the repentance shall be motivated by love, then this very deed "shall establish its abode in the depth of virtue" or source of virtue. This deed shall "drive the waves from below" to "above" in a manner comparable to the ascent "of the virtuous deeds unto virtue." The redemption of evil deeds can also be psychologically interpreted as implying that when man gains insight as to the causes and motivations of evil this fact in itself aids him toward greater self knowledge and constructively significant action in the future.

ITEM 7

Rabbi Kook strives to clarify the function of "the will for virtue." "Ratzon," or "will," is equated with the transcendence of God in Jewish mystical literature. The reason for the creation of the world is given as, "Thus did He will it." This will is a will for "tov," which may be translated as virtue or goodness. Thus the transcendent will strives for the actualization of virtue and goodness within the immanence of the world.

Man, endowed with divine qualities, is also possessed of the will for virtue. It is the profoundest and most essential aspect of his personality. Injustice and evil occur only because of a defect in the will for virtue. Repentance is the process whereby man returns to his essential self; "the important principle that the virtuous will is allness and all the talents in the world are naught but its fullfillment because a content natural to his soul by means of the light of repentance constant within him." The persons of outstanding ethical stature, or "Masters of Repentance," aid in guiding mankind toward the actualization of the will for virtue. "This teaching that all world problems are reliant solely upon the virtuous will is promulgated in the world by the 'Masters of Repentance' for the content of repentance is the constant aspiration of their souls; thereby does the will truly proceed to become refined and virtuous, and the world proceeds toward greater perfection."

ITEM 8

If man can rise to the level of viewing all existence as subject ever constantly to the effect of the will for virtue, then even the profound enigma of evil existence in the world ceases to confront him. "The defects which can be seen in the life order are discerned as folds which are straightened and leveled in the grandeur of the life of the virtuous will, which sweeps forward like an enormous river extending across generations and eras, for only fragmentary aspects of life are revealed in each individual generation, and their fulfillment comes with the passage of all generations."

ITEM 9

"The illumination of exalted wisdom" may be interpreted simply as a religious and intellectual experience whereby the recipient is endowed with insight that is both spiritually edifying and intellectually enlightening. Sin obstructs the manifestation of divine revelation in this manner. See *Likutei Amarim, (Tanya)* Chapter 18 for insight into the ethico-kabbalistic implications of this term.

ITEM 10

This paragraph refers to the sequence of Jewish holidays during the first month of the year; "the days designated for repentance" is a specific reference to the ten days of penitence commencing with Rosh Hashona, the Jewish new year, and concluding with Yom Kippur, the day of atonement. This period is characterized by "constriction of will" and "the power of life is inhibited due to the inner recoiling and the inclination to return from all sin." This repressive phase of repentance causes "that the will for virtue is also constricted, and the power of pure life is also weakened." Repression is, however, a necessary preliminary experience to the higher form of repentance out of joy. "Thus it occurs that man endures from his purification weakness comparable to that endured by a sick person who is cured by means of a strong electric charge."

The anguish of repentance is not the ultimate phase of repentance, "though it has eliminated the virus of his illness, but it has also weakened the vital and healthy power within him." True repentance is expressive and not repressive. "Therefore there return, days of sacred joyousness" is a reference to the holiday of Sukkot, or Tabernacles that follows immediately "the time of our joy," which concludes with unusual festivity on the day of "Simchat Torah," meaning "the joy of the law." Thus the highest level of repentance is achieved by "spiritual gladness to uplift the will of virtue and the power of pure life — then shall there be perfect repentance."

Man is not viewed as an egocentric being who must strive to ever constantly repress instincts toward self assertion and aggression; rather, he is perceived as capable of great creativity and self-realization if these latent powers are enabled to emerge in an appropriate manner. See also Rabbi Chaim Soloveichik's rejection of extreme repression as a life-mode, cited in Rabbi J. B. Soloveichik's classic work *Ish HaHalacha,* printed in Talpiot (April-September, 1944) p. 698.

ITEM 11

"True perfect repentance requires exalted contemplation." This exalted contemplation can only be achieved by preoccupation with the "profound aspects of Torah" or the mystical literature of Jewish tradition. To Rabbi Kook the complexity and symbolism of Jewish mystical literature is in actuality the articulation of the inarticulate, expressing that which is beyond man's intellectual apprehension and comprehension. "The radiance of intellect," (see item 9) a profound religious experience achieved by this study, is conditional upon "physical clean-liness and ethical purity to aid that the clouds of desire should not obstruct the radiance of intellect." Ultimately, by this means man achieves true unity with God and mankind "for only it can destroy all the iron barriers that stand between individual man as well as the community and their father in heaven."

ITEM 12

Sin obstructs understanding of the mystical aspects of religious knowledge by preventing "the tranquility necessary for the emanation of the world's esoteric matters." Repentance rectifies this situation. "Repentance opens the gates of understanding just as it occurs only by means of understanding."

Though intellectual repentance is the highest level of repentance, nevertheless, it is but the means for the achievement of constant union with God. "Cleaving," or "dvekut," has also been described by the term "abiding God-consciousness." Thus the truly religious personality is constantly mindful of God's presence and strives to serve him not only in praye. or ritual but also by every single conscious act performed. "Dvekut" in turn causes great humility, "for how can man be vain when standing before the source of all perfection — exalted infinite light which transcends all blessings and praise."

ITEM 13

The mystic describes the transcendence of God as "encompassing light" and the immanence of God with the term "permeating light." The medium between transcendence and immanence is described by the term "Kether," or "crown," in the mystical literature. Permeating light is characterized by ten spheres, the two highest being "wisdom" and "understanding." "Wisdom" is defined as the "spark," "point" or moment of insight, which requires the further elaboration and clarification provided by the quality of "understanding."

"Repentance occurs due to understanding." This is consistent with the view expressed in chapter one that intellectual repentance is the highest degree of repentance. For only by means of intensive introspection can man achieve true self-awareness. "Understanding" causes weakening of will due to remorse for the past. This embitterment is "transformed to joy and expansiveness of mind" because of the "exalted awareness of the transformation of intentionally evil deeds into deeds of merit," a reference to the Talmudic statement that in the case of repentance based upon love former evil deeds are regarded as transformed into acts of merit. "The light of wisdom then appears" since the barrier of evil has been removed, and man can perceive spiritual light with greater clarity. See Lekutei Amarim, (Tanya) 98b, for an explanation of "repentance occurs due to understanding."

"Even loftier than this is the manifestation of the universal Crown's radiance," a reference to the medium between the transcendence and· immanence of God. "There is revealed to its light that there is neither defect nor darkness." This is somewhat similar to the concept expressed in chapter XVI paragraph XII, wherein Rabbi Kook states that "wickedness in its entirety is naught but a veil setting aright the radiance of light." Thus though God is omnipotent he permits the existence of evil or "incompleteness" in the world so that man may strive for perfection. This is not to say that man must submit to evil and oppression. Rabbi Kook himself was an articulate champion of justice at times of pogroms and persecution. However, when men or humanity are confronted by the classic enigma of Job, suffering without a perceptible cause, then the truly religious person can only reply with his faith in the ultimate goodness of God to the effect that "there is naught but sacred light and exalted splendor."

The manifestation of the "universal crown's" radiance is above "understanding," which voids, and above "wisdom," which releases. This is a reference to the law of vows and interprets them as possessing profound metaphysical implications. A husband is empowered to abrogate a vow made by his wife freeing her from the obligation of fulfilling it subsequent to his abrogation, whereas the court has authority to nullify a person's oath as though it were never made. Thus the husband by his "understanding" voids the vow, while the court with its "wisdom" can release the individual from his self-imposed obligation if extensive inquiry can establish that the vow was undertaken due to a misconception or false premise. Beyond "understanding" and "wisdom," the two highest levels of immanence, repentance ascends to the degree of the "crown," from whence it is revealed that evil has "no existence, neither in the past, present, nor future. All that exists is the light and goodness of God." Further explication of the relationship between "wisdom" and "understanding" and the voiding and releasing from vows can be found in Rabbi M. Shneerson's *Likutei Sichos* (New York: Kehot Publication Society, 1961) Vol. IV, pp. 1076-1082. See pp. 1070-1077 for an explanation of repentance extending to the realm of the transcendental, a frequently recurring motif in *Orot Ha-Teshuvah*.

ITEM 14

The meaning of Teshuvah, the Hebrew word for repentance, is return. The religious personality perceives the universe as coming into existence due to descent from transcendence to immanence, or "Aspects or existence become manifest by means of their descent from Divine reality to worldly reality." The creation of the world entailed the manifestation of the attributes of "mercy" as well as "justice," which is synonymous with "strength" or "law." "The exalted mercy of 'a world built in mercy' (Psalms 89:2) is possessed also of the quality of strength and law of 'the spirit of God hovering over the face of the waters.' " (Genesis 1:2)

The aspiring of immanence toward transcendence is inherent within the world. "However, this descent has concealed within it the basis for exalted ascent even before the order of time, ascent is already contained therein." "The great depth of Judgment," apparently a term for immanence or the created world, and "the mighty mountains of righteousness," a term of transcendence, shall be reunited or "shall kiss each other." The mundane shall reascend to the spiritual, actualizing spirituality within the mundane world. Man actualizes this return by means of repentance, repentance being the means whereby man strives to return to his exalted source and also uplift the world with himself. This is the fulfillment of the divine will: "Thou turnest man to contrition and sayest: Return ye children of man." (Psalms 90:3)

Man is viewed as a microcosm of all existence. He is also central to the order of the universe. "Upon the orbits of individual and collective man's repentance there circles and revolves the entire order of life practical and spiritual. Out of the depths have I called thee O Lord." (Psalms 130:1) The verse from the Psalms could perhaps imply the power of man's prayer to effect divine compassion within the natural order of the universe.

ITEM 15

The significance of man's actions is "that impression which the action impresses upon the very basis of the soul; the actions are interwoven in the foundation of the actual world." Evil compels us to declare that the "actual world is nevertheless a divided world" though "all its orders are in harmony with each other." Repentance aids in the rectification of the world. "Repentance uplifts man and his world to the world of repentance, wherein all existence stands in the clairty of its spiritual content, and that world with the intensity of its spirituality prevails over our finite world" in accordance with the impressions "hewn" by means of man's thought of repentance.

ITEM 16

Though Rabbi Kook asserts that evil has no existence, this is only in terms of God's ultimate awareness. On a lower level of the spiritual cosmos there is to be found the source of virtue and evil. The sins emerging from a virtuous personality aid to bring that individual to a higher level of spirituality by means of the profound self-insight and awareness ultimately entailed in the process of repentance.

ITEM 17

This is a well known Talmudic principle, "A good measure surpassing a measure of adversity," usually referring to God's mercy surpassing the quality of retribution. (B. T. Yoma 16a.)

ITEM 18

The nature of evil is that the benefits created are only for egocentric self-interest and not motivated by a true sense of altruism. Hans Morgenthau, an eminent contemporary political scientist, has attracted much interest with his thesis that power is the primary aspiration of all nations. Martin Buber expressed a similar concept in distinguishing between world nationhood and the nationhood of Israel in the biblical ideal sense.

ITEM 19

This refers to the selling of Joseph by his brothers. The consequences of this act "sustained the world in its entirety," for Joseph predicted and directed the preparation for the "seven lean years."

ITEM 20

Even at the time of their transgression, though there will be retribution for it, "let their needs be before you," so that even at the time of divine retribution there may be the manifestation of divine mercy. (B. T. Berachot 29b)

ITEM 21

It is explained in the Jerusalem Talmud that "beneficent idolatry" is lenient even as regards Biblical laws of sacrifice. "And bring your sacrifices in the morning" is in defiance of the law forbidding any remnant of the sacrifice to be found after sunrise. "And your tithes after three days" is in contrast to the Bible, which specifies a lesser period of time. "And offer a sacrifice of that which is leavened," while the Bible prohibits the sacrifice of leaven in this context. (J. T. Avodah Zarah 1, 1.)

Rabbi Kook derives from this text the implication that in essence idolatry is a rationalization for egocentric self-indulgence even to the extent of grossly unethical behavior. "The method which departs from truth and justice which proceeds after its own heart."

ITEM 22

"Extends her Hooves" is a reference to the Biblical law regarding animals permitted to be eaten. The two requirements are the chewing of the cud and a cloven hoof. Consequently, the animal possessing only a cloven hoof which "extends her hooves and declares 'see that I am pure' " is a symbol for hypocrisy.

ITEM 23

The theme of descent and ultimate re-ascent is to be found frequently in Jewish mystical literature. In this section Rabbi Kook deals with the descent of a "thought" from its "exalted greatness." "Subsequently" violent men come and desecrate its sanctity." The righteous or "refined in heart are aroused" and "instill" in the thought "the purity of their own soul." Ultimately the thoughts shall re-ascend and "with it shall ascend all that cling to "the fringe" of the thoughts vestment. This may be another formulation of the mean-end concept dealt with in Chapter 4, paragraph VIII.

ITEM 24

"The violent men" cause corruption by desecrating the "sparks of Godliness" or ultimate ideal by using inappropriate means for their actualization. Ultimately, the righteous shall achieve "true renascence and everlasting salvation" for themselves and all humanity, uplifting the "light of God" to its source in an appropriate manner. The above is an obvious reference to the doctrine of "the fallen sparks" which occurred at the onset of creation due to "the shattering of the vessels." See *Likutei Amarim, (Tanya)* 144b.

ITEM 25

"The vestment of Israel" refers to Israel as an outer vestment garb or manifestation for the inherent "abstract Godly virtue"; Israel fulfills this function "in its own unique manner." Israel can only achieve perfection in this endeavor by "removal of every hindrance in deed from all that affects the soul of the Jew. The Torah is viewed as the medium of relationship between God and Israel, wherein there is to be found the proper mode of religious and ethical conduct.

ITEM 26

The Talmud states that man should serve God with both his virtuous and evil inclinations. This enigmatic statement has been interpreted as referring to the will for virtue and the will for evil. Thus man strives to probe deeply within the depths of his personality and redirect the will for evil toward virtue. Only ethical giants are fully capable of this great spiritual labor. This concept is in all probability referred to by the statement, the "uplifting of evil qualities and thoughts to their source." See *Likutei Amarim, (Tanya)* 35a for an explicitly mystical interpretation of "the uplifting of evil qualities and thoughts to their source."

The truly religious personality is not content with the rectification of evil but strives toward "Dvekut" or constant union with God even when preoccupied with mundane tasks and the duties of his daily life. This difficult endeavor is referred to as "the uplifting of minor qualities and thoughts," when the religious personality endows them with great personal and religious significance "they ascend to great light."

The mystic conceives of the "uplifting" as ultimately ascending from the finite world to the source of all being — to God in his transcendence. In this manner, a higher degree of unity is achieved between the imanence and transcendence of God. Thus even those "absolute in their righteousness," devoid of sin, can ascend to the degree of the penitent by uplifting "minor matters" or mundane details of their life to "grandeur" by performing these tasks with the intention of serving the Almighty.

ITEM 27

Various prominent spiritual personalities of human history have also been characterized by qualities of violence and evil. Though the charismatic personality is endowed with acute spiritual sensitivity, nevertheless, he must not be wholly reliant upon this quality for the fulfillment of his spiritual nature. He must strive toward his own ethical perfection. "Repentance with the desire for refinement of qualities of character must precede" contemplative ascent," so that a "relational medium" is created between "the body and soul." The physical and spiritual aspects of being are united with each other.

ITEM 28

The "fragments" of action refer to the minor aspects of action yet unrectified.

ITEM 29

"Regarding permissible acts" implies that even simple acts of man should be done with the thought of service to God.

ITEM 30

"At the time of nourishment" refers to the Biblical commandment regarding the reciting of grace after having eaten, which can only be fulfilled during "the time of nourishment when it is still permissible to recite grace."

ITEM 31

The priests in their eating of the sacrificial offering effect forgiveness for the person bringing the sacrifice. A similarly significant spiritual labor is effected by the "Tsaddik" who eats with pure intent or who repents "immediately after having eaten."

ITEM 32

This passage deals with two distinct personalities. The first is one "whose strivings are spiritual and mighty. When there is defect in the nature of his actions, "and the awareness of active responsibility is not very particularized," this causes "inner melancholy," since "the soul feels its inadequacy to a greater extent because the faculty of action is proximal to the realm of the soul."

The other and lesser kind of personality is one lacking in spiritual sensitivity, who, by his very nature, is only close to the realm of action and "whose defects extend, to a greater degree, in the distant world of the spirit." These persons "cannot sense their inadequacies to the extent of suffering from melancholy and are more liable to be joyful by nature."

The more sensitive personality does not depart from the realm of action; rather, he endeavors to strengthen the "spiritual flow" of spiritual contemplation and unite it with the "world of action." He strives to "illumine the vista of action by preoccupation" with "the active aspects of Torah." The spiritual flow shall thereby "develop and become a luminary of the upper level of repentance, rectifying all things, practical and contemplative life together."

ITEM 33

Jewish religious literature describes various degrees of spiritual endeavors. One classic work describing various levels of degrees is the *"Mesilat Yeshorim"* by Rabbi Moshe Chaim Luzatto. A simple example of differing degrees would be the lesser labor of a person who serves God from fear of punishment or expectation of reward; a higher level would be he who serves God motivated by selfless altruism. A person, whose "essential level" is on a relatively low level should not desist from contemplation regarding the higher levels, since "all levels of virtue and sanctity must be bound together." He thereby achieves that they all "make up one entity to enable the light to cast its rays upon him, the light of God and his exalted Torah, with the graciousness and goodness of the Lord." Though he is incapable of actualizing this high level of spiritual conduct, nevertheless, study and knowledge of this high level of spiritual attainment exerts an ennobling and beneficial effect upon him to aid toward mature and significant ethical and religious conduct.

ITEM 34

Two contrasting types of outstanding religious personalities are discussed: "there are two manners of 'grandeur of degree.'" The first is a person rich in knowledge and striving to fulfill the knowledge in deed; the other is a person endowed with "ability rooted in birth because of the greatness of his soul." Rabbi Kook describes the differences in their process of repentance.

ITEM 35

All of these are Biblical prohibitions and are cited because the transgressions occur due to absence of action on the part of the individual, rather than due to a conscious act intentionally performed. The Biblical phrase "cords of a wagon" (Isaiah 5:18) is interpreted as implying that the repetition of a forbidden act many times is comparable to the weaving of many strands into the firm "cords of a wagon." Thus habituation will exert great influence upon man's future conduct.

ITEM 36

During a profound religious experience, minor defects may have no effect, but subsequently one should take great care to cope with those matters that they should not exert any adverse influence.

This is derived from the ritual "of the high priest's sanctification of hands and feet after divesting himself of the sacred garments on the Day of Atonement." Rabbi Kook interprets the ritual of washing, or "sanctification of hands and feet," in a mystical manner, "for those fragments of impurity which break into the midst of the sanctuary, and which because of the grandeur of sacred light, strive with all their strength to cling to it but are unable to accomplish anything when sanctity dominates — yet after the passing of its radiance we must take heed against them by means of great repentance abounding with exultation, might and humility." See *Derech Mitzvosecha* by the famed Zemach Zedek, pp. 62b, 63a for a similar concept.

ITEM 37

Rabbi Kook emphasizes that Teshuvah, or repentance is not solely for transgressors. Actually Teshuvah means return; thus man is involved in an ever ascending aspiration toward Godliness. If "a person desires to be solely in the category of the perfectly righteous," this aspiration may hinder the actualization of repentance in its fullest sense. Man should strive to "become a 'penitent' — deeply preoccupied with the thought of repentance and its actualization; then can repentance exalt him above, to the degree of those perfect in their righteousness — and even beyond."

ITEM 38

A distinction is made between two differing types of personality. The first is one with a predisposition toward a life of piety. Persons possessing such a personality are endowed with the "natural gift" of being "righteous ones from the very beginning" and even if they err, they can easily revert to their former manner of behavior. But those "who by nature are possessed of such souls, that are in constant need of repentance," should strive for a high degree of sanctity by means of the "strengthening of sacred flame," or natural inherent spiritual longing, so that it may be "manifest and yearning constantly." This is done so as to avert ethical decline. "It is specifically these who are called upon to be the pious and men of sanctity." A somewhat similar differentiation is to be found in paragraph XII of this chapter.

ITEM 39

There is frequent mention in chassidic literature of states of mind known as "greatness" and "smallness." When the Zaddik's mind is in the degree of "greatness" or "grandeur," it is characterized by a high degree of inspired intellectual activity, usually marked by original and penetrating religious thoughts. In direct contrast, the degree of "smallness" is marked by apathy, constriction of creativity and originality.

When "the spirit falls into 'smallness,'" then "man must strengthen himself with the 'secret of thought.'" "Mystery of thought" may also be rendered as "wondrousness of thought," for by means of "thought" man effects constant cleavage with God and achieves the highest level of repentance — "intellectual repentance." In addition to this, the mere act of religious study is deemed highly significant in the eyes of God. Thus "he who understands one matter from another — such a person's thoughts are considered more significant before the 'Holy One blessed be He' than all sacrifices and burnt offerings." The "exalted intellectual conceptions" are possessed of all the qualities related to sacrifice as well as all the qualities of oral Torah discussion pertaining thereto. Consequently, thought encompasses the realm of speech and deed and is therefore of primary significance.

The person should "derive courage from the fact that at times the paucity of deeds and study derives only from the intensive orientation towards the mystery of thought." A person characterized by inspired flights of religious thought may subsequently suffer from the condition of "smallness of mind," inhibited intellectual activity. "It is possible that many aspects of his fall" from "greatness" to "smallness" have occurred "because he did not adequately value the basis or significance of his thought." Strengthening of "inner understanding" is required for achieving the realization that the "rectification of the entire world, as well as the healing for all souls is all contingent on the basis of thought." He should strive "to exalt his thought to the extent of which he is capable of," thereby "he shall ascend to repentance from inner love."

This paragraph is a further clarification of the highest category of repentance, intellectual repentance mentioned in Chapter I. One must also bear in mind that by means of thought man effects "cleaving" or constant relatedness to his Creator.

ITEM 40

This paragraph is a further elaboration of the concept of "cleaving." Rabbi Kook describes "cleaving" or "union" as characterized by the two qualities of love and fear. These qualities must always be in a state of balance, and if the union is only perfect in terms of one aspect — either fear by itself, or love by itself" — then the righteous already sense therein "great defect and disruption in the unity of the world's Godly order." "The exaltedly righteous" are the ones who are capable of sensing "the imbalance in their pure category of union" and, though initially incapable of achieving this balance, "they engage in repentance and return to that upper realm, from whence flows forth the treasures of sacred bounty and they find the exalted sacred balance in its place." Even an imbalance of fear and love requires repentance to the "upper realm" for rectification.

The Biblical allusion to the "limp of Jacob's side" is interpreted as reflecting the concept of balance in the state of cleaving. The "exaltedly righteous" in their ascent "rectify the defect of 'the limp of Jacob's side' (Genesis 32:32) and proceed upon upright paths."

The striving of the exaltedly righteous has significance for all humanity, "and from the radiant conception of their striving for precious worth every searching is filled with splendor and life, and the contemplation of their honor is honorable."

ITEM 41

This paragraph elaborates on the significance of truth and man's apprehension of truth. "The sensing of truth is the basis of repentance." Man must achieve the awareness that the world is an emanation from the source of truth, an emanation of "the enveloping garment of the radiance of the absolute Divine truth." By means of introspection and "self-criticism" there is a deepening of "remorse for all that is voided of the light of truth in the manifestation of human life."

"A sage must also recite one verse of prayer for mercy" (B. T. Berachot 5a), a reference to the Talmudic law which prescribes the reading of the "Shema," a short sequence of verses from Deuteronomy, prior to a layman's retiring in the evening, a "sage" only being required "to recite one verse of prayer for mercy." The specific text of this "one verse" is cited at the conclusion of this paragraph: "In Thy hands do I entrust my spirit; Thou hast redeemed me, O God of truth." (Psalms 31:6) See Rabbi Zadok HaCohen, *Zidkat HaZadik* (Tel Aviv: Payre Publishing Co. 5725), p. 61a-b.

Rabbi Kook seeks to emphasize that even at the time of sleep, when the rational aspect of man which constantly strives to determine truth is not operative, nevertheless, man places his faith in the source of truth: "Thou hast redeemed me, O God, Lord of truth."

ITEM 42

This is a religious expression of the need for growth and the pain endured by one whose soul is stationary and does not achieve self-fulfillment.

ITEM 43

"This seed-like point" refers to the belief that the soul is possessed of a Godly spark. In order to facilitate the manifestation of this spark in the world, there must be utilization of intellectuality. "There must flow upon this seed-like point great streams from the upper fountain of knowledge." Thereby shall this seed-like point "emerge into the light of the world with kaleidoscopic brilliance in grandeur and splendor" and this spark shall exert great effect in the ascent of man.

ITEM 44

"The great significance of human sanctity in the eyes of humanity" should not cause weakness of mind "because of the demands man imposes upon himself."

The significance of sanctity should evoke humility within man and this humility shall "bring about the crown of the totality of wisdom."

For "the heeding of humility" the "quality of strength" is required. The spiritual personality is strengthened by "the outer splendor," or honor, "accorded by society." "The outer splendor" or "great significance" gives power to "the basis of strength" within the virtuous personality. "The basis of strength enables the splendor to shine forth in its gleaming purity after being purged from the coarse substance of arrogance." After having undergone this process of "purification from the coarse substance of arrogance," natural virtuous man shall emerge with the quality of "strength" capable of creative behavior in a significant manner.

ITEM 45

This is a highly significant paragraph in that an explicit definition is given for the terms lower and upper levels of repentance. The upper level of repentance is primarily a religious and intellectual endeavor characterized by "sacred contemplation and the ennoblement of the perception of the Lord's graciousness." Lower repentance is the striving of man for ethical rectification and "ascent of refined character," or ever constant self-refinement and improvement. If, at times, man feels lower repentance "temporarily denied to him," then "let him hasten to upper repentance," and inevitable upper repentance will bring him unto the lesser repentance. By means of the higher form of repentance man shall ultimately achieve "the purity of character" necessary for the lower level of repentance. His very physical nature shall achieve spiritual nobility; "his heart and flesh will sing for joy unto the living God." See also Chapter XVI paragraph XI for other aspects of the "lower" and "upper" levels of repentance.

ITEM 46

See B. T. Sanhedrin, 103a, wherein we are told of the unique compassion accorded Menasseh and those comparable to him.

ITEM 47

The soul's vestment refers to the quality of thought, which is a vestment, garb or outer aspect of the essence of the soul.

ITEM 48

Once again there is an elaboration on the theme of the relationship between immanence and transcendence. "The foundation of repentance is a 'reckoning of the world' " refers to the action within the finite dimensions of existence. The origin of repentance, or reckoning, "transcends reckoning itself, just as the theory of the value of numbers transcends numbers and their particulars." Consequently, "the basic aspect of uppermost repentance" is above and transcends the world, "transcends particular reckoning, and reckoning occurs as its consequence."

Referring to a fact cited in the Midrash that the "chest of accounts" a site for commercial calculations, is to be found at the outskirts or "below Jerusalem,"

Rabbi Kook interprets this in a symbolic manner as once again reflecting the relationship between "reckoning" and the "origin of reckoning."

He further elaborates on the theme of transcendence and immanence, or the "origin of reckoning" and "reckoning," by interpreting various verses from Psalms as expressing this basic concept. His initial quotation from Psalms 92:3 is primarily for the phrase, "I will exult in the works of thy hands," which would be in the category of reckoning. This is followed by verse 6 of the same chapter, which refers to the thoughts of God, "Thy thoughts are very deep." The thoughts of God transcend all reckoning as is proven from the phrase in another chapter of Psalms: "His wisdom is infinite." The word infinite is interpreted as a synonym for "beyond reckoning." God's wisdom is "beyond the degree" of "how manifold are Thy works, O Lord." The "works" of God are subject to reckoning and finitude as seen in the verse: "The earth is full of Thy creatures." The verse is explained as implying limitations to the dimension of the earth.

Repentance transcends earth and is heavenly in its origin, "heaven" being equated with the degree "beyond reckoning." Thus the Psalmist compares the exaltedness of the heavens with the quality of God's mercy: "For as the heaven is high above the earth, so great is His mercy toward them that fear Him," mercy perhaps being evoked by the act of repentance. The next verse also speaks of the infinite, "As far as the east is from the west." This is compared to God's forgiveness resulting from man's repentance, "So far hath He removed our transgressions from us."

"The flow of repentance," or the relationship between God and man, "proceeds constantly from above to below" and also "from below above" — from the basis of reckoning to the source of world origin. "Unto the utmost bound of the everlasting hills" — this is interpreted in a temporal sense by citing the verse, "Before the mountains were brought forth," thus "the utmost bound" refers to the era preceding time. Repentance ascends to the realm beyond reckoning, which existed prior to the "reckoning" that mountains and hills are subject to, as described in the verse, ". . . and weighed the mountains in scales and the hills in a balance." God, the Infinite, turns man to contrition and reestablishes the channel between the infinite and the finite, which is created by means of repentance. By means of repentance the "children of man" are enabled to "return" to their source of origin, to God.

ITEM 49

This paragraph cites two passages from the Midrash, which are interpreted as symbolically implying a fear of self-realization on the part of two aspects of nature. Rabbi Kook extends this to the realm of the human with the assertion that man, too, is afraid of self-realization and actualization. The first Midrash quoted states that God commanded the earth to bing forth the trees in such a manner that their taste would be as the taste of the fruit they bore. The second Midrash is from the (B. T. Chulin 60b). The Midrash relates that at the beginning of creation the sun and the moon were equal in magnitude. The moon appeared before the Almighty and inquired: "Is it then possible for two kings to rule with one crown?" whereupon God told the moon to proceed and diminish itself so that the majesty of light would be possessed by the sun. This Midrash is usually interpreted as being symbolic of the consequence of vanity. Thus the moon by seeking primacy in the realm of light was compelled to relinquish the degree with which it was already endowed. Similarly, a vain person seeking to usurp that which belongs to his fellow man will ultimately be deprived of that which he already possesses. Rabbi Kook juxtaposes these two passages and interprets them as indicating that the fear of self-realization and self-emergence is to be found in nature as well as humanity. "The earth also feared and did not bring forth the tree in its perfection, so that its taste would be as the taste of its fruit. The moon was afraid of the 'contention of the two kings for one crown..' Mankind is afraid because of the clear and exalted values of freedom. This world in its entirety is afraid of the manifestation of the world to come, 'Glorious in holiness.' " By means of faith man achieves the strength to overcome this fear. However, from the treasure of faith there comes tranquility and fear is removed from its foundation.

> The Name of the Lord is a strong tower;
> The righteous runneth into it,
> And is set up on high. (Proverbs 18:10)

Faith is the quality that dispels fear and bring tranquility; "With the sanctity of trust the defects of the world and all within them shall be set aright."

ITEM 50

See Chapter IX, where the "will for virtue" is dealt with at length.

ITEM 51

Repentance is not viewed as being a primarily repressive phenomenon; rather, "repentance is united with human strength." Rabbi Kook then quotes a Talmudic explication of the Biblical verse, "Happy is the man that feareth the Lord." The Talmud (B. T. Avodah Zarah 19a) interprets this as indicating that the most significant repentance is at the time that one is "still a man," possessed of the instinctual drives impelling toward self-gratification. Rabbi Kook derives from this interpretation the implication that "happy is he who remains a man while repenting." Namely, that the process of repentance itself is joined with "human strength" and that the repentant personality should strive to give ethical expression to the instinctual forces of his personality.

ITEM 52

The "hidden longing" refers to the philosophical and mystical concept that the most elemental and inherent aspect of the human personality strives and longs for Godliness. Since this is the innermost nature of man, therefore even if one should cognitively repent with "repentance based on fear," in actuality within this repentance there is "repentance based on love." See *Likutei Amarim; (Tanya)* Chapters 18 and 19 regarding the hidden love for Godliness.

ITEM 53

"Master of inner thought" — see Chapter XIV, paragraph XXXVIII. This refers to the degree beyond scholarship of the spiritual personality characterized by inspired and original thought as well as by constant cleavage with God.

ITEM 54

This is a reference to the Talmudic passage which disparages fasting on the part of a scholar. "Let the dog consume his repast," (B. T. Taanit 11a) implying that this is not an appropriate means for the scholar's spiritual endeavor.

ITEM 55

Rabbi Kook here further clarifies the distinction between the upper and lower levels of repentance. See Chapter XV, paragraph VI for othe aspects of these concepts.

ITEM 56

The existence of evil in the world is a profound enigma to the truly religious thinker who has faith in the omnipotence of God. Rabbi Kook states that the world cannot endure the full revelation of the Godly light or the perception of God in His essence; therefore evil is the imperfection in the world which man must rectify in order to enable the ultimate radiance of Godly light. This realm of imperfection is the source of all violence and active evil. The "resplendently righteous," "exaltedly righteous" or the ethical personalities of great spiritual stature perceive "that the pure light is greater than the world's power to endure it. Nevertheless, it is necessary that it illumine in the world. It is also necessary, due to the nature of the world, that there be many veils to conceal the light. These veils are wickedness and its bearers — consequently all of these participate in the betterment of world order."

The righteous of lesser degree, or those "whose light is of a limited character," who do not perceive this function of evil, suffer from great pain because of evil's existence. "They are unable to perceive how all wickedness in its entirety is naught but a veil setting aright the radiance of light." See *Likutei Amarim, (Tanya)* Ch. 36.

The righteous of lesser degree will ultimately ascend to the "degree of upper repentance" and achieve the awareness that "were it not for the many veils which occur due to all the categories of wickedness, material and spiritual the world would dissolve as a result of the great light."

"The basic punishment of the wicked is mainly for the pain they caused the righteous in the world of condensation." This may refer to the excessive dependence of the wicked upon the Zaddik instead of their achieving ethical stature through religious self-realization. "The basic punishment" may refer to the shame experienced by the wicked who receive Godly mercy due to the merit of the righteous rather than by reason of their own worth.

"The righteous who stand in the Godly expanse come out and liberate the

wicked from all the straits of the 'nether-world.'" "Godly expanse" may perhaps be interpreted as referring to the state of cleavage with the transcendent,
which is always characteristic of "the exaltedly righteous." The righteous come
and liberate the wicked from the "straits," or imprisonment, which is caused
by the "nether-world," or egocentric concern with the self. The righteous, by
means of their spiritual guidance, direct the wicked upon an upright path, "and
all things come thereby to abound in strength and gladness."

The Biblical texts cited from Psalms 84:7, 8 can perhaps be interpreted as
paralleling the theme of the righteous rescuing and redeeming the wicked, the
righteous "passing through" the realm of the wicked or the "valley of Baca."
Baca has also been interpreted in the sense of either confusion or tears. The
valley of Baca is, therefore, the valley of suffering or tears, the aforementioned
"straits of the nether-world," from which the wicked must be rescued by the
righteous who "come and liberate them." "Yea, the early rain clotheth it with
blessing." "The early rain," or the righteous, transform the valley of Baca
from confusion or tears by clothing it with blessings and uplifting the evil. "They
go from strength to strength" — both the righteous and the evil ascend in spiritual
stature. "Every one of them appeareth before God in Zion"; all of humanity is
redeemed and is worthy of "appearing before God in Zion." This redemption
of all mankind was earlier expressed by the phrase "all things come thereby
to abound in strength and gladness."

An Aggadic explanation of this verse is to be found in B. T. Eruvin 19a. But
the context here implies general harmony with the Alshich's interpretation of this
passage in his commentary on the Psalms, namely that it is the righteous who
are passing through "the valley of Bacca" and who thereby redeem the wicked.
See also Rabbi Reuven Margulies, *Shaarei Zohar* (Jerusalem: Mosad Horav
Kook, 5716), p. 28 for references cited in relation to Rabbi Yochanan Ben Zakai's
statement "there are two paths before me" (B. T. Berachot 28a). Margulies cites
various sources regarding this passage which describe the passing of the righteous
through Gehinom in order to redeem the souls of those imprisoned there. Azulai
in his commentary on the psalms cites the famed Kabbalist Rabbi Isaac Luria who
interprets this passage similarly but in a more explicitly kabbalistic manner. See
also Isaiah B'odessa Ed. *Sefer Tehilim Im Pirushei Ha Baal Shem Tov Vetalmidov.*
(New York: Photostatic Reproduction 5713.) See *Likutei Amarim, (Tanya)* pp.
139a-b which describe different gradations of the soul, and may be relevant
to Rabbi Kook's description of two kinds of righteous personalities. Also see
B. T. Berachot 64a regarding this verse from the Psalms.

Rabbinics and Research:

THE SCHOLARSHIP OF
DR. BERNARD REVEL

by SIDNEY B. HOENIG

Prologue

THE TRANSPLANTER OF TORAH
ON THIS CONTINENT

by DR. SAMUEL BELKIN

History records many instances of personages who have transplanted Torah in new climes. Ezra, coming from Babylon, set forth the strength of the Oral law and its interpretation. Hillel, too, from Babylon, sowed the seeds of Torah Judaism. Moses ben Hanoch, also from Babylon, brought Talmud study to Spain. These luminaries made it their concern not merely to *translate* Torah to a new world but to *transplant* it there. Therefore they were successful in perpetuating Judaism. This concept explains basically the destiny of the Jewish people in its exceptional history.

It is essentially this historic aspect of transplantation of Torah which my sainted predecessor, Dr. Bernard Revel, carried forth. He was among

---

Dr. Samuel Belkin, distinguished scholar, author and educator, is now in his 25th year as President of Yeshiva University. Upon his arrival in the United States in 1929 he was immediately introduced to Dr. Bernard Revel. Pursuing graduate work at Harvard and Brown Universities and receiving his doctorate in 1935, he was then appointed Instructor in Greek at Yeshiva College and in the following year as Instructor in Talmud in the Rabbinic Department. When Dr. Revel organized the Yeshiva Graduate School (now known as Bernard Revel Graduate School) in 1937, Dr. Belkin was named Secretary of its faculty and Instructor in Hellenistic Literature.

In 1939 Dr. Belkin became a member of the three man Executive Committee governing Yeshiva College. In 1940 he was made a full professor. Upon the passing of Dr Revel on Dec.. 2, 1940, Dr. Belkin was appointed Dean of the Yeshiva (Rabbinical School) and a member of the seven man Executive Board, to exercise presidential functions. In June 1943 the Board of Directors unanimously elected Dr. Belkin to be the successor of Dr. Revel. Under his guidance the Yeshiva expanded into a full University.

Originally published by Yeshiva University Press, 1968.

the first Lithuanian Jews who came to these shores and, instead of being assimilated into the fast growing "melting pot" of the early decades of the twentieth century, he transplanted the rabbinic learning of European yeshivot to American shores.

The concept of "melting pot" was reinterpreted by him as the expression of cultural pluralities in the United States, in which each group and nationality is not only permitted but encouraged to play its own especial instruments to further, preserve and advance its own heritage. Inspired with this pioneering spirit, he not only made Yeshivat Rabbenu Yitzhak Elchanan the outstanding Torah center on this continent, but within the framework of this institution established the first High School and the first College under Jewish auspices in America. Hence Dr. Revel's name will go down in history as having contributed immeasurably to the enrichment of Jewish and general academic learning.

Dr. Revel in his personality possessed three ingredients which were essential to be the builder of our institution and thereby promote Torah learning in America. These are rabbinic and general scholarship, prophetic vision and also faith in the eternity of Israel and its sacred possessions. Above all, he had the moral courage to attain the heights under the most difficult circumstances. His was the fortitude to combine scientific training with Talmudic studies and also to maintain traditional observance without fear of backsliding. This became the strength of our Yeshiva. Orthodox Jewry in America today is greatly indebted to the genius of Dr. Revel.

All of us — at Yeshiva University and in American Orthodox Judaism — have been nurtured by Dr. Bernard Revel. He was our teacher and our guide. Individually and collectively we are beholden to him. Dr. Revel the teacher, with his wisdom has prepared all of us for the eternal life of Torah.

The course of events and destiny have directed that I humbly wear the mantle of leadership, first worn by Dr. Revel. I am eternally grateful to the great sage who encouraged and inspired me in every manner from the very moment that I stepped upon American soil. He stimulated me to pursue my academic studies and gave me the opportunity to teach. Later he invested me with dutiful responsibilities to guide others and he developed within me a total commitment to the ideals of Yeshiva.

Often do I repeat that which I first uttered in my own inaugural address:

> I shall always look upon this historic event as a tribute not to myself, but rather to the sainted memory of the sage and scholar in Israel, the founder of the Yeshiva College, the late Doctor Bernard Revel, who marched with events and often determined them, and whose contribution to the American Jewish Community was already tested by time and trial. I pray to the Almighty that I may be instrumental in the materialization of the dreams and visions of the founder.

The growth of Yeshiva in the more than two decades since Dr. Revel's demise has added glory to his name, strengthening "his bond with the living." May his memory be eternal.

The publication of this volume, *Rabbinics and Research: The Scholarship of Dr. Revel*, by a distinguished member of our Graduate Faculty, Dr. Sidney B. Hoenig, therefore is a scintillating sign of the continuum of the founder's genius. It evidences that Dr. Revel's "words" are alive and his scholarship still guides the earnest student. His rabbinics are "fountains of wisdom." Yeshiva University is built upon his foundations, and American Jewish scholarship — Talmudic and general — rests too on his direction of blending the wisdom of the *past* with the techniques of the *present*. It is hoped that this work on Dr. Revel will lead to ever greater impulse to Jewish learning in our midst, in the *future*.

Chapter 1

KARAITICA

1. *Karaite Halakhah* [32]*

Paradoxically, the champion of rabbinic, Orthodox Judaism in the United States in the first half of the twentieth century was also the keenest student of sectarianism. Dr. Bernard Revel's primary scientific scholarly interest was Karaism. His constant study and research in this area developed from his Dropsie College doctoral dissertation, *The Karaite Halakhah and its Relation to Sadducean, Samaritan, and Philonian Halakhah* (1912). Earlier scholars like Simha Pinksker had aimed to show that the Karaites "were the source of all intellectual achievement of medieval Judaism." According to this school of thought, the Massorah, with its beginnings of grammatical and biblical exegesis, belongs to the Karaites; the Rabbanites were merely imitators. This notion was challenged by Revel.

That differences in Judaism prevailed only in practice, and not in dogma, and that such divergences alone caused and sustained the divisions in Israel had been propounded by Abraham Geiger. Revel showed that this observation was particularly true of the Karaites. He reviewed the various hypotheses of their origins, as advanced by the Karaites themselves, as well as the testimony of the medieval Rabbanites that the Karaites descended from the Sadducees. This opinion, generally adopted, naturally led to the conclusion that one may trace early Sadducean halakhah in the

---

* The numbers in brackets refer to the subjects as listed in the Bibliography at the end of this volume.

Karaitic records. Revel, however, contested the entire thesis and further probed the problem of this affinity of the Sadducees and Karaites in order to trace the origin of Karaitic laws, to ascertain their common source and the reason for the differences. Upon the basis of a careful analysis of different halakhot, e.g., the "fruit of the fourth year," the "second tithe," "marriage with a gentile," etc., he subsequently refuted Geiger's "Sadducean-Karaite" theory.

Since Geiger held that Targum Pseudo-Jonathan in its divergences from accepted Halakhah represented some of the early Sadducean traditions, Revel also analyzed many of the propositions therein and concluded, contrary to prevailing views, that the Karaites basically agreed with Tradition. One must seek other origins for the divergences.

In his dissertation[1] he wrote:

> If the deviations of Pseudo-Jonathan from our Halakhah go back to ancient traditions related to Sadduceism, then we should expect the Karaites — a later name for Sadduceism, according to this view — to be in agreement with such deviations of Pseudo-Jonathan. The following examination of the main halakhic divergences of Pseudo-Jonathan from our Halakhah and of the view of the Karaites on these points will show how untenable this view is.

Revel especially reexamined the halakhot recorded in the Talmud which reveal the differences between the Pharisees and Sadducees, and set these side by side with Karaite halakhah. Contrary to Geiger's opinion that the Karaites agreed with the Sadducees, Revel concluded[2]:

> In all the differences between the Sadducees and Pharisees recorded in Talmud and Megillat Taanit, the Karaite halakhah (as far as Karaite opinion is known to us), with the exception of "on the morrow of the Sabbath"[3] and "water libation,"[4] either agrees with the Pharisees against the Sadducees, or is in itself undetermined by reason of divergent views among the Karaites themselves.

Revel also examined again the *Zadokite Fragment*, discovered by
Dr. Solomon Schechter in the Cairo Genizah. Here, too, Revel concluded that "the Karaites agree with Tradition against this sect."[5]
He further examined the influence of the works of Philo upon
Karaite halakhah, giving at least 22 instances in which Philonic
laws agree with the karaitic and are contrary to the traditional
Halakhah. Specifically in the laws of homicide the Karaites deviated
widely from Tradition; yet the Karaite laws of homicide approach
the view of Philo. For example,[6] according to Tradition, "cursing
parents" is punishable by stoning to death only when the Divine
Name is used. "Striking parents," however, is punishable only when
the blow causes a wound. Strangulation is the prescribed punishment
for the latter offense. Philo, on ·the other hand, makes stoning
the penalty for striking parents. The Karaites agree with Philo and
explain the verse (Exodus 21:15) as referring to *any* physical
violence against parents. They likewise, in interpreting Exodus 21:17,
do not limit the punishment in "cursing parents" to the use of the
Divine Name. Moreover, whereas Tradition required "intent" and
"warning" for punishment, the Karaites did not require "forewarn-
ing" for a crime. Like Philo, they maintained that intent to kill,
even if not carried out, is punishable.

Revel also showed that there was a strong affinity between
Philo and the Karaites in marriage laws. One of the many examples
cited by him follows:

> Philo and the Karaites also agree in the interpretation of
> Leviticus 21:14. Philo (II, 229) interprets this law to mean
> that the high-priest must choose his wife from priestly lineage.
> That this is also the interpretation of most Karaites was already
> observed by Azariah de Rossi.[7]

Revel reached a similar conclusion of Karaitic-Philonic affinity on
probing into the ceremonial laws:

> The Karaites also reject the traditional interpretation of Leviticus
> 23:40 and claim that the four species are for the construction of
> the booths mentioned in verse 42, deriving support for this view
> from Nehemiah 8:14...Philo, speaking of the Feast of Taber-

nacles, makes no mention of the law of the four species...He must have understood verse 40, not as a separate commandment but, like the Karaites, as prescribing material for the booths.

Revel then posed the question:

Philo, the great representative of Egyptian Jewry, knew of the existence of an oral tradition and considered it as binding as the written law...How are we then to account for the interpretations and decisions in which Philo deviates from traditional Halakhah? Are such deviations subjective opinions of Philo? Do they reflect the actual practices in vogue among Egyptian Jewry or do they go back to a peculiar tradition?

Be this as it may, the fact, which I have attempted to demonstrate,[8] that in most of Philo's deviations from Tradition the Karaites hold the same view, points to some kind of dependence of the latter on Philo, or to common descent from a particular tradition. The former view gains in probability from the following:

The Hellenic or Alexandrian method of interpretation of the Scriptures did not remain unknown to the Palestinian teachers of the law and the works and views of Philo found their way to the Palestinian schools. Moreover, the general belief that Philo and his works were lost to the Jews of the Middle ages until Azariah de Rossi, about the end of the sixteenth century, reintroduced him in Jewish literature, is now proved to be unfounded. The tenth century Karaite al-Kirkisani, in his work, written 937, speaks of a Jewish sect named "the Magarites." This sect, says Kirkisani, sprang up before the rise of Christianity. The adherents of the sect make the biblical passages that speak of attributes of God refer to an angel who, according to them, created the world.

2. *Philonic Halakhah* [63]

This point of view — that Karaite halakhah is basically Philonian halakhah — was carried on by Revel in subsequent articles. In a special essay on Philonian halakhah, he presented additional instances of agreement between Philo and the Karaites in the exposition of biblical laws:

Tradition derives from Deuteronomy 24:16: "The fathers should not be put to death for the children, neither should the children be put to death for the father," that relatives are disqualified as witnesses. Philo, in his long sermon in connection with this verse, mentions only the literal meaning of this verse and nowhere refers to the disqualification of relatives for testimony. So also the Karaites asserted that even children and parents are not disqualified from testifying against each other.

Moreover, Philo maintained that the sole reason for marriage was propagation; Anan ben David, the recognized founder of Karaism, also held this opinion, and hence forbade cohabitation during pregnancy.

3. Halakhic Differences between Babylon and Palestine [65]

The notion that Philonian halakhah, often seen as differing from the traditional norm, coincides with early Karaitic law, was carried on by Revel in many of his later studies. He suggested that since Philo had taken his ideas from the Septuagint or from practices in Alexandria which may have been influenced by Roman customs, or from Essene modes, such were not in the traditional pattern. In general Philo followed the Pharisaic view, but in criminal law he may have been influenced by the Stoics. It is not mere coincidence, declared Revel, that the Karaites agreed with Philo. There must be some affinity. Indeed, the Philonic works were known to the Karaites and the latter even adopted some notions of the *logos* or the concept of an angel creating the world.

Revel pursued this view in his assertion that the halakhic differences between Palestine and Babylon may be recognized also in the variations between the Rabbanites and Karaites. He noted that, as a rule, Palestine followed the strictest conduct in law; the Karaites, especially the Mourners of Zion, similarly adopted such approach, contrary to the Babylonian views. Revel portrayed in detail the conduct of the Mourners of Zion, particularly with reference to ablutions. Interestingly, Kirkisani noted 50 differences between Babylon and Palestine, aiming thereby to denigrate the Babylonian rabbinic tradition. The Karaites who dwelt in Palestine followed the modes of the Mourners of Zion with severity, and hence they accepted the stringent rules in laws of purity which stemmed from the Judean practices of Temple times. Many Palestinian Jews continued observance of purity law even after the Temple destruction. The Babylonian Gaonim, on the other hand, did not follow rigorously the laws of impurity. Hence the Karaites, wishing to turn the tables on the Rabbanites, asserted that the Palestinian Jews adopted the rigorous laws only from them. In truth, the reverse is correct.

The opposition of the Karaites to polygamy, notes Revel, also may be an influence of the Palestinian Halakhah. Monogamy was the mode in Palestine,[9] whereas in Babylon polygamy among Jews was not uncommon. Hence in Palestine the dissolution of the levirate marriage through halitzah was regarded as an urgency, to avoid polygamy.

To cite another example, in Babylon an unmarried priest could not pronounce the priestly benediction, but in Palestine even the unmarried could give the benediction. In Palestine, marriages were contracted later than was the custom in Babylon. Moreover, in Palestine there was greater severity against pagan cooking; the Karaites followed suit. The Palestinians did not use non-Jewish butter but the Babylonians did. The Karaites followed Palestinian practice. Similarly, many Karaites did not eat meat in the Diaspora, even as the Palestinian Jews who refrained from eating meat as "flesh of desire."[10]

The parallelism between Karaitic and Palestinian law, and the contrasts of these to Rabbinic and Babylonian halakhic conduct, indeed was one of Revel's major contributions in scholarship.

4. Differences in Customs [74]

This study of halakhic differences between Palestine and Babylon was expanded by Revel in still further essays, where additional examples were collated. Noting the practice of the Palestinians to pour the blood of the Covenant (of circumcision) on the earth, in contrast to the Babylonian practice that this blood flow into water, Revel pointed out that circumcision in Palestine was performed over the earth, even as sacrifice was performed on the altar of earth.[11] Anan ben David, the Karaite followed this practice, even deducing other laws therefrom in comparing circumcision to sacrificial conduct. When the pupils of Rav Yehudah Gaon saw that Jews were imitating the Karaitic practices, even sprinkling the blood of the Covenant on the doorposts, they set about to abolish this custom of letting the circumcision-blood drip into the earth.

In a similar manner Revel showed that the Karaites stood when the Torah was read. Basically, the custom of standing at Torah reading was in accordance with the Palestinian Talmud; the Gaonim later opposed this practice, as well as that of holding the fringes at the time of recital of the Shema, only because these became Karaitic usage.

A third item which attracted Revel's attention was the custom of standing when Kaddish is recited. The son of Maimonides, Rabbi Abraham, declared that one should stand at the recital of blessings, though his father had fought strongly against many Karaitic sectarian practices. One notes singularly that the Karaites possessed some rules of value, but that these met with opposition from the Rabbanites because of their fear of sectarianism.

Another question in this comparative study was that of the loud recital of the Amidah. In Babylonia the Amidah was a silent prayer; in Palestine it was recited aloud. The Gaonim opposed a loud recital, particularly because such was Karaitic conduct.

A still further item which occupied Revel's research was the nature of the "mishnah of the pious."[12] Examining the many talmudic reasons for a virgin to be married on the eve of the fourth day, Revel demonstrated that the Babylonian Talmud did not limit it to Wednesday. The Palestinian Talmud, however, followed the Mishnaic dictim. Revel thereupon suggested that the practice of marriage on Wednesday was one adopted by the pious. They had intercourse with their wives only on Wednesday so that there be no Sabbath violation in birth.[12*] Marriages were not held on Saturday night or on Sunday or Monday because of this same reason. Likewise intercourse was not permitted on Friday night because such involved Sabbath violation.

Though basically Sabbath infringement was permissive in child-birth, the pious aimed to refrain from it. Their notion was that anything that might lead to Sabbath transgression was to be avoided. So also they did not encourage the marriage of a niece, lest it lead to abrogation of the levirate law. In all, many of these procedures were all Karaitic, and Revel well portrayed how the Karaites assumed the manner of strictness of practice current in Palestine.

5. *Targum Pseudo-Jonathan on the Torah* [58]

The tracing of the origins of Karaitic laws and the reasons for the divergences from Tradition prompted Dr. Revel to make the text of Targum Jonathan or Targum Yerushalmi one of his greatest scholarly interests. This concern was compelling to him because many scholars used this Targum to theorize about the development of the Oral Law, arguing that this Targum was the precursor of an earlier Halakhah. In comparison, Revel devoted much attention to the nature of various earlier translations of the Bible and concluded that the early halakhot in Judaism were written in Aramaic with the specific purpose of distinguishing such traditions or halakhot from the Torah itself. He noted:[13]

> In Eretz Yisrael there did not exist a carefully arranged and acceptable Targum as in Babylon and other lands. This is mentioned by Jacob ibn Karish.
>
> The reason for this situation, according to my opinion, is that in Babylon Aramaic was the lingua franca; hence there was a necessity for an Aramaic translation for study and teaching... This did not apply to Eretz Yisrael and especially in Judea where Aramaic was not prevalent. Hebrew was widely used there not only by scholars but also in daily life... The Midrash Haggadah and *piyyutim*, which generally originated in Eretz Yisrael, as revealed in the discoveries in the Cairo Genizah, substantiate that Hebrew was the language used in Eretz Yisrael even throughout the Gaonic period.

Revel deduced that there was no necessity for an Aramaic Targum in Eretz Yisrael, as it was in Babylonia. Only much later, because of persecution in Palestine and the growth of sectarian movements, with their own variant interpretations of Torah, did the Palestinian Rabbis examine all the translations and subsequently chose those most acceptable. This translation they named Targum Jonathan. The explanations in this compilation are according to Palestinian teachers, especially Rabbi Johanan. This Targum was edited at the end of the eighth century or in the beginning of the ninth century, specifically to counteract the spirit of sectarianism. Dr. Revel stressed that this Targum contains an abundance of notions against the prevalent Karaitic views. Its acceptance in Jewry enhanced the rabbinic homiletic interpretations. It is primarily a collation of many earlier translations; hence, at times, some laws are explained differently — even contradictorily — when compared to known reports.

Whenever the Karaites disagreed on some Halakhah, Targum Jonathan would amplify the subject, even to the extent of explaining a rabbinic law as if it were of Pentateuchal origin. For example, the laws prohibiting going beyond the distance of the 2,000 cubit Sabbath limit, a rule which is rabbinic, or the Sabbath laws of courtyards, or such phases as enjoyment on the Sabbath are all explained in the Targum as Pentateuchal. The primary purpose was to offset the Karaites who did not adhere to the rules of *tehum, erub,* or *oneg* (joy) *shabbath.*

A full list of modes of interpretation in Targum Jonathan, showing the reaction to Karaitic interpretation, is found in this essay; a few examples are given here:

1) *Targum Deuteronomy* 23:22, on not delaying payment of vows, adds the phrase "three holidays," as explained by the Talmud. This is because the Karaites declared that payment must be immediate.

2) *Leviticus* 21:14 notes that the high priest shall marry a virgin of "his people." The Targum adds: "A pure virgin of the daughter of his people shall he marry." This was to counteract the Karaitic view that the high priest could marry only the daughter of a priest.

3) *Targum Leviticus* 15:29 mentions the five afflictions of Yom Kippur as being derived from the biblical verse, though the rabbis held that these, except for "eating and drinking," were of rabbinic origin. The Karaites, however, maintained that "affliction" meant only eating and drinking as forbidden; it did not apply to other matters.

Revel thus concluded that Targum Jonathan's mode of derivation of halakhot from the Pentateuchal verse had but one purpose, namely, to react against the Karaites. In that era there were many sectarian groups and, though we have no definite record of all Karaitic halakhot, the Targum's approach may indeed refer to other sectarian groups as well.

Those halakhot in Targum Jonathan which are in opposition to the traditional Halakhah were also probed. Revel explained these as laws derived from Talmud Yerushalmi which are in contradiction to the Babli, demonstrating thereby the differing practices and customs, then current. He supplied a number of examples:

1) In *Leviticus* 23:42 Targum Jonathan records the laws of Sukkot, as traditionally reported. But the Targum adds:[14] "It shall be made for a covering in designation of the festival." It was already pointed out by Rabbi Zevi Chayes that this opinion is in accordance with Bet Shammai and not Bet Hillel (Sukkah 9a). Revel suggested that Targum Jonathan followed Yerushalmi Sukkah 1.2:[15] "Something has to be put there anew." Thus the Targum, even according to Bet Hillel, felt that something *new* must be added, though the Sukkah was an old one, used for shade.

2) On the verse in *Deuteronomy* 22:5, "A woman shall not wear a man's garment," the Targum notes:[16] "Fringes or phylacteries, which are male apparel, shall not be worn by a woman." This naturally is in opposition to a tradition in the Talmud *Erubin* 96a stating that Michal, the daughter of Saul, wore Tefillin and the Sages did not oppose her. Revel held that the Targum is in agreement with Yerushalmi *Berakot* 2.3 which notes, according to Rabbi Hezekiah in the name of Rabbi Abahu, that the Sages demurred against Michal's practice.[17]

In this essay Revel also demonstrated that many early differences in practice between Palestine and Babylon continued even throughout the Gaonic period; hence they are recorded in Targum Jonathan which follows the Palestinian mode. Thus, on Numbers 19:3:[18] "The red heifer shall be slaughtered," the Targum notes:[19] "Another priest shall slaughter it before him, severing the two organs (gullet and windpipe), as in the case of other animals; he shall examine it for any of the 18 factors of unsuitability (terefot)."[20]

Rabbi Zevi Chayes had already demonstrated that examination of an animal for any of the 18 deficiencies is generally unnecessary. Even the examination of the lung, which is ordinarily required, did not apply to the red heifer, because the slaughtering itself implied wholesomeness in the animal; since the heifer was completely burnt no internal examination was necessary. Revel deduced that the Targum in its divergence followed the Palestinian practice, whereby the examination for 18 terefot was obligatory.[21] He pointed out that Kirkisani, the Karaite, already mentions this difference: "The Babylonians examine the lung; the Palestinians, the head."[22]

Revel again showed that the Targum, in its usual manner, based its perspective on the verse in order to give Pentateuchal sanction to rabbinic law and thereby counteract Karaitic theory.

Abraham Geiger had regarded this Targum as early Halakhah, designed to give prestige to the ancient priesthood. Revel, on the other hand, demonstrated the lateness of this Targum, emphasizing that it dealt only with problems that were contemporary — not obsolete — and that its purpose was solely to uphold Rabbinic Halakhah against Karaitic opinion.

The late dating of the Targum, according to Revel, is apparent, as an example, in the laws pertaining to the bringing of the first fruits. On the verse, "Ye shall come to the priest who shall be in those days," the Targum notes:[23] "Ye shall go up to the priest who has been appointed chief priest in those days." Though the Mishnaic law is that the first fruits shall be given to the Anshe Mishmar (the particular "priestly watch" of the Temple in that week),[23*] it is possible that the Targum had reference to Rabbi Judah's view that first fruits shall be given only to the *haber*, presumably a scholar.[23**] The Targumic phrase "in those days" indicated the leaders of the generation who were recognized.[23***] Philo also notes that the first fruits were given to the high priest.

This Hebrew article, one of the most scintillating of Revel's works, illustrates his keenness of mind and the ability to detect the basic roots of the Targum Jonathan. He persistently pursued his interest in Karaitic law, showing the great impact and strength of rabbinic legislation in counteracting sectarianism.

6. *Lex Talionis* [26]

These studies of the Karaitic code and its affinity to Palestinian practice were no doubt the outcome of Dr. Revel's many early articles on Karaism, authored voluminously in *Otzar Yisrael*, the first Hebrew Encyclopedia in America. As with many other scholars, the question of *lex talionis* intrigued him. He pointed out that the view held by many that the Sadducees believed in actual "eye for eye" punishment was erroneous. The Talmud would certainly have mentioned such dispute and even Josephus is not definite about it. The notion in the *Scholion of Megillat Taanit* may therefore be only a Karaitic concept.

7. *Karaism* [30]

A major introduction to the entire topic, leading into later individual Karaitica consisting of short essays, is contained in a very elaborate article on Karaism in *Otzar Yisrael*. Here the origins, opinions of Karaitic and Rabbinic writers as well as an analysis of Geiger's impression relating the Karaites to the Sadducees are reviewed. A survey of the history of Karaism till the twentieth century and the studies of Karaite scholars is presented.

Revel scrutinized the many views given by Karaitic writers that the Karaites fundamentally followed Judah ben Tabbai or the teachings of Shammai, and he set these opinions by the side of the parallel Rabbinic notions, such as those of Sherira Gaon, Yehudah ha-Levi, and Abarbanel and Simon Duran, who held that the Karaite movement originated in the time of the Gaonim. He noted that the Rabbis indeed identified the Karaites with the Sadducees, and Geiger even aimed to show that the Karaites possessed an older Halakhah, similar to that of the Samaritans. Revel insisted that this was not correct. He also held that the Damascus Fragment is not similar to Karaite Halakhah. Finally he described in this research the activities of Anan ben David and his successors, discussing the Firkovitch finds and how this "discovery" misled scholars in their objective research.

8. *Karaitic Teachers* [21-24]

Many pages in this Hebrew encyclopedia were likewise devoted by Revel to the outstanding luminaries among the Karaites. Among these were Yefet ben Ali, Joseph ben Abraham, Yeshuah ben Yehuda and Jacob ben Reuben. Revel noted the activity of Yefet ben Ali and his biblical research; he described especially the Karaitic opposition of Saadia Gaon in the interpretation of such items as the "morrow of the Sabbath," or lighting candles on Friday night. Yefet singularly attempted to prove that everything is in the written Torah and there was no need of an oral law.

Another Karaitic dignitary described by Revel was Joseph ben Abraham ha-Roeh, one of the first of the Karaites to devote much attention to philosophy. According to him the attributes of God are known through study and tradition. Joseph ben Abraham also disagreed with Saadia in the matter of the calendrical reckoning. He even held that "saving a life" does not permit Sabbath violation. He accepted a mode of observance of rigor in law, not that of lenience. On Passover non-Jewish leaven too was forbidden to be seen. Joseph even opposed views of Anan, such as based on the verse of "going out" of one's house on the Sabbath. Later Karaitic scholars, as Yehudah Hadassi and Eliyahu Basyatchi, quote Joseph ben Abraham constantly.

Joseph ben Abraham's pupil was Yeshuah ben Yehudah; he is known as the Great Teacher.[24] Following his mentor, he endorsed

the Mu'tazilite philosophy, but he also possessed a deep knowledge
of rabbinic literature and wrote polemics against Saadia. Ibn Ezra
and Abraham ibn David mention this Yeshuah often. Many of his
works were translated from Arabic into Hebrew and are still in the
Leiden Library. Finally, Revel also described Jacob ben Reuben of
the 12th century, who collated many of the writings of earlier Karaites
in his full commentary on the Bible.

9. *The Epistle of Saadia* [53]

One of the phases in Revel's intense interest in the subject of
Karaitic sectarianism naturally was the personality of Saadia Gaon.
When Dr. Nahum Slouzch brought "the Epistle of Saadia" from
Morocco, Revel published the full text, with comments. He showed
that this Epistle, wherein each item begins with the words *B'nai
Yisrael,* was a homily of guidance for the rabbinic community. In
it Saadia's battle against the Karaites is unmitigated and emphatic,
answering sectarian taunts and misinterpretations. Saadia particularly
refuted here the Karaitic notion that the Sages had changed the Oral
Law. He also warned that there be no attempt at reckoning of "the
coming of the millennium" though he himself did not refrain from
it. This mode was a contrivance of Saadia's contemporaries — the
Karaites, Salmon ben Jeruham and Yefet ben Ali. Perhaps it is
the counteraction that influenced Saadia's conduct.

This epistle was written to the Jews of Spain which was then a
haven of Torah. Yet sectarianism had already developed there too.
Hence Saadia's purpose in the epistle was basically to resist growing
Karaitic influence wherever it flared up, and to enhance the place
of ethics in Jewish conduct.

In reviewing Revel's article on this subject, Isidore Epstein made
the added comment that this epistle was Saadia's second one. He also
surmised that it had been sent to Babylon, Egypt, and to Palestine,
apparently after Saadia had become Gaon. Thus Revel's publication
of the epistle added considerably to both Saadyana and Karaitica,
stimulating further investigation by scholars.

Chapter II

NON-RABBINIC DEVIATIONS

1. *False Oaths, according to Philo* [69]

The discrepancies between rabbinic and non-rabbinic sources, as well as the differences between Palestinian and Babylonian Halakhah noted above, often intrigued Dr. Revel to seek a reconciliation. In a short article on "False oaths," he analyzed Philo's view that punishment for such infraction is death, and compared this to the Sages' declaration that the punishment is flogging. Revel deduced that basically there is agreement in the sources, for the act of false oath is primarily the utilization of the Divine Name in vain, deemed as the greatest of sins. The Sages maintained that the punishment by beating is in place of death and the administering of a lesser punishment did not at all clear the person from the transgression of taking the Divine Name in vain. The Higher Bet Din (the Divine Court, i.e., the Almighty Himself) would ultimately administer this.

2. *Priestly Emoluments, according to Jubilees* [70]

Such analysis of discrepancies in Halakhah continued in another study, specifically, on "priestly tithes." To whom did the tithe of animal flesh belong, after it had been sacrificed in the Temple — to the priests or to the owner? According to rabbinic sources, the owners enjoyed it, similar to the paschal lamb, or the second tithe. But, according to *the Book of Jubilees,* Tobit, and Philo, the tithe was to be given to the priests. To reconcile this, Revel suggested that in the Diaspora, i.e., outside of the Holy Land, the animal-tithe was to be given to the priest because, were it retained by the owner,

421

it might lead to a violation of the rule against slaughtering sacrifices outside of the Temple. Hence the Sages modified the rule that it be retained by the owners. Instead, they instituted the practice that the animal-tithe be given to the priests, who would surely not ignore the rules of sacrifice. Basically, they, as sacerdotal ministrants, better than the laity, would be more prone to visit Jerusalem, and there consume the tithe in holiness.

3. *Anti-Traditional Laws of Josephus* [56]

Not only did Revel thoroughly examine Philonian teaching and its divergence from Tradition but he was also concerned with the question of Josephus' deviation from the traditional interpretation of biblical texts and laws. He suggested that "Josephus was probably acquainted with the works of Philo and influenced by them. Though many deviations may be due to the fact that Josephus sought the admiration of his gentile reading public, finding it unnecessary to give the traditional interpretation, yet there are deviations that cannot be explained in this wise... One must account for these, especially when these interpretations of Josephus differ not only from Tradition but from Philo, the Septuagint, and from Samaritan Halakhah, and hence cannot be explained as "ante — or anti — Pharisaic tradition."

Revel propounded that the explanation is found in Josephus' estrangement from his people. Because he lived in Rome, his knowledge of Jewish sources became meager, especially since the Oral Law had not yet been committed to writing. "Therefore attempts to find in the anti-traditional interpretations of Josephus evidence of the existence of an older Halakhah must be taken with reserve." Revel then gave many examples of the "anti-traditional laws of Josephus" — one of which follows:[1]

> Josephus states that the Law forbids the priest to marry a harlot, a slave, a captive, a woman who keeps a shop or an inn, and a divorced woman.

In his explanation, following his interest in Karaitica, Revel added that the Karaites too held that every manner of insulting parents is punishable with death. *Arur*, as used here and also as pronounced against the removal of landmarks, probably implied punishment. Revel pointed out that the Romans likewise permitted the killing of any offenders who uprooted boundary-signs. His search for parallelisms never slackened; thereby he always strengthened his notion of Philonic-Josephus-Karaitic affinities.

5. *The Sadducees* [36]

When the volume, *The Sadducees*, by Rudolf Lezynsky appeared in 1912, wherein the author refuted Geiger's view that the Sadducees were the aristocratic party of priests, Revel wrote a comprehensive review of it. Lezynsky had pictured the Sadducees "not as a party but as a sect," claiming that they were the Karaites of the ancient days. Thereupon Revel fully analyzed the discussion of the Halakhot by Lezynsky, his theory of the Sadducean origin of the *Zadokite Fragment*, as well as that scholar's view that most of the Apocrypha and Pseudepigrapha were basically Sadducean works.

He then emphasized:[3]

> In general, anti-rabbinic laws in Jewish works of the Greek and Roman period do not necessarily imply Sadducean authorship. Pharisaic Judaism of that time was not entirely uniform and of one opinion on all minor questions of religious practice. At that time there was Alexandrian Jewry with its Onias Temple and its own ritual, and there were the Essenes.

This review, though short, was incisive and contained also an analysis of the apocryphal works and of early Christianity. Thus, in commenting on Lezynsky's notion that the *Testament of the Twelve Patriarchs* is of Sadducean origin, Revel asked:

> But is the expectation of a priestly Messiah sufficient to prove the Sadducean authorship of the *Testament?*

According to Lezynsky, Jesus too was a Sadducee...

That the Law enjoins a priest to refrain from marrying a shop or inn-keeper is unknown to tradition. It is possible that Josephus records here, as in several other places, as law, a custom which prevailed among the priests of his time. The priests, as we know, were very rigorous in the fulfillment of the requirements of the law in all matters pertaining to family purity, and many of them may have refrained from marrying a woman engaged in any unbecoming occupation such as inn or shop keeping. It has been suggested that Josephus interpreted *zonah* in Leviticus 21:7 to mean innkeeper (as derived from "to feed"). It seems to me, however, more probable that Josephus derived this law by interpreting *zonah* in Leviticus, according to its literal meaning, i.e., "a woman who is profaned" by being engaged in any occupation unbecoming to women, among which occupation he, like the Rabbis, included inn and shop keeping. This law of Josephus as well as the interpretation of Halakhah as meaning "one profaned by unbecoming action or occupation" is held also by most Karaite authorities.

Thus Revel showed that the Karaites, following the simple interpretation or *peshat,* agreed with or derived concepts and also laws from Josephus as well as from Philo, being fully acquainted with both of these non-rabbinic sources.

4. *Ancient Exegesis* [29]

Dr. Revel's deep interest in the origin of Halakhah and the existence of anti-traditional laws prompted him to comment on an article by Judge Mayer Sulzberger on "The Polity of the Ancient Hebrews." In a subsequent note to it[2] he added many other significant points, among which the following is most striking:

That insulting parents is punished with death is stated by Philo and Josephus. They seem to have derived this anti-traditional law from Deuteronomy 27:16, having *Arur,* as suggested by Judge Sulzberger, to mean "death sentence."

Chapter III

HISTORICAL ORIGINS

1. *Impurity of the Diaspora* [55]

Aside from the study of the sects, Revel devoted much attention to the place of the ancient Jew in the Holy Land and in the Diaspora. These were not mere theoretical investigations; they sought to uncover the historic milieu. Writing on the "Historical Background of the Levitical Impurity of the Land Outside Palestine," he reviewed the many traditions in the Talmud and in Josephus related to this subject and arrived at a conclusion:[1]

> The reintroduction of the decree of levitical impurity... eighty years before the destruction of the Temple... was due to the completion of Caesarea by Herod in that year... We know that several innovations of Herod which were in defiance of tradition or against the sentiment of the people were undone as soon as it was thought that Herod's end had come.
>
> The building of the Temple by Onias in 160 BCE may also be responsible for the declaration of levitical impurity... The Onias Temple was a local *bamah*... The Palestinian authorities did not therefore openly oppose the Onias Temple. This accounts for the vacillating views and laws concerning it, found in the tannaitic sources...
>
> It may be further suggested that the original decree of levitical impurity was confined to Heliopolis and the neighborhood of the Temple of Onias which was in the vicinity of Goshen. There were the graves of the deceased in Egypt which, according to the law, caused levitical impurity. Subsequently

Our author believes that Jesus in prohibiting divorce, except in case of adultery, follows the Sadducees. But where is the proof that the Sadducees prohibit divorce?

Here Revel displayed his precise methodology in scientific study. Even in reviewing a volume, care was taken that it be not a cursory writing but only a responsible analytical penetration.

6. The Am Ha-aretz [29; 64]

Revel's deep knowledge of the historic origins of sectarian deviation from Tradition and the composition of ancient Jewry also prompted him to write a survey of the term "am ha'aretz," as based on biblical and talmudic sources. He showed the changes in its meaning over the centuries, and accordingly examined the views of the various scholars on the subject.

Particularly revealing therefore was Revel's remark:[4]

Though ignorant of the Law, the am ha'aretz did not represent a schism or belong to a particular set. There were ammei ha'aretz among the Sadducees (Niddah 34a) and the Samaritans (Berakot 47a) as well as among the Pharisees (Horayot 3, 8). The view of Kohler and others that the haughty attitude of the scholars toward the am ha'aretz was responsible for the early growth of the Christian church is without foundation. As stated above, no fundamental cleavage existed between them.

This incidentally illustrates Revel's deep-seated notion of the traditional unity of the Jewish people, and the importance of close adhesion, despite seemingly basic differences.

("80 years before the destruction of the Temple," according to the uncertain text of the Babylonian Talmud, or "in the days of Bet Shammai and Bet Hillel," according to the Palestinian Talmud), this decree was extended to all land outside of Palestine, notwithstanding the prevailing view that the corpse of a non-Jew does not communicate levitical impurity except through contact or carrying.

2. *Pagan Settlement in the Holy Land* [68]

The emphasis on sanctity in the Holy Land prompted Dr. Revel to probe what may seem to many to be only a hypothetical question — the impurity of pagans residing in the Holy Land. In an ancient milieu this may have been a vexing problem. It was Revel's view that the decree appertaining to impurity of pagans in Palestine was imposed by the Hasmoneans, to prevent assimilation. The destruction of the Hellenistic areas was part of the Hasmonean political scheme. Though the Hasmoneans later veered from observant tradition, they recognized, from a national viewpoint, the dangers to Jewish religious exclusiveness in the land with the presence of pagan inhabitants.

Despite this zeal, the Hasmoneans hired pagan mercenaries. The Sages were definitely opposed to this, since many of these mercenaries acquired land after their term of military service. Perhaps, surmised Revel, the rabbinic opposition to John Hyrcanus and to Alexander Jannai also included the fact that these monarchs had non-Jewish soldiers. The problem of sanctity in the land thus was of vital importance, especially when Jews settled in the conquered areas where Hellenists had once lived. Therefore the Rabbis decreed impurity on all of the homes once occupied by pagans in the land.

The Second Temple era was an age of observance of the multiple laws of purity and impurity; hence such decrees had an especial effect. It included all phases of contact with pagans and was aimed primarily to strengthen Jewish tradition and solidarity. Revel suggested that this singular decree may have been issued fittingly in the reign of Queen Alexandra who was very favorable to the Pharisees.

3. Reactions to the Ancient Diaspora [41]

In contrast to the concept of a Holy Land, what was the status of the Diaspora in the eyes of the ancients? Revel evaluated the rabbinic contention of existing impurity in the lands of the Diaspora. He inquired, how could those returning from Babylon bring with them the ashes of the red heifer for their own purity, if Babylon was considered impure? His answer was that the Diaspora was not designated as impure till much later. The rabbinic decree of impurity was enacted only in the days of Jose ben Joezer. The reason for the decree was to prevent any exodus from the Holy Land during the Hasmonean wars. Many persons, particularly the Hasidim, fled the Holy Land because of the increasing troubles. In the Diaspora they lived without disturbances from the Hellenists and the pagans. When Judah the Maccabee vanquished the Syrian Greeks he wished that the emigrees return. The Sages of his time then decreed that the Diaspora land be considered as impure. Perhaps, in the subsequent Hasmonean period, when peace prevailed, this decree was nullified. However, only a few years before the destruction of the Temple in 70 CE, when many left Judea because of the war, it was found necessary to reinstate this decree. It is listed therefore among the 18 decrees,[2] enacted before the destruction.

Revel particularly noted that Katzenelesohn (Buki ben Yogli) and Dr. Solomon Zeitlin in their studies of the Second Temple Era had already suggested that, in addition to the limitation of emigration from the Holy Land, the decree in the time of Jose ben Joezer was designed as a reaction to the building of the Onias Temple, when Onias IV had fled to Heliopolis because Alcimus had become the High Priest. According to some views, the Onias Temple was constructed with adherence to divine laws; yet the Sages were not fully in favor. Indeed, that temple had no influence; even Philo made no mention of it nor is it recorded in the Apocrypha, though the interrelationship of the Holy Land and the Diaspora in that era is well known from many records.

Dr. Revel, analyzing all of these sources demonstrated that even if Onias had biblical support, this temple still was not acceptable. Hence the Sages decreed again impurity upon the Diaspora land so that the place should never be considered worthy for sacrifices. Revel also noted that though a *bamah* (high place) may have been envisaged as permitted in the Diaspora, Onias may have built his structure similar to that of the Jerusalem Temple; hence it was legally prohibitive. Moreover, the imposition of impurity on Egyptian land may have included localities near the Onias Temple because the area may have contained the Jewish corpses of Goshen. Thus, the rabbinic decree on the impurity of the Diaspora included basically the feature of corpse impurity which, in a manner, still applies today, particularly to the members of the Kohanim (priestly) family.

Revel also suggested that Herod built Caesarea in order to detract from the glory of Jerusalem. This occurred 80 years before the destruction of the Temple in the 28th year of Herod's reign (10 BCE). The Rabbis of that period therefore decreed impurity on all lands outside of Palestine, in order to lessen the possibilities of Hellenistic acculturation. Caesarea was included in the decree to prevent the spread of idolatry. Only later, in the time of Rabbi Judah, was the decree against Caesarea removed.[3] In this essay Revel cited Dr. Solomon Zeitlin's notation regarding the date of Herod's death (before Nisan, 4 BCE). To this he added that when the Sages realized that the monarch's plan to glorify Caesarea above Jerusalem did not materialize they sought to annul the original decree of impurity, so that Jews could dwell therein. Revel thus concluded that the decision to remove the impurity from Caesarea was legislated immediately after Herod's death.

This rabbinic-historic investigation also involved Revel in a discussion pertaining to the time of death of Jose ben Joezer. He favored the story according to Midrash Bereshit Rabbah and examined the problem of the textual reading "from them" or "from him"[4] in Abot 1:2 — pertaining to the transmission of the Torah from Simon the Just. He regarded "from him" as the reading of Abot, thus surmising that Jose ben Joezer lived in the time of Alcimus. To Revel a knowledge of historical dating meant a better comprehension of Talmudic lore.

4. Historic Halakhic Interpretations [72]

The deep concern with probing the historic origins, the basic meaning and mode of observance of Halakhot, never abated. Revel probed into the academic and theoretical question of a Canaanite who had accepted circumcision and immersion in order to serve an Israelite master. Is such slave now to be regarded as belonging to the category of an Israelite *per se*, obligated to observe certain commandments? Or, does such obligation of observance relate to the master only, namely, to guide the slave in his mitzvot? If this slave defected, is he in the category of a recalcitrant Israelite, or does he return to his original status of a slave? Revel demonstrated that the varied opinions depend upon differences extant between Palestine and Babylon. In Palestine the attitude toward the Canaanite slave was a salutary one; in Babylon, the slave was held with disrespect. In Palestine, as soon as the slave came to an Israelite master, he was fully regarded as a Jew and was accorded the same privileges, bearing too his own obligations. Even if he defected later, he was still Jewish. But in Babylon the slave was only chattel; he did not come under the "wings of the Shekhinah." His obligations stemmed only from his master's ownership and dominance.

Thus Revel showed that differences of opinion in the Halakhah sometimes stem historically from contemporary economic situations and social conditions. In Palestine, during the Second Temple era, slaves were owned even by the high priests; the need for observance of the laws of purity therefore enhanced their status. This feature naturally did not apply to Babylonian Jewry. After the Temple destruction in 70 CE, however, difficulties arose in Palestine. The

Church gained power in later generations; it did not allow Jews to have non-Jewish slaves and it also forbade circumcision. The holding of slaves in Palestine declined. Therefore, only if a slave voluntarily accepted the commandments could he become part of the Jewish household. In sum, the attitude in Palestine toward those slaves who were in the household was not unlike that shown to a fellow Jew, whereas in Babylon the retention of slaves was considered as holding mere chattel.

The "detention of an accused"[5] was another interesting aspect which Dr. Revel probed in this historico-halakhic study. He demonstrated that in Jewish jurisprudence there is definitely no prison punishment. How then can we explain that "meager food and water" was given to him who had committed homicide without witnesses. If the purpose was to cause death, why give bread and water, even if it is meager? Revel showed that this punishment, cited in Mishnah Sanhedrin, is not Pentateuchal law. It is only an outcome of a distinct jurisdiction, basically a residue of the ancient laws pertaining to monarchical authority. This was a distinct right, separated from any traditional court procedure. Revel then explained how this regal jurisdiction[6] functioned by the side of Torah law. It was the monarch's power to punish one, even when the courts could not do so. In fact, Revel pointed out succinctly, this Mishnah does not even mention *Bet Din*, the Jewish jurisprudence. After first enumerating the laws appertaining to the Bet Din, the Mishnah records the jurisdiction of the king and other modes of punishment not belonging to the courts; among these is the "law of the zealots."[7]

Mishnah 9:5 of Sanhedrin thus notes that if one received stripes and then repeated his evil doing, he was placed into a *Kippah* (cell) and given barley to eat until his stomach split. This passage is not to be taken literally. The *Kippah* is only a place of detention, so that the culprit remain there until the officials could be assured that he would no more repeat his offenses. The purpose of *Kippah* is only a preventive measure, not punitive. Therefore, Maimonides, in his *Code,* did not mention *Kippah* among the various court punishments.

5. *Jewish Provinces in the* 19*th Century Diaspora* [7-8]

Though Revel devoted keen attention to ancient historic Judaism and, as head of Yeshivat Rabbenu Yitzhak Elchanan, to the future of American Jewry and its academic expansion, his early interest as a youngster in European Jewry never waned. His article on the "Baltic States and Jewry" in *Otzar Yisrael* reviewed not only the historic background of the settlements in these communities and the outstanding rabbis in the area, their works and influence, but also the effect of the Emancipation upon them. He noted that in 1807 the double tax on Jews was nullified in that area.

"Bialystock," among many cities, held particular interest. Also a review of the great rabbis of that city, as well as a survey of the political situation and the effect of pogroms therein comprise this essay. It was apparent that Dr. Revel's range of studies was never limited; the universalism that permeates Judaism never was forgotten by him.

Chapter IV

THE RESTORATION OF SEMICHA

One may suggest that as the prime bestower of ordination on young Orthodox Rabbis in America in the first part of the twentieth century, Dr. Revel was particularly concerned with the background and validity of the rite of authority. His essay on the problem of the historic renewal of Semicha in Palestine about 1528 CE was designed to investigate the time of its early abolition and the attempt at its reinstatement. Examining the opinions of the great early rabbinic luminaries who studied the matter of the authority of the patriarchate and the Sanhedrin, Revel analyzed the interrelated problems of the intercalation of the calendar, the sanctification of the moon by testimony of eye-witnesses or by reckoning, and the deeds of Hillel II (320-365) in promulgating the "secret of calendation." Revel noted that Nahmanides held that from the period of Hillel II on there was no sanctification by eye-witnesses, because there was no Semicha, due to the persecutions of that time. To counteract this, the mode of calendrical reckoning was introduced. Nahmanides believed specifically that with the suppression of the patriarchate in 415 CE, in the time of Theodosius II, the Semicha institution likewise was stamped out. Revel however assumed that Nahmanides was unclear about the exact time of the eradication — whether in the period of Hillel II or before Rav Ashi (407)? He emphasized that until the period of the Crusades, Palestine was still a center of learning. We find that much Halakhah is recorded in the Piyyutim (the medieval poetic liturgy) and in 960 CE questions were still sent to Palestine, even from the Rhineland. Hence, Revel concluded, the Palestinian scholars would not have relinquished

Semicha even at that time, especially because of the presence of great scholars and continued learning in the Holy Land.

The basic feature or strength of Semicha was the power to impose fines.[1] This was limited to Palestine; in the very early period there was no Semicha given in the Diaspora. In Revel's opinion it was only in 1062 CE, with the death of the Gaon R. Daniel ben Azariah, that Semicha ceased in Palestine, according to the testimony of a late Gaon. There was an inner struggle then for Gaon Daniel's position, and it caused much academic instability. With the Crusades, coming soon after, full communal life in Palestine diminished and Semicha ultimately ceased.

Maimonides flourished about a hundred years after the abolition of Semicha in 1062. It is he who suggested its renewal, if the consent of the Palestinian scholars could be obtained. Maimonides' notion was that this problem of reenactment "needed weighty concern."[2] This may indeed have been the reason for Levi Ibn Habib's opposition to the renewal of Semicha, particularly when the problem became realistic. According to Revel, this Maimonidean expression was an addition to Maimonides' original text by one who was opposed to the idea, since such authorities as Ibn Adret, Meiri, and ha-Parhi were especially definite and persistent in their view that Maimonides had decided that Semicha could be renewed.

In the third section of this "ordination" essay, Revel dealt in detail with the attempt to revitalize Semicha in 1528 CE in Safed, based on Maimonides' judgment, namely, that with the agreement of the Sages in Eretz Yisrael the imposition of fines and flogging could be reintroduced. Jacob Berab, the eldest of the coterie, was given Semicha by twenty-five dignitaries in Safed; he subsequently ordained four more scholars. The intent was to make Palestine again the center of Jewry. The decade was presumably ripe for this act, for it was already after the period of the Spanish Inquisition and the will for continuity, to stimulate Jewry with hope of redemption and restoration, was now both manifest and essential. The Karaites, too, were then revealing their own "dates of redemption." Abarbanel also had encouraged redemption hopes, and Solomon Molcho's aspirations were widely known. Turkey had captured Palestine in 1517 and Safed now became a central point of Jewry. Hence many rabbinic authorities believed that both the time and place were fitting for the renewal of Semicha.

Not only did scholars seek such reestablishment but even the average Jew awaited it. Specifically, the Maranos welcomed this so that they could be cleansed of their previous backsliding officially by an authorized court of recognized Rabbis.

These many hopes did not materialize. Jacob Berab did not consult the Jerusalem authorities, particularly Levi Ibn Habib. Radbaz (Rabbi David ibn Zimra) of Egypt at first had agreed to the plan, but later he retracted. If, at the outset, Radbaz had shown any opposition, Revel states, R. Joseph Karo would not have acted to ordain R. Moshe Alshek.

The opposition of Rabbi Levi Ibn Habib to a renewal of Semicha was not personal, because of the dignity of Jerusalem or because he was not the first to be ordained. Rather, Revel believed, it was because Ibn Habib feared that this course would renew a pseudo-Messianic movement. Only nine years before, Solomon Molcho had begun his activities in Jerusalem.

Later upheavals in Palestine in the 16th century — the economic difficulties, hunger, war, etc. — diminished the Jewish population. Marano influx into Palestine also lessened. Ibn Habib continued to preach and stress that it was repentance, and not flagellation authorized by a Sanhedrin, that was essential; hence no Semicha was necessary to aid the Maranos. The imposition of taxes and the burden set upon officials to collect these charges may also have been among the reasons why many shunned creating an officialdom by means of Semicha.

In a fourth section of this paper on "Semicha," Revel showed that even when Semicha had been annulled, those countries which had been influenced by Palestine, such as Italy, Germany and France, still utilized a "writ of Semicha" — a permission given by a teacher to his pupil to serve as a rabbinic authority. In Spain, which was impelled by Babylon custom, there was no practice of ordination and "obtaining permission." Rabbi Isaac Ibn Sheshet already defined this geographic difference.

When the exiles from Spain settled in Italy and Turkey, a controversy developed; many were amazed at the usage of a "writ of Semicha" extant outside of Palestine. Revel recalled that the term *Minnui* was employed by the Gaonim as a parallel to *Semicha,* and he added that Samuel ben Ali, Gaon of Bagdad, held that Semicha was abolished only in the matter of fines and calendation, but not for civil cases, or for delegating authority as Gaon (head of the Yeshiva). In 1161 CE Samuel ben Ali had sent a letter upholding the practice of such Semicha, for he felt that this was most important for strengthening authority. Indeed, to traditional adherents, the sovereignty of the Sages was of greater importance to Jewry than that of monarchy, which is but temporal and transitory.

Revel continued his exploration in the fifth section of his article, by reviewing the opinions of the *Rishonim* who supported Maimonides. He analyzed many views, especially that of Nahmanides who seemed to disagree with Maimonides. Revel, however, showed that even Nahmanides, in a second estimation, did agree with Maimonides, particularly in the matter of conversion, — to wit, that it was unnecessary to have an ordained Bet Din for such religious transferral.

This Semicha essay indeed may be regarded as one of Revel's most absorbing of research papers. It displays historic insight and full talmudic profundity, especially appertaining to the perpetual question of continuing authority in Israel and the dignity of the Rabbinate.

Chapter V

RABBINIC NOVELLAE
חידוש ופלפול

Any student who was privileged to study with Dr. Revel will vividly recall the "burning fire" of academic zeal that permeated his teaching, especially when he gave a lecture (*shiur*) in Talmud. Every fiber within him thrilled, intellectually and emotionally, for this was "his life." Though trained academically and scientifically, his basic mental foundations were in Talmudic study, particularly the analysis of rabbinics in the classical manner of the European Yeshivot of Russia, Poland and Lithuania.

Such works as *Shev Shemaï'tasa, Melo-ha-Roim, Minhat Hinuch, Kesef Mishneh, Pnai Yehoshua* and *Aruch ha-Shulhan* were constantly suggested by him to his pupils for their further probing in this area, and in *sugiot* in general, by the side of their study of the interpretations of the *Rishonim* (the rabbinic sages of the medieval period before the publication of the Shulhan Aruch).

He was at home in *Pilpul* (casuistic acumen), not merely as an intellectual exercise; it was his "search for truth." This is evident in the many talmudic articles in *Yagdil Torah, ha-Pardes, Horeb* and other journals. Being close to rabbinic investigation, his numerous essays divulge the depth to which he plumbed in the sea of Talmud, emerging always with original concepts. His writings also disclose the manifold problems in the philosophy of Jewish thought or religion which stimulated him. Though he investigated most matters talmudically, the modern perspectives therein — the timeless teachings of Judaism — always reveal themselves lucidly in his work.

437

1. *The Distinction of Prominence* [54]

אדם חשוב שאני

One of Revel's unique studies was in the realm of laws related to the prominence of a person and his influence. The principle is that a man of distinction should observe his practices meticulously, so that others may not learn from him to be careless in forbidden matters. Moreover, a prominent person in his caution would not be suspect of committing a wrong. Such individuals must always be most discreet in their conduct.

Examining the various talmudic sources dealing with this subject, Revel stated that though the rigorous mode is to be followed, in order to create and to set an example of fine human deportment and an elevated spirit, one should, in general, not impose hardships on others. Some persons might be led to believe that such practices are the norm. The prominent person, by his action, might even induce and influence others, resulting in situations of defiling that which is pure, or allowing that which is not permitted. Hence, where Jewish law is flexible and broad, the policy of "prominence and rigor" should not be applied.

Revel's methodology in explaining every possible item or situation related to this topic is apparent in the following statement:

> In the Palestinian Talmud, according to my knowledge, there is no record of a difference between prominence and non-prominence, namely that a prominent individual should act with severity. Where the Palestinian Talmud mentions situations recorded in the Babli, the Yerushalmi does not make this distinction "of prominence." Apparently, Maimonides follows the Palestinian Talmud, since he disregards such distinction.

Revel also noted that, according to the Palestinian Talmud[1] he who performs an act in a disproportionate manner is a commoner (*hediot*). The Babylonian Talmud, however, maintains that one should follow a strict mode in observance.

This study involved Revel in cognate subjects, such as the regulations of impurity in public areas[1*] and *Hazakah*[2] (the rule of presumptive continuance). His diligence and precision, weighing every aspect of a problem in all the sources of the two Talmudim, led him to see even these themes as corollaries of the "observance of rigorous conduct."

2. *Certainty and Assessment* [42]
ברי ואומדנא

It is noteworthy that the academic discipline of *hilluk*[3] — "making fine distinctions in halakhic study and *pilpul*" — was Revel's forte. This is especially evident in his analysis of the norms of the "positive (certain) and the estimate (opinion by assumption)." He concluded that we follow the legal principle of "estimation" only when we are aware of the facts in a case but still do not know the circumstances or views that underlie the particular facts. If, however, the estimate or opinion is to be used to posit or establish a fact, we cannot follow such a norm, for any legal inference.

Do we rely on estimate or assumption in a decision of civil or monetary cases? Revel stressed that to impose obligations we surely cannot follow such a principle; if the purpose, however, is to strengthen any fact, then we may rely upon the norm of estimate as a sustaining opinion. In this study, all rabbinic luminaries, the *Rishonim* and *Aharonim,* and even the latest writers on the theme, were carefully scrutinized, so that his own presentation would be well balanced.

Revel also involved himself in the question whether an "equitable oath"[4] can be administered to a relative who supports given testimony in a situation where the object or money in question had been seized by the complainant. An "equitable oath" is one applied to a person who denied a debt entirely.[5] Whereas legally an oath is required only where a defendant admits part of the claim,[6] as a matter of equity the opponent may, in return, put the claimant to such "consuetudinary oath." Revel noted that no court can render a decision on the strength of its own opinion; there must always be a factual basis. An oath, however, can be administered by the court once some substantiation for its usage had already been set, as in the case of the presence of one witness. An "equitable or consuetudinary oath" fits into this category.

3. *Majority Rule in Civil and Capital Cases* [57]

רוב בממון ובדיני נפשות

Another subject often discussed by Revel in his classes and *shiurim* was that of "majority rule."[7] The principle that the majority (or major portion) is legally equal to an entirety[8] always intrigued him. Why should this rule — a problem which engaged the thought of many scholars through the ages — be applied to capital punishment and not to monetary cases?

Revel claimed that contrary to the general assumption there is no difference in following a most likely probability in civil cases or in capital cases. The distinction is rather in the circumstances of application.

Naturally, in civil matters, there was the possibility of reparations and a re-evaluation; such could not occur when capital punishment had already been applied.

In situations where witnesses could possibly clarify the issue we do not follow the rule of probability; when the issue is beyond the scope of clarification through witnesses, only then can the judges adjudicate on the basis of "most likely probability."

Revel explained that the testimony of witnesses is only in accord with what they alone know. There may be additional facts or reasons upon which judges may base their decisions. It is in these instances that one uses the norm of "majority rule." But, if witnesses give only partial evidence, knowing only a portion of the incident, such as that of a sale where only meager facts are known, the judges cannot follow the principle of majority rule. The judge's duty is primarily to clarify or substantiate[9] the testimony — not to give opinions. Hence, Revel concluded, there is apparently no value in the use of "majority rule" where the testimony is definitive; we follow here only the Biblical tenets of testimony. Where the question basically deals, however, with explaining or substantiating matters, we can then be guided by the norm of "majority." Where testimony could fully elucidate situations, we cannot and should not adhere to the "majority rule." Only where we need guidance, beyond that of testimony, does the norm of majority rule aptly function.

4. *Plausible Reason for Retracting Evidence* [5]
אמתלא

Revel's singular approach to examination of principles in Halakhah may also be noticed in his short encyclopedic review of the rules of "plausible reason."

Here he reiterated that an explanation for any factor or situation has no competence legally when confronted by witnesses to negate the original testimony. Nevertheless, "a reasonable explanation of contradictory statements or evidence" can be accepted. Even when two excuses or explanations contradict each other,[10] we can admit them to establish the truth of a fact.

5. *"A Positive Command Nullifies A Negative One"* [27]
עשה דוחה לא תעשה

The multiple phases of positive and negative commandments fascinated Dr. Revel. He emphasized that the positive can cancel the negative only if the two *mitzvot* occur simultaneously and are always combined. If, however, there is another manner of upholding the negative command, it cannot be set aside or obliterated by the concurrent positive law.

Furthermore, a positive precept does not negate any of the rules which apply to social conduct or to the rights of persons or property. Thus, one cannot efface the ordinance, "Ye shall not steal." Likewise, if a law deals with the obligation of a person toward another he is subject to the wish of that individual; there is no power to negate therewith a Biblical negative command. Primarily there must be release from the obligation in such circumstances.

6. *Property Renunciation on the Sabbath* [44]

הפקר בשבת

May one declare an article in one's possession *res nullius* (ownerless, *hefker*) on the Sabbath? Does it fall into the category of transfer by sale[11] or that of charity?[12] If by sale, it would be forbidden to perform such action on the Sabbath. On the other hand, it is recognized that designating charity is permitted on Sabbath. Is *hefker* like it or is it different? Is the giving of charity (*tzedakah*) in the category of *res nullius,* or is *res nullius* also an element which requires a mode of transfer?[13] The rule in *hefker* is that its disposal cannot be limited; it must be for rich and poor alike. Hence, it would seem that *hefker* is not in the category of charity, which is apportioned for the poor alone. Yet, according to Bet Shammai who maintained that *hefker* may be assigned to the poor alone, *hefker* is indeed in the category of charity. Or, continued Revel in this probing, shall we say that *hefker* is basically an element of changing possessions,[14] which is forbidden on the Sabbath, being a deliberate action? However, if the process is through a passive state, i.e., simply that of removing the right of possession, perhaps rendering something *hefker* would be allowed on the Sabbath, even according to Bet Hillel?

It is in this manner that Revel delved into interesting hypothetical problems with his keen pilpulistic mind. Basically the analysis and the dialectics therein are most important; not the final conclusion. The reader will often find that Revel declared at the end of many of his articles: "the rest will appear later."[15] To our regret we do not possess these further studies. Perhaps in writing, Revel realized that there were many further points of investigation that he could add to each problem. Variegated activities or communal interests, however, may have deterred him in fulfilling this aim.

7. *Retrospective Designation* [60]

בירור

A penetrating question that absorbed Revel's mind was that of "status clarification."[16] This involves the legal effect resulting from selection or disposal of objects which were previously undefined as to the mode of their usage. This question of retrospective legal effect refers both to judicial and ritual cases. Revel posed the theoretical problem: If an Israelite, together with a pagan, obtained possession of an idolatrous article, can we posit, on the basis of subsequent selection, that the Israelite renounced the possession of his own portion and hence is no more the owner of an idolatrous article. This naturally would free him from any transgression. Or, can it not be applied, once the object had been attained by both persons?

Troublesome as it might seem, this question is related to the problem of the efficacy of "a double doubt"[17] and the question of "prior presumption."[18]

8. *Material Transformations of Substances* [43]

שינוים באיסורים

A further pilpulistic question studied by Revel discussed changes occurring in forbidden things or in impurities. What is the status after the transformation? Are articles, species or elements proscribed by the Torah *per se*, i.e., only as they basically are? Hence when there is a variation in quality or in composition of the particular substance, it becomes a new entity, and consequently allowable. Shall we assert that, by adding to the primary substance permissive elements, the original prohibited element becomes as dust? Hence that which was first forbidden is now permitted. Or, does the disallowed element basically remain even after the act of mixture? Or, is it true that by combination, a new substance is created, as in changing something from a food to a beverage?

Revel stated that one cannot remove a prohibited element from a substance. There is the definite rule of "that which comes from the impure is impure."[19] However, that rule applies only where, through the life action, there is an issue from the process, such as in the case of milk of an unclean animal. Such is forbidden. But, where a fresh form of a substance appears or a new taste results — as in a chemical — one may ask: Did the Torah disallow an edible even if its form changed completely and one cannot recognize its original state? That is, even if it is something absolutely new, is it still proscribed and the prohibition (issur)[20] basically endures? Such indeed may be in case of leaven[21] where the basic element definitely abides. Or, shall we surmise that the change is like that of honey, wherein there are variations of the original ingredients by dissolution of the composition, and permission to eat the honey of the bee is not questioned? Or, e.g., if blood is varied by boiling, does it not still retain its issur? Are things only permitted when they become like "dust of the earth,"[22] but not when there is a transformation that retains its original bulk, except that only the form was changed?

Revel demonstrated that a mere modification of taste does not change the status of prohibition of a substance. In this connection he further discussed the question of nullification of something in the major bulk of extant matter,[23] and its consequent legalistic-ritualistic effect. This again was part of the academic study of "neutralization" of some material in a larger quantity.

Moreover, Revel questioned, does the Torah forbid some content only when there is a particular taste therein, following the principle that "taste is like substance?"[24] Or, is the purpose of the prohibition so designed that the stomach should not absorb a proscribed food; yet, if a thing is changed in form and taste, it is no more forbidden? Or, did the Torah also consider such a substance, even if transformed, as still maintaining the essence of interdiction?

9. Sacrificial Slaughtering [45]

שחיטת קדשים

May he who is not a Kohen (one of the priestly clan of Aaronide lineage) slaughter a holy sacrifice? Revel showed that the red heifer[25] and the leper's bird[26] had to be slaughtered only by a Kohen. Though a non-priest could sacrifice all other offerings, the practice was only for priests to perform the ritual. Revel held that in ancient days the Levites also had performed the sacrificial service. He then analyzed the question whether a nonpriest could perform worship on the Sabbath. His view was that such could not be possible, for Sabbath worship was limited to the Kohanim (priests) who were the *"chosen"* officiants.

The reason Kohanim generally performed the sacrificial ritual (though lay-Israelites could too) was that they were versed in the laws. Moreover, the average person was not always in a state of purity. Yet, with quotations from Philo, Revel demonstrated that on the eve of Passover, with the abundance of sacrifices, even the layman could sacrifice the paschal lamb. It was a time of purity for all.

The halakhic problem whether a Kohen is considered an "emissary of God"[27] or is "our messenger, bearing our gifts,"[28] also interested Revel. He affirmed that if a nonpriest could sacrifice, then the Kohen is the emissary of the person making the offering. In other Temple activities, that is, beyond the function of slaughtering, only the Kohanim performed the divine tasks. Here Revel again discussed the question of agency[29] and the transferral of rights. He demonstrated that ritual slaughter is a worship.[30] Hence the priest required priestly garments. Perhaps, he argued, even a nonpriest could perform the ritual, but such was only in individual sacrifices,[31] not in public obligations,[32] since the nonpriest was not "chosen" to minister.

This scrutiny led to still another query: Shall we infer that, since every Israelite has a share in the Temple sacrifice, our analysis becomes one of research into the category of ownership;[33] hence, even a "public" offering may be sacrificed by the nonpriest? More-over, the question whether "worship" can be performed on the Sabbath by a nonpriest led Revel also to inquire how the scapegoat[34] was dispatched on the Day of Atonement by means of a nonpriest? He concluded that this act was not considered a part of the ritual; therefore a nonpriest could function here.

Revel thus in one article collated with ease the many classical Talmudic elements of agency, ownership, priesthood, Sabbath ob-servance, sacrificial ritual and its completion, etc., and even applied these to historic episodes and contingencies.

10. Bamah Worship [76]
עבודה בבמה

The question of priesthood further involved Revel in the academic problem of a nonpriest sacrificing at a bamah (high altar). Is such permissible because no true factor of priesthood existed in those places, or shall we regard it as forbidden, since an aspect of holiness of the priesthood has remained also within the layman, even after the choice of Aaron. Israelites also are to be recognized as part of the "kingdom of priests." Hence even a nonpriest cannot defile himself by worship at a high altar.

Revel further remarked that one should not regard the priesthood as evidence of a caste system. Rather, the concept is that priesthood is associated also with the nonpriests and there is a priestly aspect extant even in the ordinary layman. The question, whether priests are "divine emissaries"[35] depends on the distinct notion whether only priests were "chosen" to do sacrificial rites. If we regard them specifically as our agents, then one must deduce that there exists sanctification even in the nonpriest, because agency is only the result of delegating one's own power. The recognition that there is a factor of sanctification within him therefore would allow sacrificial activity even for the nonpriests.

Dr. Revel inferred that tradition and historic precedent ultimately limited the functions of the laity in slaughtering.[36] All other ritual functions in sacrifice belong to the priest. Therefore on the Sabbath, when only a full and complete worship is fitting, the tasks are to be performed by the *Kohen* alone. Revel thus noted:

> It seems that a layman can even slaughter sacrifices because there has remained within him an element of priesthood; hence the Torah allowed slaughtering by laymen, though other aspects of sprinkling blood belong to priests. However, we do not say that the permission is also given to officiate on Sabbath. Such an exception belongs only to those who can complete the *entire* worship.

11. *Sequence in Tithing* [66]

הקדים מעשר

A short article on the procedure in tithing[37] included the question of "gradations in ritual worship." Is an act completed in wrong sequence acceptable? Or, must "progression" be followed as a formal order and correct conduct for the purpose of approved recognition of the performance? As often, the posing of such rabbinic, casuistic problem was more important than the actual obtaining of an answer.

12. *Transferral of Tribal Property* [67]

נחלה משבט לשבט

Another essay of depth dealt with the problem of transferral of property from one tribe to another. Though tribal intermarriage was permitted, even as Josephus and Philo demonstrate, apparently the conveyance of property of a woman who inherited from her tribe could not be effected. The Sages therefore aimed to encourage marriage only within one's own tribe. They set, as an example of merit, the marriage of one's niece.[37*] Revel further noted that in ancient days, if a woman married into another tribe, the term *zonah* (harlot) was applied to her.[38]

13. *Trustworthiness of Witnesses* [71]

נאמנות עדים

In a tribute to his mentor and friend, Rabbi Bernard Levinthal of Philadelphia, on the occasion of his 70th birthday, Dr. Revel wrote a penetrating article on the subject of "Testimony of Witnesses According to Maimonides," and the views of both Babli and Yerushalmi governing the testimony of one witness. Revel pointed out that Maimonides himself makes the statement that acceptance of two witnesses is not to be construed as a means of clarification of a matter; their acceptance is only a consequence of the divine decree.

A court (Bet Din) renders an opinion only when it cannot resolve a matter through testimony of witnesses. Likewise, the acceptance of one witness to resolve forbidden matters[39] is in the realm of clarification,[40] similar to the rules of "weighing opinion,"[41] or "majority,"[42] "signs"[43] or "prior presumption,"[44] — each in its own category.

The problem of "one" witness" may be that of *number* rather than that of *quality* of testimony. This question (number or quality), Revel stated, applies also to the subject of "alibi witness,"[45] and to the instance of marriage based on the testimony of one witness.

In all, Revel often recorded many *sugiot* (talmudic themes) under one subject of research, because to him all of these were constantly united in thought and scope. Each phase of his rabbinic research included a most interesting pilpulistic analysis, but his concern was not in reaching a conclusion or making any halakhic decision. His ardent love was Novellae as a mode of Torah study, featuring the intertwined variations that may occur in the Halakhah as a result of such a probing. To him, the constant search for the fine details — even "splitting hairs" — in determining basic principles of Halakhah, in the traditional manner of the Lithuanian Yeshivot, was the very mortar of Talmudic study or *lomdus*.

Chapter VI

PHILOSOPHICAL THOUGHT

1. *Torah and Tradition*
[50] דברי תורה ודברי קבלה

One of Dr. Revel's major works dealt with the transmission of traditional precepts and concepts. He was very much concerned with the problem of prophecy and its effect. Did the prophet have the power to introduce any new Halakhah? Examining all of the Talmudic aspects related to *Elijah, Bat Kol* (a heavenly voice) or *prophecy,* elements often mentioned in connection with decision in law, Revel pointed out that the prophet could not decide law or even turn the balance of decision. This belonged to the jurisdiction of interpretation of the law by the Sages and was decided by the majority; the prophet only explained the status and reality, if there was any doubt as to meaning.[1] That is, the prophet only pointed up the existing situation but did not render the final decision. If a prophet indicated in his writings any particular practice, we should not regard that as determinative. For example, there are records of cremation for kings or of offerings made from Amalek booty. These instances do not guide us in our religious practice. Basically, then, what is the status of laws derived from the books of the Prophets, such as "sale" from the book of Jeremiah, "laws of barter" from Ruth, "laws of mourning" from Ezekiel and Job, "concerning Sabbath-joy" from Isaiah and "female singing" from the Songs of Songs?[2] Are these to be construed as fixed criteria, valid for decision in law and practice?

Revel examined many biblical instances and sources generally cited to prove some Halakhah and weighed Rabbi Zevi Chayes' notion

449

that we can rely upon such practices mentioned in the text. His own view, however, was that all these records have only the status of rabbinic authority and are not Pentateuchal, unless the Talmud specifies otherwise. The biblical references are merely in the domain of *asmakhta* (support)[3] and hence belong only to the category of rabbinic element. They do not have the strength of Pentateuchal primacy and authority.

In this essay Revel also portrayed how pious persons introduced practices based on *Elijah* and *Bat Kol,* though generally such features could not be utilized to decide a law.

He also suggested that even the idea of the number "613" for the Torah mitzvot resulted from a concern with *gematria;* the Yerushalmi, however, makes no mention of *Taryag* (613 Commandments).

This essay on "Torah and Tradition" thus explored basic Pentateuchal sources but included many other items which, though apparently of secondary import in Judaism, ultimately became of prime significance in religious conduct.

2. *Thought and Deed*
מחשבה ומעשה [47, 49, 52]

Following the fundamental concept that all laws are "decrees of the Almighty," Revel probed a Talmudic problem, as its corollary. Is punishment meted out because of violation of the divine decree, or is it because a person, in performing an act of transgression of the Torah, causes harm to himself? Are we to regard the Almighty's warnings to mankind like those of a physician to his patient?

Revel surmised that this query may be contained in the discussion of Abaye and Rava in Temurah 4b[4]: "Does an act which Divine Law forbids have legal effect, if consummated?" Abaye said it has legal effect; else there would be no punishment. Action alone is the deciding factor. Rava said the act has no legal effect; punishment is imposed only because of violating the will of God. Since, according to Abaye, punishment is administered only when an action is effective, then, if, in the violation, one did not accomplish anything, there is no punishment. But Rava held that even one's conduct or the thought of doing wrong merit punishment.

In the question whether punishment can be administered as a result of an inference from an hermeneutic rule,[5] Abaye declared that if the conclusion is not a wrong deduction but only a classification derived from hermeneutics there is punishment, because an act was performed. Rava, however, stated that as a command is a divine decree, this must be found basically in the Torah and is not at all to be a derivative. To this Abaye retorted that though generally we do not administer punishment for precepts derived from hermeneutic rules, we nevertheless can use the inference for the clarification of a certain phrase or term,[6] because this process, too, is divine.

Analyzing this dispute, Revel probed into other Talmudic aspects, showing how Rava stressed *thought and intent* rather than *action*. Therefore, if one transgressed a rabbinic law Rava, in stressing *thought*, would regard this as part of the rules coming under divine decree. Abaye, however, who stressed *action*, would regard the violation of a rabbinic law as a deed not to be designated as sinful, because such designation applies only to Torah laws.

Here Revel continued the analysis of many cognate views of Abaye and Rava demonstrating how these belonged in this academic domain. Rava would not differentiate between actions leading to excision[7] and such which are mere prohibitions,[8] whereas Abaye would, since according to him, the *basis* for punishment is only *action*.

Concerning the question, "Do commands require intent?"[9] Rava, depending on thought, upheld the necessity of that principle. Abaye, thinking of action alone as important, did not maintain it.

Rava's reliance on thought would effectuate the rule of *muktsah*,[10] ("setting aside") applied to articles which cannot be used or handled on the Sabbath. On the other hand, Abaye on the basis of action would not depend on mere thought for "separation" of a thing. So also in the matter of a "command that has no action therein,"[11] such as "not to hate one in his heart,"[12] Rava would hold one liable for the thought; Abaye not, because of lack of action.

Similarly, in a matter resulting from a "doubt"[13] stemming from the Torah, Rava would not hold one liable, for it is not a clear divine decree. Abaye believed that even in the case of performance of the "doubt" one may be liable as a result of the action.

Following their principles, Rava would also regard both — aspects of Torah and rabbinic law — as divine decrees; Abaye, however, held that since the act depends on the evil therein, it is only Torah legislation, and not rabbinic notion that defines a thing or act as evil. Hence Abaye could accept that *muktsah* imposed by rabbinic decree is not a "separation' 'to be observed, for it has no Pentateuchal, "prohibitive status."

In this article Revel also discussed the legal principles of *miggo*,[14] "potential,"[15] "ownership"[16] and "definite determinism."[17] As a consequence of the recognition of the fine distinction and the differences resulting from *thought* and *action,* still many other talmudic principles were probed. Among these were the laws of a person's responsibility for an action likely to occur later,[18] the question of "res nullius,"[19] the "transferral of prohibitions"[20] and the "appointing of a delegate to do wrong."[21] Rava, following *thought* even in a rabbinic matter as his conceptual basis, declared that any person who appoints another to do evil is himself wicked (*rasha*)[22] and hence the appointment is not valid. Abaye, however, following the basic criterion of *action* maintained that since the conduct is only of rabbinic derivation, it is not in the category of prohibited action; such a person therefore is not a *rasha;* hence, the proxy can be an accepted as emissary to perform for others.

Involved in this talmudic analysis is also the question of the status of a minor.[23] Is he free because he is not obligated to fulfill the commands, or is he not obligated because he is not mature? Rava, depending on thought, posited that there is no punishment for the minor because he is not commanded to observe. Abaye, however, held that since action is the important element, it applies also to a minor who performed the action. One may then ask, is a minor not punished only because he is not mature, even though the action is complete? Hence, if a minor eats carcass-food,[24] Rava would maintain that since the minor had not been commanded[25] to observe the law, one does not need to constrain him in his eating.[26] Abaye, however, who stressed the effect of evil through the performance of some action, held the opinion that the Court must make effort to remove the minor from his evil performance.

3. *The Rationale of the Divine Commands*[27]

טעמי המצות

The reason for the Torah Commandments always fascinated Dr. Revel. Originally written as part of the pilpulistic study of "Thought and Deed," dealing with the perspectives of Abaye and Rava, as noted above, this historic essay was later expanded. The views of Philo, Aristeas, the Tannaim, the Gaonim, Maimonides and Karaites, etc., were all scrutinized, to understand the place of rationale in Commands of the Torah (mitzvot).

Summarizing the variant views, Revel recorded that Rava maintained there is no reason for the mitzvot, whereas Abaye held that there was a purpose in it, namely to avoid evil. Interestingly, in this monograph Revel presented a long list of passages wherein, in his opinion, the Torah indeed does give "reason."[27*] The Apocrypha too aimed to render reasons, and the Tannaim also sought to probe the question of reason for mitzvot. Philo especially labored in this area. The Rabbis, realizing the effect and the difficulties resulting from allegorical interpretation, since people could not always weigh the value of a command, consequently aimed to discourage the attempt of ascribing reasons for mitzvot. Often it led to symbolic interpretation and even to the non-performance of the command.

Revel also demonstrated that the early Gaonim likewise refrained from giving reasons. Yet Saadia, though opposed to allegorical interpretation, did indeed search for reason in the Biblical verse, because he held that such would finally reveal the eminence of God through rationalism. Perhaps, suggested Revel, Saadia's primary need for explaining the law in this manner was due to his opposition to the Karaites. Saadia had also shown that though there is general knowledge of the purpose of a mitzvah, the particular essence therein is nevertheless unknown. Revel's essay thus even contained a survey of Saadia's philosophy and the history of research in "rationale of the commands," especially as presented by the Sephardic School of thought.

One perceives in this essay the interspersion and fusion of *pilpul* with historic and academic investigation. This was unique in the rabbinic journal *Yagdil Torah*. Revel also described here the Karaites using a new hermeneutics of analogy, whereas the Rabbis declared that comparative elements for purposes of decision in law are not always valid. One cannot learn mitzvot by comparisons, as was the wont of the Karaites, was the Rabbinic retort.

In this connection Revel also analyzed Maimonides' view, particularly when the great teacher renewed the ancient allegorical approach, the coin used mostly by Philo and the Church Fathers. Even as many of Philo's disciples were misled by these investigations, so were the disciples of Maimonides. Nahmanides declared that Maimonides supplied mitzvah reasons only for those persons who were weak in their faith.

Basically there always was great opposition to rationalization of the divine decrees. The Karaites, however, pursued it; the Kabbalists also adopted it, later giving different mystical hints and esoteric suggestions for the Torah observances.

As a result of this research, Revel aimed to explain the talmudic term *homer*. He demonstrated that it was a "question and answer" method found already in Aristotle and in Philo. It was a procedure of "going from minor to major" in a subject, to explain the difficulties of thought therein. The *homer* was the difficulty and the *dorshé hamurot* were its "expounders." Thus Revel explained the methodology of exposition of difficult phrases in the Bible, according to the "question and answer" system, practiced among Jews in Alexandria.[28]

Chapter VII

ETHICS

1. *Bachya Ibn Pakudah* [20]

Interest in objective research did not only grow out of Dr. Revel's constant concern with Halakhah — its origin and practices of ancient days. Inherently he was imbued with the spirit of loftiness permeating Jewish Ethics. He sought to grasp its subjective effects. This approach long preceded even his Wissenschaft research and was no doubt in accord with the dictum, "the beginning of wisdom is the fear of God." Hence his "master's dissertation" at New York University on "Bachya Ibn Pakudah, one of the first exponents of Jewish ethics," is a profound analysis of the spiritual foundations of universal ethics and moral law, and a summary of that author's ethical work, *Hovat halevavot* (Duties of the Heart).

Revel described Bachya:[1]

> As an original thinker, a perfect master of the vast field of Rabbinical literature, Jewish philosophy and thought, thoroughly familiar with the entire philosophical and scientific Arabic literature, as well as the natural sciences, Bachya combined in a rare degree great depth of emotion and piety, a vivid, poetical imagination, noble purpose and a style of stern yet genial simplicity with a penetrating intellect and pure thought. Every line of his book reveals to us his great personality and a soul of the utmost piety, touching humility and catholic sympathy. The simplicity of his work, its eloquent, vivid language, its many beautiful sayings and gems of thought from the works of the greatest non-Jewish thinkers, as well as its deep

455

religious sentiments, loftiest moral principles, and its constant
quotations from and reference to the Bible, have made the
"Duties of the Heart" what it was intended to be — a book
for the people.

No school or system of philosophy can claim Bachya as its
disciple. He was the follower of truth wherever he found it
and he found it mainly in his own consciousness.

After presenting a general introduction to the subject of growth
and emergence of ethical works in the Golden Age, Revel devoted
a large chapter to Bachya's life demonstrating his negation of
asceticism. He analyzed specifically Bachya's philosophy, touching
upon such themes as the existence of God and the various cosmological, moral, and ontological proofs. Viewing the existence of God
from the perspective of ethics, Revel summarized his thesis:[2]

No truth is contained in the accepted belief that Bachya
followed the "Brethren of Purity," the Arabian Encyclopedists,
in their mysticism and in their belief that man can gain truth
by inner, suprarational illumination, through ecstasy and transportation, a state in which man, absorbed in himself and in the
suspension of self-perception, has visions beyond the reach of
the intellect and thereby attains the state of proximity to God,
as intermixture of being, as identification or as intimate union.

Bachya, on the contrary, insists on study and contemplation
as the only path by which man can attain his highest goal —
the knowledge and love of God — which cannot be facilitated
by external operations of the body.

2. *Jewish Ethics* [59]

It is apparent that persistent and thorough investigation of Bachya's *Ethics* prompted Revel to write some years later a comprehensive
article on Jewish Ethics, referring back to his original work. Here
he noted[3]:

The basis of morality is the belief in the existence of God,
and the love of God. But the essential condition precedent to

love is knowledge and it is, therefore, an accepted truth in Judaism that ignorance excludes piety. Reason and the Torah command us to investigate our beliefs. The Torah does not commend blind faith and devotion, but urges the proofs of reason and knowledge as to God's existence and unity.

One whose intellect is able to attain certainty on what he has received by tradition, and who refrains from investigation owing to mental laziness or because he holds God's commandments and the Torah in light esteem, will be punished and held guilty of negligence.

The attainment of man's highest goal — the sanctification of life and the dedication of man to the love and service of God — is aided by the performance of the comandments of the Law, which set a limit and barrier to man's lower natural impulses by self-dedication and through moral discipline. Obedience to the laws of the Torah, asserting the higher claims of the soul, is the portal leading to the realm of holiness. It disciplines man and guards him against the tendencies of his sensual nature and indulgence, and teaches man the right way of serving God by following the path, remote alike from sensuality and from contempt of the world. The mitzvot are thus the source of true virtue and right living.

3. *The Saadia Epistle to Egypt* [39]

Alert to any new findings that could enhance his own knowledge of Karaism, as well as bring spiritual illumination to the world, Dr. Revel became deeply interested in the epistle, bearing the superscription of Rav Saadia Gaon. A 15th century copy from Morocco, brought to America by Dr. Nahum Slouzch, deserved, in Revel's opinion, to be considered under the rubric "Ethics." He was the first to publish it[4] and he wrote:

The epistle contained a series of practical suggestions for the guidance of the individual in his daily duties and in his intercourse with God and man.

He held that Saadia wrote this epistle to early Jewish Spanish settlers to warn them against the encroaching Karaitic heresy.[5]

Saadia advises moderation and unity of action and criticizes any one who separates himself from the community.

He points out that every word of the Torah has its significance and every repetition of a word or phrase has its explanation.

This warning was perhaps directed against the Bible critics of his day such as Hivi ha-Balki against whom he wrote a separate work. He cautions against jealousy and competition. He emphasizes that, unlike the nations of the world whose ideals are conquest and acquisition of wealth, the national ideal of the Jewish people is the study of the Torah which, if abandoned, would mean our ruin. He therefore pleads that provision be made for the students of the law to enable them to carry on their holy work. He attacks the unscrupulous merchant who makes his money through dishonest methods. He asks the people to give their contributions to charity of the best and emphasizes that "we eat to live and do not live to eat." He calls upon the people not to admire his present epistle as containing so many beautiful thoughts but rather to carry out his admonitions. Finally, Saadia asks his correspondents not to be reticent in seeking his advice on all questions of the Torah.

This essay was no doubt the popularization of his more academic research on the Epistle.

4. An Observation on "The Ethics of the Fathers" [32*]

Apart from his own personal research, Revel continually guided others. It is known that scholars sought Revel's *haskamah* (approval) for their own volumes. When Rabbi Jacob Levinson, the noted Mizrachi leader in Brooklyn, New York, wrote his work on *Abot*, in which he aimed to interpret the "Ethics of the Fathers" on the basis of historic incidents, Dr. Revel added his own opinion that Abot was specifically prepared for "disciples of the wise," to teach them the mode of conduct with their teachers, colleagues and pupils in the academic school or in the rabbinic courts. Moreover, he explained why such men as Rabbi Joshua ben Levi showed interest in the study of Aggadot. Revel suggested that originally Rabbi Joshua had Essene notions but, recognizing the spread of Christianity and the errors prevalent in Essene doctrine, he later became very wary. Hence his views in the Talmud always tend to offset contemporary Essene and Christian sectarianism. To Revel, practical ethics and study of Torah are handmaidens. Hence to Yeshiva students he would often suggest that in their leisure moments they review Luzzato's *Mesillat Yesharim.*

Epilogue

THE THIRST FOR KNOWLEDGE

by LEON D. STITSKIN

Rabban Simon ben Gamaliel, in evaluating the accomplishments of his forbears, once declared, "Their words are their memorial." It is in this vein that the present volume appears, more than twenty-seven years after the death of the great teacher, Founder of Yeshiva College, Dr. Bernard Revel (1885-1940). The philosophy of this sage has crystallized within his full endeavors for realization of the ideals of "Yeshiva." He wrote:

> Yeshiva aims at unity, at the creation of a synthesis between the Jewish conception of life, our spiritual and moral teaching and ideals, and the present-day humanities, the scientific conscience and spirit to help develop the complete harmonious Jewish personality, once again to enrich and bless our lives, to revitalize the true spirit and genius of historic Judaism.

Dr. Revel consistently maintained that secular knowledge in Judaism was never separate from the study of Torah. The narrative portions of the Bible are replete with many facts of geography and history. Our medieval Jewish exegetes were not simply interpreters of Scripture. The distinctive feature of the commentaries was to read into the Biblical text general knowledge derived from philosophical, literary, midrashic and mystical sources.

Dr. Leon D. Stitskin is the editor of the Yeshiva University Special Publications. During his early years in the rabbinate he was in close communication with his teacher and mentor, Dr. Revel.

Dr. Stitskin is now Professor of Jewish Philosophy at the Bernard Revel Graduate School, associate editor of "Tradition," and the author of "Judaism As a Philosophy," espousing the thesis of "personalism."

By the same token, the potency of Judaism was manifested not alone by its affirmations of faith but by its unique mode of life. The strength and glory of that way of life was in the study and knowledge of the Torah. If Torah-true Judaism is ever to establish a foothold in this country, he said, it will be only because of a dynamic espousal of the study of the Torah. Dr. Revel often repeated to me that a rabbi who recites a chapter of the Mishnah daily before his congregation performs his duties as a spiritual leader more diligently than any sensational orator. Again and again, at every opportunity, he stressed the importance of learning. He felt that in Judaism, knowledge and the search for enlightenment was the heritage and pride of *all* people, and should be the possession of *all*. Herein lay the basis of man to lift himself to the level of divine excellence.

The "thirst for knowledge" that continually stimulated Dr. Revel has been revealed penetratingly in this book. Devoted exclusively to an evaluation of the master's scholarly research, it has brought to light the underlying themes motivating Dr. Revel's many-faceted intellectual pursuits and his methodology of combining full talmudic depth with historic background and academic orientation.

Especially fitting is it that Dr. Sidney B. Hoenig, as a disciple of Dr. Revel, prepared this academic volume. He followed in his master's footsteps in rabbinic studies as well as in scholarly research (hokhmat Yisrael), which he pursued at Dropsie College upon the advice of his teacher, who was the first graduate of that institution. Dr. Hoenig is now the Dean Pinkhos Churgin Professor of Jewish History at Yeshiva University's Bernard Revel Graduate School. He occupies a unique position in the Torah community as a scholar of note, author of the classical work on *The Great Sanhedrin,* as well as many other significant volumes and learned articles. He is also the director of YUDAE — the Yeshiva University Department of Adult Education, Community Service Division, and has helped in setting up adult Jewish programs for hundreds of congregations. The pages we have read, written by him, demonstrate the love of learning — of both master and disciple.

Today the expansion of Jewish learning in America is particularly enhanced by the growth of Yeshiva University under the consecrated and scholarly leadership of Dr. Samuel Belkin. Our distinguished President always stresses that Yeshiva — with its rabbinics and research — remains the foundation of all the other schools of learning that comprise our great institution. It is fitting then, that this volume opened with intimate and inspirational words from Dr. Belkin's pen. Most relevant and timely, they underscore the unbroken chain of tradition and learning. We are, moveover, forever indebted to our revered President for his encouragement in the publication of this series and particularly this volume.

Finally, it is important to point out that the officers and members of the Alumni of Yeshiva University, cherishing the memory of their sainted teacher, were instrumental in establishing a permanent Memorial for him. Rabbi Dr. Sol B. Friedman, one of the first of the Musmachim of the Yeshiva, spearheaded the project. It is through his tireless efforts that much was done to enhance the memory of Dr. Revel, for which task we are deeply grateful.

Equally significant is the fact that we have included tributes by close colleagues and students of Dr. Revel. These are Doctors Jacob I. Hartstein, Bernard Lander, Leo Jung and Solomon Zeitlin. This is an indication of the high esteem and veneration manifested for the sainted memory of that sage who stood courageously at the helm of Yeshiva from 1915 till 1940. In sum, these pages of Dr. Hoenig's study express devotedly and clearly the full scholarship of Dr. Revel. They reveal, too, concerning the sainted Founder, that his was the just fulfillment of the rabbinic characterization of nobility:

Torah and greatness were vested within him, as a unity.

יהי זכרו ברוך
May his memory be a blessing.

NOTES

Introduction

1. *Kiryat Chana David* (Collected Essays of Rabbi David Rackman and a selection of letters written to him by distinguished contemporaries ...) N.Y. 5727 (1967).

2. See also J.D. Eisenstein, *Ozar Ha-zikhronot* (*Autobiography and Memoirs*), New York 1929, Part II p. 363. Here is included "an example of a plan to INDEX all subjects relating to Jewish history and culture and peculiar decisions found in Rabbinical Responsa works up to the 19th century." The author claims that the "example" is his and not Revel's.

The "example" is an Index to the Responsa of Asheri (Rosh).

Ephraim Deinard (*Kehillat Ya'akov*, (St. Louis) p. 88 #527) also regarded Revel as the compiler.

A similar notion is in *Ha-yehudi*, London (Jan. 2, 1908 — 28 Tevet 5668) II #39, p. 2. Cf also *Hadoar* (N.Y.) XX #6 (Dec. 6, 1940), p. 82.

3. See Facsimile, below, p. 136.

4. *Ibid.*, p. 244 ff., 5 Shevat 5668 (Thursday, Jan. 9, 1908).

5. *Ibid.*, p. 246, 2 Adar II 5668 (Thursday, March 5, 1908).

6. This approach may be seen in Dr. Revel's acknowledgment of some error: פליטת קולמוס — האשמה בי וקצרתי במקום שהיה ראוי להאריך.

7. Cf. below Chapter VII (Ethics) sec. 2, p. 67.

Chapter I — Karaitica

1. *The Karaite Halakhah* p. 22.

2. p. 44.

3. ממחרת השבת.

4. ניסוך המים.

5. p. 50.

6. p. 64.

7. pp. 77-78.

8. pp. 86-87.

9. Yebamot 65 a: הגושא אשה על אשתו יוצא ויתן כתובה.

10. (בשר תאוה) לתיאבון.

11. מזבח אדמה.

12. משנת חסידים.

12*. Niddah 38 a.

13. *Targum Jonathan*, p. 89.

14. מתעבדא לטולא לשם חגא.

15. תני צריך לחדש בה דבר.

16. לא יהוון גוליין דציצית ותפלין דהיגון תקוני גבר על איתא.

17. See also Tosafot Erubin 96 a s.v. מיכל mentioning the Pesikta
(See Yer Ber 4 c).

18. ושחט אותה לפניו.

19. וכהגא אחרא יכוס יתה קדמין בתרין סמניא כמשאר בעורין ויבדקנה בתמני
סרי טריפן.

20. י״ח טרפות.

21. בני א״י בודקין בי״ח טרפות בני בבל אין בודקין אלא בריאה בלבד.

22. הבבלים בודקים בריאה ובני א״י בראש.

23. ותעלון לות כהני די יהו' ממני לכהן רב ביומיא האינון.

23*. See Bikkurim 3.12.

23**. See Hallah 4.9 and Yerushalmi *ad loc.*

23***. See Ramban, Deut. 26,3.

24. המלמד הגדול.

Chapter II — **Non-Rabbinic Deviations**

1. JQR, XIV, (1923-24) p. 298.

2. JQR, III (Oct. 1912) p. 315.

3. JQR, VII (1916-17) p. 433-4.

4. See Bibliography # 64.

Chapter III — **Historical Origins**

1. Jewish Forum, VII (1923), p. 566-9.

2. Shabbat 14 b.

3. *Yagdil Torah*, (1919), III, p. 146.

4. מהם — ממנו.

5. עונש כיפה. See Mishnah Sanh. 9.5.

6. דין מלך.

7. קנאים פוגעים בו.

Chapter IV — **The Restoration of Semicha**

1. ‏קנסות.‏
2. ‏והדבר צריך הכרע.‏

Chapter V — **Rabbinic Novellae**

1. Yer. Ber. 2.9(5d): ‏כל מי שפטור מדבר ועושהו נקרא הדיוט.‏
1*. ‏סומאה ברה״ר.‏
2. ‏חזקה.‏
3. ‏חילוק.‏
4. ‏שבועת היסת.‏ See I. Herzog, *Main Institution of Jewish Law* I, pp. 11, 241.
5. ‏כופר הכל.‏
6. ‏מודה במקצת.‏
7. ‏רוב.‏
8. ‏רובו ככולו.‏
9. ‏לברר.‏
10. ‏תרתי דסתרי.‏ See Gittin 88 a.
11. ‏מקח וממכר.‏
12. ‏צדקה.‏ See I. Herzog, *op. cit.* I p. 289.
13. ‏קנין.‏
14. ‏מבטל רשות.‏
15. ‏המשך יבוא.‏
16 ‏ברירה.‏
17. ‏ספק ספיקא.‏
18. ‏חזקה.‏
19. ‏כל היוצא מטמא טמא.‏
20. ‏איסור.‏
21. ‏חמץ.‏
22. ‏עפרא דעלמא.‏
23. ‏ביטול ברוב.‏
24. ‏טעם כעיקר.‏
25. ‏פרה אדומה.‏
26. ‏צפור מצורע.‏
27. ‏שליח דרחמנא.‏
28. ‏שליח דדן.‏
29. ‏שליחות.‏

30. ‎עבודה.
31. ‎קרבן יחיד.
32. ‎קרבן צבור.
33. ‎בעלים.
34. ‎שעיר לעזאזל.
35. See above notes 27, 28.
36. ‎שחיטה כשירה בזר.
37. ‎מעשר.
37*. Tosefta Kiddushin 1.4: ‎לא ישא אדם אשה עד שתגדל בת אחותו.
38. See above p. 33.
39. ‎עד אחד נאמן באיסורים.
40. ‎בירור.
41. ‎אומדנא.
42. ‎רוב.
43. ‎סימנים.
44. ‎חזקה.
45. ‎עד זומם.

Chapter VI — Philosophical Thought

1. ‎לברר מציאות הדבר המסופק לו.
2. ‎קול באשה ערוה (Ber. 24a).
3. ‎אסמכתא.
4. ‎כל מלתא דאמר רחמנא לא תעביד אי עביד לא מהני.
5. ‎עונשין מן הדין.
6. ‎גילוי מלתא.
7. ‎כרת.
8. ‎לאו.
9. ‎מצות צריכות כונה.
10. ‎מוקצה.
11. ‎לאו שאין בו מעשה.
12. ‎לא תשנא את אחיך בלבבך.
13. ‎ספק.
14. ‎מיגו — a legal rule according to which a deponent's statement is accepted as true on the ground that if he had intended to tell a lie he might have invented one more advantageous to his case.
15. ‎ראוי — capability, fit to be.
16. ‎בעלות.

17. חזקה — presumptive continuance of an actual condition until evidence of a change is produced.

18. גרמא.

19. הפקר.

20. שינוי באיסורים.

21. שליח לדבר עבירה.

22. רשע.

23. קטן.

24. נבלה.

25. לא מצוה.

26. Shabbat 121a.

27. See below, chapter XI, section A. p. 88 ff.

27*. See below Appendix I, p. 104.

28. See below, chapter XI, section B. p. 102.

Chapter VII — Ethics

1. *The Jewish Exponent,* 1909 (reprint) p. 3

2. *Ibid.,* p. 15, appendix.

3. Jewish Forum IX, (1926), p. 121.

4. See דביר I, p. 183-188; cf. ש. אברמסון, במרכזים ובתפוצות בתקופת הגאונים p. 34, for further analysis; also above p. 30.

5. Cf. Jewish Forum I, (1918) p. 77.

Chapter VIII — Jewish Notables

1. See Bibliography, p. 129.

1*. See also Gersonides and Kimhi on II Kings.

2. שבועת היסת. See above p. 49.

3. תיקו.

4. לקולא.

Chapter IX — The Pious Among Nations

1. Cf. E. Hertz, *Lincoln* and the Synagogue (1927), p. 361 ff.

Chapter X — Problems and Confrontations

1. מלקות.

2. טומאה.

3. אפר הפרה.

4. תרומה.